Africa Now

Africa Now is an exciting new series, published by Zed Books in association with the internationally respected Nordic Africa Institute. Featuring high-quality, cutting-edge research from leading academics, the series addresses the big issues confronting Africa today. Accessible but in-depth, and wide-ranging in its scope, *Africa Now* engages with the critical political, economic, sociological and development debates affecting the continent, shedding new light on pressing concerns.

Nordic Africa Institute

The Nordic Africa Institute (Nordiska Afrikainstitutet) is a centre for research, documentation and information on modern Africa. Based in Uppsala, Sweden, the Institute is dedicated to providing timely, critical and alternative research and analysis of Africa and to cooperating with African researchers. As a hub and a meeting place for a growing field of research and analysis, the Institute strives to put knowledge of African issues within reach for scholars, policy-makers, politicians, the media, students and the general public. The Institute is financed jointly by the Nordic countries (Denmark, Finland, Iceland, Norway and Sweden).

www.nai.uu.se

Forthcoming titles

Maria Eriksson Baaz and Maria Stern, *Sexual Violence in African Conflicts: Perceptions, Prescriptions, Problems*

Prosper B. Matondi (ed.), *Zimbabwe's Fast-track Land Reform*

Titles already published

Fantu Cheru and Cyril Obi (eds), *The Rise of China and India in Africa: Challenges, Opportunities and Critical Interventions*

Ilda Lindell (ed.), *Africa's Informal Workers: Collective Agency, Alliances and Transnational Organizing in Urban Africa*

Iman Hashim and Dorte Thorsen, *Child Migration in Africa*

Cyril Obi and Siri Aas Rustad (eds), *Oil and Insurgency in the Niger Delta: Managing the Complex Politics of Petro-violence*

Prosper B. Matondi, Kjell Havnevik and Atakilte Beyene (eds), *Biofuels, Land Grabbing and Food Security in Africa*

Mats Utas (ed.), *African Conflicts and Informal Power: Big Men and Networks*

About the editor

Mats Utas is associate professor and senior researcher at the Nordic Africa Institute. Between 2009 and 2011 he headed the Africa programme at the Swedish National Defence College. He has published in journals such as *African Affairs* and *Journal of Modern African Studies* and in edited books on contemporary African wars, child and youth combatants, media, refugees, gender in war zones, post-war reconstruction and urban poverty. He is the co-author of *Navigating Youth, Generating Adulthood: Social Becoming in an African Context* (2006). Utas has conducted extensive fieldwork in Liberia and Sierra Leone, and more recently researched the roles of businessmen in the Somali conflict during fieldwork in Kenya and Dubai.

African conflicts and informal power

Big Men and networks

edited by Mats Utas

Nordiska Afrikainstitutet
The Nordic Africa Institute

Zed Books
LONDON | NEW YORK

African conflicts and informal power: Big Men and networks was first published in association with the Nordic Africa Institute, PO Box 1703, SE-751 47 Uppsala, Sweden in 2012 by Zed Books Ltd, 7 Cynthia Street, London N1 9JF, UK and Room 400, 175 Fifth Avenue, New York, NY 10010, USA

www.zedbooks.co.uk
www.nai.uu.se

Set in OurType Arnhem, Monotype Gill Sans Heavy
by Ewan Smith, London
Index: ed.emery@thefreeuniversity.net
Cover designed by Rogue Four Design
Printed and bound by CPI (UK) Ltd, Croydon,
CRO 4YY

Distributed in the USA exclusively by Palgrave Macmillan, a division of St Martin's Press, LLC, 175 Fifth Avenue, New York, NY 10010, USA

A catalogue record for this book is available from the British Library
Library of Congress Cataloging in Publication Data available

ISBN 978 1 84813 883 4 hb
ISBN 978 1 84813 882 7 pb

Contents

Illustrations

Map

Boxes

Introduction: Bigmanity and network governance in African conflicts

Mats Utas

This volume invites comparisons across the African continent by presenting case studies from a variety of countries, settings and institutions with one factor in common: armed conflict.[1] The chapters that follow refer to socio-political or economic networks along a continuum from formal and open to informal and at times even illicit.[2] It has been argued that networks will rise to prominence where formal states, or other sovereign entities, are fractured, weak or barely present (Reno 1998). Informal networks of political or economic character are present in any society, whether in Africa, Europe, North America or elsewhere. The politics of intimacy, or 'the culture of intimacy', as Herzfeld (1997) would have it, is part of the everyday life of nation-states where every institution is governed by onstage and offstage politics (Shryock 2004; Goffman 1959). It is the inner workings of politics and the ever-present backrooms to the official storefronts of political and economic ventures which are central in this volume. A second theme running through the book concerns the role of Big Men, informal political and/or economic actors situated in social space.[3] Big Men will be treated here as nodes in networks, combining efforts in projects of joint action. Joint action may be economic or political, and could for instance be a war effort.

The combination of Big Men and networks is not an African phenomenon, but rather a very human enterprise. Works concerned with African neo-patrimonialism, clientelism and patron–client systems are many, but I intend in this introduction to approach from a somewhat different angle by fusing classic network studies with Big Men/Great Men research originating from Melanesia (e.g. Sahlins 1963; Godelier 1986; Godelier and Strathern 1991). The term is, furthermore, used emically; for instance, in Sierra Leone people constantly refer to Big Men and their ways of acting, systematically relating to who is, and who is not, a Big Man in all social settings.

Early in *For the City Yet to Come* (2004b), AbdouMaliq Simone notes that when working with NGOs in urban Africa, he was always bewildered that staff seldom appeared to be doing what they were hired to do; instead, the work that was in fact achieved was described as being done somewhere else. In his quest for locating this 'somewhere else', Simone notes that by engaging with these organizations 'over an extended period of time, it became clear that there were other, more provisional and ephemeral, forms of ... collective activity that association members also participated in and that seemingly had a greater impact on their life' (ibid.: 24). This is what Chabal and Daloz, although from slightly different vantage points and reaching somewhat different conclusions, talk about as *Africa Works* (1999). But in zones of conflict and war, where everything is in flux, the inner workings of 'order' are even more intricate. War in Africa does not imply the collapse of everything, a venturing into total anarchy. Alternative forms of control and management establish themselves when formal governance is diminished. These may be in the guise of rebel movements and militias, often mimicking the formal, or of more fluid forms of network. Two examples from the first war in Liberia and the early period of the war in Somalia highlight this point. The currency in the so-called greater Liberia, Charles Taylor and NPFL territory, maintained twice the value of the new, official Liberian currency introduced early in the war. By issuing a new currency and upholding a ban on trading in the old, the interim government and the international community had intended to starve Taylor and the NPFL out but, owing to informal structures of governance within greater Liberia, the result turned into the opposite. A second, related example is the way in which Somalia, without state or central bank, maintained a relatively stable currency during the first part of the war. This was possible, Peter Little (2003) remarks, because of networks of money-changers and informal finance houses. These examples demonstrate how other, and alternative, power structures maintain a degree of order in conflict zones. In fact, conflict opens up space for new alternative political and economic structures that reach far beyond the conflict zone itself, as in this recent example from Somalia:

> Somali networks criss-cross the Horn of Africa and, as states in East Africa seek to develop economic links, their experience shows that such links already exist, at least informally. Finance from Mogadishu, distribution networks fanning out from Nairobi and agents across the region paint the picture of an increasingly connected economy. The clan- and family-based nature of Somali business networks means that there is ample scope for developing new markets and connections wherever Somali communities are present. It must also be noted that Somali networks extend into Europe, North America, the Gulf states and beyond, demonstrating the continuing connectedness of this widely dispersed community. (Abdulsamed 2011: 15)

The African state and other forms of governance

There is already a considerable state-centric literature on conflicts and other outcomes of the crisis of the post-colonial Westphalian state in Africa, whether labelled failed, collapsed, weak or fragile (see, among many others, Bøås and

Dunn 2007; Bayart et al. 1999; Duffield 2001; Kaldor 1999; Reno 1995, 1998; Andersen et al. 2007; Chabal and Daloz 1999). Although many of the chapters in this volume discuss this, in this introduction I avoid such discussions. Suffice it to say that weak African states have opened up space for alternative sources of sovereignty (Hansen and Stepputat 2005) and alternative forms of governance (Utas 2009), as well as allowing ample room for violent contestations over the state in the form of military coups and armed incursions (Biró 2007; Reno 1998; Bøås and Dunn 2007; Clapham 1998). One could argue that most African states have never been more than nominally sovereign and that weak states have necessitated considerable use of violence (Mbembe 2001, 2003; Utas 2009) as well as rhizomically informal and alternative, although not necessarily opposing, structures of governance (Bayart 1993). It is essential to point out that state and civil society are intricately interconnected and interwoven and cannot be understood in opposition to each other. Neither state nor civil society is democratic in its basic set-up. The state in many African countries, Ferguson points out, 'starts to look suspiciously like civil society' (2006: 99), and civil society appears as a number of political entities, or integrated 'parts of a new, transnational apparatus of governmentality' (ibid.: 103).[4] These political entities do not replace nation-states and national governance but overlay them and coexist.

Citizens in many African states – states in the Westphalian Periphery (Biró 2007) – have an ambivalent relationship with the state. AbdouMaliq Simone remarks that in Senegal 'many urban dwellers will come to feel locked in by the frequently overbearing demands of these practices and institutions' (Simone 2004b: 36). From a predominantly economic perspective he notes that unconventional trade, involving well-off business persons, soldiers, militias, middlemen of various nationalities and petty traders, is most common within states where chronic political crisis has undermined state regulations and where civil servants in formal institutions continue to function and maintain some control by their very activities in informal trade (ibid.: 25).[5] The informal logic of daily life rests on what Simone calls 'the spectral order of things' (ibid.: 92ff.), a politico-economic blending, or a *métissage* of relations penetrating society so thoroughly that, for instance, the regime that has ruled Cameroon for the last twenty years 'increasingly recognizes that it need no longer substantially invest in the definitional aspects of rule – that is, to deliberate clearly defined jurisdictions, zones, policies, and sectors' (ibid.: 94b). The spectral order of things is deemed more efficient and possibly the only viable path.

Simone, along with many other observers, locates such 'failures' in historic perspectives and points out that, in order to make colonies productive, the objective of colonizing states was 'to access labor without encouraging wage labor' (ibid.: 144). In Central Africa it was frequently concessionary companies which carried administrative costs, leading towards more businesslike state

formations. Local order was disrupted in order to intensify authoritarian control, with the effect of '[a] loosening of the population from its former social
and political ties ... giving rise to populations accountable to no one' (ibid.: 145).
Polities, Simone further states, became 'largely based on "big man" systems
operating more as commercial firms than as states' (ibid.). This gives us a
glimpse of the roots of Big Men networks, made possible, if not necessary,
by political changes on the continent as a partial consequence of colonialism
and related politico-economic endeavours of conquest.[6]

According to Alex de Waal, the most complicated conflicts in the contemporary world are found in countries where state institutions are subordinate to
patronage networks. Without denying the fact that citizens care about political
issues and do fight over them, he states that people 'can neither organize
their political allegiances through rule-governed organizations nor resolve
them through state institutions according to the rule of law' (de Waal 2009:
99). In his view, political life in most African countries is organized as 'a
patrimonial marketplace', operating according to socioculturally established
conventions. Depending on the perspective of the viewer, the result can be
described both as 'state failure/fragility and as an alternative way in which
countries can function' (ibid.).

De Waal takes his cue from Samuel Huntington, who some forty years ago
pointed out that '[t]he most important political distinction among countries
concerns not their form of government but their degree of government' (ibid.).
In this light, it is formal organizational voids which are crucial, not differences
in socioculture per se. At this point, one could question de Waal's cultural
use of neo-patrimonialism, given his reference to Huntington's structural and
thus universally valid perspective. According to de Waal,

> [u]nder such systems, some insist that 'Africa works' and will continue to do so.
> This strand of thought does not deny that people, including political leaders,
> hold strong political beliefs. It is just that the vehicles available to promote
> these political agendas, such as political parties, legislatures and government
> ministries, operate according to socio-cultural rules, notably patrimonialism.
> (De Waal 2009: 101)

But why socioculture? Have all countries with weak states the same socio-
cultural traits? De Waal ends up with many of the same problems as Bratton
and van de Walle, for whom neo-patrimonialism is 'the distinctive institutional
hallmark of African regimes' (Bratton and van de Walle in Mkandawire 2002:
184), where 'neopatrimonial regimes [are] ... embedded in *precapitalist* societies'
(Bratton and van de Walle 1997: 89).[7] By contrast, we see Big Men and networks
of governance not as sociocultural features but rather as socio-structural ones,
where certain structural features prescribe certain social outcomes. Naturally,
networks are social and cultural manifestations as much as they are politi-

cal and economic (as Roitman points out in Duffield 2002: 160), but such manifestations differ from setting to setting. To reiterate: with weak or absent state institutions the structural alternative is more influential and stronger informal networks governance, whether in Liberia, Italy or the United States. For instance, organized criminals are connected with governance structures and formal private enterprises in every country, but the structural void created during armed conflict and war increases the space for such nodes. Yet informal Big Man networks are far from just criminal, as I argue below.

Many Africans remain sceptical about their own state; some are downright hostile. Are they citizens or subjects (Mamdani 1996), or neither (Fanthorpe 2001)? On the African continent, new groups rage against the machine (Bøås and Dunn 2007), turn abject heroes, antisocial by necessity (Utas 2008a), or just hustle the system (Christensen and Utas 2008; Utas and Jörgel 2008). In Sierra Leone and Liberia, but most recently among the Somali diaspora in Nairobi, I have researched how people affected by war arrange themselves in various local, and chiefly informal, organizations around both social and physical security, protecting themselves in part against the state and emissaries of the state. Frequently they take the form of small-scale and semi-sovereign organizations that tend to mimic the functioning state, but on a micro level. Although they organize themselves in opposition to the state to some extent, both individuals and sometimes entire organizations cultivate extensive ties with civil servants, with rhizomes reaching deep into the centre of the state (as pointed out in this volume; in particular Chapters 1, 3, 4 and 9). Such organizations are urban phenomena, although rhizomes and local cuttings certainly reach into rural areas, in particular into resource-rich mining areas, rural towns and borderlands (see Chapters 1, 2 and 5 in this volume) connected not only to urban but also to global networks (see Chapters 6 and 10).

In what might appear fleetingly, especially to a scholar of government, to be the ruins of urban life, a social infrastructure still exists, says Simone. Such infrastructure facilitates *intersections of socialities* used by citizens who possess limited other means (Simone 2004a: 407). He points out how 'residents' reciprocal efforts are radically open, flexible, and provisional' and thus 'a specific economy of perception and collaborative practice is constituted through the capacity of individuals to circulate across and become familiar with a broad range of spatial, residential, economic, and transactional positions' (ibid.: 408). Simone proposes that we should see people themselves as *infrastructure* (ibid.: 407, 410–11).

It is always possible to do something different with the city, or the state for that matter, from what it is intended for; it is possible to keep the official structure operative, using official space for private entrepreneuring (ibid.: 409). For instance, the minister of aviation in an African country formally prevents illicit goods going through the national airport, but informally uses the same structures to facilitate the smuggling of cocaine. Commonplace traders are using an official storefront to sell construction material but double as dealers in so-called blood diamonds, and get a cut from the prolific trade in arms and ammunition destined for a neighbouring country in armed conflict. It is the combination of activities and people which is creating alternative modes of production. Such institutional forms constitute

> highly mobile and provisional possibilities for how people live and make things, how they use the urban environment and collaborate with one another. The specific operations and scopes of these conjunctions are constantly negoti-ated and depend on the particular histories, understandings, networks, styles, and inclinations of the actors involved. (Ibid.: 410)

It is, in this telling, the reweaving of connections, both local and international, which makes Africa work, and it is these conjunctions and network textures which are of interest in this book, networks that are systems of both 'politics and resource provision' (Simone 2004b: 42). If networks are alternative modes of governance, then Big Men are alternative governors of *peopled infrastructures.*

Big Men

Marshall Sahlins, in an article from 1963, states that '[t]he Melanesian big-man seems so thoroughly bourgeois, so reminiscent of the free enterprising rugged individual of our own heritage. He combines with an ostensible interest in the general welfare a more profound measure of self-interested cunning and economic calculation' (Sahlins 1963: 289). There are a number of characteristics that he attaches to the Big Man, many universally valid and easily adaptable to African scenarios. '[T]he indicative quality of big-man authority', he states,

> is everywhere the same: it is *personal* power. Big-men do not come to office; they do not succeed to, nor are they installed in, existing positions of leader-ship over political groups. The attainment of big-man status is rather the outcome of a series of acts which elevate a person above the common herd and attract him a coterie of loyal, lesser men. (Ibid.: 289)

The Big Man has the ability to command, to instigate mass action, where authority is not structurally ascribed and socio-historically motivated but based on the Big Man's ability to create a following and to a large extent dependent on his informal abilities to assist people privately. The creation of his own faction is absolutely crucial for his power and standing (ibid.: 290f.), and upward mobility occurs when he connects other men and their families to his faction, 'harnessing their production to his ambition' (ibid.: 292). Building renown and power is based on amassing wealth and redistributing it with 'astutely calculated generosity' (Godelier 1986: 163).

Sahlins asserts the fragility and the temporality of Big Man power, as loyalty must continuously be reinforced and dissatisfaction among followers may have grave consequences for his authority (Sahlins 1963: 292), which leads to what Sahlins calls a 'comparative instability' (ibid.: 293). The death of an important Big Man, for instance, may lead to a regional political 'trauma' as factions are built around a particular Big Man and a whole network may temporarily dissolve, eventually being rebuilt around other Big Men. A further source of instability is what Sahlins calls 'the Melanesian contradiction' (ibid.): economic reciprocity between the Big Man and his followers on one side, but on the other hand there is cumulative build-up of a Big Man that eventually will lead to extortion of the faction (ibid.). There is thus an obvious risk that a Big Man will overburden his followers, leading to 'the generation of antagonisms, defections, and in extreme cases the violent liquidation of the center-man' (ibid.). As Godelier notes, the Big Man is thus 'little by little undermining his social base' (1986: 163). If we take these factors into account, it may for instance help to explain the relative instability of many African rebel movements resting on Big Man/warlord logics.

There will inevitably be regions, or localities, where the idea of who, or what, a Big Man is will differ from the overarching framework. Thus, while we aim to employ the Big Man concept in case studies across the continent, one must expect that the definition given here will fit in some settings better than in others. Médard (1992) has explicitly used Sahlins' Big Man model in exploring African politics, pointing out how African Big Men convert economic resources into political authority (cf. Chapter 7 in this volume) and how state affairs become quintessentially personal (cf. Chapter 8 in this volume). However, other authors focusing on Africa use the term as a rather loose label and in a variety of ways. To give a few examples: in Burundian refugee camps in Tanzania, liminal experts or brokers who operate in the space in between refugees and humanitarian aid agencies such as UNHCR are referred to as Big Men by Simon Turner (2010: 86–7). Johan de Smedt employs the term when discussing election violence and vote manipulation in Kenya's 2007 elections. Highlighting the fact that 'local "big men" exercised authority by sharing out their wealth – the recipients of this redistribution, the poor, then "inevitably owed obedience"' (de Smedt 2009: 583) – he explains how British-created 'tribes' continue to function as political avenues for ethnic patronage that ties local Big Men to the 'ultimate Big Man', the president (ibid.). In his book *Big Men, Small Boys and Politics in Ghana* (1995), Paul Nugent situates Big Men of the political arena in open-ended hierarchical relations. 'The "big man" issues commands, normally from a seated position, while subordinates do the running,' states Nugent (ibid.: 3). A Big Man is primarily, but not only, a political figure associated with opulence. Bigness is in part measured in status symbols and the ability to fill that Big Man role according to social criteria. In Ghanaian politics, Big Men 'sought to win over potential voters by insinuating that some of this wealth would rub off on them – either directly (through patronage) or indirectly (because of the application of their business acumen to national affairs)' (ibid.: 5). Despite different usage of the term, Bigmanity can be said to hold a number of key characteristics:

1 Bigmanity is based on social relations. 'A big-man is one who can create and use social relations which give him leverage on others' production,' says Sahlins (1963: 292). Big Men transform social relations into strategic power and control (Médard 1992). Bigmanity forms loose social webs based on the ability to gather followers. In some settings this form of gathering is more important than economic wealth, access to land or formal political power. This has been called 'wealth in people' (Guyer 1993) or a rights-in-person complex (Kopytoff and Miers 1977), or has been linked with the notion of 'being for' someone (Bledsoe 1990; see also Utas 2008a).

2 Big Men do not generally control followers. Quite the opposite; it is in the interest of followers to maintain ties with a Big Man (and it is rarely just one) because Big Men provide economic possibilities as well as protection and social security. Bigmanity is far from mere wealth gathering. Big Men are not merely rational-choice wealth-generating positions; to maintain a Big Man position, one must extend solidarity within a moral framework. Gathering of power and its maintenance are built on forms of reciprocity, and if the Big Man does not distribute enough largesse he will eventually lose his supporters. Bigmanity is unfixed and multiple. Bigmanity is not a matter of inherited patron–client structures, but rather fluid and ever-changeable webs of relations. Some Big Men endure a lifetime at the centre of things while many others come and go. Followers may discard Big Men when they do not deliver. At the same time a follower is not loyal to just one Big Man, but typically enjoys different relationships with different Big Men.

3 Bigmanity is a response to a lack of formal structures. Typically, Big Men wield a great deal of social power in situations where there is a structural void. Big Man power should be seen as an alternative form of governance, where the national state doesn't reach, or where local forms of formal governance do not have sufficient sovereign powers. Formal structures are typically weakened during conflicts which thus give increased room for Bigmanity. Big Men networks may or may not involve the façades of the state. Big Men ought not to be seen as an opposing system to that of the state – quite the contrary. Politicians as well as civil servants use their positions within the state to engage business and cultivate relationships 'based on their role in tendering contracts, issuing licenses, and approving land use plans' (Simone 2004b: 81). The fewer functioning checks and balances there are, the more room there is for the Big Man to manoeuvre.

4 Being a Big Man is not a fixed label but rather a term that highlights a

position within social relations. It implies that a Big Man may well have his own Big Man. Furthermore, 'small' systems of Big Men and followers also occur at the grassroots level of a society (even the boy has his boy). There is a structural tension between the Big Man and 'the small boys', coming to the fore in studies such as Richards (1996) and Jackson (2004), where Big Men aim at controlling the production of their followers and this tension gives rise to the desire of underlings to slip the leash, as well as radicalizing discourses and in some cases sparking revolutionary engagements. Violent conflicts open up possibilities for underlings to contest power and climb the social ladder (Utas 2008a, 2009).

Network

Mark Duffield discusses war as a network enterprise (2002) using Manuel Castells' ideas of the new information society as a basis, when he defines the *network enterprise* as 'the generic institutional expression of the new global/informational economy' (ibid.: 154). He draws conclusions about certain aspects of networks from Castells' *The Rise of the Network Society* (1996), seeing networks not as oligopolistic, but rather interconnected groups of decentralized components with significant autonomy making room for competition within shared strategies (Duffield 2002: 154). Networks are not primarily concerned with territorial control but aim at 'constructing flexible relations between sets of information-sharing companies in different institutional or spatial environments' (ibid.); thus such networks come to resemble business projects, as we shall see below. New information technologies have played a seminal role in the success of 'the network' in this broader sense. Somalia may be the prime case of a Castellsian war where a diaspora community is directly connected through new media and information flows to friends, family and business community within the war zone itself. Alongside information flows run intricate transfer networks of money, goods and people that in many ways sustain the war (Little 2003; Lindley 2009). However, all African wars do not look the same; the wars in Sierra Leone and Liberia, for instance, differed substantially from the Somali experience in that new media communication flows played much less of a role.

The idea of the networks often prompts associations of social threat. We tend to think of networks as illicit (see, e.g., Eilstrup-Sangiovanni and Jones 2008). Al-Qaeda is the contemporary example par excellence, with semi-independent cells and terrorist goals. Rhizomic networks with tacit underground derivations make these structures seem the opposite of 'up in the air' information networks, although information hubs and flows are today crucial for illicit activities to prosper. Other 'threatening networks' could be networks of curiously successful Japanese firms in 1980s and 1990s USA (as discussed in Podolny and Page 1998), but also Freemasonry across the world, or secret societies in, for instance, West Africa. Secret society networks such as the Poro in Liberia and Sierra Leone have been obsessively studied. Although the heyday of such study has passed, many have continued to fear the informal powers of societies based on secret networks. A few years ago, I met a UN police officer who was preoccupied with unmasking the members and informal activities of the secret male Poro of Nimba County in rural Liberia, certain that everything damaging that happened in the county had its origin within that secret realm. Elsewhere, examples of 'malevolent' networks that come to mind are drug cartels (see Chapter 6) and economic networks extracting resources in conflict areas (cf. Chapters 1 and 10).

Duffield's study of wars as network enterprises focuses on emerging global rather than local structures. Although the emphasis of this volume is on the latter, there are clear resemblances and also a profound connectedness between a local conflict and global networks, as most chapters in this volume demonstrate. By making Castells' information networks the starting point for his analysis, Duffield, however, implies that network society (and war) is something new, made possible only in and by the information age, but other researchers have at least since the 1950s pointed out the importance of social networks. There is a rich history of network studies starting with Barnes' study of the Norwegian island parish Bremnes, published in 1954 (Barnes 1954). By the end of the 1950s and early 1960s, social anthropologists were anticipating great things from the study of social networks. Hopes were raised that network studies would enhance an understanding of social change (Kapferer 1973: 83). Clearly, the study of networks has since then experienced ups and downs, and researchers continue to consider networks important but hard to pin down with precision. Podolny and Page (1998) point towards a vogue of network studies in organizational economy in the 1990s, where they filled a theoretical void in explaining economic patterns that did not fit the classic duality of market and hierarchy.

Clyde Mitchell (1973; see also Mitchell 1974), in his overview of network studies within social anthropology, identifies Barnes as the first venturing beyond the classic understanding of kin and family networks when he described the social network as 'a set of personal relationships which interfused and crosscut the set of relationships in the industrial [work-related] and territorial [place-related] systems' (Mitchell 1973: 15). Mitchell points out that social class and neighbourhood are typical variables that influence the 'connectedness' of social networks. Such factors are, however, not straight determinants and typically networks cut across villages and across kin- and identity-based groups. Thus the network deviated from (in his words) 'traditional' social systems (ibid.: 17, 21). Although he posits a theoretical differentiation between the boundedness of a social group and the unboundedness of networks, in practice they are interconnected and not easily separated (ibid.: 20).

Quoting Srinivas and Béteille (1964), Mitchell defines a social network as 'a set of concrete individuals who are members of diverse systems of enduring groups and categories' (Mitchell 1973: 21). Srinivas and Béteille look at the network from an actor-centred perspective. Bruce Kapferer, in his work on social networks in Zambia, proposes a similarly actor-centred approach: 'The concept network for my purpose refers to a set of points (individuals) defined in relation to an initial point (ego) and linked by lines (relationships) either directly or indirectly to this initial point of focus' (Kapferer 1973: 84). Mitchell argues that '[f]or a deeper understanding it is necessary not only to chart concrete networks of different individuals but to relate these different networks to one another, to draw up, so to say, a master chart, in a coherent and systematic manner' (Mitchell 1973: 22). But to study networks and relate them to each other is hard enough in a study localized to a neighbourhood (e.g. Kapferer (1973) and Epstein (1961)). The networks of conflict economies with which we are preoccupied in this volume are much wider, ranging over neighbourhoods and cities, into the rural, and over the national and transnational. They frequently, but not always, range into the clandestine, if not illicit. Most assuredly, it is not possible to draw up complete master charts of such complexity. It is a tough enough task to describe temporary nodes, Big Men and how they work and combine efforts for social, political and economic action in the form of joint projects. The very fluidity of conflict networks is an obstacle to any systematic study. Still, we must attempt a shift from 'the subjective network of the actor to the objective one of the observer' (Mitchell 1973: 22), maintaining a suitable degree of humility in taking on this challenge.

Returning to the practical/functional aspect, a network should be 'thought of as the actual set of links of all kinds among a set of individuals' (ibid.: 22). Graphically, the social relationships of individuals in networks are drawn as lines with individuals as connected points, but as Mitchell points out, this is not sufficient, as we need also to observe what kind of relationship every single line stands for (ibid.: 23) – is it a political tie, an economic relationship, or both? To add to the complexity, not all ties remain the same over time. Ultimately we must also identify the nodes/Big Men and take into account their multiple roles in addition to the plethora of links they maintain. Adrian Mayer (1966), for instance, studied 'action sets' in elections, tracing sets of offers of services that were exchanged for support during an election (Mitchell 1973: 25). Voters were connected to political candidates through expectations of patronage. Mayer observed thirty-eight links between a particular candidate and voters. Ten of them were kinship based, seven were economic links, four were caste based and the rest had other characteristics: 'the state, the wrestling club, trade union membership, occupational links, village links and so on'. Mitchell points out that Mayer's study involved three kinds of network: the exchange network, a communications network and a social network (ibid.: 25).

This variety of network forms and functions is highly relevant to conflict networks (as perhaps becomes especially clear in Chapters 2, 3 and 5 in this volume). Furthermore, common interests and goals tend to incorporate certain norms and values that form the basis for a social network (ibid.: 32–3). Rules to play by are important in networks and formations of trust or control appear central for the network to function, but also present a built-in disadvantage compared to formalized enterprises or governance structures, as is obvious in post-conflict power-sharing agreements (see Chapter 8 in this volume).

Common values have become the focus of more recent research into networks of corporations and businesses. Podolny and Page, in their study of network organizations, speak about a network as a 'moral community' guided by joint ethics (Podolny and Page 1998: 61) where '[e]ach member of the network feels a sense of obligation to the other party or parties rather than a desire to take advantage of any trust that may have been established' (ibid.: 60). Walter Powell points out that, in network forms of resource allocation, individuals are more dependent on others (Powell 1990: 303) and that some forms of exchange are more social than others – 'that is, more dependent on relationships, mutual interests, and reputation – as well as less guided by a formal structure of authority' (ibid.: 300). These researchers contrast market and hierarchy, as per classic organization theory, but argue in addition for the network as a third mode of organization. Networks consist of reciprocal patterns of communications and exchange (ibid.: 295) with network shapes being based on 'lateral or horizontal patterns of exchange, interdependent flows of resources, and reciprocal lines of communication' (ibid.: 296). Networks can, then, be described as an 'intricate latticework of collaborative ventures with other firms, most of whom are ostensibly competitors' (ibid.: 301). From this strand of research, we can draw the notion of networks as complex organisms in free-market-like relations, which 'involve neither explicit criteria of the market, nor the familiar paternalism of the hierarchy' (ibid.: 303). Networks are thus not only horizontal, and patron–client relations are not just vertical. A combination of both gives Big Men networks. It is interesting to see how de Waal's concept of African countries as patrimonial marketplaces, as previously discussed, communicates neatly with these ideas.

'From a structural perspective every form of organization is a network, and market and hierarchy are simply two manifestations of the broader type,' state Podolny and Page (1998: 58). Market relations are not enduring but, rather, episodic and, conversely, hierarchies consist of relations that are enduring but by no means permanent (ibid.). From a governance perspective, a network form of organization is 'any collection of actors that pursue repeated, enduring exchange relations with one another and, at the same time, lack a legitimate organizational authority to arbitrate and resolve disputes that may arise during exchange' (ibid.). This fact caters for flexible network solutions

allowing innovation and adaptation to new methods as 'network forms allow participating firms to learn new skills, gain legitimacy, improve economic performance and manage resource dependencies' (ibid.: 66). Flexibility and innovation are in particular key elements to understanding the success of both economic and social networks in times of conflict, as is clearly pointed out in most chapters of this volume. Below, I list factors that appear to be essential for our study of networks in conflicts. If we stay with the graphic idea of a network with nodes/Big Men and connecting lines between them representing ties of all kinds (economic, political, social and so on), then the points at which they cross each other are common projects, and this network exhibits a number of characteristics:

1 The success of a network project does not depend solely upon the number of Big Men involved but also on the degree of power that individual Big Men invest and the resources – including human resources/followers – they possess. Weight and density of a network are thus central to how efficient the outcome will be (Duffield 2002: 155; Kapferer 1973: 84), although it should be noted that '[a] potential network of relations is maintained that need not be activated right away but that exists in some immanent state for future mobilization when necessary' (Simone 2004b: 227).

2 Networks are unstable, changing and constantly adaptable. As such, social networks are in its double meanings nervous systems (Taussig 1992). Clandestinity of networks makes them efficient, flexible and adaptable to new functions, where new nodes/Big Men can be added while older ones can be subtracted with great ease. Furthermore, few formal, transparent mechanisms at either state or regional level can function without the support or authorization of informal networks and Big Men. Network logic is based on a spectral order of things, as Simone (2004b) puts it. Socio-economic networks are very much part of the daily cut-and-paste activities of the bricoleur (Lévi-Strauss 1966). '[A]ctors may assume one point of view or position within a local context, but take a very different position outside the locality' (Simone 2004b: 236), and Simone further notes that 'it is rare that any African urban resident is without some kind of external network that can be plied or mobilized in some way' (ibid.: 238).

3 Networks cut across social and economic groups as well as geographies (ibid.: 235) but still rest on common interests, although not necessarily the same goals. When Big Men from different backgrounds and with different capacities share the same goals (although not necessarily for the same reasons) – that is, have interest in the same project – then a network becomes strong. Networks do not need to have the same socio-cultural background, beyond the capacity to communicate. Rather, difference is an advantage for network operations because they can work across virtually any divides.

At the same time, this fact makes them more vulnerable, fragile and less durable. It should be noted that network ties connecting actors from different areas and social backgrounds may counteract identity-based conflict as they draw strength from heterogeneity. Networks are not simply horizontal systems and Big Men hierarchies cannot simply be understood as vertical ties of patron–client relations but Big Man networks must be understood as intricate webs of power – accounts of 'African patrimonialism' frequently fail to show this.

4 As networks cut across social space it is only natural that criminal actors are involved as well. Some networks concentrate more on criminal activities than others (see Chapter 6 in this volume). However, in an efficient network it is often an advantage to involve criminal nodes, or at least players who are less morally concerned. The Jago and the Preman in Indonesia are good examples of actors taking a natural part in larger socio-economic networks (Schulte Nordholt 1991; Ryter 1998; Schulte Nordholt and van Till 1999),[8] while politically and economically connected mafia organizations are well-known examples of networks across the world (see, e.g., Blok 1972, 1974). Yet it is important to point out that although some Big Men are criminals, most are not. Conflict networks are far from only about illicit commodity extraction and trade, but also about providing security, development and peace initiatives. Networks are alternative governance structures in particular in settings where other forms of governance are weak. Big Men and networks are not the prototypical form of governance in Africa any more than elsewhere in the world. Network forms of governance are a response to certain organizational factors in present-day Africa. Big Men appear in structural voids of the state, skilfully combining network governance, social control and economic activities. In this volume, we point out that Big Men and networks play particularly prominent roles in war and conflict.

Big Men and networks of governance in African conflicts

African wars in the post-Cold War era have commonly been dubbed New Wars, after Mary Kaldor's influential book *New and Old Wars: Organised violence in a global era* (1999), although critical voices have been raised, questioning the validity of this old/new distinction (e.g. Kalyvas 2001; Chan 2011). De Waal points out that '[t]he term "new wars" utilized by Mary Kaldor describes conflicts in less governed countries, rather than truly new forms of conflict' (de Waal 2009: 101). And Duffield contends that what is in fact 'new' is the security terrain shaped by network war (2002: 153, 156).[9] Network wars are rhizomatic, anti-institutional in character (ibid.: 161) and typically associated with shifts in social life (ibid.: 154). Instead of 'failures of modernity', Duffield, following Ulrich Beck (1992), proposes that we view these new network wars as an 'ambivalent and violent form of reflexive modernity' where '[w]ar as a reflexive and network enterprise does not follow the traditional state-based pattern of escalation, stalemate and decline' (Duffield 2002: 158).

Current networked wars in Africa involve not just national but hordes of external (African or non-African) actors. It is crucial to study networks of such actors in order to understand these wars. External actors, such as business-men, peacekeepers and aid donors, function as Big Men and connect in one way or another to national and regional networks. This is more pronounced in countries marked by conflicts than those not. Conflict countries are in fact soaking up international capital, according to William Reno (in Ferguson 2006: 41). In 1994 and 1995, half of private capital inflows to Africa south of the Sahara (except for South Africa) went to four countries with weak states, and three with ongoing civil wars: Liberia, Sierra Leone, DRC and Nigeria (ibid.). War economies link local resources illegally or legally to global markets in a variety of ways (Duffield 2002: 157; cf. also Chapters 1, 4, 6 and 10 in this volume). Blood diamonds and other conflict minerals have received widespread atten-tion, timber and foodstuffs less, although they are equally important. There are also flows of human resources in the form of conflict-related migrants as well as more directly conflict-related labourers, such as mercenary soldiers in the booming business of private security companies in, for instance, Iraq.[10]

Duffield notes that 'war economies, terrorist networks and criminal syndi-cates have increasingly become interconnected, not only among themselves, with legitimate businesses and established systems as well' (ibid.: 158). This is a central tenet of this book, yet we should be cautioned here by Reno's claim that many scholars conflate war and crime but tend to forget how peacetime politics may be even more conflated with crime than are the politics of war (Reno 2010: 128) and also keep in mind that conflict and post-conflict networks are not merely criminal, but also forms of alternative governance (as most chapters in this volume clearly point out). Yet fears persist that the illegal trade networks of wartime will jeopardize the fragile peace in several West African countries. Reno holds that drugs with a wholesale value of around $1.8 billion pass through West Africa on a yearly basis. Profits of an esti-mated $450 million end up in the pockets of traffickers, incomes that exceed the entire state budgets of several West African countries. Furthermore, an estimated ten million small arms circulate in West Africa (ibid.: 128–9). But organized crime is rife also in states that have not experienced direct civil war. For instance, in Nigeria, according to Nigeria's Economic and Financial Crimes Commission, the 'state is not even corruption. It's organized crime' (Watts 2008, cited in Reno 2010: 141). Reno correctly points out '[t]he irony ... that some of the actors who are held to be responsible for misdeeds in war and the exploitation of illicit commerce turn out to be best suited and most motivated to cater for the interests of young ex-combatants while those who participate most fully in postconflict reconstruction present the most risk of repeating patterns of behavior that are blamed for hindering the life prospects of young people' (ibid.: 145). This is a paradox to which I shall return in the concluding remarks of this introduction.

Few have done more for our understanding of the shadow side of African conflict networks than William Reno. However, some of the revelations of Carolyn Nordstrom are equally important and challenging, especially as her work on illicit war economies is poignantly global, beginning in African war zones, but ending up in the backyards of Europe and the USA. That there is a 'thin line between criminal traffic and government-inspired trade' (Castells 1998: 178, in Nordstrom 2007: 15) is something that Nordstrom's research makes intelligible, in *Shadows of War* (2004) and more so in *Global Outlaws* (2007). For the purposes of this book, I see the story of the Angolan 'governor' and his red tractors as particularly instructive, among a number of imperative examples of how social transaction, political power and economic wealth are interlaced and accumulated in the global shadows. The governor uses his political position and global connections with economic actors and the international aid busi-ness, involving local labour on close-to-slave contracts, INGO food-for-work arrangements and hordes of internally displaced peoples (IDPs); INGO tools, including heavy equipment such as tractors; and European air carriers – all to accumulate extreme personal wealth (ibid.: 27–35). What Nordstrom in particular underlines is how illicit Big Men play important roles in most networks, whether in conflict zones or well beyond. Many socio-economic networks list at least some criminal elements. These actors are often Big Men in their own right. Schulte Nordholt, for instance, as briefly mentioned above, has looked at the semi-criminal character of the Jago on Java, a figure that turned out to play a significant role in colonial Indonesia. He states that 'The *jago* was not a bandit ... He did not stand outside society but instead formed a crucial link with the political system. There was no transition from crime to rebellion, because the *jago* was part of the colonial power structure' (Schulte Nordholt and van Till 1999: 68). Borrowing from Anton Blok's historical work on the Sicilian Mafia (Blok 1972, 1974), Schulte Nordholdt points out that Jago figures gain importance in 'a process of unfinished state development in which local order breaks down and new groupings set themselves up violently as political entrepreneurs' (Schulte Nordholdt 1991: 89). What I want to stress with this comparison, albeit from an entirely different geographical context, is that criminal elements are important as components within political networks around the state as well as in direct contestation with the state. Jagos are clearly Big Men in their own right and have the capacity to grow considerably in times of socio-political unrest.[11]

The moral ambivalence of Big Men, the porosity and fluidity between legal and illegal, crime and politics, is pinpointed in several of the chapters in this volume. The following example is particularly connected to Anders' study (Chapter 7): Gus Kouwenhoven, a Dutch national and long-time resident of

Liberia, personifies the criminal Big Man of African conflict networks in many ways. After committing a variety of crimes in Europe and the USA, he fled justice and headed to West Africa. There, by pretending to be an international businessman, he conned his way into leasing Hotel Africa, the largest Monrovia hotel, from Liberian president Samuel Doe in the mid-1980s. From this position, he worked his way into the centre of the political economy in pre-war Liberia. When the war started, he smoothly changed sides and became a close ally of Charles Taylor, rebel leader and later president. Under Taylor's presidency, Kouwenhoven remained a key player, brokering a deal, among many others, with the Oriental Timber Company, which subsequently exported large quantities of hardwood from Liberia's virgin rainforest. Kouwenhoven allegedly also brokered arms deals for Taylor despite an international embargo. While clearly on the radar for international crimes, he simultaneously continued to run Hotel Africa and a whole complex of villas in its vicinity. During much of this time, the hotel and villas were rented by the United Nations for a presumed fortune. Kouwenhoven's broad international network, along with his standing as a Liberian Big Man, was essential to his success. In perfect keeping with the rules for a local Big Man, he was not just known for being a businessman. At the time I was living in the country, many Monrovians told me that Kouwenhoven helped people by paying children's school fees and making other redistributive efforts. Together with other key players around Charles Taylor, he was placed under a UN travel ban, but apparently still managed to travel to Europe on a number of occasions. After the fall of Charles Taylor, he could no longer reside in Liberia and was finally arrested by Dutch police in the town of his birth, Rotterdam, in 2005. In June 2006 he was sentenced to eight years in jail for arms smuggling. The court, however, did not find him guilty of war crimes despite his role in Liberia during the Taylor years. Were it not for well-connected Big Men criminals such as Kouwenhoven, war endeavours like Taylor's would make limited headway.

Informal wartime networks consist of a multitude of actors: politicians and political parties, military, finance, NGOs, national and international actors, religious leaders, businessmen, warlords and trade union leaders. As I have pointed out above, network analysis is taking us beyond simple identity-based categorizations of ethnicity, regional attachments and religion as key factors behind conflict. Many chapters in this book propose alternative logics to such categories, as well as demonstrating other driving forces (see, e.g., Chapters 4 and 9). It is clear that informal networks characteristically transgress the political landscape and, rather than pitching individuals against each other, exist alongside politicized identities. Yet conflicts rarely unfold owing to the existence of informal networks. Indeed, at certain times informal networks do manipulate differences, but from the viewpoint of economic logic this is seldom a choice preferred by conflict-based Big Men.[12]

Networks themselves are social creations, guided by common cultural codes, as noted above. Duffield points out how, during conflicts, '[e]ach of the components and nodes in a networked system such as those associated with reflexive forms of resistance and organized violence, are sites where new identities emerge, roles are reinvented, and novel forms of social legitimacy become established' (Duffield 2002: 160). Networks are reshaped by violence, but are also actively reshaping social space itself. Big Men who at the onset of a violent conflict may be marginal will move to the centre of networks owing to their knowledge of violence and access to potential soldiers and arms. Often, illicit Big Men take positions in networks where they previously played marginal roles. Once peace is restored, the network may morph back into its previous shape, or previously marginal Big Men may remain central, but aiming at more peaceful roles (although at times failing to do so, as discussed in Chapter 7 in this volume). Wars and conflict have at times made marginal Big Men even bigger in the post-war period. Typically, they will rise in power in political networks (cf. Chapters 2 and 5), but also in business networks where control over people is crucial (cf. Chapters 4 and 6).

De Waal, in his study of conflicts as marketplaces, states that 'political life can be described as an auction of loyalties in which provincial elites seek to extract from one or other metropolitan centre the best price for their allegiance' (de Waal 2009: 103). In fact, 'the marketplace of loyalties also operates at a lower level, whereby provincial elites secure support, including votes and guns, of their constituents in return for money, jobs and licenses to trade or pillage ... a similar market also operates within each metropolitan elite' (ibid.). Big Men, or what he calls provincial elite members, have in their turn their own Big Men, or metropolitan elites, with whom they bargain over loyalty compensated for by votes, money or violence (ibid.: 103–4; cf. also Chapter 8 of this volume). De Waal goes on to show how political bargains between metropolitan elites and provincial elites are quite short-term – often covering only two to three years – and then need to be renegotiated (ibid.: 104), stressing how network systems are nervously changing and flexible. In conflicts, changes appear even more rapidly: loyalties change overnight and rebel factions merge and fall apart (see Chapter 3). Big Men within the rebel armies, the commanders, take their men and join other factions, while foot soldiers change Big Man, rather than making individual political or identity-based moves (Utas 2008a; cf. also Chapter 9 in this volume); on the other hand violent conflict is a landscape of opportunity for subaltern Big Men motivated by individual socio-economic mobility (Utas 2009; cf. also Chapters 3 and 5 in this volume).

Big Men, networks and post-conflict

There is little doubt that liaisons between Big Men on different levels and in different settings within a conflict zone, but also outside in a broader warscape (Nordstrom 1997), have implications for the possible success of peace negotiations (as pointed out in Chapter 8 of this volume) and the sustainability of peace accords. Peace accords, de Waal states, 'will work only if the formal negotiations over constitutional provisions and power-sharing takes place in support of a patrimonial buy-in' (de Waal 2009: 108).[13] According to the logic of the marketplace, failing to do so implies that agreements end up as simple 'bargains that stick for as long as it suits the interest of both parties' (ibid.). As such provisions are chiefly viewed as pacts between government and provincial elites, hinged on security and patronage, there is actually a risk that they may increase violence. In addition, other Big Men, such as military and rebel commanders, have an equal interest in the possible end points of conflicts and so their informal investments and interests must also be taken into account. Moreover, it is imperative to emphasize that warfare is in some places the typical arena for Big Man politics (Utas 2008a, 2009). Warlords and other Big Men regularly enter not just conflicts, but also peace processes, as a result of personal socio-economic opportunities and prospects for personal advantage. Frequently such actors are aware of risks for their own safety and prosperity in the post-conflict setting (cf. Chapters 7, 8 and 10 in this volume).

As previously pointed out, conflict networks, in the eyes of the international emergency aid/post-war recovery industry, are seen only as a danger to the stability in war-ridden African states. Such observers fail to understand that these networks are far from simply criminal and a danger to stability but are, rather, extensions and reconfigurations of informally governing networks working in peacetime as well. Networks cannot simply be destroyed as they are multifaceted institutions governing, protecting and supporting most aspects of life in these countries. In many cases they are the very structures on which the government itself is resting. If Big Men are structurally as important as authors in this volume suggests, does this fact justify the efforts of the international justice system to indict war criminals? Are the International Criminal Court's indictments of President Bashir in Sudan and of a number of rebel and militia leaders in the DRC, or the Special Court for Sierra Leone's indictment of Charles Taylor from neighbouring Liberia, efficient methods for change and peace, or merely justice to victims only? (Further discussed in Chapter 7 of this volume.) Here, we need to reflect on what we know about the functioning of networks of Big Men, who partly combine efforts and partly compete over power. If a central Big Man disappears another Big Man will move into his/her position. In Liberia the removal of Charles Taylor, and his forced absence from the scene as the 'Biggest Man', did not lead to the death of his network. His loss of might was military, rather than diplomatic or legal, and occurred on the Liberian battlefield. He left the country owing to the military victory of the LURD and MODEL rebel movements, not as a consequence of his indictment by the Special Court for Sierra Leone. Other Big Men around Taylor maintained much of their powers after his removal; in fact, many of the financial Big Men, and to a lesser extent the political ones, moved their interests from around Taylor and later re-emerged as supporters and partially financial backers of the new Biggest (Wo)man, Ellen Johnson Sirleaf, elected president and cherished by the entire international community. In many ways, it could be argued that Taylor and Johnson Sirleaf had throughout the political commotion (and war) been part of the same network, although in competition (Utas 2008b). When Taylor lost out militarily, Big Men loyal to him regrouped around Johnson Sirleaf. 'Like a living organism, if you change its environment, in order to survive it will mutate – even to the extent of becoming a different life-form altogether,' states Duffield (2002: 158). And thus many Big Men maintain their grasp on socio-economic and political power, albeit by less violent means.

William Reno raises doubt as to whether the destruction of wartime militia networks is a viable path to a more stable and peaceful future in West Africa – and, by extension, in much of Africa – pointing out that 'instead of leading to chronic instability, violent commercial networks are seen playing important roles in creating new versions of sustainable order in communities and in creating new commercial opportunities that persist after a war' (2010: 129).[14] When politics is an extension of business and the interests of Big Men dominate state structures, then 'predation and plunder' may in fact contribute to 'new sustainable political economies' (ibid.: 130). But in places such as Liberia and Sierra Leone, Reno argues, the old local elites which have been restored to power in the aftermath of the civil wars are more corrupt, although less dependent on outright violent methods, and actually closer to the organizational logic of drug traffickers in Guinea-Bissau or corrupt civil servants in Nigeria than are wartime leaders and members of rebel groups in Liberia and Sierra Leone (ibid.: 131, 136). Indeed, state corruption in non-conflict countries is not random corruption, but in many cases the way government works; it is not incidental, but structural. Rebuilding centralized bureaucratic hierarchies

> ... does not necessary replace the logic of patronage-based rule in West Africa. Instead, these state agencies risk institutionalizing such relations in new form. If new hybrid forms of formal institutions, patronage politics, and commerce result in a greater level of local exploitation and illicit international transactions, then it may be better to de-emphasize the construction of European style state administrations in postconflict West Africa and to work more intensively to assist what already works to varying degrees for people on the ground. (Ibid.: 132)

Many wartime militia networks do survive in post-war environments (and it is rather obvious, from discussions here, that they will) 'as commercial organizations, as community based NGOs, and in quasi administrative roles, depending on their positioning vis-à-vis broader developments within their country's political situation' (ibid.: 135). Such networks clearly demonstrate capacities in the post-war arena (cf. Chapters 2, 4 and 9 in this volume). If they are closer to the grass roots, ought they not to be supported instead of destroyed? asks Reno. 'Uncritical top-down approaches toward the process of restoration risk restoring centralized patronage networks that control less powerful people's economic prospects and diminish their chances to influence their fates through their own decisions' (ibid.: 141). De Waal has similar thoughts regarding peace negotiations: 'The logic of the political marketplace means that an internationally guaranteed peace agreement may actually be less durable than a purely domestic one, not more' (2009: 109). Both Reno and de Waal highlight the need both to understand and to allow the local/domestic when studying and working with African conflicts; this, I would argue, is central to all chapters in this book.

The chapters

This volume is divided into two sections, one with country studies (Chapters 1–5) and one with thematically comparing chapters (6–10). The book is based on primary field research conducted by the authors themselves and has a multidisciplinary approach, combining scholars of political science, peace and conflict studies, political sociology, law and social anthropology.

In Chapter 1 Koen Vlassenroot and Sandrine Perrot scrutinize the semi-privatized military-economic networks that controlled the borderlands of DRC in the second Congolese war (1998–2003). Looking beyond criminalized descriptions that have been commonplace in UN reports, they focus on a trans-border military-commercial nexus tying the Ugandan military elite, with close connections to the Ugandan government, to the Congolese war, leading to refigurations of local regulation, power and control. Big Men within the Ugandan army used their military positions and great entrepreneurial skills to control both populations and resources in DRC. Two examples are very illustrative of this military entrepreneurialism. One is the case of Salim Saleh, Ugandan president Museveni's brother, who together with his wife and Museveni's son, Muhoozi Kainerugabe, developed a strategy of resource accumulation based on endless diversification of activities and the mixing of civilian and military businesses, charity, corruption and regional trading operations. Another example is General James Kazini, who initially led the operations of the Ugandan army in the DRC. Kazini evolved into a key actor in Congo's war economy, for which he constantly manipulated local actors and networks. The chapter by Vlassenroot and Perrot also challenges the argument that Big Men operate at the margins of the state and represent alternative power structures. Rather than weakening the Ugandan state, Ugandan military entrepreneurship and the semi-informalization of security structures created additional opportunities for regime consolidation. This brings the authors to the conclusion that there is a paradox between the constant undermining of state authority by parallel networks and the contribution of the same forces to the viability of the Ugandan state.

In Chapter 2 Maya Mynster Christensen focuses on events in the aftermath of the ten-year civil war in Sierra Leone. Here several former military commanders of both national army and rebel forces have in democratic processes carved out political space for themselves. Christensen is presenting a case study from a geographically remote area of Sierra Leone bordering Liberia and Guinea, where Tom Nyuma, a well-known 'warlord' in the civil war, was appointed chairman of the district council in Kailahun district after the national elections in 2007. The chapter shows how he has made shrewd use of his networks of ex-combatants, many of whom do not originate from the area, and thereby established himself as a prominent political and socio-economic Big Man. Nyuma is thus using both informal networks for his formal political ambitions and his formal political position for informal socio-economic profit. In classic Big Man fashion he is promoting his followers, and Christensen shows how junior commanders under his wing in the civil war make use of the space created by him to establish themselves as junior Big Men with both economic and political aspirations, most commonly with an aim not just to control local politics but to gain future positions in the Sierra Leonean capital Freetown.

In Chapter 3 Karel Arnaut deals with the proliferation of militias in the recent conflict in Côte d'Ivoire (2002–11). By placing specific emphasis on subaltern mobility of youngsters in urban Abidjan, he guides us through the waxing and waning of a myriad of militias. The latter are largely shaped by juvenile networking and vested in the *Nouchi* street culture of Abidjan, but also utilized by and closely connected to political and military Big Men in the country. The author is particularly interested in the youth militias' relationship with the *corps habillés* – army, police, etc. – that militia youth first and foremost relates to as support units, boosting its crippled capacity, but also aiming at integration into it as a major step towards social maturity and stability. Looking deeper into the dynamics of militia formation as impersonation of *corps habillés*, or, stated otherwise, as apprenticeship without real chances of full incorporation into the military, Arnaut scrutinizes the mutual complicity as well as the structural inequality of the two fellow armed forces in both war and post-war (or pre-peace, as he calls it) topographies. Arnaut is offering two key examples of militia Big Men and their manoeuvring of the fragile political environment of Abidjan during the reign of Laurent Gbagbo: that of the late Ato Belly and 'Marcus Garvey'. Both are young men who rose to a certain prominence during the past decade of conflict but in the end were not capable of transcending their subaltern position. The case of Ato Belly is that of a militia leader (who attained the rank of 'general' and was camp

22

commander of two important militia barracks) whose success largely resides in the way he engages in building and managing his '*gbôhi*' – the Nouchi label for 'gang': the kind of transient and yet socially consequential network that has become prototypical of urban juvenile life in Côte d'Ivoire during the last decade. Above all, the story of 'General' Ato shows how during that period the militarized *gbôhi* featured in larger constellations of patronage and political-military Bigmanity in Côte d'Ivoire. This also applies to the case of the militia member and *gbôhi* leader of lesser weight whose *nom de guerre* and *nom de plume* is 'Marcus Garvey'. In his autobiographical writings 'Marcus Garvey' reveals the intricacies of militia activity as the impersonation of *corps habillés*. As such, Garvey instantiates the militia membership of thousands of Ivoirian youths as a vital tactic of subaltern social mobility.

With case studies from post-war Liberia, Mariam Persson, in Chapter 4, shows how former commanders and soldiers from different rebel factions are carving out occupational niches in informal security and business sectors, by reutilizing chains of command and rebel networks maintained from the war years. Political Big Men, she points out, have gone a long way, not to demobilize and reintegrate, but rather to maintain such structures as means of power and security in an uncertain post-war terrain. Where the formal state has limited control, informal actors – although far from not being connected to Big Men within the state – become significant players. In the first part of the chapter Persson describes a vigilante group in Lofa County, where the leader is best portrayed as a local Big Man, connecting to more powerful people, but at the same time catering for and controlling groups of ex-combatants from within the Liberians United for Reconciliation and Democracy (LURD) rebel group. The Big Man's preference for including ex-combatants is due to the fact that they are already organized according to a military logic, and 'feared' in the local community. The second part of the chapter concerns the informal governance of one of the larger rubber plantations in the country. After the fall of Charles Taylor's government in 2003, LURD commanders took control of the plantation in a bid to maintain economic opportunities. LURD commander General X established himself as a Big Man in the area with control over business, with approximately five thousand ex-combatants as rubber tappers, as well as over socio-political life on and around the plantation. General X is a good example of the hybrid breed of a post-war Big Man successful in such a setting, where he commands and controls people beneath him, but is mandated his position by Bigger Men from within the political elite. In the case of General X these Bigger Men were Boakai Sirleaf, deputy minister of agriculture, and a relative of the Liberian president, and not least Fombah Sirleaf, director of the National Security Agency and stepson of the president, clearly pointing out that Liberian Big Man politics is a combination of political might, economic interest and violent control administrated through far- and deep-ranging informal networks criss-crossing geographic and social terrains.

Morten Bøås, in Chapter 5, takes us to northern Mali, where from a historical perspective he scrutinizes the 2006 Tuareg rebellion. He shows how emerging illicit trade, smuggling of contraband cigarettes, emerging drugs trade and trafficking of people destined for Europe have created not only new regional networks, but also novel types of Big Men contesting local power. In previous Tuareg rebellions the Malian state has managed to co-opt old elites by involving them in state bureaucracy. Rebel leaders and key commanders saw both armed resistance, often using the rhetoric of fighting for an independent Tuareg nation, and cooperation with the Malian state as means to maintain local control.

Decentralization efforts after the second Tuareg rebellion, which took place between 1990 and 1996, however, created resources to organize new networks around Big Men controlling political constituencies and the extraction of resources, the building of fresh 'castles in the sand', to paraphrase the title of Bøås' chapter. Yet when peace dividends failed to materialize, Big Men, such as Ibrahim Ag Banhage in the Kidal district, with a combination of political will and personal ambitions, fought their way into the local political scene. A new feature was that these Big Men did not come from noble or royal lineages, and thus contested long-standing power in the region. The May 2006 rebellion was made possible in part by local discontent and in part by the aspirations of these new Big Men. Much is in flux in northern Mali, and Bøås states that it is the combination of Malian politics played out on the local scene and a re-emergence of the importance of old trade routes into Algeria (now chiefly with illicit goods, new regional networks with, for instance, al-Qaeda in the Land of Maghreb (AQIM) – although he is downplaying connections with al-Qaeda – and the Niger Justice Movement (MNJ)) which accounts for the emergence of these new Big Men.

Henrik Vigh's Chapter 6 is centred on local political consequences of international trade in illicit drugs. Political power and large-scale drugs smuggling have become intimately intertwined in many West Africa coastal states, now by some called the cocaine coast. Vigh's material is, however, from the most gravely affected country, Guinea-Bissau, a country that has been dubbed Africa's first 'narco state'. With a focus on cocaine connections, Vigh argues that global networks have particularly targeted the country owing to the crisis of the Guinea-Bissauian state, which has made it a perfect drug hub where illicit goods and smuggling routes can be protected, but not interfered with. The cocaine trade is maintained through networks around Big Men that in many instances first rose to prominence during the struggle for independence and subsequently during the civil war that began in 1998. Vigh pinpoints how the *homi garandi*, the local Creole term for Big Man, lent their political offices and networks to Colombian cocaine cartels, creating a booming business for the few, yet still a forceful network economy which many citizens are forced to relate to. It is a well-known secret that the former president, Nino Vieira, was, up until his murder, the Biggest Man in the cocaine trade. However, the decapitation of Vieira and several other drug kingpins hardly affected the business. Vigh is highlighting how both armed factions during the civil war and drug networks are loosely ordered and based on transaction rather than issues of principle (quoting Adrian Meyer's work on quasi-groups). Reordering within Big Man networks is part of their nature, and when one Big Man passes another slips into his shoes, yet if the basis for existence changes a whole network may cease to function, although in the case Vigh considers the cocaine economy maintains its continuity.

In Chapter 7 Gerhard Anders examines to what extent the advent of international criminal justice and the criminalization of the African modes of warfare it entailed affected politics in Sierra Leone and Liberia. He describes how former leaders and commanders of armed factions attempted to convert their wartime exploits into social status, economic wealth and political influence. The period between 1999 and 2003 was characterized by intense, often violent, political conflicts as military and economic Big Men repositioned themselves after the end of the war in Sierra Leone. The Special Court for Sierra Leone, an international ad hoc tribunal established in 2002 to hold accountable those bearing greatest responsibility for war crimes committed in Sierra Leone, played an important role in these domestic power struggles both in Sierra Leone and Liberia by preventing Sam Hinga Norman, former militia leader and Sierra Leone's minister of internal affairs at the time of his arrest in 2003, and Charles Taylor, former rebel leader and Liberian president between 1997 and 2003, from further pursuing their political careers. In court, both men tried to adapt to the requirements of legal fact-finding, but while Taylor performed extremely well in the witness stand, Norman failed to conduct his own defence. This shows how difficult it is to perform Bigmanity in the arena of an international war crimes trial. Anders' analysis traces the complex interplay of external and internal forces shaping contemporary African Big Man politics in the shadow of international criminal law's growing influence.

Ilmari Käihkö's Chapter 8 focuses on power-sharing and informal governance in conflicts around the African continent, ranging from full-scale wars to more limited forms of violent conflict. Käihkö's chapter starts off with a comprehensive discussion of Big Men and networks in relation to state power and political opposition in contemporary Africa – in some ways fleshing out points that I have only hinted at in this introduction. In the main body of his chapter the author observes that a major problem with the literature on power-sharing and co-option is that it seldom takes informal structures into account, but maintains a simple focus on the political party, the rebel group or militia, without observing that in most African countries these are rarely managed by a centralized administration, or have a single political agenda, but are rather fractured and made up by groups, or often individual Big Men with diverse and far from formal motives and agendas. On political parties, Käihkö notes that in reality they are often networks built around Big Men, constituting little more than façades for individually based interests. The same goes for many military movements and rebel factions on the continent, he further argues. As much of the real politics happens far from the formal façades, a deeper understanding of the informal realities of local contexts becomes of utmost importance. Käihkö concludes that a better understanding of contemporary African political realities can be gained only by combining the formal and informal perspectives, and therefore ending the strict categorization of politics into formal and informal.

Anders Themnér, in Chapter 9, points out that long after armed groups have been disarmed and demobilized, informal military networks continue to be a reality for many war-torn African societies. Often these structures are upheld by Big Men who see them as assets in their political and economic struggles with other elites. For Big Men it is especially important to gain access to ex-combatants. Accustomed to taking orders and possessing military skills, former fighters can be used for any number of socio-economic and political purposes, including warfare. For this reason, informal military networks constitute a significant challenge when building sustainable peace. However, in order to address the threat posed by such structures, it is necessary to acknowledge the role played by a post-conflict actor that is often forgotten – former mid-level commanders (MiLCs). As gatekeepers into ex-combatant communities, they possess a near-monopoly on interaction between Big Men and ex-fighters. Post-war elites are therefore often obliged to enlist ex-MiLCs as intermediaries in order to represent them in their dealings with former combatants. For this reason, any peace-building efforts failing to take ex-MiLCs into consideration run the risk of sowing the seeds of new violence.

Ruben de Koning, in Chapter 10, deals with the uses, or abuses, of natural resources in African conflict zones. By presenting examples from recent conflicts in Central and West Africa, the author starts with a discussion on so-called conflict resources and how Big Men with business, military and political backgrounds in times of conflict operate through controlling and administrating resources. He points towards a clear continuity in governance of resources over pre-war, war and post-war times, whereby rebel leaders in the conflicts often had direct stakes in the pre-war state, or were part of resource-full networks connected to pre-war governing structures. In other words, in most cases conflict resources are controlled by the same socio-economic Big Men as before the outbreak of civil war. De Koning is using DRC as an in-depth case, showing a variety of Big Men and networks set up around the management of conflict resources, with military commanders becoming informal governors, tax officials or mine guardians, and where Big Businessmen create militias, if not themselves transforming into rebel leaders. In the case of North Kivu he points out that a trading elite, together with local civil groups, managed to sideline rebels by creating its own militia, the Mai Mai, and thus maintained its grip over prosperous business and a level of socio-political leverage. On the other hand he also shows how in Kivu and elsewhere in the eastern DRC, networks headed by military Big Men control resources through taxation of mines and/or transport of minerals – for instance, the 85th brigade of the FARDC, the reformed national army, is believed to have levied informal taxes to the tune of US$350,000 monthly from a single mine in 2007. The brigade did not just function as tax collectors controlling through violent means, but also to some extent protected civilians and helped settle local conflicts. De Koning also gives examples of how, in the process of army reform, through the inclusive *brassage* procedure, military Big Men refused, or delayed, the movement of their troops to new designated regions on the ground that they would lose control over resource rewards in strategic areas, a fact that has been a serious problem for successful army reform in the country. A final case of particular interest to this volume is how the Forces démocratiques de libération du Rwanda (FDLR) have not just been collecting revenues but have also given credits for commercial activities to actors both within and outside the FDLR, a typical Big Man form of redistribution.

Notes

1 The African continent is huge; Africa cannot be explained in a single and comprehensive way as differences abound when it comes to economy, politics or sociology. By focusing broadly on the continent of Africa in this book, we are not arguing for Africa as a cultural region (it is not a 'culturology of African politics', in James Ferguson's phrase (2006)), nor for Africa as the result of a singular history.

2 Many writers have, justifiably, questioned the use of formal/informal distinctions, especially from an economic vantage point (Meagher 2010; MacGaffey 1991; MacGaffey et al. 2000; Hansen and Vaa 2004; Lourenço-Lindell 2010), but for the sake of simplicity we use 'formal' in this book to mean state-governed or state-controlled, and 'informal' for what is governed by other institutions, or partly ungoverned. Simone points out that, rather than a coherent category, the 'so-called informal sector is a kind of umbrella for a multitude of "stories"' (Simone 2004b: 24).

3 Big Man is not a gendered concept; despite the gender specificity of the term, women can also be Big Men.

4 Very much in line with what Hardt and Negri call the (new) *Empire* (2001).

5 Here we have what Christian Lund describes as the twilight institutions at work (2006).

6 Certainly also dependent on other structural conditions, but entering into more detail is beyond the scope of this book.

7 My emphasis. See critique by, for instance, Mkandawire (2002: 184); Erdmann and Engel (2006); and Olukoshi (2001, 2005). The latter has been one of the most vociferous critics of neo-patrimonial explanation. He points out how neo-patrimonialism in itself becomes a catch-all paradigm that obstructs a wide

diversity of explanations needed to understand African societies (Olukoshi, keynote speech, Uppsala, 28 October 2010).

8 See below for an extended discussion on the Jago and Preman in relation to criminal actors in conflict areas.

9 It is also worth pointing out that for some individuals war is a direct entry point to modernity (Utas 2008a).

10 On former Sierra Leone soldiers in Iraq, see, for example, Christensen and Utas (2008) and Utas (2010).

11 Loren Ryter shows the continuity of the Jago in the more recent Indonesian Preman (Ryter 1998).

12 On the other hand, it may be a method used by international businessmen and conglomerates forming part of conflict networks in a particular country or region.

13 There is still no guarantee that it will work.

14 Reno is describing how similar kinds of violent structures were a large part of the creation of European states, referring to the work of Charles Tilly (1992).

References

Abdulsamed, F. (2011) *Somali Investment in Kenya*, Chatham House Briefing Paper, Africa Programme, March.

Andersen, L., B. Møller and F. Stepputat (2007) *Fragile States and Insecure People? Violence, security, and statehood in the twenty-first century*, New York: Palgrave Macmillan.

Barnes, J. A. (1954) 'Class and committees in a Norwegian island parish', *Human Relations*, pp. 39–58.

Bayart, J.-F. (1993) *The State in Africa: The politics of the belly*, London and New York: Longman.

Bayart, J.-F., S. Ellis and B. Hibou (1999) *The Criminalization of the State in Africa*, Bloomington: Indiana University Press.

Beck, U. (1992) *Risk Society: Towards a new modernity*, London: Sage.

Biró, D. (2007) 'The (un)bearable lightness of ... violence: warlordism as an alternative form of governance in the "Westphalian periphery"?', in T. Debiel and D. Lambach (eds), *INEF Report 89*, Duisburg/Essen: INEF.

Bledsoe, C. (1990) '"No success without struggle": social mobility and hardship for foster children in Sierra Leone', *Man*, 25: 70–88.

Blok, A. (1972) 'The peasant and the brigand: social banditry reconsidered', *Comparative Studies in Society and History*, 14: 494–503.

— (1974) *The Mafia of a Sicilian village, 1860–1960; a study of violent peasant entrepeneurs*, Oxford: Blackwell.

Bøås, M. and K. C. Dunn (2007) *African Guerrillas: Raging against the machine*, Boulder, CO: Lynne Rienner.

Bratton, M. and N. Van de Walle (1997) *Democratic Experiments in Africa: Regime transitions in comparative perspective*, Cambridge: Cambridge University Press.

Castells, M. (1996) *The Rise of the Network Society. The information age: economy, society and culture*, Malden, MA: Blackwell.

Chabal, P. and and J.-P. Daloz (1999) *Africa Works: Disorder as political instrument*, London/Oxford/Bloomington: International African Institute in association with James Currey and Indiana University Press.

Chan, S. (2011) 'On the uselessness of new wars theory: lessons from African conflicts', in C. Sylvester (ed.), *Experiencing War*, London: Routledge.

Christensen, M. M. and M. Utas (2008) 'Mercenaries of democracy: the "politricks" of remobilized combatants in the 2007 general elections, Sierra Leone', *African Affairs*, 107(429): 515–39.

Clapham, C. (1998) *African Guerrillas*, Oxford: James Currey.

De Smedt, J. (2009) '"No Raila, no peace!" Big Man politics and election violence at the Kibera grassroots', *African Affairs*, 108: 581–98.

De Waal, A. (2009) 'Mission without end? Peacekeeping in the African marketplace', *International Affairs*, 85: 99–113.

Duffield, M. (2001) *Global Governance and*

the New Wars: The merging of development and security, London: Zed Books.

— (2002) 'War as a network enterprise: the new security terrain and its implications', Journal for Cultural Research, 6: 153–65.

Eilstrup-Sangiovanni, M. and C. Jones (2008) 'Assessing the dangers of illicit networks: why al-Qaida may be less threatening than many think', International Security, 33: 7–44.

Epstein, A. L. (1961) 'The network and urban social organization', Rhodes-Livingstone Institute Journal, pp. 29–62.

Erdmann, G. and U. Engel (2006) 'Neopatrimonialism revisited – beyond a catch-all concept', Giga (German Institute of Global and Area Studies) Working Papers no. 16, pp. 1–38.

Fanthorpe, R. (2001) 'Neither citizen nor subject? "Lumpen" agency and the legacy of native administration in Sierra Leone', African Affairs, 100: 363–86.

Ferguson, J. (2006) Global Shadows: Africa in the neoliberal world order, Durham, NC: Duke University Press.

Godelier, M. (1986) The Making of Great Men: Male domination and power among the New Guinea Baruya, Cambridge: Cambridge University Press.

Godelier, M. and M. Strathern (eds) (1991) Big Men and Great Men: Personifications of power in Melanesia, Cambridge: Cambridge University Press.

Goffman, E. (1959) The Presentation of Self in Everyday Life, Garden City, NY: Doubleday.

Guyer, J. I. (1993) 'Wealth in people and self-realization in Equatorial Africa', Man, 28: 243–65.

Hansen, K. T. and M. Vaa (2004) Reconsidering Informality: Perspectives from urban Africa, Uppsala: Nordiska Afrikainstitutet.

Hansen, T. B. and F. Stepputat (eds) (2005) Sovereign Bodies: Citizens, migrants, and states in the postcolonial world, Princeton, NJ: Princeton University Press.

Hardt, M. and A. Negri (2001) Empire, Cambridge, MA: Harvard University Press.

Herzfeld, M. (1997) Cultural Intimacy: Social poetics in the nation-state, New York: Routledge.

Huntington, S. P. (1997) The Clash of Civilizations and the Remaking of World Order, New York: Touchstone.

Jackson, M. (2004) In Sierra Leone, Durham, NC: Duke University Press.

Kaldor, M. (1999) New and Old Wars: Organized violence in a global era, Stanford, CA: Stanford University Press.

Kalyvas, S. N. (2001) '"New" and "old" civil wars a valid distinction?', World Politics, 54: 99–118.

Kapferer, B. (1973) 'Social network and conjugal role in urban Zambia: towards a reformulation of the Bott hypothesis', in J. Boissevain and C. Mitchell (eds), Network Analysis: studies in human interaction, The Hague: Mouton.

Kopytoff, I. and S. Miers (1977) 'African "slavery" as an institution of marginality', in I. Kopytoff and S. Miers (eds), Slavery in Africa: Historical and anthropological perspectives, Madison: University of Wisconsin Press.

Lévi-Strauss, C. (1966) The Savage Mind, London, Weidenfeld & Nicolson.

Lindley, A. (2009) 'Between "dirty money" and "development capital": Somali money transfer infrastructure under global scrutiny', African Affairs, 108: 519–39.

Little, P. D. (2003) Somalia: Economy without state, Oxford: International African Institute in association with James Currey.

Lourenço-Lindell, I. (2010) Africa's Informal Workers: Collective agency, alliances and transnational organizing in urban Africa, London: Zed Books.

Lund, C. (2006) 'Twilight institutions: an introduction', Development and Change, 37: 673–84.

MacGaffey, J. (1991) The Real Economy of Zaire: The contribution of smuggling and other unofficial activities to national wealth, Philadelphia: University of Pennsylvania Press.

MacGaffey, J., R. Bazenguissa-Ganga and

International African Institute (2000) *Congo-Paris: Transnational traders on the margins of the law*, London/Bloomington/Oxford: International African Institute in association with James Currey and Indiana University Press.

Mamdani, M. (1996) *Citizen and Subject: Contemporary Africa and the legacy of late colonialism*, Princeton, NJ: Princeton University Press.

Mayer, A. (1966) 'The significance of quasi-groups in the study of complex societies', in M. Banton (ed.), *The Social Anthropology of Complex Societies*, London: Tavistock.

Mbembe, A. (2001) *On the Postcolony*, Berkeley: University of California Press.

— (2003) 'Necropolitics', *Public Culture*, 15: 11–40.

Meagher, K. (2010) *Identity Economics: Social networks and the informal economy in Nigeria*, Woodbridge and Rochester, NY: James Currey.

Médard, J.-F. (1992) 'Le "big man" en Afrique: esquisse d'analyse du politicien entrepreneur', *L'Année Sociologique*, 42: 167–92.

Mitchell, C. (1973) 'Networks, norms and institutions', in J. Boissevain and C. Mitchell (eds), *Network Analysis: Studies in human interaction*, The Hague: Mouton.

— (1974) 'Social networks', *Annual Review of Anthropology*, 3: 279–99.

Mkandawire, T. (2002) 'The terrible toll of post-colonial "rebel movements" in Africa: towards an explanation of the violence against peasantry', *Journal of Modern African Studies*, 40: 181–215.

Nordstrom, C. (1997) *A Different Kind of War Story*, Philadelphia: University of Pennsylvania Press.

— (2004) *Shadows of War: Violence, power, and international profiteering in the twenty-first century*, Berkeley and London: University of California Press.

— (2007) *Global Outlaws: Crime, money, and power in the contemporary world*, Berkeley: University of California Press.

Nugent, P. (1995) *Big Men, Small Boys and Politics in Ghana: Power, ideology and the burden of history, 1982–94*, London: Pinter/Mansell.

Olukoshi, A. O. (2001) *West Africa's Political Economy in the Next Millennium: Retrospect and prospect*, Dakar: CODESRIA.

— (2005) 'Changing patterns of politics in Africa', in A. Boron and G. Lechini (eds), *Politics and Social Movements in an Hegemonic World: Lessons from Africa, Asia and Latin America*, Buenos Aires: CLASCO.

— (2010) 'Democratic governance and accountability in Africa: in search of a workable framework'. Inception workshop of the NAI research cluster on conflict, displacement and transformation, Uppsala, 28/29 October.

Podolny, J. M. and K. L. Page (1998) 'Network forms of organization', *Annual Review of Sociology*, 24: 57–76.

Powell, W. W. (1990) 'Neither market nor hierarchy: network forms of organization', *Research in Organizational Behavior*, 12: 295–336.

Reno, W. (1995) *Corruption and State Politics in Sierra Leone*, Cambridge: Cambridge University Press.

— (1998) *Warlord Politics and African States*, Boulder, CO: Lynne Rienner.

— (2010) 'Transforming West African networks for postwar recovery', *Comparative Social Research*, 27: 127–49.

Richards, P. (1996) *Fighting for the Rain Forest: War, youth and resources in Sierra Leone*, Oxford: James Currey.

Ryter, L. (1998) 'Pemuda Pancasila: the last loyalist free men of Suharto's order?', *Indonesia*, 66: 45–73.

Sahlins, M. D. (1963) 'Poor man, rich man, big-man, chief: political types in Melanesia and Polynesia', *Comparative Studies in Society and History*, 5: 285–303.

Schulte Nordholt, H. (1991) 'The Jago in the shadow: crime and "order" in the colonial state in Java', *RIMA*, 25: 74–91.

Schulte Nordholt, H. and M. van Till (1999) 'Colonial criminals in Java, 1870–1910', in V. L. Rafael (ed.), *Figures of Criminality in Indonesia, the Philippines, and Colonial Vietnam*, Ithaca, NY: SEAP/Cornell University.

Shryock, A. (2004) *Off Stage/On Display: Intimacy and ethnography in the age of public culture*, Stanford, CA: Stanford University Press.

Simone, A. (2004a) 'People as infrastructure: intersecting fragments in Johannesburg', *Public Culture*, 16: 407–29.

— (2004b) *For the City Yet to Come: Changing African life in four cities*, Durham, NC: Duke University Press.

Srinivas, M. N. and A. Béteille (1964) 'Networks in Indian social structure', *Man*, 64: 165–8.

Taussig, M. (1992) 'Culture of terror – space of death: Roger Casement's Putumayo report and the explanation of torture', in N. B. Dirks (ed.), *Colonialism and Culture*, Ann Arbor: University of Michigan Press.

Tilly, C. (1992) *Coercion, Capital, and European States*, Oxford: Blackwell.

Turner, S. (2010) *Politics of Innocence: Hutu identity, conflict, and camp life*, New York: Berghahn Books.

Utas, M. (2008a) 'Abject heroes: marginalised youth, modernity and violent pathways of the Liberian Civil War', in J. Hart (ed.), *Years of Conflict: Adolescence, political violence and displacement*, Oxford: Berghahn Books.

— (2008b) 'Liberia beyond the blueprints: poverty reduction strategy papers, Big Men and informal networks', Lecture Series on African Security, 150.227.5.137/upload/projects/Africa/Utas%20Liberia%20Beyond%20the%20Blueprints.pdf, accessed 11 December 2009.

— (2009) 'Malignant organisms: continuities of state-run violence in rural Liberia', in B. Kapferer and B. E. Bertelsen (eds), *Crisis of the State: War and social upheaval*, Oxford: Berghahn Books.

— (2010) 'The rewards of political violence: remobilizing ex-combatants in post-war Sierra Leone', in Graduate Institute of International and Development Studies (ed.), *Small Arms Survey 2010: Gangs, groups, and guns*, Cambridge: Cambridge University Press.

Utas, M. and M. Jörgel (2008) 'The West Side Boys: military navigation in the Sierra Leone civil war', *Journal of Modern African Studies*, 46(3): 487–511.

PART ONE

Country case studies

1 | Ugandan military entrepreneurialism on the Congo border

Koen Vlassenroot and Sandrine Perrot

In early August 1998, Ugandan troops re-entered the Democratic Republic of the Congo, as part of a joint strategy with Rwanda to oust the Congolese president, Laurent-Désiré Kabila.[1] Very soon, media sources and Ugandan parliamentary representatives started reporting the involvement of semi-privatized military-economic networks, including high-ranking Ugandan People's Defence Force (UPDF) officials, that would be described as 'entrepreneurs of insecurity' (Perrot 1999b) or committing acts of 'military commercialism' (Dietrich 2000).[2] Hardly three years after the beginning of this second Congolese war (1998–2003), senior UPDF officers, linked to local militias and international commercial networks, were singled out by a UN Panel of Experts report on the illegal exploitation of Congolese resources. The head of the Ugandan expeditionary corps in the DRC, the late General James Kazini, the chief of military intelligence, Colonel Noble Mayombo, Uganda's presidential adviser on Congo, Colonel Kahinda Otafiire, President Museveni's brother and UPDF lieutenant general (retired) Salim Saleh, his wife Jovia Akandwanaho and Colonel Peter Karim were all named as key players in what was referred to as an 'elite network' (United Nations 2002). James Kazini and Salim Saleh particularly could be considered as Big Men. Both held a key position within the Ugandan regime, from which they skilfully exploited the opportunities offered by the Congolese war to further expand their economic and political power. Their capacity to mobilize regional networks was a key condition to get access to Congo's vast natural resources. The same networks played a pivotal role in Congo's war economy, linking local zones of production to regional and international markets and local to regional actors, and reconfiguring the local economic space, with local and regional Big Men and politico-military entrepreneurs as key actors.

In most explanations of Uganda's military involvement in the DR Congo conflict, these informal networks have taken centre stage but have hardly been defined.[3] Political scientists tend to see these economic and political networks as non-state forms of organization or informal institutions. These networks are considered as predatory forces and socially destructive forms of organization, undermining political stability, the functioning of state institutions and economic efficiency (Reno 2000; Bayart et al. 1999). Based on his research in Sierra Leone, Reno also introduced the term 'shadow state', which relates to the informal commercial networks that operate parallel to state bureaucracies and undermine formal governance. Even if state agents are involved, according to Reno, these networks have their own channels of exploitation and commercialization outside of the state (Reno 2000).

Other authors have argued, though, that these networks, which in most cases are understood as very centralized structures of control and regulation, can shape political processes and political authority (Lund 2007; Roitman 2004b; Callaghy et al. 2001), particularly in Africa's war-torn societies or fragile states. The seminal research of Janet Roitman on the Chad Basin's unregulated commerce in this sense is inspiring for the evaluation of Uganda's intervention in the DRC. Wrong-footing dominant literature, Roitman described these emergent forms of economic regulation as a 'productive moment' that does not blur the functioning of the state. According to her, militarized shadow networks may not undermine state power but take part in the reconstitution of its authority through informal actors emerging in the interstices of the state system. She explains these unregulated economic activities as moments of reconfiguration of social regulation. 'Generally interpreted as existing beyond the state or even anti-state, their tactics of mobility and misdemeanour are essential to the reconstitution of state power today. As part of the genealogy of that indeterminate and ever-elusive category, the flottante population (those who are on the frontiers of wealth creation in this time of indebtedness and austerity) has become a new target of state regulation' (Roitman 2004b: 16).

This perspective on trans-border networks as 'alternative forms of governance and authority' is the starting point of our evaluation of the informal political structures and networks linking Uganda's political centre to Congo's war complex. In this chapter we do not want to question the validity of the different motives of Uganda's second intervention in the DR Congo. Nor do we want to evaluate Uganda's occupation in relation to a larger internal process of state-building (Reno 2002) or to unravel the structures and mechanisms that made it possible for UPDF's 'entrepreneurs of insecurity' (Perrot 1999b) to accumulate profits from their military presence on Congolese territory. Rather we want to document the scope and content of different trans-border networks and how these have been exploited by a number of Ugandan Big Men. This perspective on Congo's war helps to explain how military intervention has shaped and reshaped existing patterns of trans-border economic exchange and political processes.

One particular issue of discussion will be the relationship between these Big Men and the Ugandan state. It will be argued that these Big Men and networks do not necessarily lead to further state fragmentation and can be an important tool for regime consolidation. Beyond the criminalized description given by the UN reports, we want to contextualize these networks from a historical perspective, to evaluate their embedment in *longue durée* localized and trans-border networks, and to analyse and illustrate the 'military-commercial nexus' (Roitman 2004b) that has developed along the Ugandan–Congolese border as part of UPDF's involvement in the Congolese wars. We will use both the notion of 'Big Men' and of 'military-political entrepreneurs' (Perrot 1999b; Giustozzi 2005) to highlight the personalization of these networks, and the accumulation of economic but also political resources through straddling positions (Médard 1992) and a legitimation strategy based on the redistribution of resources and political exchanges. We will insist on the horizontal and vertical connections linking the actors of these networks and raise the question of the perpetuation of these networks in the state, both during and after the end of the war. Our reflection will not be based on why they were created, but on how they were perpetuated in the state system, and what it tells us about the nature and functioning of the Ugandan state. In doing so, this chapter questions the common perspective on Big Men and networks as alternative forms of governance at the margins of the state, as well as the perspective that Big Men and networks mainly operate in fragile formal contexts. As will become clear from the analysis of Ugandan military entrepreneurialism in the Ugandan–Congolese borderland, the informal networks operating in this environment are not necessarily alternative power structures in opposition to the state, but to a considerable extent depend on their integration in the formal Ugandan political space, which thus includes different, parallel centres of authority and sovereignty.

Pre-war trans-border networks

Key to the success of the military-commercial nexus is the historical process of informalization of both Uganda's and Congo's borderlands and the existence of pre-war trans-border networks of economic and social exchange. During the Congolese wars, these networks could be mobilized and exploited by new coalitions of army commanders, rebel leaders, traders and local authorities. Also, UPDF commanders increasingly traded protection and security for economic gain with local, Congolese politico-military elites, smugglers and traders, with existing trans-border networks being continuously manipulated. So-called 'elite networks' replaced pre-existing local informal networks that developed during Mobutu's regime because of porous borders (MacGaffey 1991) and weak local state institutions (Reno 1998). These pre-existing transnational networks had already destroyed the formal economy and used state power to instrumentalize the potentialities of informal trade (gold and diamond smuggling), through a subversion of the state regulatory authority (Vlassenroot 2003: 342; MacGaffey 1991).

In this sense, the manipulation of the Congolese–Ugandan borderland during the Congolese wars offers an interesting example of how unregulated economic activities can be moments of reconfiguration of local regulation and reconstitution of public authority and state power. As is illustrated by recent developments in the Ugandan–Congolese borderland, these zones can also be understood as regions of inventiveness, creating their own institutional arrangements and regulatory regimes that eventually (re)define their relationship with the central state (Raeymaekers 2009). Here, at least one paradox can be observed, though. While the further development of these trans-border networks during the Congolese wars hardly affected regime stability in Uganda, the survival of some of these networks in the DR Congo after the start of the peace process overshadows the functioning of the reinstituted state administration and turns the Congolese state into a very weak centre of power (Vlassenroot 2008).

The dramatic increase in cross-border economic transactions, both in volume and in their illicit character, had already started during the 1980s and consolidated the emergence of a vast regional network of informal trade that became 'the means by which seemingly disastrous national economies managed to keep going' (MacGaffey 1987: 22). Where official international treaties in the Great Lakes Region failed to create regional economic integration, unrecorded cross-border trade resulted in unofficial market integration beyond the state limits yet with the complicity of state agents. In the mining sector specifically, the Mobutu regime liberalized the grip of state societies or state shareholding on the production, exploitation and commercialization of the main national natural resources in 1982. This privatization accelerated the informalization of the trans-border economy. Hundreds of private small-scale exploitation structures were created and absorbed by local and foreign private gold-diggers and diamond exploiters in Kasaï, Katanga, Kivu and Orientale Province. In the 1990s, in Kilo Moto gold mines (Ituri District), for example, exploitation of resources was increasingly taken over by Congolese gold-diggers, selling 'their production to Hema (Ituri) and Nande (North-Kivu) traders, who themselves fraudulently export gold via Kampala and mainly Bujumbura' (Willame 2007).[4] Not only local entrepreneurs profited from these smuggling activities: 'private businesses, transportation companies, and tax-collecting bureaucracies throughout the region benefited significantly from the informal sector and the income opportunities it provided' (Mwanasali 2000: 140). This explains why already prior to the Congolese war, a vast network of informal trading had sprung up, connecting Ugandan and Congolese markets. Disrupting agricultural economies, informal networks increasingly interfered with violence and conflict areas.

Intervening in the DR Congo: the rise of 'entrepreneurs of insecurity'

Already during the military campaign against Mobutu in 1996–97, UPDF commanders discovered a veritable 'Mini Eldorado' in the eastern parts of Zaire (Vlassenroot and Raeymaekers 2004b) and concluded alliances with

Kabila's networks, already involved in violent and illegal mineral exploitation (Schatzberg 1997, in Clark 2001a: 275). In Kisangani and Ituri, both flourishing centres of informal diamond or gold trade, UPDF officers started exploiting Congolese minerals for their own benefit. Initially, the smuggling activities of the UPDF were mainly organized on an individual basis.[5] UPDF commanders quickly learned, though, how to turn their military control into a profitable enterprise by developing a lucrative modus vivendi with Congolese business communities in Orientale Province. The result was that local Congolese traders, even if they did not benefit directly from the war, could continue their economic activity or could even profit from it if they were able to establish a position in the military trade mechanisms. But Ugandan traders also took advantage of UPDF's presence in the DR Congo and were offered free passage to sell goods such as soap, metal roof sheeting, fuel, canned food and clothing to the Congolese consumer market in exchange for natural resources and agricultural produce. The fact that UPDF's military intervention in 1997 was a lucrative enterprise also for the Ugandan economy was illustrated by the country's gold exports, which in 1997 became the second-largest source of export income (Clark 2001a).[6]

After Kabila took power in May 1997, economic relations between both countries intensified with several visits of Ugandan delegations of businessmen and government officials to the DR Congo and a bilateral agreement on a number of development projects. One of these projects, which was never realized, included a railway that would connect Ugandan and Congolese markets. Both countries also concluded an agreement on military cooperation. The Alliance of Democratic Forces for the Liberation of Congo-Zaire (AFDL) campaign succeeded in ousting Mobutu from power but did not put an end to the Allied Democratic Forces–National Army for the Liberation of Uganda (ADF-NALU) operations in eastern DR Congo, which continued to pose a security concern to Uganda. In April 1998, an arrangement that allowed the UPDF to conduct operations in eastern DR Congo against several Ugandan militias was formalized with a Protocol on Security along the Common Border. As a result, on the eve of the second Congolese war, the UPDF presence in DR Congo had already increased to three battalions (Fahey 2009).

In spring 1998, the Ugandan–Congolese relationship started to deteriorate. Already prior to the start of the second Congolese war, the Congolese minister of economy and oil, Pierre Victor Mpoyo, caused a deep rift in relations between Congo and Uganda when accusing Ugandan government officials of warlord practices in a provocative statement, broadcast by Congolese radio on 22 May 1998. According to Mpoyo, top Ugandan officials were involved in the smuggling of gold, diamond and timber from north-eastern DR Congo (Ayeabare 1998). Kinshasa also denounced the existence of a Rwandan–Ugandan plot to assassinate the Congolese president. Inspired by the fears of a Rwanda-led *coup d'état* and in search of local power bases, on 27 July 1998 the Kabila regime urged all foreign troops to leave the country within two weeks. This decision was the final trigger for a second Rwandan–Ugandan military adventure in the DR Congo. Six days after Rwandan and Ugandan troops were expelled, the same troops re-entered the country in support of the Rassemblement Congolais pour la Démocratie (RCD), a Congolese rebel movement created in Kigali a few days after the start of this military operation.

During this second Ugandan intervention (1998–2003), the exploitation of Congolese resources became much more systematic, and trading networks, linking mining centres in Congo's hinterland to international traders, drastically expanded. As part of UPDF's presence in the DR Congo, these patterns of military commercialism evolved from a parasitic structure of military businessmen and petty thieves already active in northern Uganda, for example (Perrot 1999a), to a feverish entrepreneurial logic of conflict economy linked with international illegal and criminal networks: 'Over the months, successful businesses and petty corruption (petty theft, smuggling, as well as the sale of gasoline, uniforms, the mixing of different qualities of coffee) – after all typical in conflict areas – expanded to evolve into an entrepreneurial organization adept at a large scale business of war, led by a military businessmen clique, whose very pillars were the government structures, of the bellicose states'[7] (Perrot 1999b).

The existence of these networks (which involved Congolese, Rwandese and Ugandan political leaders, military commanders, businessmen, leaders of armed groups, local administrators and international commercialization networks) would be presented as an illustration of a new type of warfare aimed at maximizing profit through military control over resources and based on a new type of partnership between military commanders and businessmen. It was observed that 'privatised networks of individual army officials, local warlords, and international enterprises are orchestrating the plundering of the Congo for their personal benefit in order to finance their war. They gave birth to a new political economy, in which national sovereignty and state boundaries have become almost completely irrelevant' (Raeymaekers 2002: 4). These 'structures of opportunity' included formal and informal elements and could best be described as militarized shadow networks with a clear interconnectedness between public and private logics.

Even though authors disagree on the initial motivation of this Ugandan intervention (see Prunier 1999; Prunier 2004; Clark 2001a; Reno 2000), it is unquestionable that after a few months the security objectives were also diverted or manipulated for financial and economic stakes. The economic benefits of these military entrepreneurs brought to light the lucrative dynamic of the Congolese conflict. It could be argued that these individuals, assured of their political position at home, continuously exploited a context of insecurity in the DR Congo as a source of private income. For several observers, these strategies point at an informalization of politics and the military in Uganda (Reno 2000; Clark 2001a). Eriksen even states that 'because the regime is politically dependent on support from the army, it has been unable or unwilling to control the behaviour of its armed forces in Congo and to prevent private profiteering' (Eriksen 2005: 1106).

Realities on the ground suggest a more sophisticated reading, though. As will be illustrated in the next section, the UPDF developed a larger strategy of politico-economic and military control in the DR Congo. This strategy did generate resources for the somehow paradoxical strengthening of the domestic state regime, even if it can be argued that the private agendas of individual UPDF commanders eventually conflicted with this objective. Also, UPDF commanders were dependent upon the local realities (including existing trading networks, local political agendas, etc.) yet they were not able to fully control them. Before evaluating this merging of local and regional agendas in the DR Congo, the dynamics of the military entrepreneurialism of the UPDF need some further illustration.

The dynamics of military entrepreneurialism: Big Men, Big Women

At their arrival in the DR Congo, the Ugandan military tried to take a grip on trade and business in the territories they controlled. A main target was the exploitation of natural and strategic resources (gold, coltan, diamonds and cassiterite) but also timber, coffee, copper, cobalt, ivory and vanilla. To consolidate control and guarantee continuous production, several alternative structures were put in place. In the Kilo Moto area, the old mining guards of the Zairean state company were replaced by UPDF-controlled elements, while individual recruits started monitoring access to the mining sites by guarding bridges and strategic roadblocks and by levying taxes from local miners and traders. Through the control over the pre-war chain of transactions and intermediaries between mining centres and urban trading posts, or through direct exploitation of mining centres, top-ranking officers from Rwanda and Uganda could lay their hands on considerable shares of the local artisanal mining production. Price-fixing, forced monopoly and direct or indirect control of customs helped to consolidate a total control of the exploitation of resources. Different financial networks had to back this system and to guarantee the financing of the war efforts, while new networks of transportation, increasingly based on air transport, eased the exchange of goods with the Congolese interior.

The gap between the Ugandan production of mineral and strategic resources and its exports in 1997 and 1998 was a clear sign of the fraudulent re-exportation of Congolese resources via Kampala. Uganda had become a diamond exporter without producing a single carat; in 1998 more than 11,000 carats were exported for a total value of about US$1.5 million (PANA, 28 September 1999).

The exports of nobium, which were non-existent before 1997, had a value of US$782,000 in 1999 (United Nations 2001: 19). In addition to the export of natural resources, the Ugandan military controlled imports and distribution of goods from Entebbe (beer, cigarettes, soda, toilet paper, etc.) around Gbadolite (northern DR Congo) and Bunia (Ituri).[8] This economic production was largely generated through individuals closely linked to the Ugandan regime, sometimes via straw societies or dummy companies (examples include the Victoria Group, Trinity Investment, CONMET and Sagricof). The careers of Big Men Salim Saleh and James Kazini are particularly symbolic of the rise of a new class of 'entrepreneurs of insecurity' (which included military senior officers closely linked to the regime but also with a considerable stake in business activities in Uganda and elsewhere) and of the economic dimensions of Uganda's second intervention in the DR Congo.

The reports by the UN Panel of Experts and human rights organizations were particularly critical of UPDF's role in the exploitation of natural resources in the DR Congo. In its first report, the UN Panel of Experts described Presidents Museveni and Kagame as the 'godfathers of the illegal exploitation of natural resources and the continuation of conflict in the DRC' (United Nations 2001: 41). At the end of August 1998, General James Kazini was singled out as the principal holder of timber looted from the stockpiles of Amex-bois and La Forestiere. In January 1999 Kazini, who was by then closely associated with Congolese rebel leader Jean-Pierre Bemba, confiscated hundreds of tons of coffee stocks from Bumba, Lisala, Bosonzo, Binga and Mindembo (ibid.: 8). This traffic required large redistribution and network offshoots, including international commercialization channels, 'comptoirs d'achat' and intermediaries.[9] General James Kazini was 'the master in the field: the orchestrator, organizer and manager of most illegal activities related to the UPDF presence in north and north-eastern DRC' (ibid.: 89). In Equateur and Orientale Provinces, James Kazini constituted the link between UPDF officers and the Congolese leaders of armed groups. As UPDF overall commander in the DR Congo from 1998 to 2000, he became a close collaborator of Congolese rebel leaders – Mbusa Nyamwisi, John Tibasiima (RCD-ML – RCD-Mouvement de Libération), Roger Lumbala (RCD-National) and Jean-Pierre Bemba (MLC) – all of whom facilitated his illegal dealings in diamonds, coltan, timber, counterfeit currency, gold and coffee.

A key role was also played by Salim Saleh (President Museveni's brother and between 1996 and 1998 a senior adviser on defence and security as well as commander in the reserve force). Saleh is one of the most famous representatives of these military entrepreneurs. Endlessly diversifying his activities, he developed a resource accumulation strategy that skilfully mixed civilian and military business, charity and 'legitimate corruption', as well as national development and international capitalism. Dismissed from the military in 1989 for indiscipline, he made a fortune buying shares in various firms. He was at the head of a financial holding exploiting natural resources (Branch Energy), a private security company (Saracen) and several local airlines, among other things (Perrot 1999b). In 1999/2000, Salim Saleh opened a trading post for the commercialization of gold and diamonds in Kisangani, as well as a number of aviation companies that operated commercial flights from Uganda to the DR Congo. At least two Ugandan airlines claimed a quasi-monopoly on the flights to Equateur and Orientale Provinces: Air Alexander belonging to Salim Saleh's wife (Jovia Akandwanaho), and Uganda Air Cargo, which operated in Gemena, Basankasu, Isiro and Buta. A third company that is often mentioned is Air Navette, which was hired regularly by Salim Saleh and the leader of MLC (Jean-Pierre Bemba), and operated in Gbadolite, Gemena, Kisangani and Bunia. The Saleh couple, together with Kazini, were also linked to Trinity Investment, a company that transported among other items agricultural products, wood and cattle on behalf of the Gegere families from Bunia to Kampala exempt from UPDF toll barriers and export taxes.

The most striking structure of exploitation was the Victoria Group. Salim Saleh, with his wife and his nephew, Museveni's son, Muhoozi Kainerugabe, were the major shareholders of this group, which in reality was an unregistered company. The group was managed by a Lebanese long-term diamond trader based in Kisangani and Gbadolite who was also associated with two other Lebanese traders linked to the MLC and UPDF officers in the control of the diamond business. Based in Kampala and founded in 1999, this export company was well established in Bunia, Beni and Butembo. Through the military control of production areas, the Victoria Group had specialized in the export of gold, timber and diamonds and re-exportation from Kampala to international markets. It was General Kazini, who was associated with Congolese rebel groups and some administrative officials, who in July 1999 issued a safe conduct for the Victoria Group to export diamonds, coffee and gold from the DR Congo (*La Lettre de l'Océan Indien*, 11 September 1999). He wrote a letter to the tactical headquarters of the MLC and UDPF in north-eastern Congo, in which he authorized Victoria to trade in coffee, diamonds and gold in territories under their control. This safe conduct proved also to be an interesting tool for several Congolese businessmen who were operating under the UPDF's cover to freely expand their commercial enterprise.

Altogether, these societies ran a wide range of activities, including tax-exempted import and export, counterfeit currency and arms trafficking. They became crucial elements in militarized trans-border trading networks that were based on a complex system of protection and exploitation and which linked mining sites to international networks through rebel forces and military officers, who had replaced pre-war intermediaries. Each of these companies concentrated its activities on a number of commercial niches, which often changed, but always had to secure control of trading activities between Uganda and the DR Congo. At the same time, they consolidated the links between local business elites and their Ugandan patrons: 'These networks ... have enabled local warlords to forge a shadow economy that cuts right through the national level. By linking up local and global economic networks, the participants in this war economy are increasingly successful in blurring and dissolving the conventional distinctions between people, armies, and governments' (Raeymaekers 2002: 10).

The vacuum left by pre-war local authorities in the regulation of economic activities and competition conditioned the use of violence and the 'militarization of economic activities' (Vlassenroot 2003: 355). As will be discussed in the next section, local actors played a crucial role in these power games, in which protection was increasingly traded for economic gain. The role of these local actors clearly illustrates the dependency of Big Men. As is argued in the introduction to this volume, Big Men do not control followers but followers try to create and maintain ties with those Big Men who offer them the best economic opportunities, power or protection. In the case of the Ituri crisis, as will be illustrated, it was even extremely difficult for Ugandan Big Men to have any impact on their local followers.

Reconfiguration of domestic political powers

A closer look into these arrangements reveals that Uganda's military presence in the DR Congo was largely based and depended on close collaboration between UPDF commanders and Congolese rebel leaders, traders and political elites. In order to consolidate its military position, the Ugandan regime concluded security arrangements with local elites which went much farther than territorial and border control and also comprised private business deals. New arrangements have restructured or replaced pre-war networks and instigated a new process of regional economic integration, with businessmen, traders, local bureaucracies, tax administrations and military leaderships as their main actors. The outcomes of these arrangements caused additional contestation on a local level, though, while the UPDF commanders never had the capacity to fully control local power struggles. This forced them to continuously adapt to changing contexts and identify alternative partners and alternative strategies to protect their business interests.

Developments in the Ituri district (Orientale Province) during DR Congo's second war offer a good example of the merging of local and regional interests and the emergence of alternative security arrangements (Vlassenroot and Raeymaekers 2004a). Between 1999 and 2003 this district, which shares borders with Uganda and Sudan, witnessed one of the most severe episodes of the Congolese war as a result of the exploitation, by local and regional actors, of a deeply rooted local conflict over access to land, economic opportunity and political power. Local antagonism, which in origin centred on control over vital livelihoods, including land, was skilfully manipulated by UPDF commanders for the development of alternative trans-border networks. One of the key players was General James Kazini, who understood the benefits of an alliance with the local Hema (Gegere) community. In 1999, a number of Hema landowners threatened to evict Lendu farmers from their land, based on fraudulently acquired property titles. Revenge acts by local Lendu leaders led to a first series of violent clashes. Hema landowners started recruiting defence groups that soon acquired the support of some UPDF units, who started acting as private security guards for Hema elites. This security arrangement became the backbone of an emerging Hema politico-economic power base. Hema traders started operating under the protection of the UPDF and succeeded in expanding their commercial enterprise, which ultimately connected local markets to Ugandan and international traders. One of the beneficiaries was the Savo family, which was generally considered one of the instigators of the illegal appropriation of land. Its agricultural products, wood and cattle could be carried from Bunia to Kampala exempt from toll barriers and export taxes (United Nations 2001). The issuing of the letter by Kazini that granted the Victoria Group a monopoly over trans-border commerce was clearly also advantageous to Hema interests.

This economic partnership was further consolidated on the politico-administrative level with the appointment by General Kazini of Adèle Lotsove Mugisa, a Hema-Gegere, as the governor of the newly created province of Kibali-Ituri. Kazini's decision met with fierce resistance from the governor of Orientale Province, who technically still had control over Ituri (the creation of a separate province was a personal decision taken by Kazini as part of a larger strategy to install an alternative power structure under his protection). For non-Hema communities, this was a clear move to exclude them from the local decision-making process and trans-border trading networks, and consequently led to the formation of additional militias for the defence of these communities' interests and further complicated the local politico-military landscape. For the Gegere, the alliance with the UPDF proved to be essential for the creation of an alternative power structure. Relying on existing bonds of kinship and trust, the Hema-Gegere families became very successful in fostering new and flexible relations with regional and global markets and in consolidating political and military dominance. In Mahagi, Bunia and Aru, where traders of Nande origin had for a long time been trading goods with Sudan and Uganda, the combination of a favourable administration and foreign military back-up made it possible for Hema-Gegere traders to undercut these existing links. Control over illegal trade in gold, diamonds and other resources served as a financial basis for a new generation of local ethnic leaderships. The monopoly claim over the local economy was also protected by the Uganda People's Congress (UPC), a Gegere-dominated militia that served the interests of the Gegere elite and community. This structure of control was intended to prevent traders from other ethnic communities accessing their trading activities.

The interconnection between military occupation and economic enterprise in Ituri was fuelled and made possible to a large extent by the existence of pre-war trans-border trading networks, yet at the same time has strongly transformed economic regulation in the Ugandan–Congolese borderland. The Congolese war only further reinforced existing dynamics: 'the double opportunity of withering state authority and insecurity at its margins had generated the foundations of a vast network of trading relationships' (Raeymaekers 2009). It also economically integrated Ituri into the regional markets, with an important stake in (some argue quasi-monopoly of) Ugandan traders in local Congolese markets. The vast production of commodities such as gold and timber today is fraudulently exported to Uganda, often with the compliance of official state representatives on both sides of the border. As elsewhere in Congo's borderlands, these trading activities are subject to constant negotiation between traders, custom agents, security officials and provincial departments.

What after war?

The developing politico-economic enterprises in the Ugandan–Congolese borderland soon proved to have their limits, though. First, economic stakes generated substantial competition, both within the UPDF and between Ugandan and Rwandan army commanders. It is generally believed that Kazini and Joviah Akandwanaho's decision to take over the informal diamond trade in eastern Congo marked the beginning of the so-called 'Kisangani wars' between the Ugandan and Rwandan armies, which would inflict a serious blow on Ugandan–Rwandan relations. As part of an attempt to expand its sphere of control in northern and north-eastern DR Congo, the Ugandan regime preferred to mobilize a number of proxies, including Bemba's MLC but also parts of the RCD. This rebel movement eventually split into a number of factions, leading to a military fragmentation and the carving up of the rebel-held territories into different zones of control. In 2000, the UPDF high command unsuccessfully attempted to unite the factions under its influence into the Front de Libération du Congo (FLC). Also, tensions rose between UPDF units, mainly because of Kazini's strategic choices. At a certain point, these standing differences even resulted in an open confrontation between two opposing UPDF units in Ituri: while one unit was supporting the Lendu, the other (probably sent by Kazini and Adèle Lotsove) unsuccessfully tried to stage an attack on the Lendu-controlled town of Rety.[10]

Secondly, the UPDF was never in control of local realities, partly because of the complexity of the Ituri conflict but also because of a lack of political leadership over the expeditionary corps, which eventually led to an open rift within the UPDF itself. The Ugandan regime thought it could consolidate its control through the supporting of different factions, in what came down to a divide-and-rule strategy in the pure sense. This strategy has not proved to be as successful as hoped, which is illustrated by the division of the Hema-led militia UPC and the formation of split-offs (Parti pour l'Unité et la Sauvegarde de l'Intégrité du Congo, PUSIC, and Forces Armées Populaires du Congo, FAPC) at the beginning of 2003. Not long after the creation of the province of Kibali-Ituri, Thomas Lubanga – the nephew of administrator Lotsove – established the UPC (Union des Patriotes Congolais), which successfully took control over Bunia in August 2002. From there, it instituted its own governance apparatus and structures of control, which forced other ethnic groups to establish their own armed groups. Initially supported by General Kazini in pursuing its exclusivist agenda, the UPC's shift to Rwanda urged other UPDF officers to develop a different military strategy towards the Ituri conflict. Colonel Peter Kerim – who had already expressed his dissatisfaction with Kazini's ethnic tactics in Ituri – created a new alliance between non-Gegere militias (PUSIC, FAPC and Force de Résistance Patriotique d'Ituri, FRPI) in the hope of stimulating a dialogue between Ituri's fractioned communities. Meanwhile, Kazini continued to blacken Kerim's name, labelling him the protector of the Lendu in their brutal quest for power in Ituri (Vlassenroot and Raeymaekers 2004a).[11] These tensions also fomented armed clashes between UPDF-supported militias in resource-rich areas (particularly for control over gold mines around Mongbwalu) and further complicated the local politico-military landscape. As the United Nations Mission in the Democratic Republic of the Congo (MONUC) concludes in one of its security reports, the 'Ugandan army commanders already present in Ituri, instead of trying to calm the situation, preferred to benefit from the situation and support alternately one side or the other according to their political and financial interests' (MONUC 2004). After Ugandan troops eventually withdrew from the DR Congo in May 2003 as a result of growing international critiques of the UPDF's role in the Congo war, some members of the Ugandan regime tried to keep a foot in the door through the creation of additional local proxy forces. In 2005, a new rebel group was instituted in Kampala, which settled in north-east Ituri and could mobilize support from Ugandan sources. Other Ituri-based groups that started operating more recently are believed to get assistance from allies based in Uganda as well, though it is deemed that this support is mainly generated through private networks.[12]

One question remaining unanswered so far is what the interconnection between military occupation and economic enterprise means in terms of regime stability and what it tells us about the nature of the Ugandan state. On the domestic scene, the opposition was counting the human toll of Uganda's intervention in the DR Congo while small traders were complaining about their loss of income. The military itself was divided on the issue of the legitimacy of the intervention. The UPDF cadets criticized the unnecessary tension created with Rwanda. The second intervention created dissent and open clashes inside the UPDF between cadets and the 'Historicals' (the original members of the National Resistance Army (NRA), which had fought in the bush during the 1981–85 civil war), but also among the Historicals themselves (see the role of Kiiza Besigye, Museveni's bush doctor, who became a fierce political opponent and took part in the presidential race in 2001) (Perrot 2003). In the longer term the state authority was hardly affected, though, even if it can be argued that it caused a political crisis at the end of Uganda's intervention, that it meant a loss of formal economic revenues and that the state proved to have limited control over the military, as was revealed by the different military confrontations between Ugandan and Rwandan troops in Kisangani. To comprehend this seeming paradox, it is crucial to get a better understanding of the particular links between the shadow networks of politico-military and economic control that became visible during the intervention and the Ugandan regime.

The proliferation of privatized trading networks and the development of military-economic enterprises at the Ugandan–Congolese border suggest an informalization of security management and political control also on the Ugandan side, with shadow networks weakening 'the state control over private patronage' (Giustozzi 2005: 1). According to Clark, the involvement of individual Ugandan Big Men 'in the market for Congo's natural resources only raises specific questions about the relationship between the original motivation for Uganda's intervention and the UPDF's continuing presence in Congo, about Uganda's ultimate purposes in Congo, and about the extent to which President Museveni has been truly in control of the Ugandan national army' (Clark 2001a: 275). In other words, are we talking about the behaviour of individual and undisciplined officers (a 'moral' issue, as Prunier suggests; 1999: 58) or do our observations suggest a deliberate strategy on the part of the Ugandan regime? With other authors, Prunier raises some questions about the future of these networks once back in Uganda (ibid.: 56; see also Perrot 1999b). The relationship between the state and these privatized networks is far from being as clear as it may seem. At the end of the 1990s, there were fears that once these informal networks were back home, they would threaten Museveni's regime through their independence of the central high military command and that they could potentially ally with Uganda's political opposition. The increasing autonomy of these informal networks through predation and criminalization in the DR Congo does indeed raise questions about the future of these networks. Were the UPDF commanders in the DR Congo becoming a 'corps social guerrier', built by war and socially reproduced in war (Geffray 1990) and thus a potential source of domestic destabilization? Or should it be doubted that these entrepreneurs of insecurity or Big Men really could 'act financially and politically in the international system without interference from the state in which [they are] based?' (Duffield 1997). Contrary to what has been stressed since the end of Uganda's military intervention in the DR Congo (Reno 2002; Clark 2001a; Prunier 1999), we argue that these networks did not act without interference from the political centre in Kampala and (in the longer run) did not weaken the Ugandan regime, but they do illustrate a strong interconnectedness of parallel networks with formal state structures and with the formal centre of power helping to consolidate the power and resources of the shadow structures and the shadow networks being exploited by the political centre.[13]

One element that has been suggested to illustrate the loss of control of the political centre over these shadow networks is the decrease in Ugandan gold and other exports supposedly originating from the DR Congo from 1998 onwards. This would confirm the increased capacity of the aforementioned entrepreneurs of insecurity to bypass the state authority and to grant a degree of autonomization to their commercial networks. According to Reno, privatized networks had developed their own channels of exploitation and commercialization outside the state, leading to a considerable decrease in exports from the Ugandan state (Reno 2002). However, it could also be claimed that this decrease suggests that the Ugandan regime, under international and internal pressure, purposely prevented the profits of the illegal exploitation appearing in its accounts. It is now clear that some shadow networks, either the same ones or new ones, survived after the official end of the war and the departure of Ugandan troops from Congolese soil (United Nations Security Council 2009).

Also, the clashes between Ugandan and Rwanda troops in Kisangani epitomize how private interests prevailed over public ones and dramatically weakened the Ugandan state, prominently illustrating a privatization of Uganda's foreign security policy by UPDF commanders. Clark and the International Crisis Group argued that the Kisangani clashes had to be localized within an entrepreneurs' network that was trying to extend its control over the local diamond trade and increasingly was out of the Ugandan and Rwandan governments' control (Clark 2001a: 282; International Crisis Group 2001). This argument needs reconsideration, because these clashes were also caused by differences in perceptions of the Congolese conflict, regarding the most suitable strategies to solve it and the issue of profits made from the conflict. For Morten Bøås, the clashes were the result of a long meta-narrative about treason and the victimization of Rwandese Tutsi dating back to 1989, when the Rwandese officers in the Ugandan military were dismissed (Bøås 2004). It was revived by the acerbic disputes between Ugandan and Rwandese high military officials. Colonel Kahinda Otafiire accused the Rwandan officers of being thieves (*The Monitor*, 24 August 1999). In return, the Rwandese newspaper published articles about the 'shameful degeneracy of UPDF. You just have to look at the list of UPDF commanders deployed in Congo. This is a group of men rotten to the core' (*New Times*, 12–18 October 1998). The Kisangani wars probably had as much to do with growing disagreement and distrust between Ugandan and Rwandan army commanders as with private business interests. Nevertheless, the Kisangani clashes also caused tensions within the UPDF high command. According to Clark, 'It may even be the case that President Museveni "negotiated with" his own army in some instances, rather than commanded it, as some evidence suggests' (Clark 2001a: 282). The final withdrawal of the UPDF from the DR Congo would have depended more on the 'war trade union' conviction that the return to peace and to the barracks in Bombo would not mean a dramatic loss of their profits than on strategic choices.

The privatized commercial activities of UPDF officers in the DR Congo were considered to have weakened the Ugandan regime to such an extent that it became more and more dependent on external aid. Ironically, the positive effects of the economic activities being developed during the first Congolese war on Uganda's national accounts had softened donors' tolerance towards the increasing defence budget. In increasing its GDP (mainly as a result of the export of Congolese natural resources), the government could maintain its defence expenses under 2 per cent of its GDP, as recommended by the donors (Reno 2001: 31). This also allowed the Ugandan government to lighten the debt service (ibid.: 19). But it has to be noted that not all state organs benefited from this in the same way. Even though the Ministry of Defence gained benefits from this externalization of its revenues (Perrot 1999b), some state organs, such as the Uganda Internal Revenue in particular, worried about the impact this would have on their own administration of the tax-exempted imports and exports (United Nations 2001: 13).

Moreover, the disappointing economic results (poor performance of the coffee industry, lack of transparency in the privatization process, corruption in the banking system, decrease in fiscal revenue, etc.) concomitant with the beginning of the second Congolese war irritated donors. The second Congolese war created an unprecedented crisis of confidence in Museveni's regime; some donors, including the IMF, suspended their aid in 1999 (Prunier 1999: 55), which was the start of a long-term rift in Uganda's relations with its main donors (only in 2006 could some changes be observed). For the first time, in December 1998 defence expenses (relative to the war in the DR Congo specifically) and corruption were at the heart of discussions at the World Bank consultative group meeting. In February 1999, during a visit, IMF representatives decided not to proceed with the disbursement of the allocated aid fund (US$18 million) owing to the overwhelming size of the defence budget (which had increased by 60 per cent between 1998 and 1999). The IMF reconsidered its position after an opportune ministerial reshuffle. Likewise both the Netherlands and Finland had frozen part of their aid in September 1999 to protest against Uganda's second intervention in the Congo (*Uganda Newsline*, 1 September 1999; *Marchés tropicaux et méditerranéens*, 21 May 1999). In contrast, official US development assistance tripled between 1998 and 2003, mainly in order to support the war against the Lord's Resistance Army in northern Uganda, which had been added to the US State Department's list of terrorists in December 2001.

And yet, even though donors and UN agencies realized the limits of the regime's good governance records, they continued to pursue a collaborative approach with the Ugandan government. In 2005, they had already expressed their discontent with the undemocratic developments of the regime by partly and temporarily cutting aid, but they were not geared up to cut additional funds for security reasons.[14] After only a few months, and when there was a window of opportunity to end the conflict in northern Uganda through the Juba peace negotiations, they put their short-term threatening and uncoordinated strategy aside to largely support and collaborate with the government. It is clear that the persistence of the vision during the 1990s of Uganda being a success story still affects the perceptions of the donors. But 'fundamentally, the UN and donors shifted back to a pragmatic and realist diplomacy because there is really no other option than conciliating with Museveni. Most of the external aid in Uganda is provided through budget support, therefore linked to the government's willingness to allot and manage it properly. Moreover, the absence of credible political alternatives as a state leader makes any confrontational policy with the incumbent regime vain and pointless. Museveni won the February 2006 presidential elections with more than 60% of the votes', and his main opponent, Kiiza Besigye, was discredited by his inability to mobilize rural Uganda and to muster the opposition representatives (Perrot 2010).

More interestingly, rather than becoming a threat to Uganda's political stability, most of the entrepreneurs of insecurity or Big Men who have been involved in Congo's war economy have been recycled or reintegrated into the state machinery.[15] Apart from a few arrests and lay-offs (as in the case of Peter Kerim, for example) the main leaders of the shadow networks who were involved in Congo's resource trade are still in charge of public affairs. Salim Saleh was first recycled as minister of state for micro-finance (*Bonna Baggawale*) and later became senior presidential adviser. Kahinda Otafiire was appointed minister for local government. As such, he helped other veterans from the DR Congo acquire plots of land (La Lettre de l'Océan indien 2007). James Kazini was a clear exception, though. Despite strategic mistakes committed by Kazini in Kisangani, he was promoted (Mwenda 2002) and deployed to southern Sudan for Operation Iron Fist on return from eastern Congo. Already accused of perjury by the UN Panel of Experts, he was dismissed after the publication of the Porter Report, which accused him of disobedience to President Museveni's order not to help Congolese businesses. Major General James Kazini had been on '*katebe*' (undeployed) since 2003 and was fired as army commander in June 2003; in March 2008 he was finally convicted and sentenced to jail.[16] This affair seems to prove that Museveni never fully lost control of these entrepreneurs of insecurity. Even more, the arrest of James Kazini was believed to be linked to his political ambitions and not to his role in the shadow economic structure in the Congo.

In the end, the shadow networks perpetuated themselves. Interestingly, Colonel John Mugyenyi, former commander of a UPDF brigade in eastern Congo, maintained his business activities in Kampala and bought a large part of the Kisekka market via his firm Rhino Investments. He had been accused in a UN report of plundering gold in the Congo and also of infringing the military code of conduct by not declaring his goods (including several luxurious cars). As a close ally of Museveni and more especially of Salim Saleh, he financed Museveni's presidential campaign in 2006 (La Lettre de l'Océan indien 2007). In 2009, rumours circulated that training camps of Ituri militias were based on the Ugandan side of Lake Albert on Ugandan islands in the same lake. Also, shipments of arms from Uganda to these militias have been reported, indicating that informal contacts between Ugandan elements and Congolese militias continue to exist, even if it could seriously be questioned whether these contacts are part of a deliberate strategy on the part of the Ugandan regime. A November 2009 report to the Security Council disclosed again the existence in Uganda of illegal private networks involved in gold exports from the DR Congo (United Nations Security Council 2009). The recorded and un-recorded mineral trading networks from Ituri and North Kivu are still passing through Uganda, where there is no tax on exports. And even though the UPDF pulled out of the extracting sector, to the benefit of Congolese gold traders, the Ugandan military is definitely still involved in the trading of gold once exported to Entebbe (Cuvelier 2010).

Conclusion

Uganda's interventions in the DR Congo have often been presented as being guided by greedy UPDF commanders who have all tried to develop and consolidate private business interests through trans-border networks by connecting Congo's resource-rich areas to markets in eastern Africa, there-fore largely escaping the control of the political centre in Uganda. Moreover, these parallel networks are believed to have weakened the Ugandan regime considerably. For Reno, the Ugandan state was unable to centralize control of this violent accumulation. He underlines a possible backlash effect: '[it] creates violent entrepreneurs within the military and government who will resist institutional efforts to control them and may defy the ruler's personal authority to get what they want' (Reno 2002). The analysis presented in this chapter illustrates that this reading of Uganda's military involvement in the Congolese wars only partially corresponds with realities on the ground. Even if it can be agreed that a number of Ugandan Big Men played a central role in and skilfully exploited the UPDF interventions in the Congo, this did not really weaken the Ugandan regime. Moreover, most of these 'violent entrepreneurs' or Big Men have been recycled and reintegrated into the state machinery.

From the example of Uganda's military adventures in Congo, a number of conclusions can be drawn, both about the strategies of Big Men and informal networks in conflict environments and their impact on state stability. First, the intervention of the UPDF in Congo gives us some perspectives on how Big Men try to consolidate their power in volatile contexts. While it is often argued that their potential success in contexts of war depends on their capacity to mobilize and control violence, the trajectories of some of these Ugandan Big Men reveal that they are also able to survive in a post-war, non-violent context. Another issue is their capacity to control followers. As has been illustrated in this chapter, Big Men rely on the support of local actors, which in the case of Ituri have proved to be very unpredictable in their choices and strategies. This made it extremely difficult for Ugandan Big Men to maintain their economic stakes and consolidate their politico-military power at a local level. Even if originally Kazini was very successful in creating a local power structure and exploiting existing trading networks, he eventually lost control over his local partners. So in other words, the success of Big Men depends not only on their own mobilizing capacities but also on the choices and strategies made by their followers.

Secondly, there is a strong connection between informal networks and formal political spheres. Even if Ugandan Big Men involved in Congo's war economies could be largely considered as representing alternative power structures, they remained strongly connected to and integrated in Ugandan formal political structures. Rather than posing a threat to regime stability, the activities of Ugandan military entrepreneurs and the networks under their control could even be considered an integral part of the Ugandan governance regime. The military shadow networks under the control of these Big Men could not flourish without their links with the state machinery (protection, commercialization networks, resources, etc.). The established interactions, interlocking and straddling shadow networks and the political centre, have called into question 'the natural inclination of criminal networks to subvert political order by imposing their own rules. The entrepreneurs of violence often meet the rules of the political and economic context in which they operate, including detecting opportunities that will enable them to develop their business' (Briquet and Favarel-Garrigues 2008: 12).[17]

Thirdly, the case of Uganda's intervention in Congo also teaches us that an informalization of security structures can create additional opportunities for regime consolidation. The paradox here is that while state regulatory authority is constantly undermined by parallel networks, the same forces also seem to contribute to the viability of the state: 'Officially relegated to the margins of the legitimate social order, opposed to democratic standards and models of good governance promoted by international organizations, the illegalities and the misuse of violence nonetheless constitute levers of accumulation of economic resources, political, social and territorial control, and *in fine* instruments for the exercise of power' (ibid.: 12)[18]. Rather than including an often suggested 'privatization of the state' (Bayart et al. 1999), these processes thus are characterized by more indirect forms of political control, which drive 'the middle-ground between formal and informal, state and non-state spheres of authority and regulation' (Raeymaekers and Vlassenroot 2008). The question here is whether, in the case of Uganda, new governance frameworks are developing that include parallel power structures and institutions (with UPDF officers becoming powerful in the field through private patronage networks and yet still remaining loyal to the Ugandan regime) and which force the political centre into strategies of mediation in order to regain or maintain its authority. The threatened brutalization of the military and development of autonomous 'warlords' within the Ugandan state (as was suggested by Prunier, Reno and others) never materialized. Rather, the continuing straddling of public and private functions helped these entrepreneurs of insecurity face the transformation of their environment once they left the DR Congo. By simultaneously keeping one foot in the 'bush and border' (Roitman 2004b) and another in the state bureaucracy and national economy, they could thus both consolidate their private economic interests and serve the political centre.

Notes

1 Two weeks prior to this military campaign, President Kabila, who had come to power in May 1997 with Rwandan and Ugandan military support, had urged his former allies to leave the Congolese territory as part of an attempt to gain domestic legitimacy and consolidate power.

2 For Dietrich (2000), military commercialism describes 'an increasing utilization of national militaries as tools for private financial gain by the political elite in these countries. ... While militarised commercialism refers to the entrance of military functions (such as contract soldiers) into international commerce, military commercialism refers to the strong influence of entrepreneurial considerations as a key component of foreign military deployment.'

3 Even if in 1998 security concerns had been raised as the official reason for Uganda's armed intervention in the DR Congo (Uganda's western border areas witnessed continuous infiltrations and attacks from the Ugandan 'Allied Democratic Forces'), some observers argued that this campaign was mainly inspired by economic incentives (see Clark 2001a; Reno 2000). Different perspectives on these economic reasons have been articulated, though. For Clark and Reno, economic resources generated in the DR Congo were of crucial relevance to its regime-building process and national economy. For Prunier, in order to help explain Uganda's intervention, dynamics of regional economic integration should be taken into account (Prunier 1999). According to some more questionable explanations, Uganda's involvement in

the DRC war was proof of an ambition to create a Hima or Tutsi empire in the Great Lakes Region (see Maindo Ngonga 2003).

4 '... *leur production à des commerçants hema (Ituri) et nande (Nord-Kivu) lesquels exportent l'or frauduleusement via Kampala et surtout via Bujumbura'.*

5 An example was the case of Colonel Peter Kerim, who was caught stealing two pick-up trucks loaded with fuel from a Zairean businessman. Following this incident, Kerim was forced to go on leave. Nevertheless, he managed to reappear as a trainer for Jean-Pierre Bemba's Movement for the Liberation of Congo (MLC) and a commander in Mahagi District in Ituri during the second war in 1998 (United Nations 2002).

6 In 1997, gold exports amounted to US$81 million, compared to US$12.4 million in 1994/95 and US$35 million in 1995/96 (Clark 2001; Reno 2002).

7 '*Au fil des mois, les commerces fructueux et les logiques de petite corruption (petits vols, contrebande, revente d'essence, d'uniformes, mélange de cafés de différentes qualités ...) – en somme tous classiques dans les zones de conflit – prirent de l'ampleur pour évoluer vers une organization entrepreneuriale de* business *de guerre à grande échelle, dirigée par une clique militaro-affairiste, dont les structures gouvernementales des États « agresseurs » étaient les piliers'.*

8 In Kisangani, Bukavu and Goma, consumer goods were imported from Rwanda and Burundi (United Nations 2001: 12).

9 The UN report (United Nations 2002: 31) names Belgium, France, China, Germany, India, Israel, Japan, Kazakhstan, Lebanon, Malaysia, the Netherlands, Russia, Switzerland, Thailand, the Arab emirates, Great Britain and the USA as transit points for this traffic. For more information on these offshoots, see the different reports of the UN Panel of Experts.

10 It was also suggested that the other UPDF unit may have been motivated by its participation in the Lendus' coffee-smuggling practices (Human Rights Watch 2001).

11 To prevent a total breakdown of military discipline, President Museveni eventually had no choice but to dismiss Kazini as the overall commander of Operation Safe Haven (the official name of the Ugandan intervention in the DRC) and replace him with Colonel Peter Kerim, who was generally considered more moderate in military matters.

12 Authors' interviews with international observers in Brussels, Nairobi and Ghent, July 2009. In a recent paper, Dan Fahey adds that Uganda also allowed Congolese rebel leaders and Congolese businessmen to stay in exile and took no action against Congolese individuals subjected in 2005 to UN sanctions because of their ties to the arms trade in eastern Congo (Fahey 2009).

13 Interestingly, the Ministry of Water and Forests during the second Congolese war issued a certificate for imported timber from DR Congo, which highlights the integration of this informal traffic into the official state economy (United Nations 2001: 10–11).

14 At the end of 2005 again, Norway, Ireland and later the Netherlands, Sweden and the UK reduced their financial budget support over concerns about Uganda's political transition, freedom of the press, and public administration expenditure. They partly reallocated the funds to humanitarian relief. DfID had already cut budget support by £5 million in May 2005 to show its concern about the political developments in the regime. In total, the UK cut its aid by £20 million, followed by Norway and Ireland (£2 million), the Netherlands (£5 million) and Sweden (around £7 million) (DfID 2005).

15 One reason could be the juridical threat of the ICC. The arrest of Jean-Pierre Bemba by the ICC created tensions among the circles of Ugandan officers pinned down by the UN reports (La Lettre de l'Océan indien 2008).

16 A three-man committee (General Tinyefuza, Hon. Mbabazi and General Salim Saleh) investigated him from June to September 2003 over the existence

of ghost soldiers on the UPDF payroll, financial loss and embezzlement and the creation of a semi-autonomous military unit (the 409 Brigade) in West Nile. He was suspected of plotting a coup against Museveni, together with the former Alpine Brigade commander Lieutenant Colonel Muhindo (Afedraru 2009). This three-man commission of inquiry convicted him in March 2008 and sentenced him to a three-year jail term for causing financial loss by creating ghost soldiers on the army payroll (Wakise and Mukasa 2008). He was released on bail from the Luzira prison but was accused of disobeying the commander-in-chief in relation to deployment of troops (Atuhaire 2008). Kazini petitioned the Constitutional Court to challenge the constitutionality of his trial. He could have been jailed for life (Afedraru 2009). But in November 2009, he was killed by his girlfriend.

17 '... la volonté naturelle du milieu criminel de subvertir l'ordre politique en imposant ses propres règles. Les entrepreneurs de violence se satisfont bien souvent des règles du jeu politique et économique dans lequel ils évoluent, en y décelant les opportunités qui leur permettront de développer leur activité.'

18 'Officiellement relégués aux marges de l'ordre social légitime, opposés aux standards démocratiques et aux modèles de bonne gouvernance promue par les organizations internationales, les illégalismes et l'usage irrégulier de la violence n'en constituent pas moins des leviers d'accumulation de ressources économiques et politiques, de contrôle social et territorial, in fine, des instruments d'exercice du pouvoir.'

References

Afedraru, L. (2009) 'Judge saves Kazini from court martial', *The Monitor*, 16 April.

Atuhaire, A. B. (2008) 'Uganda: Kazini offered to resign', *The Monitor*, 6 April.

Ayeabare, A. (1998) 'Kabila falls out with his allies', *East African Alternatives*, September/October.

Ballentine, K. and J. Sherman (eds) (2003) *The Political Economy of Armed Conflict*, Boulder, CO: Lynne Rienner.

Bayart, J.-F., S. Ellis and B. Hibou (1999) *The Criminalization of the State in Africa*, Bloomington: Indiana University Press.

Bøås, M. (2004) 'Uganda in the regional war zone: meta-narratives, pasts and presents', *Journal of Contemporary African Studies*, 22(3): 283–303.

Boone, C. (1994) 'Trade, taxes, and tribute – market liberalizations and the new importers in West-Africa', *World Development*, 22(3): 453–67.

Briquet, J. L. and G. Favarel-Garrigues (eds) (2008) *Milieux criminels et pouvoir politique*, Paris: Karthala, coll. Recherches internationales.

Callaghy, T. M., R. Kassimir and R. Latham (2001) *Intervention and Transnationalism in Africa: Global-Local Networks of Power*, Cambridge: Cambridge University Press.

Clark, J. (2001a) 'Explaining Ugandan intervention in Congo: evidence and interpretations', *Journal of Modern African Studies*, 39(2): 261–87.

— (2001b) 'Foreign policy making in Central Africa: the imperative of regime security in new context', in G. K. T. Lyons (ed.), *Foreign Policy Making in Africa*, Boulder, CO: Lynne Rienner.

Collier, P. (2000) 'Doing well out of war: an economic perspective', in M. Berdal and D. M. Malone (eds), *Greed and Grievance: Economic Agendas in Civil Wars*, Boulder, CO, and London: Lynne Rienner, pp. 91–111.

Cuvelier, J. (ed.) (2010) *The Complexity of Resource Governance in a Context of State Fragility. The Case of Eastern RDC*, IPIS, International Alert.

Das, V. and D. Poole (eds) (2004) *Anthropology in the Margins of the State*, Santa Fe, NM/Oxford: School of American Research Press/James Currey.

DfID (2005) 'UK cuts direct budget aid to Uganda by £15 million, withholds further £5 million'. Press release, 20 December.

Dietrich, C. (2000) 'The commercialization

of military deployment in Africa', *African Security Review*, 9(1), www.iss.co.za/pubs/ASR/9No1/Commercialisation.html.

Duffield, M. (1997) *Post-modern Conflict, Aid Policy and Humanitarian Conditionality*, Birmingham: University of Birmingham.

— (2001) *Global Governance and the New Wars: The merging of development and security*, London: Zed Books.

Eriksen, S. S. (2005) 'The Congo War and the prospects for state formation: Rwanda and Uganda compared', *Third World Quarterly*, 26(7): 1097–113.

Fahey, D. (2009) *Explaining Uganda's Involvement in the DR Congo, 1996–2008*, Paper presented at the annual meeting of the ISA's 50th Annual Convention, 'Exploring the past, anticipating the future', New York Marriott Marquis, New York, 15 February.

Geffray, C. (1990) *La Cause des armes au Mozambique. Anthropologie d'une guerre civile*, Paris/Nairobi: Karthala/CREDU.

Giustozzi, A. (2005) *The Debate on Warlordism: The Importance of Military Legitimacy*, London: Crisis States Development Research Centre, London School of Economics.

Hovil, L. and E. Werker (2005) 'Portrait of a failed rebellion: an account of rational, sub-optimal violence in western Uganda', *Rationality and Society*, 17(1): 5–34.

Human Rights Watch (2001) *Uganda in Eastern DRC: Fuelling Political and Ethnic Strife*.

International Crisis Group (1999) *The Agreement on a Cease-fire in the Democratic Republic of Congo – an Analysis of the Agreement and Prospects for Peace*.

— (2000) *Uganda and Rwanda: Friends or enemies?*

— (2001) *Rwanda/Uganda: A Dangerous War of Nerves*.

Juma, L. (2007) '"Shadow networks" and conflict resolution in the Great Lakes region of Africa', *African Security Review*, 16(1), www.iss.co.za/static/templates/tmpl_html.php?node_id=2597&slink_id=4939&slink_type=12&link_id=29.

Kayunga, S. S. (1993) *Islamic Fundamentalism in Uganda: A case study of the Tabligh youth movement*, Kampala: Centre for Basic Research.

Keen, D. (1998) *The Economic Functions of Civil Wars*, Adelphi Papers 320, London.

La Lettre de l'Océan indien (2007) 'Les officiers dans l'immobilier', 22 September.

— (2008) 'La grande peur des généraux', 14 June.

Lund, C. (2007) *Twilight Institutions: Public Authority and Local Politics in Africa*, Oxford: Blackwell.

MacGaffey, J. (1987) *Entrepreneurs and Parasites*, Cambridge: Cambridge University Press.

— (1991) *The Real Economy of Zaire: The contribution of smuggling and other unofficial activities to national wealth*, Philadelphia: University of Pennsylvania Press.

Maindo Ngonga, A. (2003) '"La République de l'Ituri" en République démocratique du Congo: un far west ougandais', *Politique africaine*, 89: 181–92.

Meagher, K. (1990) 'The hidden economy: informal and parallel trade in northeastern Uganda', *Review of African Political Economy*, 17(47): 64–83.

Mwanasali, M. (2000) 'The view from below', in M. Berdal and D. Malone (eds), *Greed and Grievance*, Boulder, CO, and London: Lynne Rienner.

Mwenda, A. (2002) 'How UPDF lost Kisangani I, II, III', *The Monitor*, 23 June.

Niemann, M. (2007) 'War making and state making in Central Africa', *Africa Today*, 53(3): 21–39.

Obbo, C. (2002) 'M 7's "dog" broke away from the pack', *East-African*, 29 April–5 May.

Otunnu, O. (2003) 'Uganda as a regional actor in the Zairian War', in H. Adelman and G. C. Rao (eds), *War and Peace in Zaire/Congo*, Trenton, NJ: Africa World Press Inc.

Perrot, S. (1999a) 'Les forces de sécurité dans l'Ouganda de Museveni: un monstre domestiqué?', *Les Cahiers de l'IFRA*, Special issue on Uganda, pp. 37–89.

— (1999b) 'Entrepreneurs de l'insécurité: la face cachée de l'armée ougandaise', *Politique africaine*, 75: 60–71.

— (2003) *La reconstruction d'un ordre politique dans l'Ouganda de Yoweri Museveni (1986–2001): de la réversibilité du chaos?*, PhD dissertation, Centre d'études d'Afrique Noire, Institut d'Études Politiques, Bordeaux.

— (2010) 'Northern Uganda: a "forgotten conflict", again? The impact of the internationalization of the resolution process', in T. Allen and K. Vlassenroot (eds), *The Lord's Resistance Army, Myth or Reality?*, London: Zed Books, pp. 187–204.

Prunier, G. (1999) 'L'Ouganda et les guerres congolaises', *Politique africaine*, 75: 43–59.

— (2004) 'Rebel movements and proxy warfare: Uganda, Sudan and the Congo (1986–99)', *African Affairs* (London), 103(412): 359–83.

— (2008) *Africa's World War: Congo, the Rwandan Genocide, and the Making of a Continental Catastrophe*, Oxford: Oxford University Press.

Raeymaekers, T. (2002) *Network War: An Introduction to Congo's Privatised Conflict Economy*, Antwerp: IPIS.

— (2009) *The Central Margins. Congo's Transborder Economy and State-making in the Borderlands*, Working Paper, Copenhagen: Danish Institute for International Studies.

Raeymaekers, T. and K. Vlassenroot (2008) 'Reshaping Congolese statehood in the midst of crisis and transition', in U. Engel and P. Nugent (eds), *Respacing Africa*, Leiden: Brill, pp. 139–67.

Reinikka, R. and P. Collier (2001) *Uganda's Recovery: The Role of Farms, Firms, and Government*, Washington, DC: World Bank.

Reno, W. (1998) *Warlord Politics and African States*, Boulder, CO: Lynne Rienner.

— (2000) *War, Debt and the Role of Pretending in Uganda's International Relations*, Occasional Paper, Copenhagen: Centre of African Studies, University of Copenhagen.

— (2001) 'The politics of war and debt relief in Uganda', *Conflict, Security and Development*, 1(2): 5–23.

— (2002) 'Uganda's politics of war and debt relief', *Review of International Political Economy*, 9(3): 415–35.

Roitman, J. (1990) 'The politics of informal markets in sub-Saharan Africa', *Journal of Modern African Studies*, 28(4): 671–96.

— (2004a) *Fiscal Disobedience: An anthropology of economic regulation in Central Africa*, Princeton, NJ: Princeton University Press.

— (2004b) 'Productivity in the margins: the reconstitution of state power in the Chad Basin', in V. Das and D. Poole (eds), *Anthropology in the Margins of State*, Santa Fe, NM/Oxford: School of American Research Press/James Currey, pp. 225–52.

Ruffin, J.-C. (ed.) (1994) *Les économies de guerre*, Paris: Livre de Poche/Pluriel.

United Nations (2001) Letter dated 12 April 2001 from the Secretary-General to the President of the Security Council.

— (2002) Letter dated 15 October 2002 from the Secretary-General addressed to the President of the Security Council.

— (2005) Letter dated 26 July 2005 from the Chairman of the Security Council Committee established pursuant to resolution 1533 (2004) concerning the Democratic Republic of the Congo addressed to the President of the Security Council.

United Nations Mission in the Democratic Republic of the Congo (MONUC) (2004) *Special Report on the Events in Ituri, January 2002 to December 2003*, S/2004/573, 16 July.

United Nations Security Council (2009) *Final Report of the Group of Experts on the Democratic Republic of the Congo*, S/2009/603, 29 November.

Utas, M. (2007) *Informal Security Structures in the Mano River Region: Guinea, Liberia, Sierra Leone*, Research project, Nordiska Afrikainstitutet, www.nai.uu.se/research/areas/informal/, accessed 16 June 2009.

Van Schendel, W. (2005) 'Spaces of engagement: how borderlands, illicit flows, and territorial states interlock', in W. van Schendel and I. Abraham (eds), *Illicit Flows and Criminal Things: States, borders, and the other side of globalization*, Bloomington and Indianapolis: Indiana University Press.

Vlassenroot, K. (2003) 'Economies de guerre et entrepreneurs militaires: la rationalité économique dans le conflit au sud-Kivu (République démocratique du Congo)', in P. Hassner and R. Marchal (eds), *Guerres et sociétés: Etat et violence après la Guerre froide*, Paris: Karthala, pp. 339–70.

— (2008) 'Négocier et contester l'ordre public dans l'Est de la République Démocratique du Congo', *Politique africaine*, 111: 44–67.

Vlassenroot, K. and T. Raeymaekers (2004a) 'The politics of rebellion and intervention in Ituri: the emergence of a new political complex?', *African Affairs*, 103(412).

— (2004b) *Conflict and Social Transformation in Eastern DR Congo*, Ghent: Academia Press.

Wakise, A. and H. Mukasa (2008) 'Uganda: who is Major General James Kazini?', *New Vision*.

Wennmann, A. (2008) *What Is the Political Economy of Conflict? Delimiting a debate on contemporary armed conflict*, Paper presented at the World International Studies Conference, Ljubljana, 23–25 July.

Willame J.-C. (2007) *Insecurité, violences et resources naturelles au Congo-Zaïre*, Unpublished paper, Madrid, 25 May, www.eurac-network.org/web/uploads/.../20070601_9230.doc.

2 | Big Man business in the borderland of Sierra Leone

Maya Mynster Christensen

At the checkpoint

A truck overburdened with goods is ordered to stop at a strategic check-point in Kailahun District, the eastern borderland of Sierra Leone. It is late at night – a favoured time to cross the checkpoint when travelling with goods to the major cities. The security officials are half asleep. As the truck driver and his two young workers get out of the vehicle, the police officers remove the tarpaulin covered with red dust from the long drive on the dirt roads. The truck is loaded with coffee and palm oil.

After the inspection of the truck for 'suspicious objects' – weapons, drugs or bodies – the revenue collector finally interrupts. He is excited, as this might be his catch of the day. He signals for the truck driver to follow him to his small office and asks to see his documents. The revenue collector underlines the fact that he is in charge of the checkpoint now, and that he has been officially appointed by the chairman of the district council – an (in)famous warlord and coup maker. The truck driver is unable to pay the requested evaluation fee for his produce, but as it turns out that he is closely related to a town chief in the district, negotiations are smooth. The checkpoint barrier is lowered and the truck continues into the dark.

Introduction

Alex, the revenue collector, has been rewarded for his loyalty to retired military commander Tom Nyuma, who serves as the district council chair-man in Kailahun, and with his new responsibilities at the checkpoint he has moved from marginality into being a representative of official authority. While he would previously refer to himself as 'a jungler', referring to his long-term experience of combat during the civil war, he now claims to be 'the eye of the government'. Moreover, occupying a legitimate and officially recognized position, he claims the power to exercise control over the circulation of goods and bodies, and the right to regulate economic relations.

Despite being regarded as a newcomer and stranger in the border district, Alex has learned how to negotiate with local authorities, and how to tactically manoeuvre ambiguous positions of both an official and unofficial nature. He has learned how to go about Big Man business in the borderland, and has now himself become a Big Man.

This chapter addresses Big Man business in the rural borderland of Sierra Leone by exploring the role ex-soldiers and ex-combatants have come to play in performing statehood practices in a context of absent centralized state power. Focusing on how militarized patrimonial networks facilitate the mobilization of ex-soldiers and ex-combatants into official and less official politico-economic domains, the chapter illuminates how sovereignties are negotiated and fragmented by a multitude of actors with competing claims to power and wealth.

In order to unravel how Big Man networks are instrumental in dissolving lines denoting distinctions not only between official and unofficial spheres but also between military and civil political practices, and between licit and illicit activities, I draw on Jean and John Comaroff's theories on the coexistence of law and organized lawlessness in the post-colony (2006), and on Janet Roitman's (2004, 2006) writings on the pluralization of regulatory authority in the interstices of the state – in limit zones such as borders and the bush.

My empirical point of departure is a case study of Tom Nyuma, the district council chairman, and his loyal group of 'task force' members – Alex being one of them. Building on ethnographic fieldwork conducted in Sierra Leone from 2006 to 2010, I trace the mobilization of Nyuma's task force members over time, and through spaces, from when they were first appointed as unofficial security guards in Freetown during the 2007 presidential elections to their later incarnation as representatives of official authority in the Kailahun borderland.

Borderlands are often conceived of as territorial limit zones detached from the political centre; as marginal to central state formation. Yet they are also spaces that shape political and regulatory practices at regional, national and international levels (Roitman 2004). As such, border zones can act as 'magnifying glasses focalising the hazy normativities of heartland society'[1] (Arnaut and Højbjerg 2008: 10). In this chapter I treat the margins as essential to the centre (Das and Poole 2004), arguing that a borderland perspective offers important insight into the complex nature of patrimonial politics also at a national level. And it is also against this background that I will conclude by reflecting on what I argue is a general tendency influencing current state formation and governance in Sierra Leone: the redirecting and consolidation of militarized patrimonial networks for post-war politico-economic purposes.

Sovereignties unsettled, patrimonial networks consolidated

> In many parts of Africa, the territorial sovereignty of postcolonial states has been eroded to such an extent that it only exists in a formal sense, devoid of any monopoly of violence and replaced by zones of unsettled sovereignties and loyalties. (Hansen and Stepputat 2005: 27)

Post-colonial Sierra Leone is often considered to be the ultimate symbol of state failure. The lack of a clear distinction between the official and unofficial spheres, and the significance of informal patrimonial networks in organizing the formal realm, are key features that make the Sierra Leonean state deviate from Western notions of political modernity (Jörgel and Utas 2007). The crucial role of what we usually term 'non-state actors' – be they chiefdom authorities, religious groups, secret societies, warlords or other Big Men – in providing in/security and organizing economic and political networks, and as such acting on behalf of or in the absence of a state, radically challenges the Weberian definition of an ideal state maintaining a monopoly on legitimate violence. And if we accept the idea that the state can be approached as a sovereign, unitary power centre our fantasy will, indeed, collapse when looking at the case of Sierra Leone. As in other post-colonial states, in Africa and beyond, the 'dispersal of state authority into patchworks of partial, horizontal sovereignties' is what characterizes the dominant mode of governance (Comaroff and Comaroff 2006: 41).

The outbreak of the long-lasting civil war (1991–2002) has been explained as a product of injustice (Archibald and Richards 2002: 344) and with references to the weakness of a nation-state that was unable to offer physical and economic security to the majority of its citizens (Keen 2005). It is also against this background that the reform of a failed state became a key target for international agencies when former president Tejan Kabbah officially declared the civil war to be over on 18 January 2002. In order to prevent a renewal of conflict, and in accordance with an intense desire for statehood, the promotion of 'good governance' became an important agenda set by international donors. What was considered a state of lawlessness – or even a criminal state – governed by patrimonial elites was to be reformed and reformalized.

Renewed demands for governmental accountability and substantial efforts to weaken patronage systems have, nevertheless, not resulted in fundamental change in post-war politics, at least not when we consider the significance of patrimonial networks and the dispersed nature of sovereignty. Rather, as Steve Archibald and Paul Richards argue (2002: 358), interventionist programmes have in some instances become a resource for the renewal of patrimonial politics. As humanitarian aid has been distributed along specific political lines and through local chiefly authorities, existing patrimonial networks have, to some extent, become consolidated and strengthened in the process of post-war recovery (Keen 2005: 304; Fanthorpe 2003).

The obstacles to rebuilding a failed state must also be understood in a context in which the civil war was not simply a collapse and breakdown of a system but rather a reorganization of existing orders of profit, power and protection (Keen 2005: 286–97). As the central state was unable to deliver sufficient security, local defence forces, mobilized around existing patronage networks, became important providers of protection. Rather than being replaced during wartime, patronage networks that dominated everyday existence in pre-war Sierra Leone became militarized (Hoffman 2007: 660).

As this chapter illuminates from a rural borderland perspective, the militarization of patrimonial networks has extended into post-war governance, though perhaps in a more 'soft' or domesticated form adapted to peacetime possibilities and purposes. This continuity becomes evident when looking at the role former military personnel and militia combatants have come to play in state-making performances and practices – in the capital as well as in the rural borderland.

Post-war borderland governance: in need of a warlord?

> In a rebel-infested district people need a hardliner, somebody they used to be afraid of, to be on top of them ...

When I ask the newly elected chairman of Kailahun District Council whether post-war society is in need of retired military leaders to restore 'good governance', he addresses his own position by replying with the above statement. Nyuma argues that 'military-minded' governance structured around networks of powerful patrons is the only way to handle the current state of unrest in Kailahun District.

Nyuma is one of several retired military commanders who influence politics in Sierra Leone today. He was one of the young army officers who staged a coup against former President Momoh of the All People's Congress (APC) on 29 April 1992. Subsequently, he came to serve as the commander of the Eastern Province during the military regime of the National Provisional Ruling Council (NPRC) from 1992 until 1996. With this military-historic background, Nyuma is a well-known, almost mythic figure among the people of Kailahun District. He is admired by some, pictured as a brave and powerful military commander who protected the eastern region from the rebels, but is simultaneously feared, as it is said that his soldiers were responsible for a series of atrocities committed against the civilian population (see also McGreal 1995 in Keen 2005: 120).

The district council chairman describes himself as a 'real sincere saviour', not only for the people of Kailahun but for the whole nation. Though he admits that his expertise was not valued in the aftermath of the military regime – and especially not by international agencies – Nyuma argues that the post-war society is now in need of a man like him to restore governance. And he is not hesitant to proclaim that he is, indeed, the leader the people are requesting: 'Today, everybody wants to see the wonderful Tom Nyuma as their leader and that is why I volunteered to take this post as the chairman.'

The rationale Nyuma employs in order to legitimize his own position, and to advocate for military-minded governance, is clearly linked to discourses of security, which in turn produce experiences of insecurity (Bubandt 2004: 4–5). In a district locally referred to as 'the last corner of the world' – a district where 'the state' is at least to some extent absent – Nyuma regards himself as a source of protection, a self-image he fought hard to consolidate among the civil population while campaigning for the chairmanship.[2] Lack of trust in the police to enforce law and order, corrupt government representatives and a minimal presence of military security officials at the numerous border-crossing points are key factors contributing to a continuous experience of insecurity among the citizens of the district. Popular myths about cannibalism, chaos and savagery – produced and narrated also locally within the border district – are extremely powerful in reinforcing the production of fear, and hence in creating the request for a 'saviour'. Yet it is especially by looking at historical experiences of rebellion and civil war that we understand how Nyuma attempts to secure his position in the political sphere.

It was in Kailahun District that the civil war initially broke out on 23 March 1991, when a group of rebels called the Revolutionary United Front (RUF), led by army corporal Foday Sankoh, crossed the border from NPFL-controlled territory in Liberia.[3] Within a month, large parts of Kailahun were under rebel control (Keen 2005: 36), and the district came to serve as an RUF stronghold, and as a key base for the recruitment of rebel fighters. Government troops intervened, but following failed attempts to defeat the RUF, civilians began to consider their own means of protection. It was against this background that the Civil Defence Forces militia (CDF),[4] formed around groups of local hunters and secret societies, was established (ibid.: 90). In Kailahun the largest ethnic faction of the CDF, the 'Kamajors', came to be instrumental in fighting against the RUF, partly in cooperation with the government troops. Following a decade of violent confrontations between the various armed factions and a series of atrocities committed against the civilian population, it was also in Kailahun District that the last armed factions finally agreed to disarm.

Though this brief listing of the wartime history in Kailahun does not offer any insight into the complex dynamics of civil war in the border district, and particularly not into the lived experiences of fear, violence and loss, it does, however, give us a sense of the prolonged state of emergency that still influences the present situation in the most war-affected district of Sierra Leone.

Simultaneously with attempts to disarm, demobilize and reintegrate a large population of young ex-combatants into so-called 'civilian life', a number of standard 'humanitarian packages' have been introduced to rebuild what is considered a collapsed system. Despite well-intentioned efforts – and positive steps towards peace-building – Kailahun District is continuously plagued by insecurity. Today most international organizations have migrated to other conflict zones, but the remains of the civil war – burned-down houses, empty tanks, ammunition and a slaughterhouse stained with human blood – stand as reminders of a violent past. Porous borders facilitating the flow of illicit goods, arms and bodies, and the current political instability in Guinea following the December 2008 military coup, are some of the factors contributing to this state of insecurity. Combined with extensive poverty and a lack of employment facilities, especially among the youth, there is a potential for riots and rebellion.

As suggested by Henrik Vigh (2006: 108), it is exactly in such a context, characterized by scarcity and decline, that patrimonial politics secures its influence and dominance. The shortage of resources consolidates the power bases of patrimonial networks as their dependants have few alternative options at hand other than linking up with Big Men who can secure their access to material and social needs (ibid.). Moreover, it is in such a context that Nyuma and his allies are able to create a sense of protection among certain groups of the local population in Kailahun. Though this was particularly the case during wartime emergency, Nyuma still claims to offer a degree of security to the civilian population, though he is feared by the very same group. He portrays himself as a liberation hero, a ruler, who through the exercise of disciplining performances possesses the power to 'secure the ground' of Kailahun.

The district council chairman and his 'task force' of remobilized combatants

It was during the 2007 presidential elections that ex-combatants and retired military personnel re-entered the political arena. After being morally condemned and marginalized from the political sphere following the declaration of peace, the so-called 'ex-servicemen' (as both ex-soldiers and ex-combatants usually refer to themselves) were once again invited into the power centre.

It was also during the 2007 elections that Nyuma made his way back into politics after ten years of exile in the United States. Following the handover of power to former president Tejan Kabbah of the Sierra Leone People's Party (SLPP) in 1996, Nyuma went to the United States with other military colleagues. But just as the campaigning for the 2007 elections kicked off, he was deported as a result of domestic violence.

Rather than echoing the public worries and criticism regarding his return, Nyuma points out that it was his former NPRC companion, Brigadier General Maada Bio, who convinced him to return home. Bio, who was head of state during the last phase of the NPRC regime, had also been in the United States for several years but had managed to make his way into politics upon his return.[5] And though Nyuma – retrospectively – argues that he had not planned on getting involved in politics upon returning to Sierra Leone, he quickly changed his mind when he realized he could still navigate and profit from the networks of post-war patrimonial politics. As he expressed it during an interview conducted shortly after he was appointed to the post of chairman of Kailahun District Council:

When I came back I didn't want to go into politics. I came just before the election. But then Maada Bio convinced me to come on board. I had my own worries. But I realized that I have a lot of fans in the military and I also had fans in the civilian sector. I fought in almost every corner of this country and I have a remarkable record. But those records were not recognized when we were here. But when we left for the USA in 1996 people saw how things evolved and they started to realize that we were good. And then they came to realize that I was a saviour – the real sincere saviours were members of the NPRC.

Like Bio, Nyuma linked up with the SLPP during the 2007 presidential elections. Having staged a coup against the other dominant political party – the APC – and coming from an SLPP-dominated area in the south-east, his choice of political affiliation did not come as a surprise, though he argues that the APC would have loved to include him in their party.

Together with Bio, Nyuma incited an intense campaign mobilized around networks of rival military and militia factions. While RUF combatants were mainly recruited into the APC, most members of the West Side Boys,[6] a splinter faction of the army, and retired military personnel governing during the NPRC regime decided to link up with the SLPP.[7]

Alex, the revenue collector recently appointed by Nyuma, was one of a large group of former militia members who were remobilized into the SLPP 'task force' in order to organize in/security and mobilize votes. Like most of his companions, Alex was released from prison just as the political campaigning began. Being a member of the West Side Boys, he was arrested under the 'public emergency order' in 2000, charged with murder, conspiracy to murder and other offences. After six years in 'protective custody' in the maximum security prison in Freetown, Alex and his companions were acquitted and released in February 2006. Although it was not officially stated, it was a common belief among them that their release was closely connected to their expected remobilization into the political sphere and their presumed loyalty to specific political Big Men (Christensen and Utas 2008).

The political remobilization of ex-combatants and ex-soldiers was conducted through chains of command established during the war and, consequently, Alex was one of the West Side Boys called in for the initial negotiations with the SLPP presidential candidate, Solomon Berewa. While his former commander became the key security adviser for the entire SLPP task force and the presidential candidate, Alex came to work closely with Nyuma.

After several months of campaigning that resulted in violent clashes between rival task force members, it was announced that Ernest Bai Koroma of the APC had won the election.[8] Being positioned not only as losers of the presidential election but also as key organizers and performers of the political violence against APC supporters, Tom Nyuma and his 'task force' of remobilized combatants retreated to the SLPP stronghold in Kailahun to campaign for the chairmanship during the 2008 local council elections.

Being 'a son of the soil' in Kailahun District, where APC supporters are hardly allowed to organize, and belonging to the Mende ethnic group, which makes up the great majority of the population in the south-eastern region, Nyuma defeated his APC rival at 399 of 401 polling stations.[9] Despite widespread protest not only within the APC government but also among civil society organizations and donor agencies, combined with a fear of the possibility of another coup attempt, Nyuma was elected to the post of chairman of the district council in July 2008.[10]

Though they felt betrayed and neglected by politicians who did not fulfil their promises, Alex and his task force colleagues did not hesitate long before deciding to follow their former NPRC boss to Kailahun District. At a very basic level, this choice was a matter of personal security, as they feared they would be targeted by APC task force members, who were now in power, and be held responsible for the electoral violence. But furthermore, following long-term imprisonment and a lack of alternative post-war survival options in a strongly hierarchical system in which loyalty to specific Big Men is often one's only prospect of getting benefits, they hoped this would finally be their chance to improve their future lives and obtain the position of 'a somebody'. They hoped their support for Nyuma would be rewarded once he was back in power. As one of Nyuma's task force members underlines, linking up with Big Men in the political sphere is crucial when one is seeking to improve future prospects: 'I am looking for my future; if you are not a politician you cannot live in Sierra Leone. For now, I don't have anywhere to succeed, except for inside politics. Tom is my "Sababu" [a Big Man offering opportunities] inside politics so I know that he will do something for me.'

Apart from expectations of benefit and reward, loyalty and a strong sense of belonging among combatants who have fought together during the war were also important aspects facilitating the remobilization, from the centre to the margins. Referring to Nyuma not only as their former NPRC commander but even as family, his task force members all indicated that they would never turn their backs on him as this would be regarded as betrayal. Echoing this consideration, Nyuma stresses that he regards his supporters as family who are to benefit from their loyalty: 'They are my boys, I treat them like my children. … They are loyal and they are hard working. I reward loyalty.'

From militias to officials: civil–military shape-shifting

While initially acting as unofficial security guards, surviving from small handouts from their boss and other related Big Men, Alex and his colleagues were appointed as revenue collectors to work at strategic border-crossing points in the district when Nyuma took office at the district council following the local elections in 2008. As Alex points out, the political remobilization and his loyalty to Nyuma were, indeed, rewarded: 'I am an official man now, I have my identity card. I know the reason I decided to get involved in politics. I know what I am after, I have my purpose, I know why I find myself at the last station [Kailahun].'

Alex is proud to declare that he is not a soldier now but rather a council representative with 'real official documents'. If asked during the 2007 elections, he would not have hesitated to describe himself as a 'jungler' or a 'guerrilla'. And at that time, violent military skills were rewarded by presidential candidates who made use of ex-combatants not only to secure party offices but also to intimidate opposition voters. Today, however, Alex prefers his past as a soldier and militia member to remain unspoken for strategic purposes – at least sometimes. Moving from the military into the civil sphere as a result of his position as a revenue collector, Alex seeks to act in a manner that he believes suits a representative of official authority in the civil sphere, as he in fact was instructed to do by his boss upon arriving at the Kailahun borderland.

Alex has always been a master of chameleonic skills, the art of shape-shifting. He moved from one armed faction to another during the civil war. Back then, he spied on the enemy camps, sometimes dressing up as a schoolboy and at other times as a woman, using fake hair and make-up. Today, walking around with his briefcase and neatly polished shoes, Alex is aware that it is this mastery of camouflage skills which aids him in adapting to a radically different position in a new environment. 'When in Rome we do as the Romans do,' he says, and adds – using military language to describe his adaptation strategies – 'we always live according to the terrain.'

The transition from military to civilian rule, and the apparently radical shift in moving from being militia to official, does, however, pose certain obstacles. Not least for the district council chairman. It is with a sense of nostalgia that Nyuma refers to the 'good old days' of the military regime, when people respected military command and hard policies were implemented without protest. And it is with great admiration that he talks about his heroes: Winston Churchill, Mu'ammer al-Gaddafi and other military-minded leaders. Talking about his experience of moving from being a military commander to a government representative, and the related difficulties he has in managing the civilian population in times of peace, Nyuma complains:

> You cannot do hard and fast policy when dealing with the civilian population. Because of bureaucracy it is hard to fire them, it is hard to punish them.
> That's one of the difficulties I have, I cannot really take hard action. They don't respect punctuality, being on time is not part of them. They do not have discipline. Of course, in the military I tell you what to do ... I am a disciplined man and I always practise my discipline, also at home when it comes to my kids and

my spouse. I am using my military discipline in the civilian sector and I think it works really well.

Though stressing that it is through discipline and punishment that he most effectively exercises control over the local population, Alex and his colleagues were soon faced with different realities as local authorities began to protest about the violent methods Nyuma's task force members employed. They complained that Nyuma had brought along his squad of 'rarray boys' (footloose urban youth)[11] and undisciplined ex-soldiers. As a member of one of the ruling chiefdom families in Kailahun town complained:

> Tom Nyuma brought these street boys to collect taxes. They were beating people. He brought some sort of ex-combatants and he gave them uniforms. They were flogging people here, molesting people. They were working as tax collectors but at the same time as security. When you wanted to see Tom Nyuma, they would not even permit you to see him.

Pointing to the ambivalent role of simultaneously occupying the positions of unofficial security guards and official tax collectors, this authority expresses a general concern about the employment of 'ex-servicemen' in the civil sphere, and most importantly dissatisfaction with the violent methods Alex and his colleagues were using to force people to pay their taxes. This scepticism was expressed not only by authorities who were worried about the task/tax force's use of intimidation and violence. As I will illustrate below, other local authorities with competing claims to power and wealth argued that Nyuma should replace his loyal supporters from Freetown with some of their kin.

Negotiating local power constellations and competing claims to authority

In spite of their long-term experiences of combat, moving from district to district during the war, Alex and his colleagues were regarded as outsiders when they arrived in Kailahun. In contrast to their boss, none of them belong to the Mende ethnic group, and consequently not only were they unable to understand the local dialect but also local cultural norms and customs were foreign to them. As such, they were automatically positioned as 'strangers', or, as Alex formulates it, 'second-class citizens'. While this position intensified their sense of being out of place among what they considered 'primitive' and 'uncivilized villagers', more importantly it made them unable to easily make claims to the same entitlements as the local population.

Even before Nyuma's election to the post of district council chairman they were faced with their status as strangers who could not be fully included in Mende society. When they were campaigning for their boss in one of the villages, members of the powerful secret society – the Poro – gave strict orders that they not move around in the streets as the masked Poro devil was due to come out.[12] To non-initiated members, the witnessing of the Poro ceremony was strictly forbidden, even dangerous, they were informed. Forced to hide in a house until the ceremony had finished, they felt humiliated, degraded to the status of children.

Following similar confrontations, Alex and his colleagues became aware that they would not be allowed to carry out their job as revenue collectors if they did not belong to the Poro society. This must be understood against the background that the Poro society not only serves to initiate its members into adulthood but also regulates socio-economic and political practices in close collaboration with the local chiefdom administrations. In Kailahun District, the paramount chief is automatically the head of the Poro society, with the responsibility of authorizing all initiation rites within the chiefdom in close collaboration with senior politicians (Fanthorpe 2007: 10). Considering the significance of such local power constellations, and the obstacles his task force members would experience in performing their duties if they were not included in the secret society, Nyuma reacted quickly by urging one of the local chiefdom authorities to initiate them.

Pointing to the fact that most employees in the district council are members of the Poro society, Alex explains the significance of belonging to their society:

> The district council administration is only for the Mende people. The Mendes are full of advantages – if you don't belong to their society you are nobody, you are zero to them. So my boss talked to the council administration, and they told him that if we are not members of their society they cannot allow us to work on the district council. And sometimes they can send me to work in some areas where they have the society, where the devil will come out. If you are not part and parcel you have to stay away, otherwise it will be dangerous for you. That is why he [Nyuma] advised us: gentle guys, stay cool – go for it.

As indicated in Alex's statement, not being in the Poro society results not only in a lack of recognition and exclusion but also in a lack of protection and security. As mentioned above, the Poro society became an important provider of security during the civil war. Today, in times of relative peace, the society is still regarded as an important source of protection among its initiated members as the society leaders are, for instance, important mediators in disputes and conflicts at the local level. Yet to the uninitiated, the Poro society is often perceived as a source of insecurity. Records of forced initiation, intimidation and violent attacks on non-members and opposing authorities are some of the factors contributing to this insecurity.

Following almost three months of initiation rites in the bush, Alex and his colleagues returned to the district headquarters in Kailahun town as recognized members of the society, initiated into Mende manhood. As the district council chairman had not only organized their initiation but had also paid a large amount of money to the society elders, Alex and his colleagues were granted the prestigious rank of 'chief' through their initiation. As such, they had indeed taken a positive step towards adaptation and integration into Mende society.

Referring to his initiation into the Poro society, Alex claims that he is now a 'full member' of society, a 'citizen' of Kailahun, entitled to the rights and privileges of all other chiefs and Big Men. Yet being mandated to collect taxes and issue licences and evaluation fees at strategic border-crossing points, Alex and his colleagues also came to occupy the position of potential enemies. While their initiation into the secret society reduced the resistance to their presence in some circles, they would still encounter groups of local residents who refused to pay their taxes to outsiders.[13] With Alex and his colleagues occupying sought-after and well-paid positions, local authorities, including employees on the district council, complained about Nyuma's favouring of loyal ex-combatants from Freetown. As will become evident below, they demanded that he replace them with some of their kin, 'a son of the soil'. Having their own relationships of dependence to maintain, these authorities wanted to secure their status as Big Men by providing jobs to their supporters. As also captured in the Mende expression of 'standing for others', it is crucial to nurse such relationships of dependence when seeking to consolidate one's power and authority as a Big Man (Hoffman 2007: 551). Alex is well aware of this; yet he does not allow anyone to challenge the position of revenue collector he has fought so hard to attain. 'Politics is not a drink – when you get power, you want to hold on to it,' Alex emphasizes, and adds that if people should try to challenge him, he is still able to make use of his military skills: 'Let them not take any chance – if they do, we'll let people know that we are ex-fighters, if anybody tries the shit we are ready for them.'

With time, however, Alex has learned how to more pragmatically (and less violently) create modes and means for enacting his claim to power. As will be discussed below, he has learned how to manoeuvre interconnected and overlapping networks of both an official and an unofficial nature, which enables him to maximize personal profit and to simultaneously better handle some of the authorities who attempt to challenge his position.

Manoeuvring intertwined networks and zones of ir/regularity

In the absence of a centralized state maintaining a monopoly on violence, we often witness attempts to make state power highly visible (Hansen and Stepputat 2005: 29). The above discussion shows how a multitude of competing actors, with equal claims to power and wealth, seek to act in the absence of a unitary state. As we get a sense of from Nyuma's statements about discipline and punishment as instruments for exercising authority, he attempts to counter such competing claims by commanding what can be termed 'zones of local sovereign power' (ibid.: 30). As the example of his appointed revenue collectors demonstrates, taxation and regulation are, among other issues, significant instruments for the enactment of such a claim to sovereignty. Not least when taxation is policed and enforced by military-minded regulators like Alex.

Referring to a specific case in which some police officers at the checkpoint attempted to challenge his right to collect revenues and evaluation fees, Alex explains how Nyuma serves as a guardian over lawmaking – and how he as a revenue collector represents the 'law' of his boss, and moreover the Kailahun District as a whole:

> ... whatever law or anything – it is the district council chairman who has the responsibility, and I am a representative of the council – as far as Kailahun District is concerned. And above all, I am the eye of the chairman, you know. He put me here for certain purposes ... certain reasons and certain activities, you know. Because this is a strategic point. They have to recognize that this is a political district and the district council chairman is the head of that district. ... These guys [the police officers] are under my feet now, they are presently under control.

As indicated in this statement, the 'law' Alex refers to, and the sovereign power he asserts on behalf of the district council chairman, also extends into the unofficial and sometimes illicit sphere. Alex not only occupies the position of council representative; he simultaneously serves as an unofficial spy ('the eye of the chairman'), reporting any 'dubious movements' to his boss. Covered by his official status, he is able to access information, especially about border-crossing activities, with relative ease. This ambiguous position enables his access to networks of both an official and an unofficial character, and consequently multiple spaces for generating wealth.

Being well aware that revenue collection and economic regulation constitute a main arena for disputes in the border district, Nyuma has advised his 'tax force' to work with 'incentives' – that is, to allow a certain degree of flexibility, what donor agencies would probably call 'corruption' or perhaps even 'criminality'. When working as a revenue collector, Alex officially receives 25 per cent of the money he collects from issuing licences and charging evaluation fees at the border-crossing point.[14] The speed at which he is able to 'eat money' depends not only on harvesting seasons – and the time for produce to be transported and traded – but also on the way he 'moves the collection'. And here, he argues, it is sometimes necessary to 'get dry eye' (be rude) while other moments call for diplomatic 'sensitization in that official way'. Sometimes Alex enforces the law by making people pay their revenues – whatever (violent) means this takes; at other times, he accepts a small 'token' (in this case money/a bribe), a symbolic exchange serving to maintain positive reciprocal relations. This way of tactically manoeuvring lawmaking and regulation not only allows Alex to better handle some of the local authorities who attempt to challenge his position, and the power he claims to hold, but also enables him to establish his own networks of dependants. By creating zones of irregularity, and also facilitating flows and means for socio-economic mobility across the border when people are reluctant to pay their taxes, Alex accumulates favours from networks of people who rely on his position and the 'incentives' he provides. In this way, by creating his own network of dependants, he gradually establishes his own position as a Big Man.

In a context in which lines between the official and the unofficial, and between the licit and the illicit, are fluid, and in which the networks regulating border economies are interconnected and overlapping, Alex and his colleagues are not the only agents who tactically manoeuvre between ambiguous positions in order to establish and maintain profitable networks. On the contrary, it is the rule rather than the exception that official agents perform a multiplicity of roles, also extending into the unofficial and illicit realms.

As Jean and John Comaroff suggest in their reflections on the dialectic of law and disorder in post-colonies, regulations and irregularity, law and organized lawlessness coexist, and are in fact conditions of each other's existence (2006). This also applies to the borderland of Kailahun, where military officers and custom officials seek to regulate illicit cross-border trade while simultaneously profiting from organized criminal activities, such as cocaine trafficking. As also pointed out by the Comaroffs, there can be no smuggling without border control (ibid.: 21). That is, illegal forms of profiteering, such as the drug trade, require that laws be there to be broken.

Carolyn Nordstrom highlights a similar point in her discussion of the nature of 'shadow networks'. She argues that these networks are not completely distinct from the state, despite their non-state character; rather, they work 'through and around formal state representatives and institutions' (Nordstrom 2000: 36). As such, 'states and shadows exist simultaneously' (ibid.) and, as the case of Alex illustrates, at times even through the very same regulatory figures.

When I ask Alex about the moral implications of involving himself in, for instance, the illicit diamond trade when he simultaneously claims to represent 'the law', he first reacts by legitimizing his right to resources. Pointing to his 'time of predicament' (imprisonment), he argues that it is finally his own time to enjoy, 'to eat money', and that no one should deny him this right: 'I have suffered for this land [Sierra Leone], I have been detained unlawfully. Today I strive hard for my dignity, my bigmanity [Big Man status], and I know what I'm after. I don't care about anybody as long as I know what I'm doing! What is yours is yours, what is mine is mine! I work according to my own ideology ...'

Yet immediately following this outburst, and remarks about how he can make use of his violent skills if necessary – in the above quote simply referred to as 'ideology' – Alex more reflectively explains to me about the intertwined nature of licit and illicit spaces, the blurring of official networks and shadow networks, and about the navigational options such ambiguous networks offer.

In order to skilfully manoeuvre and profit from such networks, it is vital to maintain a delicate balance between enforcing law and order on the one hand, and allowing a certain degree of organized lawlessness on the other. This is the case not only when regulating the illicit diamond and drug trade – or strategically choosing not to do so in order to increase production and profiteering – but also when regulating trade and transactions in the licit domain.

As Janet Roitman concludes from her study of economic practices in the borderlands of the Chad Basin, focusing on competing figures of regulatory authority, the 'code of officialdom' and the 'code of trafficking' are deployed simultaneously and are mutually constituted (2004, 2006: 264–5). In making this point she draws on long-term fieldwork among what she – translating from a local expression – terms 'military-commercial figures', or 'customs officials-soldiers'. Like Nyuma's 'task/tax' force members, these 'officials' have become guarantors of access to wealth for certain groups of the local population despite being associated with the use of violent means (Roitman 2004: 18). Hence, the 'commercial-military bind' comes to constitute a 'site of transfers and redistribution'; a mode of sociability and productivity (ibid.: 181). Roitman argues that while circumventing government, 'customs officials-soldiers' do not regulate an autonomous economy in opposition to official government, or a mode of resistance to 'the state'. As state institutions equally participate in illegal economic practices, the 'customs officials-soldiers' themselves suggest that their activities are licit in the sense that they are ways of 'participating in forms of reasoning that constitute a particular political economy' (Roitman 2006: 265) – a suggestion resembling the rationale Alex employs to explain his regulatory practices.

While Roitman is mainly concerned with the interdependent relationship between non-state regulators and the constitution of state power, her argument also contributes to our understanding of the dynamics of regulation and irregularity enforced by Nyuma and his revenue collectors. In their case, it is through maintaining states of irregularity – what Nyuma would probably term 'flexibility' – that they create a mode for exercising power over politico-economic relations. As such, it is not simply through enforcing law and order, but perhaps more importantly through being able to suspend 'the law', that Nyuma and his allies facilitate the maintenance of local sovereign power in Kailahun District.

Redirecting militarized networks

Tom Nyuma and his 'task/tax force' do not represent an exceptional example of how ex-soldiers and ex-combatants have managed to move from the military to the civil sphere, and have come to occupy the positions of official authorities making claims to power and wealth in post-war society. On the contrary, I argue that their case demonstrates a general tendency influencing current state formation and governance in Sierra Leone: the redirecting of militarized patrimonial networks for post-war politico-economic purposes.

While this chapter has explored the role so-called 'ex-servicemen' play in performing statehood practices at a local level in the SLPP-dominated rural borderland, a similar pattern emerges when we look at the centre. In parallel with Nyuma's mobilization of loyal military/militia colleagues, President Ernest Bai Koroma of the APC has appointed a large group of ex-combatants and ex-soldiers as presidential guards. Enrolled in the armed wing of the national police, these guards are now officially mandated to enforce law and order, through the use of violent means if necessary. Their official employment has become an indicator of legitimacy – as is also the case with Nyuma and his revenue collectors. Though it is important to note the difference between mobilizing militia/military networks into the security sector and, as in the case of Nyuma, into the civilian sector, both processes document how informal militarized networks have been absorbed into the formal sphere. And as discussed above, networks in the formal or official sphere are closely intertwined with informal or unofficial networks. They are, in fact, interdependent and mutually constitutive.

International agencies and local media have expressed concern about the current process of absorbing militarized networks into the official sphere, and thereby 'militarizing politics' or 'politicizing security'. Pro-SLPP journalists in particular have complained about 'violence and organized lawlessness perpetuated by members of the Presidential Guards', and advised the president not to treat 'ruthless killers' with 'kid gloves'.[15] Representatives of State House, including the presidential press secretary, do, however, emphasize that this is a step towards positive reintegration and inclusion. Responding to the criticism, they argue that it is through the absorption, and domestication, of these networks that political stability is ensured in Sierra Leone. In contrast to the perception that the overcoming of patronage is a prerequisite for successful state-building, they suggest that militarized patrimonial networks can actually serve to stabilize state power.[16] Yet approaching the 2012 general elections, it remains to be seen whether this holds true. Alex and his colleagues are awaiting what they refer to as the 'die minute', hoping that their favoured SLPP candidate – Julius Maada Bio, head of state during the NPRC regime – will become the next president. Picturing their return to State House, they hope their loyalty will once again be rewarded by Big Men, and that they themselves will advance to even greater levels of 'bigmanity'.

Notes

1 Translation from French.

2 For instance, he showed a video reportage of how he freed Kailahun District from the rebels.

3 The National Patriotic Front of Liberia was led by Charles Taylor.

4 The Civil Defence Force is an umbrella term referring to various militias

from different ethnic groups: the Kono (*donsos*), the Temne (*gbethis* and *kapras*), the Kuranko (*tamaboro*) and the Mende (*kamajoisia*) (Hoffman 2007: 642).

5 Despite widespread protest within the military concerning the transfer to civilian rule – usually referred to as 'elections before peace' – Maada Bio ceded power to the democratically elected SLPP government of Tejan Kabbah on 29 March 1996. As a reward for this he received a generous 'retirement package', including an educational scholarship in the USA (Keen 2005: 198). Many Sierra Leoneans speculate, however, that Kabbah also promised him a return to political power at a later stage.

6 See Utas and Jörgel (2008) for an analysis of the history and military trajectory of the West Side Boys.

7 For a more detailed discussion of the mobilization of combatants during the 2007 elections, see Christensen and Utas (2008).

8 The election results were announced by the National Electoral Commission (NEC) on 17 September 2007.

9 Generally, the SLPP secures its support from the Mende ethnic group while the APC is mainly backed by the Temne ethic group from northern Sierra Leone.

10 Pro-APC newspapers blamed Maada Bio and Tom Nyuma for being the architects of a letter written by disgruntled military officers threatening the security and peace of Sierra Leone. Many thought this letter was simply a warning signal for another overthrow and their return to power (see, for instance, *We Yone*, 6 February 2009).

11 See Abdullah (2002) for a historical discussion of the 'rarray boy' phenomenon.

12 For studies of the Poro secret society, see, for instance, Fanthorpe (2007) and Bellman (1984).

13 Here it should also be noted that though the Local Government Act 2004 spells out what level of government is responsible for the collection and administration of different taxes and revenues,

it remains somewhat unclear to the local population who is actually entitled to collect revenues and taxes in the district. This uncertainty is mainly a result of unclear relations between the central government, the local councils and the chiefdom administration in terms of their roles in tax and revenue collection.

14 The remaining money will go to the district council.

15 *Standard Times*, 9 February 2010.

16 Interview conducted with the presidential press secretary, 20 May 2009.

References

Abdullah, I. (2002) 'Youth culture and rebellion: understanding Sierra Leone's wasted decade', *Critical Arts*, 16(2).

Archibald, S. and P. Richards (2002) 'Converts to human rights? Popular debate about war and justice in rural and central Sierra Leone', *Africa*, 72: 339–67.

Arnaut, K. and C. K. Højbjerg (2008) 'Gouvernance et ethnographie en temps de crise: de l'étude des ordres emergent dans l'Afrique entre guerre et paix', *Politique Africaine*, 111: 5–21.

Bellman, B. L. (1984) *The Language of Secrecy: Symbols and Metaphors in Poro Ritual*, New Brunswick, NJ: Rutgers University Press.

Bubandt, N. (2004) *Vernacular Security: Governmentality, Traditionality and Ontological (In)Security in Indonesia*, DIIS Working Paper no. 2004/24, Danish Institute for International Studies.

Christensen, M. M. and M. Utas (2008) 'Mercenaries of democracy: the "politricks" of remobilized combatants in the 2007 general elections, Sierra Leone', *African Affairs*, 107(429): 515–39.

Comaroff, J. and J. Comaroff (2006) 'Law and disorder in the postcolony: an introduction', in Comaroff and Comaroff (eds), *Law and Disorder in the Postcolony*, Chicago, IL, and London: University of Chicago Press, pp. 1–56.

Das, V. and D. Poole (2004) 'State and its margins. Comparative ethnographies', in Das and Poole (eds), *Anthropology in the Margins of the State*, Santa Fe, NM/

Oxford: School of American Research Press/James Currey.

Fanthorpe, R. (2003) *Humanitarian Aid in Post-war Sierra Leone: The politics of moral economy*, Overseas Development Institute (ODI), February.

— (2007) *Sierra Leone: The influence of secret societies, with special reference to female genital mutilation*, Writenet Report commissioned by the United Nations High Commissioner for Refugees, Status Determination and Protection Information Section (DIPS).

Hansen, T. B. and F. Stepputat (2005) 'Introduction', in Hansen and Stepputat (eds), *Sovereign Bodies: Citizens, migrants, and states in the postcolonial world*, Princeton, NJ: Princeton University Press, pp. 1–38.

Hoffman, D. (2007) 'The meaning of militia: understanding the Civil Defence Forces of Sierra Leone', *African Affairs*, 106(425): 639–62.

Jörgel, M. and M. Utas (2007) *The Mano River Basin Area: Formal and Informal Security Providers in Liberia, Guinea and Sierra Leone*, FOI, Swedish Defence Research Agency.

Keen, D. (2005) *Conflict and Collusion in Sierra Leone*, New York: Palgrave.

Nordstrom, C. (2000) 'Shadows and sovereigns', *Theory, Culture and Society*, 17(4): 35–54.

Roitman, J. (2004) *Fiscal Disobedience: An anthropology of economic regulation in Central Africa*, Princeton, NJ: Princeton University Press.

— (2006) 'The ethics of illegality in the Chad Basin', in Comaroff and Comaroff (eds), *Law and Disorder in the Postcolony*, Chicago, IL, and London: University of Chicago Press, pp. 247–72.

Utas, M. and M. Jörgel (2008) 'The West Side Boys: military navigation in the Sierra Leone civil war', *Journal of Modern African Studies*, 46(3): 487–511.

Vigh, H. (2006) *Navigating Terrains of War: Youth and soldiering in Guinea Bissau*, New York and Oxford: Berghahn Books.

3 | *Corps habillés*, Nouchis and subaltern Bigmanity in Côte d'Ivoire

Karel Arnaut

The last time I spoke to 'General' Ato Belly was on Thursday, 31 March 2011. It was the first night of the battle for Abidjan between armed forces defending the incumbent president Laurent Gbagbo and those dedicated to instating the elected president Alassane Ouattara.[1] This battle heralded the tragic finale of the post-electoral crisis which took a decisive turn with the arrest of Laurent Gbagbo, ten days later. The pro-Ouattara offensive was launched both from the rebel-held northern territories by the recently raised Republican Forces of Côte d'Ivoire (FRCI), and from within Abidjan by the so-called 'Invisible Commando' led by Major Coulibaly, alias IB. This urban guerrilla group had been active in Abidjan for more than a month when at the end of March, simultaneously with the final FRCI offensive on Abidjan, it began attacking strategic sites in the heart of the city: army camps and headquarters, the presidential palace and residence, and not least the buildings of the national radio and television, RTI.[2] In response, the pro-Gbagbo, so-called 'patriotic' armed forces stepped up their mobilization efforts by recruiting youngsters and/or handing out arms (mainly Kalashnikovs) to them.

At about midnight on that Thursday, the 31st, Ato Belly was defending the RTI against the Invisible Commando when the deafening noise of detonations forced us to break off our (last) telephone conversation. Previously Ato had expressed his dismay about the speed of the FRCI blitz and (related to that) the alacrity with which the majority of the regular armed forces – called the FDS (Defence and Security Forces) – had abandoned their positions. Forestalling an imminent military debacle for the pro-Gbagbo camp, Ato Belly took up the arms which he had officially put down back in May 2009. Then he was formally disarmed as a member, with the rank of 'general', of Abidjan's largest militia, the Grouping of Patriots for Peace (GPP, Groupement des Patriotes pour la Paix). Even when earlier that month patriotic youth leader Charles Blé Goudé urged youngsters to sign up for immediate recruitment into the army, Ato had declined the offer. Nonetheless, he told me how he found pride in assisting in the enrolment of many members of his *gbôhi*. The latter is the Nouchi term for gang or group and, as we will see soon, it can refer to different types of networks, bands and fractions, as well as formal militia groups (see also Banégas 2011). The junior militia members of Ato's *gbôhi*, he reported, were quartered at the prestigious infantry camp of Akouédo, and he reckoned they were finally very close to becoming real soldiers: 'they have a bed, a uniform, and a firearm of their own'.

Ato Belly's reluctance to join the patriotic battle this time around was largely due to his resentment of the Gbagbo administration for lack of recognition and remuneration for his participation in the previous patriotic battles (following the *coup d'état* of 2002). Among other things, his long-standing pro-Gbagbo militantism had resulted in the creation in 2004 and 2007 of GPP militia barracks in different parts of Abidjan. Instead of official appreciation, Ato had seen both barracks being forcibly shut down by the FDS on direct orders from the president, whose embattled nation he was trying to defend. On top of that, the 500,000 CFA (approximately 900 euro) demobilization fee promised to every formally demobilized militia member was never disbursed by the Gbagbo administration. This was all too much for Ato, who not only needed this money for his young family – living in a ramshackle house with a ten-month-old disabled daughter – but also for the hundreds of youngsters of his *gbôhi* who kept on hassling him for financial support or urging him to raise the matter of this broken promise among the militia leadership and its patrons in presidential circles. But against all odds, Thursday, 31 March offered the occasion for ultimate redress.

During our last telephone conversation, Ato explained that he was rigged out in full battledress, put together from the uniforms, boots, berets and belts left behind by the many FDS who had abandoned the RTI premises. He had even succeeded, he added, in procuring a number of shoulder marks (*galons*) which he would put on later. Also, he had an impressive number of weapons at his disposal: Kalashnikovs in great numbers as well as anti-tank RPG-7 grenade launchers. Finally, Ato did not miss the opportunity to point out that all this took place in the presence, and with the support, of Gbagbo's finest and manifestly bravest army unit, the Republican Guards (Gardes Républicaines). They made this sudden transformation 'real': vouching for his value as a soldier, turning his hasty dressing-up into an official act of instantaneous conscription, and converting his seized weaponry and insignia into bestowals complementing his last-ditch, 'well-deserved' career move.

Militias and pre-peace networking

The above section recounts one of the many tragic micro-moments in Côte d'Ivoire's recent post-electoral drama which formed the violent denouement of a long decade of political-military strife. The latter started with the 1999 *coup d'état* removing Henri Konan Bédié from power, followed by a turbulent military transition under General Guéï. Laurent Gbagbo's seizure of power in late 2000 and the (half-successful) *coup d'état* which ensued from this in

September 2002 resulted in the creation of a rebel-held northern zone. The recent post-electoral crisis began when Laurent Gbagbo and Alassane Ouattara both claimed victory in the November 2010 presidential elections. After four months of fruitless mediation the crisis took a decisive turn when the two protagonists had recourse to military force and Ouattara won owing largely to the support of the international community.

The types of armed forces engaged in the conflict from 1999 were many and diverse. Apart from the regular military and security forces (FDS, and later the FRCI), and the international peacekeeping forces – the UN peacekeeping force ONUCI and its French counterpart Licorne – there were mercenaries, (gangs of) thugs, youth militias, hunter-warriors group (the so-called *dozos*), ad hoc armed youth groups and activist civilians providing shelter and food for the various combatants.

Although estimates vary widely and (will) remain extremely difficult to make, one may posit that up to 40,000 people, mainly youngsters, were active in so-called parallel forces on both sides of the conflict. An estimated 25,000 of them belonged to the pro-Gbagbo patriotic militias. The latter emerged in late 2002/early 2003 within widely differing contexts of local and national mobilization. Although the large majority of the militia members waited for their official demobilization and disarmament until the end of 2009, many were active in military operations only prior to 2005 and only for a couple of months in total.

With a few notable exceptions, the operations in which the patriotic self-defence groups participated were of limited military significance. Ironically perhaps, but quite typical for the Ivorian situation, militia organizations were mostly established in the aftermath of the early decisive combats in the west (Chelpi-den Hamer 2011), and anticipated post-war registration and so-called communal reinsertion programmes which began to materialize in a haphazard way from 2009 onwards. All this time many remained mobilized or kept in contact with their units and commanders while attending to other activities. As we will see in more detail below, throughout the short decade of political-military conflict (2002–11), the patriotic militias were the locus of extensive networking and, to the extent that this was informed by political or ideological choices, vast enterprises of civil society building. On the latter dimension of militia formation I have written elsewhere (Arnaut 2008b, 2008c). In this chapter, I focus more on its social dimension: the intricate processes of networking and the emergence of subaltern Big Men in the form of militia leaders. After all, the post-war, or rather pre-peace, multiplication of militias and their growing impact on social and political life constituted a protracted, multifaceted and multi-sited process, which this chapter tries to begin to disentangle in terms of social mobility of a juvenile and subaltern kind.

Military triangulations

The dynamics of expansion, dissemination and mobility of militias in southern Côte d'Ivoire during the preceding decade had at least three dimensions: (a) the flexibility of militia members as regards their resourcefulness and entrepreneurship, (b) the changeability of militia structures within strategies of clientelism and low-key elite formation, and (c) the proximity to the regular defence and security forces. The latter are commonly referred to as *le(s) corps habillé(s)*, meaning 'corps in uniform' (literally, 'the dressed-up corps'), and comprise several categories of uniform-wearing, arms-carrying civil servants: police, state police (*gendarmes*), specialized police units (such as environmental police), army and customs (*douanes*). By 'proximity' to the *corps habillés*, I mean either the latter's physical co-presence during training, on the front lines, and in various sites and schemes of 'violent labour', or their omnipresence in the aspirations of the youngsters – as holders of secure employment and as icons of social success. As we will see at the end of this chapter, this proximity situates the *corps habillés* and the militias in a common 'field'. Theorizing this will allow us to get a firmer grip on youth, their social mobility and networking as dimensions of subaltern agency in times of crisis and violent conflict. But first, we need to grasp the basic entangled dynamic of militia members, their chiefs and patrons.

Coming back to the issue of militia mobility, 'General' Ato Belly was definitely a stationary type, both geographically and in terms of militia membership, but that did not make his calculations about his own and his fellow militiamen's social mobility any less judicious. Ato was an Abidjanese local taxi (*woroworo*) driver until in late 2002 he joined the patriotic movement. In early 2003 he joined the Abidjan-based GPP militia and remained active in its networks until his death. Within the GPP Ato played a central role in successive attempts to establish camps (*cantonnements*) in Abidjan. He took the lead in transforming the girls' school Institut Marie-Thérèse into a GPP barracks. Between August 2004 and March 2005 this camp, branded the First Battalion of Commando Legionnaires (1er BCL), housed up to four hundred youngsters. Much later, in mid-2007, Ato made another successful attempt to accommodate several hundred militiamen who were out on the streets of Abidjan after having been chased from their camps and from the police and gendarme barracks in which they had been housed for several months. This time around, Ato chose the deserted run-down Hotel Akwaba along the Abidjan beach as his self-styled 'naval' base – located in Vridi, the neighbourhood where Ato was raised and spent most of his life. According to Ato, his sustained attempts to muster and accommodate his ex-combatants were meant to keep up their public visibility in anticipation of announced demobilization and reinsertion schemes. However, as we will see presently, given the inveterate uncertainty of these programmes, militiamen also bet on other horses.

Both from the Akwaba 'naval' base (until it was dismantled in November 2008) and, even more so, from the above-mentioned First BCL camp in Adjamé, Ato observed and supported the to-and-fro movements of 'his' troops. On an individual basis or in groups of variable size (also called *gbôhi*), combatants were seizing all sorts of opportunities to valorize their 'violent labour' (Hoffman 2011) or other skills. In between answering one call or another for support on the front lines, they carried out often very short-term contract work in as diverse areas as construction work and development projects, but mostly in security and vigilantism in very different sectors such as transport (or transport regulation) and politics.

While serving as a dispatching centre for thousands of militia members in different war sites in the interior, the GPP in Abidjan increasingly fragmented. While in action along the so-called front lines, GPP members formed new groups and networks which on return to Abidjan did not (fully) reintegrate into the parent organization. These new networks, referred to as *gbôhi*, sometimes took the form of new militia fractions with new leaders who proclaimed themselves 'general' or 'commander'. Such was the case of the CNLB of Watchard Kédjébo, the FLP of Oliverson le Zoulou, and the GCLCI of Jimmy Willy, to name only three.[3] The clearing of their only centralizing camp at the Institut Marie-Thérèse and the relative failure of subsequent camps such as the ones at Azito (Yopougon) and Biabou II (Abobo), as well as the aforementioned camp at Vridi (Port-Bouët), reinforced this process of disintegration which, in turn, was countered by subsequent attempts to regroup the militia factions. These federalizing attempts were either undertaken by long-standing GPP leaders such as President Bouazo Yoko Yoko Bernard or 'Chief of the Defence Staff' Jeff Fada, or by newcomers with relevant resources in the form of political contacts and financial means. Such was the case of 'General' Jimmy Willy, who capitalized on his contacts with Gbagbo's FPI (Ivorian Popular Front) party in order to create the very influential federation Union of Self-defence Groups from the South (UMAS).[4]

From the above description one can already infer that the fragmentation of militias was not only the outcome of grassroots militia mobility and networking but also of intervention 'from above' – *in casu*, of sustained attempts by political and military entrepreneurs to raise militias or federations thereof and become officially recognized as their chiefs. The general dynamics of the Ivorian patriotic activism in general and militancy in particular are those of mobility, of fission and fusion. These processes started within days of the outbreak of the conflict in September 2002 and, as far as we can discern, are still going on in the post-conflict period with militia leaders repositioning themselves and building new constituencies in the peace process. If Eugène Djué is now (May 2011) a figurehead of the reconciliation of patriotic militias with the new Ouattara regime, it is mainly due to his more or less consolidated status as a Big Man of patriotic militantism: in order to mark his senior position as a militia paramount chief among the many militia 'generals', he labelled himself 'marshal' (Arnaut 2006).

Further to this point, it is significant that the GPP, the self-declared 'mother of all patriotic militias', is itself the offshoot of an earlier patriotic organization, the UPLTCI (Union des Patriotes pour la Libération Totale de la Côte d'Ivoire), created by Eugène Djué in the immediate aftermath of the September 2002 insurgency. Almost at the same time, Djué's fellow former student leader and competitor in patriotic activism Charles Blé Goudé created the eventually hegemonic patriotic federation the Alliance des Jeunes Patriotes pour le Sursaut National. When, after a couple of months, Charles Groguhet and Touré Moussa Zéguen left Djué's activist UPLTCI and founded their own, more belligerent and instantly very popular, GPP militia, both Goudé and Djué recruited some of the GPP's trained combatants, while at the same time trying to incorporate the GPP and other organizations into their respective patriotic federations. The same double operation of patronage underlies the overall dynamics of the patriotic militias: (a) emerging patrons trying to draw together networks of adventurous and peripatetic juvenile militants (from below) while (b) capturing through federation (from above) the networks that escape their control.

In order to illustrate how the above processes were also at work in other militias, but above all in order to introduce the aspect of the proximity of *corps habillés* as the third factor of militia dynamics, I introduce another character, a militia member called 'Marcus Garvey'. His case, in combination with that of Ato Belly, provides the core empirical ground for further theorizing subaltern mobility and networking in conflict situations.

'Marcus Garvey', networker and 'Nouchi'

Like Ato Belly, 'Marcus Garvey' took up arms again in the tragic finale of post-electoral conflict, after having been demobilized or waiting to be demobilized for almost seven years. Also like Ato Belly, Marcus Garvey saw himself very much as part of the so-called reserve pool or support base (*base arrière*) of the FDS, not by dispatching 'violent labour' or by accommodating its 'labourers' in barracks (as Ato Belly did) but by executing such violent labour first as a combatant and later as the foreman (*chef de dispositif*) of a group engaged in security operations. In sum, both Ato and Garvey were Big Men of sorts, managing a network (*gbôhi*) of (ex-)combatants around them. Of both their networks nothing much is presently left: Ato's *gbôhi* has lost its leader (and in all probability most of its members), while Garvey's is entirely dispersed, reduced to a dozen friends trying to keep in touch by mobile phone.

In March 2003, at the age of twenty-eight, Garvey left Abidjan, where he was born and raised, in order to join the western front near Guiglo. After a stay of about eight months, during which he was enrolled by the FLGO (Front for the

Liberation of the Great West) militia, Garvey was flown home in the company of exactly 677 Abidjan-based FLGO recruits. Following a short stay-cum-forced-removal at the Akouédo army camp, half of the returnees, including Garvey, took up residence in the vicinity of the camp, in the unfinished houses of a gigantic building site on the outskirts of Abidjan called Lauriers. Later on, for about seven months (November 2004–May 2005) Garvey ran a large-scale vigilante operation around the radio and TV transmitting station of Abobo (northern Abidjan) in collaboration with the FDS. For this, he employed, according to himself, more than two hundred (ex-)combatants, most of whom belonged to his already unravelling *gbôhi* at Lauriers. One year on, Garvey returned to Guiglo, where he associated himself with the MILOCI (Ivorian Movement for the Liberation of the West of Côte d'Ivoire) militia, which, in the meantime, had won a certain notoriety and was first in line to receive demobilization fees. In late 2008, after more than two years in Guiglo waiting fruitlessly to be demobilized, Garvey returned to Abidjan and joined what was left of his *gbôhi* at Lauriers. As before (2003–04), he and his dispirited gang survived on small jobs, mostly in building, security or petty trade, until the violent denouement of the post-electoral crisis made him and the remaining sixty members of his group take up arms again.

On 3 March 2011 Garvey got hold of an AK-47 rifle from one of the many deserting trainees at the Gendarmerie School and joined the armed forces who were defending the residence of the incumbent President Gbagbo at Cocody. When, one week later, heavy UN and French bombardments destroyed the entire defence infrastructure around the presidential residence, and the arrest of Gbagbo was imminent, Garvey abandoned the battle. He also walked out on what was left of his *gbôhi*, most of whom had decided to continue the struggle from the marine base at Yopougon, seconding the notoriously intrepid marine forces loyal to Gbagbo. Two months after this naval base was 'pacified' by national and international forces, in April 2011; only two members of Garvey's *gbôhi* have returned home. As before, Garvey now (May 2011) shares a squat in a storage container with his old mate Aubin (who was too ill to partake in the recent fighting). Garvey's girlfriend, who takes care of their three-year-old daughter, has been refusing to join her partner in this makeshift abode.

Having no proper job, no proper house and no family in whose midst he resides, Garvey labels himself a 'noussi'. Going against the standard spelling of 'Nouchi', which refers to a broad category of (juvenile) urban vagrants and their slang (de Latour 2001; Newell 2009a), Garvey employs an idiosyncratic etymology to stress the word's composition from the French morphemes '*nous*' (we) and '*si*' (if), while explaining that: 'We the unemployed, we the students who have diplomas but no jobs, we, children whom the street has given birth to without checking into the maternity hospital, it is us; if you could accept us in your society without too many *arrière-pensées* about us.'

This passage, in which Garvey tries to grasp the predicament of his exclusion from mainstream society, is an excerpt from one of his many writings, which total about 350 pages of manuscript telling of his life during the 2002–11 violent conflict. His story, as well as that of Ato (which is enshrined in about eight hours of recorded interviews), forms the core of the empirical basis for exploring what I have called the proximity of the *corps habillés* as a first step towards addressing the central questions of subaltern mobility and networking in times of conflict.[5]

Corps habillés

The relationship between the youth militias and the *corps habillés* during the 2002–11 conflict in Côte d'Ivoire entails (a) the latter's physical co-presence during training, on the front lines, and in various other sites and schemes of 'violent labour', and (b) their importance in the imagination of youngsters as icons of successful people with a (potentially) honourable profession, secure employment and a flourishing social life. This does not mean that youth militia members have an unqualified admiration for the *corps habillés*. Rather, the relationship between militia members and their professional counterparts is riddled with ambiguity.

Reading through the writings of Marcus Garvey, it is difficult to miss the fact that, as for so many of his fellow combatants, proximity to the army is the alpha and omega of his engagement with militias. In the first pages of his war journal, Garvey reports a short conversation with a friend which instantly made him volunteer for the patriotic battle. When informing Garvey that an organization was being set up in order to dispatch youngsters to the front lines, the friend explained its modus operandi as follows: 'You go, they train you, they drop you off on the battle front in order to fight alongside the FANCI [Ivorian regular army] and after the war, they put you in the army, at least those who survived' (Garvey 2011: 7).

The plausibility of this causal link between militia membership and entry into the regular army largely followed from the appeals of popular politicians in the early months after the insurgency of 2002, calling on youngsters to join the regular army, which was diagnosed as ageing, depleted, disheartened and in urgent need of reinforcement. Officially in late 2002 about three thousand of those who volunteered were incorporated into the army while thousands of rejected youngsters kept roaming the streets and public places of Abidjan for several months, hoping fruitlessly to become part of future recruitment campaigns. That is where the process of militia formation took off.

Once they were incorporated in one or other self-defence group based either in Abidjan or on the front lines in central and western Côte d'Ivoire, these volunteers immediately came into direct contact with members or former members (either retired or dismissed) of the *corps habillés*. Among the earliest recruits of the GPP were a group of sixty-five marines who had recently been dismissed for insubordination (Njabehi 18/6/2008; Shao 4/4/2009).[6] Rather than becoming plain militia combatants, most (ex-)members of the FDS took more responsible positions and acted as trainers and coaches, exceptionally as militia leaders and in a few cases also as gatekeepers. In all, members of the *corps habillés* occupied vital positions in the intricate patronage structure surrounding the militias.

With few notable exceptions, such as that of 'Commander' Nahui Lazare, leader of the self-defence group MI-24, who was an ex-member of the Ivorian army (Nahui 26/3/2009), (former) soldiers and policemen acted most often as coaches and trainers of the militia groups. To start with the former category, the late Koré Moïse, alias 'Ministre de la Défense', was a military officer effectively attached to the Ministry of Defence, who acted as a coach to the GPP leadership during the first years of the conflict (2002–05) (Ato 25/3/2009; Saintgbal 21/3/2008; Delta and Assoumou 3/4/2009). A typical example of a trainer is 'Colonel' Zagbayou, who was a sergeant of the Ivorian army. In Abidjan he was one of the GPP's most important trainers from the very early days (Lago 8/4/2009; Njabehi 18/6/2008). Zagbayou continued his training of militia volunteers in Yopougon into the post-electoral crisis, and even ended up fighting alongside his trainees until the final days of patriotic resistance to Ouattara's election (*Le Patriote*, 11 January 2011; *Times Live*, 30 April 2011). On the western front sergeants like Koulaï Roger and Oulaï Delafosse played a similar role. Unlike Zagbayou, who appeared to have had good connections with the presidency, Koulaï and Delafosse were detached by their respective superiors, Colonel Oulé Yedess and General Denis Bombet, to train and coach the FLGO recruits. Importantly, higher officers such as Yedess and Bombet were less patrons than gatekeepers. As Big Men of the armed forces they warranted the temporary permeability of the military sector for enterprising and zealous youngsters. In this role the military gatekeepers were endorsed by political Big Men-cum-agitators such as presidential security councillor Kadet Bertin and patriotic youth leader Charles Blé Goudé, who regularly proclaimed the state's receptivity to juvenile input for its *corps habillés.* In fact, Bertin's and Blé Goudé's rapid rise to national prominence in itself indexed the new possibilities for youngsters. On top of the politicians who made public appeals, there were those whose occasional public encouragement of youthful patriotic activism was complemented by moral, material and financial support for certain militias. Among these sponsors featured members of parliament of Gbagbo's FPI party, such as Nko Marcel and William Attéby, and fellow party member Geneviève Bro Grébé, president of the patriotic women's organisation (Ato 26/2/2010; Bouazo 19/3/2008). Together, the military gatekeepers as much as the politicians and propagandists who either represented or supported the militant youngsters inscribed the militias into the larger story of the emergent 'rejuvenation of the nation' under President Gbagbo by showing them concrete pathways leading from militias into the military and by extension the *corps habillés* (see Arnaut 2005).

More concretely, it is no exaggeration to say that all ex-combatants of the self-defence groups I have spoken to could name at least one member of the *corps habillés* who was involved in their training or in important military operations in which they partook (such as Dignité or Léopard). Moreover, many of the militia members spent some time in military precincts on the front lines or in Abidjan. In and around Abidjan the prestigious marine base of Adiaké and the spacious 1st Battalion camp at Akouédo were important sites in that respect, and so were the two so-called war schools of Abidjan: the Ecole de Police and the Ecole de Gendarmerie (e.g. Guéï, KRR and Ato 10/4/2009). In all of these places militia members received extremely variable treatment – a puzzling alternation between being glorified and being humiliated, being nurtured and accommodated one moment and starved and chased at gunpoint the next. As we will see presently, a similar ambivalence was at play in the core signifier of the *corps habillés*: the uniform, which could connote dignity and righteousness as much as cowardice and travesty.

One of the central items of proximity between the *corps habillés* and patriotic militias was the outfit they wore. References and anecdotes relating to the uniform or battledress (*treillis*), including the shoulder marks (*galons*), beret (*beret*), boots (*rangers* or *rénaux*) and belt (*ceinturon*), crop up in almost any conversation with ex-combatants. This is also the case in Garvey's autobiography. Merely four months after his arrival on the western front line, he reports that militia members from Guiglo went out demonstrating half naked in military drill (*pas-gym*) while chanting 'Give us uniforms.'[7] This incident heralded ever-growing tensions between the militia rank and file on the one hand and its leadership and the *corps habillés* units at Guiglo on the other. Eventually, as mentioned, this resulted in the deportation of more than six hundred FLGO youngsters to Abidjan in early October 2003. Also, as I explain below, this event exemplarily revealed the broader meaning of 'dressing up' in the context of the Ivorian conflict and the participation of militant youngsters in it.

To 'dress up the militia members' (*habiller les éléments*) does not simply mean providing them with uniforms or authorizing them to wear them, but falls nothing short of giving them official employment, including registration, monthly salary, healthcare and pension schemes, etc. That is what Sergeant Koulaï Roger, the FLGO's main trainer and Yedess's aide-de-camp, referred to when in response to the nude *pas-gym* he promised that his trainees would all 'be dressed', while several months later, just days before their deportation to Abidjan, he broke down in tears, admitting: 'I have lied to you, you will not be dressed here' (Garvey 2011: 21). This strongly indicates that the militia's focus on uniforms is much more than a (juvenile) obsession with outward appearance. As we will see presently, apart from considering the uniform as indexing a potentially critical move regarding social mobility, for its aficionados it also functioned as a marker of moral distinction.

As could be expected, the military leadership gave preference to its regular troops when it came to the distribution of battledresses and equipment. Garvey reports on the frustration this sometimes caused among his fellow FLGO members, but while explaining this he also provides us with some clues as to how this combines with a more general disdain for the FDS's (in)significance in the maintenance of public order in a front-line city like Guiglo. During the rainy season of 2003, he writes: 'The policeman at his roadblock could sleep throughout, the gendarme commuted between the Mini Shop bar and his desk, while the soldier was busy managing his women's business when he wasn't attending to the roadblock.' In order to measure the degree of Garvey's low esteem for all three categories of the *corps habillés*, it is important to know that not only was drinking at the Mini Shop and flirting considered to be of little benefit to national security, but also hanging around the office was despised as a futile wartime activity, and occupying a roadblock even more so. This is also explained by Ato Belly (25/3/2009), who, in a long narrative about the day he decided to abandon his job as a taxi driver in order to 'liberate his country', insulted the policemen who approached him at the central junction (*le grand carrefour*) of Abidjan's important commune of Koumassi: 'I told them: this country is dying and you are here busy racketeering along the road; one asks us to go and liberate Bouaké, you have the required arms but you use them to force taxis to stop.' The fact that, as a taxi driver, Ato had been undergoing the racketeering-at-gunpoint of these police officers for many years certainly added to his frustration and to the ferocity of his scolding. However, it is probably not so much the practice of roadside racketeering itself at which Ato took offence – after all, that was also one of the militias' favourite activities – but the fact that the *corps habillés*' arrogance towards helpless citizens masked a proven lack of courage when it came to facing an armed adversary. This was also exemplified in the way the FDS dealt with their uniforms.

The most obvious sign of the cowardice among the FDS was what 'General' Ato Belly witnessed in 2002–03 as much as in 2011: imminent attacks by rebel forces were preceded by massive desertions. As Ato experienced on 31 March 2011 at the national radio and television site, these desertions began with a hasty change of clothes. In 2003 Richard and Eric (10/4/2009), two members of Ato Belly's *gbôhi*, identified this as the reason for their own recruitment into a special commando to attack a rebel stronghold near Daloa: the FDS who were stationed there 'had taken fright, they undressed … they took their rifles and threw them away, they put on civilian clothes and fled'. Consequently thirty-five GPP members such as themselves and fifteen professional commando troops from Akouédo formed a new commando which received the same red (marines') berets, the same uniform and the same weapons – for Richard and Eric a source of profound job satisfaction.

Finally, uniforms were a way of distinguishing oneself not only from the non-uniformed civil servants or from civilians, but also from different armed units, and most of all from enemy troops. Recounting his admission to the GPP, Ato explains that he feared confusion and infiltration when he observed that GPP militia members were dressed in the same way as the rebels he had seen on TV: wearing no proper boots (*rangers*) but plastic sandals (*lèke*), and merely uniform trousers plus T-shirt (*bas treillis*) (Ato Belly 7/6/2008).[8] As the late GPP 'general' Shango (14/6/2008) explains, dressing up like the rebels was sometimes part of the tactics used mainly on the western front (see Utas and Jörgel 2008 for parallels). In other circumstances, wearing the full uniform was indispensable and an important part of the military etiquette. During the military crisis of November 2004, Ato Belly (26/2/2010) explains, his troops started seconding the elite Republican Guards to assist in their task of defending the presidential residence. The way Ato recounts it, the trustworthiness and the dedication of both groups as expressed in their sharing full dress (*treillis complet*) warranted the fraternal co-presence of both formal and informal armed forces. This brings us to the 'social' dimension of the relationship between both groups.

Militia members generally refer to the *corps habillés* as their 'elder brothers' (*grands frères*). This relationship carries the full ambiguity of their rapport: it combines familiarity with respect and, at times, resentment, which in practice underlies their mutual complicity as much as inequality and the militia's subjugation. The deep sense of complicity is well illustrated by, for instance, a whole series of mutual engagements with the FDS, which Garvey reports in his writings. One typical example relates to the arrangements for the roadblocks or checkpoints (*corridors*) and patrols (*patrouilles*) which Garvey and his *gbôhi* set up in the vicinity of the transmitting station of Abobo during the time they were responsible for its protection. At four so-called passageways (*corridors*) members of Garvey's group undertook the rather lucrative activity of checking the identity papers and luggage of passers-by while taking bribes from them. By doing this they entered into direct competition with the surrounding *corps habillés*, who were happy to be cut in on the deal. 'The elder brothers agreed,' Garvey (2011: 90) notes with satisfaction.

At certain dramatic moments this complicity between militias and the military was reversed by the latter, who used their power and position to discipline or punish their 'younger brothers'. In late 2006 and early 2007 more than three hundred GPP youngsters experienced this during their time at the aforementioned Abidjanese war schools. While initially the militias were well received there, the relationship rapidly deteriorated in the run-up to the March 2007 Ouagadougou peace accord, and resulted in the militia members being chased at gunpoint from their guest abode. However humiliating such forced evacuations and other reprimands were, they were sometimes glossed over as the legitimate right of 'elder brothers' to correct or admonish their younger siblings (Delta and Assouma 3/4/2009). Finally, such reprimands were all the more humiliating when they involved uniforms. When in November 2008 Ato Belly's so-called naval base at Vridi was evacuated by the chief of staff, General Philippe Mangou, himself, the sad climax was that all uniforms, boots and military gear were put on one big stack and set alight in the presence of television cameras (Ato Belly 25/3/2009). In spite of deeply traumatic events such as these and other camp evacuations, many militia members maintained the desire to join the military one day. Such tenacity requires our theoretical attention, presently.

Subaltern mobility: going in circles?

The above detailed description of the complex and ambivalent relationship between the military and the militias through the prism of *corps habillés* allows us to safely speculate that for militia members FDS uniforms and military gear were important markers of a prospective transition process which could lead into the heart of the *corps habillés*. Such a process starts, quite plainly, with a change of clothes, as described in graphic terms by the late GPP 'commander' Roger Njabehi (26/3/2009): 'because we were civilians, we had to put on a military uniform ... in order to help the military ... and the military were aware of that, and the gendarmes were also aware of that: that these kids there are helping us; so we are going to fight along with you, "dress them", and they have dressed us'. However, as we know now, with the exception of a few lucky ones, thousands saw their military dreams unfulfilled for some time (Banégas 2008).

The magnitude of this disillusion is certainly proportional to the recursivity of the false promises expressed by many important political and military entrepreneurs, and at critical moments echoed by the militia leaders themselves in a desperate attempt to keep their *gbôhi* mobilized and rallied behind them. However, the impact of these messages 'from above' must be qualified by considering the tactics 'from below' – the sustained attempts by youngsters to infiltrate the *corps habillés* in spite of the successive disillusionments and even downright rejections over a period of many years. For many of the militia members, as for Ato Belly and Marcus Garvey, these disillusionments repeated themselves over a period of eight long years and ended some time in March 2011, in a decisive if not fatal bid to enter the *corps habillés*. By then the latter were perceived as stripped of the weak, the cowards and the impostors who, in an ultimate *démasqué*, had abandoned their battledresses. The militia members' adherence to the uniforms in itself became a demonstration of their unabated loyalty and the proof that they deserved what they had been asking for since day one: 'being dressed'.

In the remainder of this chapter, I want to further explore the effects and, above all, the mechanisms of these tactics of impersonation within broader frames of apprenticeship, on-the-job training and social mobility. As a starting point, it is important to be aware that the youngsters were somehow conscious of the fact that by putting on some military garb and hanging about in the vicinity of the *corps habillés* they were playing a big game, with all the ambiguity that came with it. Near the end of 2007, after yet another six months of waiting for the demobilization and reintegration programme in Guiglo to resume, Garvey noted:

> I am 32 years old, it is true that without having served in the army, I have served in the army. I have frequented it so much that I can claim I was with it, this army, it is beautiful, impressive but hypocrite and treacherous. When I recall the words of sergeant Koulaï Roger I feel myself suffering, regretting. I still see him sobbing, telling us that he merely executed orders. That makes me feel like throwing up: to offer hopes of beauty and of strength, and shatter these in such a hypocritical way. In one word, I have walked alongside this beauty, this imposing and betraying hypocrite and I have come to detest it in the end. (Garvey 2011)

The central metaphor of this paragraph – companionship – provides some guidance for starting to devise an analytical framework for subaltern (social) mobility in times of crisis. Garvey looks back on a trajectory in which he became entangled with the army, learned much about it, but never really became part of it, never fully inhabited the corps he so eagerly wanted to belong to. Instead, in phrases such as 'I was *with* it' (my emphasis), Garvey positions himself as a (travelling) companion of the army. This matches the general theme of his autobiography, which he entitles 'The Companion', and in which he addresses the reader throughout as 'my companion'. Companionship has at least two strings of meanings which relate to social mobility and networking respectively. In the realm of social mobility, the companionship implies an enduring situation of initiation or apprenticeship without ever reaching full proficiency. Garvey sees himself lingering in a situation of truncated mastery which for some time constitutes a source of hope but eventually also of desperation. Equally so in the realm of networking – the enduring co-travelling produces 'company' in many forms, albeit mainly of a rather ephemeral and cursory nature. The companions of the army and *corps habillés* in their capacity as elder brothers have a large stake in regulating the seesaw movement of nearing (complicity) and distancing (subjugation) between the militia dilettantes and the properly 'dressed' FDS professionals. Furthermore, militia members seek the company of friends or *'compagnons de route'* and more often than not consider themselves as belonging to a *gbôhi*. Although at certain times the *gbôhi* can be a strong locus of identification and solidarity, it has very permeable boundaries and is in constant flux as people join and leave. Finally, militia activity creates conduits to the bigger world of national politics, magistrature and top-level administration. The web of military and political patronage surrounding the self-defence groups in Côte d'Ivoire in the preceding decade resulted both in occasional contacts and short- or long-term contracts between members of both realms. Having addressed Gbagbo directly in the course of a protest action was a source of pride for Marcus Garvey, as much as it was a source of prestige for Ato Belly to have met the army chief of staff, Philippe Mangou, on several occasions. More durable and lucrative were the special operations or long-term bodyguard contracts for politicians, judges or top-level civil servants which certain militia members were able to secure for themselves and their *gbôhi*. A good example of this was the two-month contract Ato Belly concluded with the Mauritanian ambassador in February 2011 whereby he and a dozen of his 'elements' protected the embassy and the hundreds of Mauritanian refugees it accommodated at that time.

In all, the networking as much as the on-the-job training of militia apprenticeship was rather shallow and elusive, and, for the large majority of the militia members, never resulted in full mastery, a stable professional or patronage network, or a far-reaching identification with the coveted *corps habillés*. Instead, the relationship with the latter largely boiled down to a fascination for what Garvey calls its 'beauty and strength' – that is, its outward appearance epitomized by the uniforms and paraphernalia, and its strength indexed by the firearms and the direct impact of carrying weapons in public. Thus, in spite of their tenacity and dedication, militia members remained forever 'outside' and hierarchically 'below' the army 'corps' – enduringly peripheral and subaltern. Any further theorizing should start from here.

Incrementalism, impersonation and the field

Tens of thousands of youngsters who try to supplement the state's *corps habillés* can be taken as an instance of what AbdouMaliq Simone describes as 'incrementalism' (Simone 2008a: 17). In his usage, this refers to the gradual albeit sometimes rapid process of haphazard extension in the construction of houses, markets and other urban infrastructures (ibid.: 16). When applied to institutional contexts such as the *corps habillés*, incrementalism alerts us to the proliferation of 'state'; what Aretxaga (2003: 369) identifies as 'an excess of statehood practices: too many actors competing to perform as state'. This enables us to further develop the idea launched in the introduction to this volume, that the absence of the state in Africa leaves voids that are filled by entrepreneurs of different sorts. 'Incrementalism' does not start from possible voids but from the supplementing or multiplying of operations in the vicinity of state institutions, which may either condense and extend them or drain them and trim them down. As one of Hibou's seminal texts on state transformation

– in accord with founding texts such as that of Bayart (Bayart et al. 1999) and Reno (1995) – points out, the privatization of the state does not simply concern its '*décharge*' (discharge) but also its '*dédoublement*' (duplication/multiplication) by way of the 'intensive use of intermediaries' (Hibou 1999: 13–14). More recent studies in domains as diverse as administration (Blundo 2006) and conflict transformation (Engel and Mehler 2005; Mehler 2009; Menkhaus 2008) show the empirical potential of exploring this multiplication or refraction, resulting in the creation of vast terrains of hybrid state-related activity. The mediation that takes place there falls within the formal/informal networks evoked in the introduction to this volume. The networks described in the preceding sections of this chapter consist of *gbôhi* and militia structures with shifting degrees of formality as well as the patron networks that surround them. Central nodes in these hybrid mediating structures are Big Men of different scales and weight who occupy equally ambivalent positions in transition zones between state and non-state activity.

In order to understand such zones of state mediation it is important not only to acknowledge the pull factors of state '*décharge*': formal (guided by, say, the World Bank or the Washington Consensus) as well as informal privatization. The obvious 'push factors' of state mediation are youth unemployment or, more generally, lack of opportunities. This situation has been rightly identified as 'social death' (Vigh 2006) or 'blockage' – as a lack of mobility and opportunities 'to keep the options open' (Simone 2008b). The (auto)biographies of Ato Belly and Marcus Garvey offer us a certain insight into the tactics of setting out on a voyage that could open the possibility of entering the composite state institution of the *corps habillés*. The tactical movements of the militant youngsters take place in the vague terrain situated between a state-in-crisis which is outsourcing its military force and a vast group of youngsters engaged in what Mitchell (2007) would perhaps call a 'counter-inscription of the state'. In sum, it seems proper to suggest that the main juvenile tactics, those of impersonation and dressing up, are above all an 'art of being in between' (De Certeau 1984: 30). Like '*la perruque*' – De Certeau's *locus classicus* of the subaltern tactics of the detour: the diversion of labour time in government and commercial administrations as much as in factories – the militia activity of so many militant Ivorian youngsters during the past decade can best be understood as a sustained 'act of camouflage, of counterfeit and make believe' (ibid.: 37) aimed at helping them insinuate themselves into the state and its institutions.

These provisional remarks on impersonation are meant to indicate that we are dealing with a particularly complex phenomenon which requires the kind of empirical and theoretical grounding which this chapter is merely able to begin to provide. After all, we need to account for the reflexive dialectics involved in dressing up (from below) and being dressed up (from above), or, more broadly, in the appropriation and registering of forms, types and postures which circulate within the urban, national and transnational Ivorian space – to the extent that, in themselves, these forms come to stand for circulation, (social) mobility and advancement in life. Any proper interpretation of impersonation as a subaltern tactic must avoid slipping into simplistic, supremacist, if not downright (neo)colonialist conceptions of subaltern mimicry (Apter 1999; and see Fabian 2002; Ferguson 2002).

The broader empirical grounding for juvenile impersonation in patriotic militantism and activism in Côte d'Ivoire must be sought within popular culture and popular politics (see also McGovern 2011), which in the preceding decades had been vested in new urban culture, sometimes labelled 'Nouchi'. To describe the success of Nouchi in Ivorian public life over the last two decades is beyond the scope of this chapter. It suffices to situate the expansion of Nouchi street culture in the period of fast urbanization of the 1980s, and, most importantly, its take-up by the student 'revolutionary' movements of the 1990s. This, in turn, led to the introduction of street culture and discourse into opposition politics, mainly in the hands of the leftist FPI party and its leader Laurent Gbagbo; and, when the latter came to power in 2000, to its sedimentation in mainstream politics (Arnaut 2005, 2008a). By and large, what many Ivorians seem to observe in politics is comparable to what Newell (2009b) describes as 'bluff' in economic and sexual exchange in Abidjanese urban street culture, and what before him Banégas and Warnier (2001: 8) identified as 'mischievousness, astuteness, [and] the right of the strongest ... in a moral economy of shrewdness and "débrouille"'. What makes the bluff particularly interesting is 'the incorporation of deceitful illusion and illocutionary performance into economic transactions, gender roles, and claims to modernity' (Newell 2009b: 384). Very important for our purposes is the fact that in typical bluff settings none of the participants is completely fooled: 'It was at once based on the idea of deception and prestige of illusion, yet at the same time no one was fooled, the audience was aware of the hoax before the show even began. And yet, everyone acted as though the bluff were real' (ibid.: 385). In conclusion, Newell (ibid.: 385) claims: 'the audience's awareness of fakery was irrelevant, it was the aptitude for artifice that earns respect and praise, and had transformative potential'.

The politician who embodied this 'aptitude for artifice' most cogently was President Gbagbo, the Biggest Man in the country at the time, in his capacity as 'the baker' (*le boulanger*), who, according to the French expression to which this epithet refers, 'rolls everyone in flour' (*il roule tout le monde dans la farine*) – that is, takes everyone (his colleagues, and his opponents as much as his electorate) for a ride. However, if streetwise bluffing is a youth competency, so are its political and activist variants. One of the most flagrant instances of juvenile political 'bluff' was the so-called 'Versailles Accord' signed in July 2006 by 'warring' youth leaders such as Charles Blé Goudé and Karamoko

Yayoro six months before the senior politicians signed a new peace agreement at Ouagadougou. Adding to the 'artifice' was the fact that 'Versailles' in the aforementioned accord did not refer to the French town where the post-First World War peace agreement was signed, but to Café de Versailles, a bar-restaurant in a posh part of Abidjan owned by Ivorian reggae superstar Alpha Blondy. The juvenile 'Versailles Accord' had all the makings of a successful 'fakery': a peace accord named after a world historical event, discussed in a trendy Abidjanese pub by youth leaders who not only impersonated senior national and international negotiators and simulated the drafting and signing of the peace agreement, but who also anticipated the latter and, thus, imposed themselves as political players to be reckoned with.

The well-frequented popular parliaments were another example of youthful political bluff involving more than a handful of junior political leaders. The flippant use of 'Versailles' resembled in this respect the use of 'La Sorbonne' as the name of Abidjan's most notorious people's parliament. 'La Sorbonne' was created in Abidjan's administrative centre (Le Plateau) in the 1980s and served as a model for hundreds of other popular parliaments set up since 2000 (Bahi 2003, 2004: 59; Yao Gnabeli 2005). Like the renowned Parisian university, to which they relate through the Abidjanese 'La Sorbonne', the many parliaments employed self-styled 'professors' who delivered 'scientific' analyses, thus claiming some sort of 'open university' status for their political propaganda (Atchoua 2008; Bahi 2001: 159). A final example of juvenile activist 'bluffing' is that which took place on a grand scale in the urban militias and the southern youth militant groups in general. As we have seen, the simulations of 'real' military life were manifold and pertained to matters of rank, outfit and attire, and, of course, activities. Among these the use of military titles by the GPP leadership was the most flagrant, since not only did GPP members recognize them but also civilians and the FDS acknowledged them publicly, whether in tongue-in-cheek fashion or more or less seriously – depending on the power balance at the moment of interaction (Arnaut 2006).

Lastly, in a recent paper Newell (2009a) invites us to situate impersonation and 'bluff' at the very heart of Nouchi culture. Bluffing, he argues, as the appropriation of alterity, is also central to the urban slang called Nouchi. Taking most of its lexical material from French, Nouchi also incorporates lexical material from English and a number of national languages such as Dyula, Baule and Bété. By dethroning 'metropolitan' French and venturing into trans-local and transnational linguistic terrains, Nouchi indexes urban cosmopolitism and modernity (ibid.). But there is more to it. Nouchi is in constant flux and its speakers take pride in using the latest new words or even try to introduce them themselves by transferring lexical material from other 'languages' within their repertoires. This is illustrated by Marcus Garvey's autobiography, in which he enriches 'standard' Nouchi with expressions which he himself identifies as 'military slang' or 'builder's idiom'. Taken together, his repertoires index his 'walks of life': the different sectors of society and of professional activities which he straddles. In other words, his linguistic agility is a function of his (professional) flexibility, and his potential social mobility. Taking our lead from Mbembe (1992; Mbembe and Roitman 1997), who saw the multiplication of identities as a performative tactic in what he calls the post-colony, the impersonating behaviour of Ivorian youngsters can be seen as an attempt to insinuate themselves into different spheres of activity in order 'to keep the options open' (Simone 2008a; Simone 2008b). The ultimate task, which this chapter can merely initiate, is to conceptualize this.

The theoretical frame of the topography and performativity of the kind of juvenile impersonation observed above consists of three related analytical concepts: articulation, navigation and fields.

Taking her lead from Gramsci and Hall, Tania Li (2007: 22) looks at identification as well as the social practice of 'political subjects' in terms of articulation – that is, 'the multiple positions that people occupy, and the diverse powers they encounter'. For research purposes, articulation 'points rather to the necessity of teasing out, historically and ethnographically, the various ways in which room for manoeuvre is present but never unconstrained' (Li 2000: 153). Navigation, as used by Vigh (2008) and Utas (2005; Utas and Jörgel 2008), partly based on Honwana (2000: 77–8) and De Certeau (De Certeau 1984), is precisely conceived in order to account for this 'room for manoeuvre'. Situations of crisis, according to Vigh (2008: 18), 'force agents to take into account not only how they are able to move within a social environment, but also how the social environment moves them, and other agents within it, as they seek to traverse envisioned trajectories'. Navigation implies a dialogical relationship between actors and their social environments; hence more attention needs to be given to the actual constitution of the terrain on which it takes place. Between overstressing stability and predictability and merely characterizing actors' mobility as 'motion within motion' (ibid.), an intermediate position seems possible, acknowledging that flow and fixity constitute each other as much as mobility rests upon structures of immobility (Hedetoft and Hjort 2002; Lien and Melhuus 2007: ix). In order to make this into more than a truism, we need some concept of 'field' without – and here I agree with Vigh – adopting the rather heavy and static concept Bourdieu made of it. Instead, our analyses of tactical agency may profit from a rather open, dynamic notion of field which helps to identify and map 'terrains' in terms of the stakes and opportunities they contain, the competencies they value and the expectation they nourish. Taken as such, a field largely corresponds with Turner's definition of it as 'an ensemble of relationships between actors antagonistically oriented toward the same prizes or values (in this case control over the state apparatus)' (Turner 1974: 135). The dynamic and open nature of such a field allows us, above all, to register how these fields alter through the incursions of 'navigating' actors – as well as other external interventions (Martin 2003). As far as the identification of fields is concerned, contemporary field theory allows us to define fields rather loosely and according to specific analytical needs, more or less as 'spheres of activity' or 'registers of social action' in the Weberian sense (Lahire 1999), even related to particular social networks (Breiger 2004). In this chapter I have focused mainly on the *corps habillés* as a field and ventured into interrelated fields such as popular culture, media and popular politics.

Afterthoughts in lieu of a conclusion

The first months of the new Ouattara administration have witnessed a series of far-going interventions into public space. Within days of taking power, Alassane Ouattara ordered the FRCI to clear out and destroy La Sorbonne, signalling the imminent demise of the dozens of popular parliaments in Abidjan and other urban centres in Côte d'Ivoire. More recently (August 2011), Yopougon saw the demolition of large sections of the Rue Princesse, Abidjan's archetypal nightlife hot spot and breeding ground of world-famous music genres such as Mapouka, Coupé-Décalé and Ivorian rap. The destruction of these sites of popular culture and popular politics makes us realize the extent to which over the last decade public life, at least the pro-Gbagbo part of it, had been flourishing in a novel and vigorous human infrastructure and built environment. Two items of this public culture – generally labelled 'Nouchi' – which rose to prominence and proliferated in many different guises in this milieu were *gbôhi* and 'bluff'.

In this chapter, 'bluff' was presented as a key performative tactic in a broader politics of impersonation of subaltern urbanites concerned with their ever-threatened social mobility. In the hands of the thousands of members of patriotic youth militias, 'bluffing' had the *corps habillés* as its target and took the form of a tenacious and sometimes fatal impersonation of military postures, discourse and practices. The cases of Ato Belly and Marcus Garvey demonstrate how unrewarding this politics of impersonation was and how it merely resulted in a state of enduring apprenticeship without full mastery, or ongoing 'companionship' without a proper 'joining in'. The latter observations bring us to the *gbôhi*, the second important item of urban public life which flourished during the Gbagbo era. *Gbôhi* thrived in Nouchi in the 2000s as a new term for 'gang' derived from the Dyula term for 'house', '*gbo*'. Simultaneously, it was adopted in militia circles as the key term for referring to the intricate process of networking: the fission and fusion of groups and 'groupuscules', the continuous fragmenting and merging of formal self-defence groups as well as the formation and disintegration of smaller fractions, of bands of friends and of ad hoc squads of youth militia members offering their 'violent labour' to state and non-state actors. The cases of Marcus Garvey and Ato Belly not only illustrated the vibrancy of networking but also revealed the double dynamics of bigmanity involved in this: the search of groups for leadership and patronage as well as the quest of Big Men to gather and coach 'elements', merge fractions and federate militia groups.

By choosing to approach the problematic of this volume on networks and Big Men in conflict situations within a perspective of impersonation and social mobility, I have tried to bring out both the geographical and the historical specificity of militia formation in the Ivorian conflict of the preceding decade *and* its universality in terms of juvenile subalternity and post-colonial urbanity.

Acknowledgements

I owe a large debt of gratitude to Marcus Garvey and the late Ato Belly for sharing their life histories, their dreams and disillusions. Many others assisted me in researching this chapter: Gadou Dakoury, Téhéna and Mariam Koné, Adjallou and the numerous 'patriotic' militia members and militants of which so many have since disappeared. The field research was funded by MICROCON. I thank Koen Vlassenroot, Anne Walraet and Timothy Raeymaekers for many years of collaboration.

Notes

1 It was the last telephone conversation because Ato Belly died soon after. It appears that Ato was severely wounded during that night's battle and spent a couple of days in hospital before being acquitted. Less than one week into his convalescence, Ato was shot dead in his house by people who have so far remained unidentified.

2 The history of IB and his Invisible Commando remains to be elucidated. His role in the battle against Gbagbo is as murky as his participation in the *coup d'état* of 2002. On 27 April IB was killed and his Invisible Commando dismantled.

3 CNLB = Comité National pour la Libération de Bouaké; FLP = Front pour la Libération du Peuple; GCLCI = Groupement des Combattants pour la Libération de la Côte d'Ivoire.

4 UMAS = L'Union des Mouvements d'Autodéfense du Sud.

5 The entire corpus of formal and informal interviews on which this chapter is based amounts to approximately 110 conducted with seventy-four interlocutors during four spells of fieldwork between March 2008 and March 2010. In order to document the post-electoral crisis of November 2010–May 2011, I kept in touch with about seventeen former interlocutors, mostly by telephone and sometimes by email.

6 The standard format for referring to formal field interviews is 'Name d/m/y'.

7 The full song is '*Donnez treillis oooh ça va finir* (2x)' (Give us uniforms oh it will finish), adding 'han got the natty dread'. The word 'dread' is an interesting contamination of dress (the expression 'natty dress') and dreadlock, which together with the rest of the English, 'got the', indexes the presence of Liberian fellow combatants (mercenaries as well as members of the LIMA militia) on the western front. Garvey could not explain the meaning of the word 'han'.

8 Having observed this confusion, Ato Belly proposed to the militia leadership that they create and supervise a GPP intelligence service.

References

Apter, A. (1999) 'Africa, empire, and anthropology: a philological exploration of anthropology's heart of darkness', *Annual Review of Anthropology*, 28: 577–98.

Aretxaga, B. (2003) 'Maddening states', *Annual Review of Anthropology*, 32(1): 393–410.

Arnaut, K. (2005) 'Re-generating the nation: youth, revolution and the politics of history in Ivory Coast', in J. Abbink and I. van Kessel (eds), *Vanguard or Vandals: Youth politics and conflict in Africa*, Leiden: Brill, pp. 110–42.

— (2006) 'Two meetings with Eugène Kouadio Djué, Marshall', Paper presented at the EASA 9 conference, Bristol, 21 September.

— (2008a) 'Les hommes de terrain: Georges Niangoran-Bouah et le monde universitaire de l'autochtonie en Côte d'Ivoire postcoloniale', *Politique africaine*, 112: 18–35.

— (2008b) 'Marching the nation: an essay on the mobility of belonging among militant youngsters in Côte d'Ivoire', *Afrika Focus*, 21(2): 89–105.

— (2008c) 'Mouvement patriotique et construction de "l'autochtone" en Côte d'Ivoire', *Afrique et Développement*, 33(3): 1–20.

Atchoua, N. J. (2008) 'Discours politique et dynamique de communication dans les espaces publics ivoiriens: l'exemple des "agoras et parlements" et des "grins" des quartiers populaires d'Abidjan', Université de Cocody.

Bahi, A. (2001) 'L'Effet "titrologue": étude exploratoire dans les espaces de discussion de rues d'Abidjan', *En Quête*, 8: 129–67.

— (2003) 'La "Sorbonne" d'Abidjan: rêve de démocratie ou naissance d'un espace public', *Revue Africaine de Sociologie*, 7(1):1–17.

— (2004) 'Approche sémio-contextuelle des communications dans les forums populaires d'Abidjan', *Revue Ivoirienne d'Anthropologie et de Sociologie*, 5: 52–72.

Banégas, R. (2008) '"La république oublie-t-elle ses enfants?" Milicianisation et démilicianisation du champ politique en Côte d'Ivoire', in *Regards croisés sur les milices d'Afrique et d'Amérique latine en situation de violence*, CERI.

— (2011) 'Post-election crisis in Côte d'Ivoire: the gbonhi war', *African Affairs*, 110: 457–68.

Banégas, R. and J.-P. Warnier (2001) 'Nouvelles figures de la réussite et du pouvoir', *Politique africaine*, 82: 5–21.

Bayart, J.-F., S. Ellis and B. Hibou (1999) *The Criminalization of the State in Africa*, Bloomington: Indiana University Press.

Blundo, G. (2006) 'Dealing with the local state: the informal privatization of street-level bureaucracies in Senegal', *Development and Change*, 37(4): 799–819.

Breiger, R. (2004) 'The analysis of social networks', in M. Hardy and A. Bryman (eds), *Handbook of Data Analysis*, London: Sage, pp. 505–26.

Chelpi-den Hamer, M. (2011) *Militarized Youths in Western Côte d'Ivoire: Local processes of mobilization, demobilization, and related humanitarian interventions (2002–2007)*, Leiden: African Studies Centre.

De Certeau, M. (1984) *The Practice of Everyday Life*, Berkeley: University of California Press.

De Latour, E. (2001) 'Métaphores sociales dans les ghettos de Côte d'Ivoire', *Autrepart*, 18: 151–67.

Engel, U. and A. Mehler (2005) '"Under construction": governance in Africa's new violent social spaces', in U. Engel and G. R. Olsen (eds), *The African Exception*, Aldershot: Ashgate, pp. 87–102.

Fabian, J. (2002) 'Comments on "Of mimicry and membership"', *Cultural Anthropology*, 17(4): 570–71.

Ferguson, J. (2002) 'Of mimicry and membership: Africans and the "New World Society"', *Cultural Anthropology*, 17(4): 551–69.

Garvey, M. (alias) (2011) *Le Compagnon: journal d'un noussi en guerre: 2002–2006*, Unpublished manuscript, Abidjan.

Hedetoft, U. and M. Hjort (2002) 'Introduction', in U. Hedetoft and M. Hjort (eds), *The Postnational Self: Belonging and identity*, Minneapolis: University of Minnesota Press.

Hibou, B. (1999) 'La "décharge", nouvel

interventionnisme', *Politique africaine*, 73: 6–15.

Hoffman, D. (2011) *The War Machines: Young men and violence in Sierra Leone and Liberia*, Durham, NC: Duke University Press.

Honwana, A. (2000) 'Innocents et coupables. Les enfants-soldats comme acteurs tactiques', *Politique africaine*, 80: 58–74.

Lahire, B. (1999) 'Champ, hors-champ, contrechamp', in B. Lahire (ed.), *Le Travail sociologique de Pierre Bourdieu: dettes et critiques*, Paris: La Découverte, pp. 23–56.

Li, T. M. (2000) 'Articulating indigenous identity in Indonesia: resource politics and the tribal slot', *Comparative Studies in Society and History*, 42(1): 149–79.

— (2007) *The Will to Improve: Governmentality, development, and the practice of politics*, Durham, NC: Duke University Press.

Lien, M. E. and M. Melhuus (2007) 'Introduction', in M. E. Lien and M. Melhuus (eds), *Holding Worlds Together: Ethnographies of knowing and belonging*, Oxford: Berghahn.

Martin, J. L. (2003) 'What is field theory?', *American Journal of Sociology*, 109(1): 1–49.

Mbembe, A. (1992) 'Provisional notes on the postcolony', *Africa*, 62(1): 3–37.

Mbembe, A. and J. Roitman (1997) 'Figures of the subject in times of crisis', *Public Culture*, 7: 323–52.

McGovern, M. (2011) *Making War in Côte d'Ivoire*, Chicago: University of Chicago Press.

Mehler, A. (2009) 'Hybrid regimes and oligopolies of violence in Africa: expectations on security provisions "from below"', in M. Fischer and B. Schmelzle (eds), *Building Peace in the Absence of States: Challenging the discourse on state failure*, Berghof Handbook Dialogue Series no. 8, www.berghof-handbook. net.

Menkhaus, K. (2008) 'The rise of a mediated state in northern Kenya: the Wajir story and its implications for state-building', *Afrika Focus*, 21(2): 23–38.

Mitchell, J. (2007) 'A fourth critic of the Enlightenment: Michel de Certeau and the ethnography of subjectivity', *Social Anthropology*, 15(1): 89–106.

Newell, S. (2009a) 'Enregistering modernity, bluffing criminality: how Nouchi speech reinvented (and fractured) the nation', *Journal of Linguistic Anthropology*, 19(2): 157–84.

— (2009b) 'Godrap girls, Draou boys, and the sexual economy of bluff in Abidjan, Côte d'Ivoire', *Ethnos*, 74(3): 379–402.

Reno, W. (1995) *Corruption and State Politics in Sierra Leone*, Cambridge: Cambridge University Press.

Simone, A. (2008a) 'Emergency democracy and the "governing composite"', *Social Text*, 26(2): 13–33.

— (2008b) 'Some reflections on making popular culture in urban Africa', *African Studies Review*, 51(3): 75–89.

Turner, V. (1974) *Dramas, Fields, and Metaphors: Symbolic action in human society*, Ithaca, NY, and London: Cornell University Press.

Utas, M. (2005) 'Victimcy, girlfriending, soldiering: tactic agency in a young woman's social navigation of the Liberian war zone', *Anthropological Quarterly*, 78(2): 403–30.

Utas, M. and M. Jörgel (2008) 'The West Side Boys: military navigation in the Sierra Leone Civil War', *Journal of Modern African Studies*, 46(3): 487–511.

Vigh, H. (2006) 'Social death and violent life chances', in C. Christiansen, M. Utas and H. Vigh (eds), *Navigating Youth, Generating Adulthood: Social becoming in an African context*, Uppsala: Nordiska Afrikainstitutet, pp. 31–60.

— (2008) 'Crisis and chronicity: anthropological perspectives on continuous conflict and decline', *Ethnos*, 73(1): 5–24.

Yao Gnabeli, R. (2005) 'Reconstruction identitaire chez les orateurs des sorbonnes, sénats et parlements des quartiers d'Abidjan', *Revue Ivoirienne d'Anthropologie et de Sociologie*, 7: 33–45.

4 | Demobilized or remobilized? Lingering rebel structures in post-war Liberia

Mariam Persson

Introduction[1]

Over the years there have been numerous examples of how formal security institutions in contemporary Africa have proved incapable of providing, or unwilling to provide, its citizens with basic security. Not surprisingly, mistrust of these formal institutions and authorities has made people turn to alternative solutions to cope with their everyday lives and safeguard their basic human security. What is surprising, however, is how little we still know about these informal security mechanisms in Africa. International donors and others who seek to contribute to the strengthening of the security context in African states have repeatedly failed to look beyond the official façade of the state and its formal security institutions in order to gain a deeper and more comprehensive understanding of security and insecurity in Africa. But without acknowledging the informal we will undoubtedly be unsuccessful in recognizing the very actors, mechanisms and networks ordinary African citizens often rely on for their basic security. Accordingly, we may fail to acknowledge and support security structures and initiatives that actually do work while providing assistance to inefficient or unavailable security mechanisms. By searching beyond and beneath the official state structures and formal institutions for security provision, we will be able to recognize the importance of informal security providers and come closer to an understanding of how informal security networks operate. While doing this we will also be able to identify influential, yet informal, actors of power that may not be visible from a formal state-centred perspective, and more importantly, perhaps this will enable us to identify hidden links between the formal and informal power structures shaping the security reality of many African countries.

In August 2003 the warring parties of Liberia signed the peace agreement that after two civil wars (1989–96 and 1999–2003) ended years of brutal fighting in the West African country. The war-torn republic now faced enormous challenges. Liberia was to be rebuilt, and security inaugurated. Since then Liberia, with major assistance and funding from the international community, has undergone a disarmament, demobilization, reintegration and rehabilitation (DDRR) process of ex-combatants to restore peace and stability, and security sector reform (SSR) in an attempt to reform the state security institutions, such as the Liberian National Police (LNP) and the Armed Forces of Liberia (AFL), as a means of improving overall security. President Ellen Johnson Sirleaf announced in July 2009, almost six years after the war ended, the formal closure of Liberia's DDRR programme, noting that the success of the programme was testimony to the return of peace and security (UNMIL Today 2009). However, insecurity has prevailed in Liberia and, as suggested in this chapter, so have the former chains of command and rebel structures, yet mobilized for new purposes and in new informal security settings. In order to understand how and why these former rebel structures linger on in Liberia it is herein suggested that the often neglected informal security context plays a key role.

This chapter aims to shed light on some of the informal structures that shape Liberia's contemporary security context by examining different networks of informal security providers, namely vigilante groups in Liberia and 'the monitors', a network of informal security providers at the Guthrie rubber plantation in Bomi and Grand Cape Mount counties. Guthrie is of significant strategic importance since rubber is one of Liberia's main exports. In addition to examining how and why these networks operate, this chapter more specifically seeks to explore how former chains of command and rebel structures are used in contemporary security settings in post-war Liberia and in these networks. It sets out to explain how these chains of command and rebel structures of war, which officially have been demobilized, at the same time, within the informal sphere, for different reasons, are maintained and mobilized. At times, this was made possible with the support of political 'Big Men'. Hence, this chapter aims to show that the informal and formal security structures of Liberia must not be understood as each other's antithesis, but rather as an intertwined, interacting web of official and unofficial links, shaping Liberia's contemporary security context.

Informal security networks

The Western notion of formal and accountable security systems as the sole providers of individuals' security often fails to correspond with the reality ordinary citizens face in many contemporary African states. In fact, security provision in many non-Western societies has never been a monopoly of the state and its formal institutions (see, for example, Baker 2008). As suggested by Migdal, social control is fragmented and heterogeneous. Still, when we look at states from a Western perspective we tend to be solely focused on the examination of politics in the capital city in order to identify those in power, without acknowledging that there might not be just one single manager involved (Migdal 1988: 180). Hence, the use of a mere state-centred approach when analysing security provision poses a great risk of misunderstanding complex power relations in non-Western states. As Ebo has pointed out, state security is only an element, albeit a crucial one, in the broader spectrum of security. In other words, the extent to which a state is secure is a function of the security of the entire society (Ebo 2005: 1–2).

Hill et al. argue that in most cases individuals and communities in fragile states, where formal and public security is often inefficient or scarce, create their own security mechanisms or accept compromised and unaccountable security provided by non-state actors. In addition, individuals and communities that are forced to take security into their own hands are often remarkably effective and creative in doing so (Hill et al. 2007: 38). Accordingly, when a state cannot offer a system that protects people from crime, and when it cannot guarantee to detect and punish occurring crimes, people are likely to resort to their own policing and courts (Baker 2008: 45). Yet few African citizens see formal and informal security provision as mutually exclusive categories. People constantly move from one sphere of security agency to another, formal or informal, in order to safeguard their protection at any particular moment (ibid.: 27). However, despite the importance they have for many African citizens, the dynamics of informal networks of security provision appear to be largely unknown to the outside world.

According to Jörgel and Utas, who have examined security providers in Guinea, Sierra Leone and Liberia, informal structures decide both the importance and the real use of the formal structure as actors within the informal structures use the formal system as vehicles to achieve their own goals. Thereby, in real political terms, the formal structures instead become the shadow image of the informal reality. Nevertheless, mapping informal security networks is a challenging undertaking, mainly because there are no simple structures to unravel. They are just a complex web of constantly changing links, which are difficult to understand and trace. Furthermore, actors operating in the formal system most often wish to keep their links to the informal sphere hidden, owing simply to the importance of presenting to the Western donor world an official picture free from such links (Jörgel and Utas 2007: 12). Yet in West Africa informal networks play such a crucial role in all activities that no formal process would function without the support of some form of informal network authorization (ibid.: 8). Accordingly, not only must the informal sphere be further examined in order to understand the complex security context in Liberia, so must the hidden links and interactions between the actors within the formal and informal structures which subsequently affect security and political development in the whole region.

Vigilantism – the antithesis of formal security provision?

Vigilantism can be understood as a form of informal security provision people choose or are forced to rely on for their basic human security. Yet in contemporary media and among the international donor community, vigilantism tends to be described as undisciplined mobs or crowds of young men without any clearly defined social or political identity, acting spontaneously on emotional impulses. Viewing vigilantism from such a narrow perspective is, however, not helpful when trying to understand this complex phenomenon. Vigilantism can arguably in many cases be seen as a form of local, everyday policing (Buur and Jensen 2004: 139–40).

Vigilantism can emerge and further be encouraged as a result of deep mistrust of the state and formal security providers. Daniel Nina, for example, has argued that vigilantism arises from the perception that the state is doing nothing to guarantee the safety of a community. The state in this light is thereby seen as a limited player with regard to crime prevention. Accordingly, the notion of the state as the sole guarantor of safety and security becomes little more than a myth (Nina 2000). However, this type of security provision should not be understood as something entirely separated from the formal security sphere. These organized attempts to defeat crime or enforce norms and law and order, sometimes with violent measures, are often claimed to be outside of, and in opposition to, an inefficient and even predatory state. Yet Buur and Jensen argue that the links between these informal groups and the state are often more complex than that. These groups operate at the frontier of the state, blurring the boundaries of what normally falls within and outside the formal sphere. For instance, formal security providers sometimes take part in informal security provision, such as police officers in vigilante groups, while state representatives, on the other hand, have used vigilante groups for legally sanctioned violence (Buur and Jensen 2004: 144–5). Pratten, in the case of Nigeria, gives further examples of the blurring boundaries between vigilantism and state activities. Here, the state itself and individual state governors have provided a significant impetus for vigilante practices. This can be illustrated by the actions of the state governors, who argued that the federal police were unable to deal with local conflicts and therefore sponsored vigilante groups as a substitute for autonomous state-level police forces (Pratten 2008: 5).

Nevertheless, the links between informal security providers and the formal sphere are for different reasons often kept hidden. As Lund points out in the case of Niger, vigilante groups, along with various informal actors, portrayed the state as their antithesis, as the state was considered distinctly removed from the local arena. These groups had an ambiguous position as they searched for credibility. On the one hand, they emphasized their non-state status and, on the other, they operated using the formal language of the state. Vigilantes could, for example, sometimes involve themselves in police matters. In this sense these groups, by vying to establish their own public authority, paradoxically become part of the very state they depict as distinct, distant and exterior (Lund 2006: 688).

State-sanctioned use of informal security networks and rebel groups

African governments have not only used vigilante groups to achieve political ends. In fact, other informal-security-providing networks and even rebel groups have unofficial links to formal states. An example of this is the Kamajors in Sierra Leone, which Hoffman describes as a web of social relations or patronage networks that became militarized during the war. This ethnically Mende-based network constituted the largest force of the country's 'Civil Defence Forces', which served as an umbrella term for Sierra Leonean disparate militias. When the Mende-dominated Sierra Leone People's Party (SLPP) won the election in 1996 the Kamajors gained greater influence. Sam Hinga Norman became a key figure in the Kamajor movement but was also appointed the SLPP's deputy minister of defence. The Kamajors thereby became widely perceived, particularly by the Sierra Leone Army, to be the SLPP government's de facto security force, Hoffman argues. Later on, in 1998, the Kamajors, together with other irregular forces under the banner of the CDF, helped to reinstate the SLPP during the war (Hoffman 2007: 642–3; for more on Norman, see Anders in this volume). Another example of the unofficially state-sanctioned use of informal networks in Sierra Leone can be illustrated by the role of the militia West Side Boys (WSB) towards the end of the civil war. Here the military commanders and politicians employed the WSB as a tactical instrument in a larger plot to safeguard their own military and political interests (Utas and Jörgel 2008: 488). The WSB was one of several military actors in the Sierra Leone civil war which became a useful tool for politicians and which was partly encouraged and managed in a way that benefited sections of the political elite (ibid.: 491). As, in 2000, President Kabbah and his government grew increasingly afraid of the rebel movement the Revolutionary United Front (RUF), the government of Sierra Leone made the WSB part of an 'ad-hoc security force' that was successfully used against the RUF, which was eventually forced to lay down its weapons (ibid.: 502–3). This gives further evidence of how informal security networks are strategically used and how formal and informal actors interact in order to gain mutual benefits and to reach strategic, political, military and economic goals, in times both of war and peace.

Liberia: from war to demobilization

The first Liberian civil war began on Christmas Eve in 1989 when Charles Taylor and his rebel group, known as the National Patriotic Front of Liberia (NPFL), entered the country from the Ivory Coast. It ended after seven years of war between the Armed Forces of Liberia and several rebel factions, when Taylor took power in the democratic elections of 1997. But peace did not last long with Taylor as president. The security situation remained uncertain, and parts of the country soon returned to war. In late 1999 the situation was further aggravated when Lofa County experienced the first series of renewed armed rebellions (Utas 2009: 269). The Liberians United for Reconciliation and Democracy (LURD) was the first of several new rebel movements that fought during the second civil war, which eventually came to an end in 2003 when Taylor was forced to leave the presidency and go into exile. In 2005 Ellen Johnson Sirleaf took power in democratic elections. International and national hopes and expectations were high that she would be able to break the war structures, consolidate peace and rebuild the state.

The Comprehensive Peace Agreement (CPA), signed on 18 August 2003, called for the United Nations to deploy an international stabilization force to Liberia to support the implementation of the CPA. This resulted in the establishment of the United Nations Mission in Liberia (UNMIL) in September 2003. The UNMIL was mandated to develop and implement the DDRR strategy in coordination with the National Commission for Disarmament, Demobilization, Rehabilitation and Reintegration (NCDDRR), and started the disarmament process in December 2003. At this point it was estimated that 48,000–58,000 ex-combatants were to be disarmed (International Crisis Group 2004: 1). However, by November 2004, when the disarmament and demobilization phase ended, 103,019 persons had been disarmed (NCDDRR 2005). When President Ellen Johnson Sirleaf announced the formal closure of the Liberian DDRR programme in July 2009, about 98,000 of the demobilized ex-combatants were said to have received reintegration assistance in the form of vocational training and formal education (UNMIL Today 2009). Nonetheless, as has been argued by Utas, among others, ex-combatants in Liberia faced remarginalization rather than reintegration after the war. Extreme poverty and lack of employment opportunities have maintained the continuum of war and peace in Liberia (Utas 2005).

Liberia's security reality

In June 2009, in the special report of the secretary-general on the United Nations Mission in Liberia, the situation was described as follows:

> The dysfunctional justice system perpetuates a culture of settling disputes through mob violence, and the thousands of unemployed youths, ex-combatants, deactivated former soldiers and other retrenched security personnel constitute an incendiary mix of disaffected people with a proclivity to violence that could easily be exploited by spoilers. The country is still plagued by a high incidence of violent crime, particularly armed robbery and rape, and many Liberians informed the mission that, six years after the end of the conflict, they still do not feel secure. (United Nations Security Council 2009: 3)

Insecurity has prevailed in Liberia and structurally deprived youth and ex-combatants still remain a threat to peace and stability. Bøås and Hatløy point out that groups of ex-combatants have been known to stage protests claiming that the DDRR programme has not improved their situation and that a large number of them remain unemployed, despite having received DDRR. In their opinion, this may indicate a disconnect between individuals' experiences in the DDRR programme and its relation or importance to daily life (Bøås and Hatløy 2008: 48). Furthermore, Liberia's formal security agencies, such as the army and the police, have mostly been a source of insecurity and troubles for Liberian citizens. The internationally driven attempts to reform the security sector in order to prevent destabilization, which have been ongoing since 2004, have had mixed results. The police are still widely regarded as ineffective and corrupt, and a recent spate of armed robberies has been blamed on their poor performance (International Crisis Group 2009: i–ii; see also Kantor and Persson 2011).

According to Bøås and Hatløy, interviewing nearly five hundred Liberian ex-combatants, what caused Liberian youth to fight in the civil wars and join armed factions were mainly security concerns – for themselves, their families and communities. Regardless of which armed group they belonged to, security was given as the most important reason for joining, based on various ideas regarding protection and opportunity (Bøås and Hatløy 2008: 45). Following this rationale, and given that insecurity still prevails in Liberia, joining informal security networks such as vigilante groups seems like a rational strategy for individual, family or community protection, despite the fact that the war is officially over. In other words, ex-combatants might have the same incentive to join new informal security networks as they did during the war. Furthermore, given that many ex-combatants in the aftermath of war have faced unemployment, joining an informal security network can be a way of fighting economic and societal insecurity.

Former rebel structures in post-war vigilantism

Whether in rural Voinjama or the urban neighbourhoods of Monrovia, security provisions occur beyond the formal security institutions as groups of citizens (usually young men) organize themselves into vigilante groups. In these groups ex-combatants often play a significant part, as well as former rebel structures and chains of command. While their modes of operation or organizational structure may differ, all individuals studied for this article agreed that the state-provided security was far from enough to protect them and their communities. They felt that the state had failed them; therefore, they had taken security into their own hands.[2]

Vigilante groups in Voinjama and Monrovia

Voinjama, the once prosperous capital city of Lofa County, bordering Guinea and Sierra Leone, was heavily affected by the civil wars. From here the LURD launched their rebellion against President Taylor in late 1999, and the city served as the rebel movement's headquarters during the second civil war. When the war finally ended in 2003, Voinjama lay in ruins, devastated by fierce battles. Today, burnt-out and bullet-scarred houses, painted with the names of the rebel groups, bear witness to the many years of war. This city now harbours the third-largest number of ex-combatants in Liberia. After the war, rebels aligned with LURD remained active in Lofa County as ex-combatants were increasingly frustrated with the slow pace and rewards of the DDRR programmes. LURD combatants continued to enjoy significant influence in the region when the villages started to be repopulated in 2004 and 2005, when former commanders, assisted by young combatants, assumed policing roles in Voinjama and several larger villages. Lacking supervision, these well-armed ex-rebels in many parts of the county remained a security risk, yet several communities accepted such security arrangements during this period, probably under the assumption that this would decrease the risk of renewed LURD attacks (Hill et al. 2007: 43–4). Furthermore, one could speculate whether President Ellen Johnson Sirleaf more or less silently accepted the active role and influence of the former LURD combatants in the region. In June 2009 the Liberian Truth and Reconciliation Commission (TRC) found Johnson Sirleaf to have sponsored NPFL and Charles Taylor in order to overthrow the government of Samuel Doe (Truth and Reconciliation Commission 2009). Moreover, Ellen Johnson Sirleaf is believed to have been supporting LURD openly in order later to oust Taylor from power.[3] Given this, President Johnson Sirleaf is likely to have given LURD's lingering influence in Voinjama silent approval.

As elsewhere in Liberia, insecurity has prevailed in Voinjama with an under-resourced police force with an apparent lack of capacity to respond to criminal activities. Economic and societal insecurity also remains as the city struggles with poverty and unemployment. In this post-war context, people have organized themselves in vigilante groups for their own and their communities' protection, and within these formations ex-combatants and former rebel structures are of clear significance.

In Voinjama a group of ethnic Mandingos had organized themselves into what they referred to as a community watch group. This was a highly organized group with clear hierarchical structures. The initiator of the group, a relative of the Mandingo chief in the area, coordinated approximately fifteen young men who met after dusk and patrolled the streets of their community until the early morning hours. Since each family and business in the community contributed with a small payment each week for the community's protection, the young men could earn a little money or food for their work. The vigilante leader, rather than being described as an elder, could be seen as a 'Big Man'.[4] He was characterized by his ability to create a network of dependants, both among the vigilantes and those they protected, by his strong ties to the chief, and by his high social status. The leader was married and could afford a house, something that was impossible for the social category of youth that took part in the vigilante activities. In this setting there were clearly mutual benefits for the vigilante leader and the participating youth in the formation of this informal security group. The leader explained that this was a way to keep the youth of his area occupied. Many of them were ex-combatants. Being a vigilante group member kept the youth out of crime and made them feel that they were contributing to their community, he argued. Nonetheless, the leader himself gained and maintained influence over his community by controlling the vigilantes. That Voinjama had been a former LURD stronghold with a large majority of its fighters being Mandingo was still evident in the vigilante group's lingering military organizational structure. Alongside the vigilante leader a former high-level LURD commander functioned as the vigilante group's security adviser. The former rebel general, who had begun the war as an officer in the Liberian army, was both well known and feared in Lofa County. Despite the fact that the war was over, his influence over security matters in Voinjama remained. Together with the vigilante leader, the security adviser was responsible for choosing, organizing and training the young vigilantes. When selecting the group he preferred former LURD combatants, since they already had training and were organized.[5] Some of the rebel structures were thereby maintained in Voinjama's post-war informal security setting.

Interviews with the vigilante groups in Monrovia revealed that the ex-combatants appeared to have a special position, even though their participation involved both perils and advantages. A former vigilante leader from Monrovia explained that he always made sure that he had ex-combatants among his vigilantes because of their fearless attitude and ability to use violence when necessary. The knowledge of him having ex-combatants in his group also made others less prone to commit crimes in his neighbourhood, fearing the retaliation they knew ex-combatants were capable of, he argued. The mere presence of ex-combatants had a deterrent effect.[6] Nevertheless, the Monrovian vigilantes saw not only benefits in having ex-combatants among their number. A young vigilante explained this by referring to a former NPFL combatant who took an active part in his group. 'He hasn't been rehabilitated so he is very unpredictable and aggressive. You can see it in the way he moves and talks. But he is also popular, but he is not respected, he is feared.'[7] The former NPFL fighter had a central role in the vigilante group, and the others said that they needed men like him because they feared nothing and had the ability to be violent when facing criminals. Yet as the young vigilante member explained, this man also often caused problems as he readily attacked people without making sure they were guilty of a crime, especially when he was under the influence of drugs.[8]

Former rebel structures in the post-war rubber industry

That neither the end of the war nor the subsequent DDRR process managed to destroy former rebel structures or chains of command became clearly evident as ex-combatants after the war took control of Liberia's rubber plantations and thereby one of the country's main exports. The government-owned Guthrie rubber plantation in Bomi and Grand Cape Mount counties had been operated by the Malaysian Guthrie Rubber Company since 1981, until Charles Taylor, as the new president of Liberia, in December 2000 installed an interim management to control Guthrie. The new management mainly comprised the same management team as before, but now Charles Taylor had direct control of the Guthrie plantation. When the second civil war started, LURD rebels carried out several attacks against Taylor's forces in and around the Guthrie plantation during 2002 and 2003, and in July 2003 they finally succeeded in establishing full control and management of the Guthrie plantation under the leadership of a former LURD general[9] (United Nations Mission in Liberia 2006: 78).

In June 2006, three years after the signing of the peace agreement and LURD's takeover of Guthrie, an estimated five thousand ex-combatants were still in full control of the rubber plantation area. The command structures were still intact as the ex-combatants maintained allegiance to their former commanders. Rank determined control over rubber tapping. No one could operate at Guthrie without the permission of General X, and taxes had to be paid to the self-established NGO, the National Veteran Rehabilitation Project (NVRP), which was run by a five-member committee of ex-combatants also controlled by General X, as well as another ex-LURD general. Control over Guthrie implied control over great economic interests. The NVRP was said to generate up to US$18,000 a month, in addition to significant sums made by individual ex-combatant tappers. The ex-combatants themselves claimed that the rubber tapping was their only means of survival while waiting for the RR component of the DDRR process to take effect (Global Witness 2006: 10). In February 2006 President Ellen Johnson Sirleaf and the Special Representative of the Secretary-General (SRSG) of UNMIL, Alan Doss, established the Rubber Plantation Task Force (RPTF) in order to assess the situation of Liberia's rubber plantations and to make recommendations for future action (Joint Government of Liberia/United Nations 2006: 1). The RPTF concluded that the illegal occupation of rubber plantations had to be stopped and the recommendations included that the government should evaluate options for implementing reintegration and rehabilitation packages for registered ex-combatants in Guthrie so that they would hand over the plantations in order for the government to be able to establish interim managements (ibid.: 9). President Johnson Sirleaf formally requested the RPTF to concentrate its efforts on re-establishing state authority and rule of law on the plantations occupied by ex-combatants or other illegal management. Negotiations between the RPTF and the ex-combatant leadership followed. After promises of reintegration benefits for the ex-combatants, the government, with UNMIL military and police support, claimed to have repossessed Guthrie, under an interim management team (IMT), on 15 August 2006. Following negotiations between the Liberian government and the Malaysian company Sime Darby, an agreement was finally signed in April 2009 (Tamagnini 2009). The takeover was delayed, but Sime Darby finally took over the Guthrie rubber plantation on 1 January 2010.

According to a UN report from October 2009, individual negotiations launched by the RPTF with ex-combatants helped to break down the ex-combatants' chains of command in order to repossess the Guthrie plantation in 2006 (ibid.: 18). However, as this chapter aims to show, the chains of command and the former rebel structures were far from broken at the Guthrie rubber plantation, even though control officially lay in the hands of the Liberian government and the current IMT.

Lingering chains of command at Guthrie

The role ex-LURD general X played at the Guthrie rubber plantation should not be underestimated. For three years, from 2003 until 2006, Guthrie and the nearby villages were completely under his command. Such influence, during this relatively long period, would have been impossible if General X did not have the ability to satisfy, or to a certain extent coerce, dependants below and the Big Men above. First, by relying on the former rebel structures and chains of command, General X could maintain control and loyalty by keeping lower-ranking former commanders in key positions under his direct control. Furthermore, General X's organization structure went beyond LURD's former chains of command. Within his ex-combatant network at Guthrie, former rebels, as well as followers from NPFL and MODEL (Movement for Democracy in Liberia), were organized and fully integrated into the command structures.[10] In this way, General X avoided internal divisions. Secondly, Guthrie generated significant amounts of money. As mentioned above, Global Witness estimated that General X's ex-combatants' organization made up to US$18,000 a month in addition to the money the individual ex-combatant tappers earned (Global Witness 2006: 10). A large number of authorities, including local and central top officials of the transitional government, were known to receive bribes from ex-combatants in order to ignore the situation at Guthrie (Tamagnini 2009: 17). Accordingly, since General X had the ability to keep the plantation running while at the same time generating a significant income, he had gained the crucial unofficial political support needed to remain in power. In the words of General X himself, 'I was the government, the management, everything. You see, I created a system that everybody was benefiting from. In that way I could keep the control and everybody was satisfied.'[11]

'The monitors' – the informal security providers at the Guthrie rubber plantation

When I conducted research at Guthrie in October 2009, men and women guarded the entrances to the plantation day and night and kept a record of all persons and vehicles entering. They were called 'monitors' because that was what they were supposed to do: monitor, observe and report suspected illegal tapping without taking any action themselves. Those who entered Guthrie unauthorized or who were caught stealing rubber or tapping illegally were to be immediately handed over to the police. As I was told by several UN officials, the IMT and the police during my stay at Guthrie, the monitors were not to be considered a security force. In reality the situation was much more complex than that.

During my stay at Guthrie, the workers and inhabitants at the plantation were once again under the management of a new IMT. The IMT was led by Boakai Sirleaf (deputy minister of agriculture and a relative of President Johnson Sirleaf) while awaiting the expected, but delayed, handover to Malaysian investors. Since the government's takeover from General X in 2006, new IMTs had come and gone. They were often characterized by mismanagement and regularly failed to pay the workers, causing tensions and occasional violent demonstrations. Yet when it came to informal security provision some structures appeared to have lingered. The current monitors had worked for the new IMT only for a couple of days in early October. Nevertheless, this was not a new constellation. The IMTs all needed to protect their interests at Guthrie, and apparently the small unarmed and under-resourced police force, the monitoring UN police force and the present UN peacekeepers were not considered capable of fulfilling this task satisfactorily. Already during Taylor's time in power he had brought in ex-combatants to attend to security at Guthrie, and the IMTs, following the government's takeover, had chosen to take the same action. A significant constituent of the monitors had always been ex-combatants, operating under former rebel structures.

The Guthrie rubber plantation is divided into three estates: Grand Cape Mount Estate, Lofa Estate and Bomi Estate, which is divided into two sections, Bomi 1 and Bomi 2. Each estate is then further divided into divisions and camps where the inhabitants live and work. The monitors numbered nearly 160, including three women. They live and work in all sections of the plantation and are organized somewhat like a military unit. Each estate has one commander (in total there are four commanders), who in turn has responsibility for the lower-ranking monitors. However, the estate commanders are all accountable to three main commanders, the first commander and his two deputies.[12] Yet another man also appeared to be influential; that is, ex-LURD general X.

The monitors were not all ex-combatants; indeed, many were not. Yet ex-combatants were present in every monitoring group at Guthrie. Many had been working as monitors for years, some since the government takeover in 2006, and for different IMTs. Others had been there since the war or even before it. The current IMT had simply kept most of the monitors. Yet following UNMIL's advice, the IMT was said to have excluded the most notorious ex-combatants. However, this was evidently not entirely the case since the presence and influence of two men in particular, Commander Y and General X, proved otherwise.

Commander Y

Commander Y first came to Guthrie in 1998. The civil war was over and Charles Taylor had taken office as the new Liberian president. In so doing President Taylor also assumed direct control over Guthrie and the interim management. To secure the area against illegal tappers and rubber thieves, then as now, a security force was installed. The security providers were called the Plantation Protection Department, or simply the PPD. Commander Y, a former NPFL general, was installed as head of the PPD with the title of Chief of Security. In this position Commander Y remained until the Taylor regime relinquished power in 2003.

At the age of twenty, in 1990, Commander Y joined Taylor and the NPFL rebels. After three years with Taylor's forces, Commander Y had advanced within the ranks of NPFL and become a general. However, despite his new status, Commander Y was still outranked by his twin brother, a well-known NPFL general (but who eventually was executed after orders by Taylor in 1994).[13] The twin brothers early gained a reputation. A former PPD member who worked at Guthrie under the command of Commander Y for a year described the twin brothers as

> really notorious and well known. Those who have lived beyond the NPFL
> lines during the war know them. Commander Y's twin brother was one of the
> NPFL generals and a close friend to Charles Taylor, and therefore Taylor chose
> Commander Y as head of the PPD. But I think it was mostly because he was so
> notorious. You know, that was needed to keep the security at Guthrie. When
> you saw him you wouldn't believe what he was capable of doing, Commander Y
> could be very violent.[14]

Commander Y is still well known at Guthrie. Some workers at the plantation told me that he was power-hungry and corrupt, others that they respected him as their leader. Nonetheless, Commander Y's influence and authority were never questioned. According to UNMIL officials, Commander Y was one ex-combatant they certainly did not want to see at Guthrie since they said he was known to cause trouble and harass workers and inhabitants at the plantation. Nevertheless, in October 2009 Commander Y was the deputy commander of the monitors. He claims that he had already returned to Guthrie in 2006, after having been called upon by the former interim management to provide security in the same way that he was now providing it.

General X

In early October 2009 I heard a rumour among the plantation workers; General X was back at Guthrie. He had been seen in several camps and the atmosphere became immediately tense when the matter of the former general was brought up. That General X once again was present at Guthrie was clear; however, not many knew why he was there and this caused worry and distress among the workers. Yet the monitors were better informed than the regular tappers. One of the young monitors told me that General X had come to their headquarters a few days earlier and said that he was now responsible for security at Guthrie and that the monitors were once again under his command. The monitor had not had this information confirmed by his monitor commanders. When I discussed the return of General X with one of the plantation workers' supervisors, he not only confirmed the rumour but also claimed that the very person who had brought General X back was in fact the head of the new IMT, Deputy Minister of Agriculture Boakai Sirleaf. The supervisor himself was not surprised at all by Sirleaf's actions. General X possessed the ability to make tappers and monitors obey, either out of fear or respect. With him on his side Sirleaf could control Guthrie. According to the supervisor, General X had already started to reassume his commanding position, as he supervised the plantation at night, driving around the camps in one of the estate manager's cars, and he knew of at least one recent incident when General X had threatened a plantation worker suspected of illegal tapping. Sirleaf's relationship with General X was, at least at Guthrie, not a well-kept secret since the monitors as well as the LNP commanders and the UNMIL soldiers stationed there confirmed seeing them together. According to one of the UNMIL soldiers at Guthrie, Sirleaf had said that General X had been brought back to offer him advice on which of the ex-combatants were trustworthy and therefore should be included in the new security structures for Guthrie. This, he said, had caused deep tensions among the workers at the plantation, who feared the return of the ex-combatant leadership. Sirleaf himself denied that General X had, or was to have, anything to do with security provision at Guthrie when I had the opportunity to ask him about this matter. He claimed that the only reason he had brought General X back to Guthrie was so that the workers could see a good example of an ex-combatant who was now a fully reintegrated man.

I met General X in mid-October 2009 in Monrovia. He came accompanied by those he called his 'boys', a couple of ex-combatants he always kept around him for his security. He had always organized his personal protection in the same way during the war and when he controlled Guthrie. The ex-combatants in his network were not all former LURD fighters. His ability to unite the ex-combatants irrespective of their previous allegiances during his years at Guthrie was still prevalent, as some of his closest 'boys' came from other warring factions. General X and his boys had once again been active at Guthrie for a couple of weeks. He had returned because he was requested to do so, he said. In September, when the new IMT took over responsibility for Guthrie, Boakai Sirleaf had called General X, telling him that the Liberian government needed him to secure peace at the plantation. Otherwise they risked new demonstrations among the plantation workers. Since then General X had travelled back and forth to Guthrie, showing his support for the new IMT by 'encouraging' tappers and monitors to remain loyal to the new management. According to General X himself, his new position in no way implied that he was now inferior to the monitor commanders; instead he claimed that they once again were under his command. General X reported directly to Boakai Sirleaf. However, he was not the only person General X reported to. As we talked, General X's phone rang, and according to General X, it was Fombah Sirleaf (the stepson of President Ellen Johnson Sirleaf and the director of the government's National Security Agency) who had called and requested a meeting, wanting the latest report on the situation at Guthrie.

Concluding remarks – political Big Men as mobilizers of informal security networks

This chapter has aimed to show that the informal and formal security structures of Liberia must not be understood as each other's antithesis, but rather as an intertwined, interacting web of official and unofficial links, shaping Liberia's contemporary security context. Even though the official links to the informal security structures are seldom publicly expressed, they are clearly present. As Utas argues in the introduction to this book, it is the informality and inaccessibility of these networks which on the one hand make them difficult to discover and address, but on the other hand render them so effective (Jörgel and Utas 2007: 8). The dismantling of former war structures is often considered crucial for post-war reconstruction and the establishment of security. DDR processes in war-torn countries are seen as important steps to achieving such development. Accordingly, President Johnson Sirleaf, during the official closing of the DDRR programme in Liberia, noted that the success of the programme was testimony to the return of peace and security (UNMIL Today 2009). However, rebel structures have remained active in Liberia, yet in new informal security settings. It is herein argued that one reason for this is the fact that formal security structures provide insufficient protection for ordinary citizens. Therefore informal security-providing networks, to which ex-combatants often affiliate themselves, become important. The other explanation for the lingering rebel structures in Liberia, as illustrated by the case of the Guthrie rubber plantation, is that the Liberian political elite has intentionally kept parts of these networks mobilized in order to attain control and make economic and political gains.

First, if we accept that security concerns (for themselves, their families and communities) caused Liberian youth to fight in the civil wars and to join an armed faction, as argued by Bøås and Hatløy (2008), it is not surprising that parts of these networks are still active. As insecurity still prevails in Liberia, joining security networks such as vigilante groups seems like a rational strategy for individual, family or community protection, despite the fact that the war is over. In other words, ex-combatants might have the same incentive to join new informal security networks as they did during the war. Furthermore, with inefficient formal security structures ordinary citizens have to rely instead on informal security providers for their everyday protection. There are also compelling incentives for vigilante groups and other informal security-providing networks to involve ex-combatants as active members. Even though employing ex-combatants involves risks owing to their past war experiences, they are for the very same reasons considered valuable assets.

Secondly, as shown by the case of Guthrie, it appears that it was never the true intention to completely demobilize all of the former rebel structures. In the words of Jörgel and Utas, politicians are Big Men with powers only as great as their networks. Party politics can therefore be seen as a form of patronage, whereby politicians obtain 'wealth in people' in exchange for assuming responsibility for their followers (Utas in the introduction to this volume). This could be further illustrated by the findings of Christensen and Utas, who claim that politicians in Sierra Leone strategically remobilized the ex-combatants before and during the general elections in order to protect themselves and to mobilize votes. At the same time, it is argued, politicians feared the consequences of *not* mobilizing the ex-combatants since they knew the extent of the destabilization they were capable of causing (Christensen and Utas 2008: 521). Thus, the Liberian government, rather than demobilizing all of the ex-combatants, appears to have remobilized influential ex-combatants such as General X and Commander Y as informal security providers at the Guthrie rubber plantation. Considering Liberia's violent past and history of power being obtained through war or coups, this strategy should not be underestimated. Ex-combatants are by definition potential destabilizers; given that they were once able to cause war, they could just as easily cause a war again. Therefore, by unofficially using the violent potential of the ex-combatants, President Johnson Sirleaf and the ruling political elite can secure their political and economic interests in order to remain in power. The Guthrie rubber plantation has the potential of generating a significant income for the Liberian state, yet the government is unable to provide employment and basic social services for the workers. Therefore demonstrations and strikes are a constant threat to the government's authority. In such a context the influence of notorious ex-combatants can be used in order to make people work. Paradoxically, the very networks of former rebel structures that President Ellen Johnson Sirleaf has officially set out to dismantle are the same ones she and the Liberian government unofficially appear to be using in order to maintain control and stay in power.

Notes

1 This chapter draws heavily on the author's fieldwork in Liberia during March and October of 2009. Interviews were mainly carried out with members of vigilante groups in various neighbourhoods in Monrovia, Montserrado County, and the city of Voinjama in Lofa County, and with several members and leaders of an informally organized security network at the Guthrie rubber plantation in Bomi and Grand Cape Mount Counties.

2 The findings here are based on interviews with members of six different vigilante groups (three in Monrovia and three in Voinjama), conducted in March 2009.

3 Personal communication with Mats Utas, who was given this information by Sierra Leonean combatants fighting in Liberia during the second civil war. Assistant Professor Chris Blattman also supports the notion of Johnson Sirleaf's support for LURD; chrisblattman. com/2009/07/03/news-flash-there-are-no-angels-and-demons-in-politics/.

4 In line with what Utas proposes in the introduction of this book.

5 Interviews with members and leaders of vigilante groups in Voinjama, March 2009.

6 Interview with a former vigilante leader in Monrovia, March 2009.

7 Interview with a vigilante group member in Monrovia, March 2009.

8 Ibid.

9 I have chosen to refer to the former LURD general as General X in this chapter.

10 Interview with ex-LURD general X, Monrovia, October 2009, and Global Witness (2006).

11 Interview with ex-LURD general X, Monrovia, October 2009.

12 I have chosen not to refer to the three main commanders of 'the monitors' by name in this chapter. However, one of the two main deputies will hereafter be referred to as Commander Y.

13 The twin brother of Commander Y had been one among the top commanders of the NPFL, who included Taylor's Gbaranga 'Executive Mansion Commander' Cassius Jacobs, whom Taylor ordered to be executed in 1994.

14 Interview with a former PPD member, Monrovia, October 2009.

References

Baker, B. (2008) 'Multi-choice policing in Africa', Nordic Africa Institute.

Bøås, M. and A. Hatløy (2008) 'Getting in, getting out: militia membership and prospects for re-integration in post-war Liberia', *Modern African Studies*, 46(1): 35–55.

Buur, L. and S. Jensen (2004) 'Vigilantism and the policing of everyday life in South Africa', *Africa*, 78(1).

Christensen, M. M. and M. Utas (2008) 'Mercenaries of democracy: the "politricks" of remobilized combatants in the 2007 general elections, Sierra Leone', *African Affairs*, 107: 515–39.

Ebo, A. (2005) 'The challenges and opportunities of security sector reform in post-conflict Liberia', Occasional Paper no. 9, Geneva Centre for the Democratic Control of Armed Forces (DCAF).

Global Witness (2006) 'Cautiously optimistic: the case for maintaining sanctions in Liberia', Global Witness Briefing Document, June.

Hill, R., J. Temin and L. Pacholek (2007) 'Building security where there is no security', *Journal of Peacebuilding and Development*, 3(2).

Hoffman, D. (2007) 'The meaning of militia: understanding the civil defence forces of Sierra Leone', *African Affairs*, 106(425): 639–62.

International Crisis Group (2004)

'Rebuilding Liberia: prospects and perils', *ICG Africa Report*, 75, 30 January.

— (2009) 'Liberia: uneven progress in security sector reform', *ICG Africa Report*, 148, 13 January.

Joint Government of Liberia/United Nations (2006) 'Rubber Plantations Task Force', May, www.laborrights.org/files/Rubber_TF_Report.pdf.

Jörgel, M. and M. Utas (2007) *The Mano River Basin Area: Formal and Informal Security Providers in Liberia, Guinea and Sierra Leone*, FOI, Swedish Defence Research Agency.

Kantor, A. and M. Persson (2011) 'Liberian vigilantes: informal security provision on the margins of security sector reform', in M. Ekengren and G. Simons (eds), *The Politics of Security Sector Reform: Challenges and opportunities for the European Union's global role*, Ashgate.

Lund, C. (2006) 'Twilight institutions: public authority and local politics in Africa', *Development and Change*, 37(4): 685–705.

Migdal, J. S. (1988) *Strong Societies and Weak States – State–Society Relations and State Capabilities in the Third World*, Princeton, NJ: Princeton University Press.

NCDDRR (National Commission on Disarmament, Demobilization, Rehabilitation and Reintegration) (2005) *DDDRR Consolidated Report Phase 1, 2 & 3*.

Nina, D. (2000) 'Dirty Harry is back: vigilantism in South Africa – the (re) emergence of "good" and "bad" community', *African Security Review*, 9(1).

Pratten, D. (2008) 'The politics of protection: perspectives on vigilantism in Nigeria', *Africa*, 78(1).

Tamagnini, A. (2009) 'End-of-assignment report', from the director of the Reintegration, Rehabilitation and Recovery (RRR) Section, United Nations Mission in Liberia, 1 October.

Truth and Reconciliation Commission (2009) *Consolidated Final Report*, 30 June, www.trcofliberia.org/reports/final/volume-two_layout-1.pdf.

United Nations Mission in Liberia (2006) 'Human rights in Liberia's rubber plantations: tapping into the future', May.

United Nations Security Council (2009) *Special Report of the Secretary-General on the United Nations Mission in Liberia*, 10 June.

UNMIL Today (2009) 'DDR wraps up', *UNMIL Today*, 6(2), July.

Utas, M. (2005) 'Building a future? The reintegration and remarginalisation of youth in Liberia', in P. Richards (ed.), *No Peace, No War: An anthropology of contemporary armed conflicts*, Athens/Oxford: Ohio University Press/James Currey.

— (2009) 'Malignant organisms: continuities of state-run violence in rural Liberia', in B. Kapferer and B. E. Bertelsen (eds), *Crisis of the State: War and social upheaval*, Oxford: Berghahn Books.

Utas, M. and M. Jörgel (2008) 'The West Side Boys: military navigation in the Sierra Leone civil war', *Journal of Modern African Studies*, 46: 487–511.

5 | Castles in the sand: informal networks and power brokers in the northern Mali periphery

Morten Bøås

Northern Mali – the home of the country's Tuareg minority – comprises the broad part of the Sahara that borders Algeria, Burkina Faso, Mauritania and Niger.[1] Resisting external intervention in their way of organizing their livelihoods, the Tuareg have fought several wars of autonomy – during colonialism as well as after it ended. With the arrival of the French, whom their religious leaders declared infidels, the Tuareg spearheaded resistance to colonial rule. However, by the early twentieth century the French had managed to establish some nominal control over northern Mali and the Tuareg lost several of their privileges, including their right to tariff collection and protection services for trans-Saharan caravans. Today, northern Mali may seem like an isolated and forlorn place 'at the end of the universe', but it used to be an important frontier region, well integrated into the global economy, and a similar process is taking place today: this time through the economic power of the illegal world of trafficking of contraband, migrants and drugs.[2] Thus, to a certain extent, the current increase in informal and/or illicit trade also represents a revitalization of the ancient routes of trade, commerce and pilgrimage connecting West Africa to the Mediterranean, and to the Middle East and the Persian Gulf, that used to pass through this area.

Taking the National Pact of 1992 as its point of departure, this chapter analyses how what at face value seemed to be a relatively well-planned decentralization arrangement aiming at co-opting Tuareg rebel leaders in fact just cemented the beginning of a new conflict into the solution of the previous one. Big Men in the form of senior Tuareg commanders, almost exclusively originating from noble and royal families, were given access to power and economic resources on the local level as well as in the national government and administration. Both formally and informally, these Big Men therefore benefited from the peace agreement. This strategy of co-option worked remarkably well for several years, but as more widespread peace dividends failed to materialize a new undercurrent of discontent started to emerge, first and foremost among former junior rebel commanders from non-ruling lineages in Kidal, the most isolated of the three Tuareg regions (see Map 5.1). Formally speaking, Kidal is a marginalized area, completely off the beaten track, but informally and illicitly it is well connected

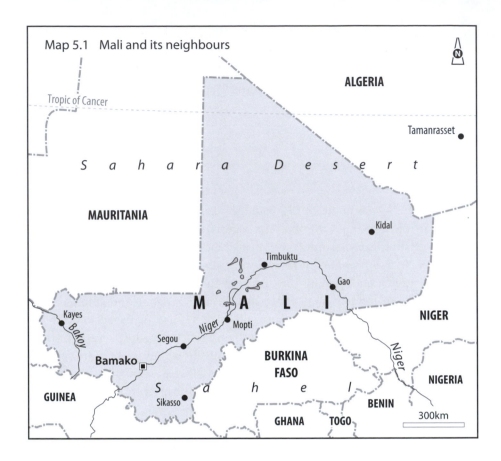

Map 5.1   Mali and its neighbours

to the world of globalization through the new economic opportunities of the trans-Saharan trade. The violent discontent that has emerged is clearly related to the fact that ancient trade routes through the Sahara have regained some of their old importance. The sudden influx of cash – one successful smuggling trip can earn the driver as much as 3,000 euros – is altering the traditional power configurations of Tuareg society, leading to competing informal regimes of power, locally and regionally (Bøås and Hatløy 2008).

The Tuareg rebellion and the National Pact

June 27 1990 is a significant date in the contemporary history of Mali, as it marks the beginning of what is known as the Second Tuareg Rebellion. The first had taken place only two years after Mali became independent in 1960, and lasted from 1962 to 1964. This rebellion was harshly suppressed by the Malian army, but the Tuareg continued to nurture grievances. The Second Tuareg Rebellion was much better planned, organized and equipped, but also took place during a turbulent period in Malian politics (Keita 1998). In March 1991 General Amadou Toumani Touré overthrew the president, Moussa Traoré, in a coup, and started a process of democratization. This made it all the more important for the new policy-makers in Bamako to end the Tuareg insurgency in a peaceful and cost-efficient manner. By the mid-1990s Mali had apparently found that solution, and the 'flames of peace' ignited in Timbuktu on 27 March 1996 – the symbolic setting on fire of some three thousand guns – were heralded as a model for conflict resolution in Africa. However, as part of northern Mali, and particularly the isolated Kidal region, remained as politically marginalized and economically unattached to the Malian state as ever, a new revolt started in 2006. Some of the underlying causes were the same as in previous times. However, the current conflict is also being played out within a different context: it is framed not only by the Tuareg rebellion in neighbouring Niger, but also by the 'war on terror' logic and the fact that this part of the Sahel has become a new hot spot for drug trafficking through Africa to Europe – thus setting in motion a complex competitive struggle among current and aspiring Big Men to become the very nodal points in emerging shadow-like semi-hidden informal networks of governance and control (social, economic and political).

The rebellions The first post-colonial conflict lasted from 1962 to 1964. It began, much like the present one, with small 'hit and run' raids against government targets in the Kidal area. It escalated throughout 1963, resulting in extremely volatile conditions in northern Mali. In this regard the rebellion was successful, but it did not reflect a unified leadership, a well-coordinated strategy or a coherent political programme. It even failed to mobilize the majority of the Tuareg. It was also insufficiently stocked with arms, ammunition and means of transportation. The insurgency depended upon camels for transportation, and its fighters – numbering no more than about 1,500 – relied on unsophisticated and old small arms (see Keita 1998). In the end the Malian army harshly crushed it, and the Tuareg provinces were placed under military administration.

The Second Tuareg Rebellion took place between 1990 and 1996, and aspired to achieve autonomy for Azawad, the northern part of the country.[3] However, even if the leaders of the insurgency appealed to the Tuareg to unite under the identity of a common language as much as an ethnic banner, the rebellion must be understood as diverse in social origins as well as economic interests. This is vividly illustrated by the very fact that the Tuareg rebels were split among four factions: the Popular Movement of Azawad (MPA); the Popular Front for the Liberation of Azawad (FPLA); the Revolutionary Army for the Liberation of Azawad (ARLA); and the Islamic Arab Front of Azawad (FIAA).[4] These movements represented different well-established and aspiring Big Men networks based on kin and geography as well as different political alignments and economic interests, and whereas they all fought against the Malian army they also fought each other at times. References to the Tuareg as *Kel Tamacheq* (the people who speak Tamacheq) apart, the Tuareg have never constituted one entity. They have instead historically been divided among a number of sultanates, ruled by various royal families, sometimes in cooperation and at other times in conflict with each other.

The war officially ended on 26 March 1996, and the peace agreement allowed for approximately seven thousand Tuareg rebels to be incorporated into the national army and other government bodies (see also Seely 2001). The 120,000 Tuareg refugees living in camps in neighbouring Mauritania, Algeria, Burkina Faso and Niger were also repatriated. Based on these agreements the four rebel factions mentioned above, which by now jointly constituted the United Movements and Fronts of Azawad (MFUA), agreed to disarm and demobilize, and again permit free movement across Mali's northern region (Humphreys and Ag Mohamed 2003; Berge 2002; Maïga 1997; Lode 1997). For a long time, Mali was seen as a successful post-conflict country that had effectively solved the underlying causes of conflict (ICG 2005a, 2005b).

However, as the benefits of the 1996 peace agreement failed to materialize as widely as envisioned by most Tuaregs, tensions in northern Mali increased, particularly among the young rank and file and junior commanders from the civil war, and ten years later, in 2006, some Tuareg groups took up arms once more. Thus, in a situation of increased discontent, the Democratic Alliance for Change (ADC) of 23 May was organized around former MPA fighters in Kidal. Initially the three main leaders were Ibrahim Ag Bahanga, Hassan Ag Fagaga and Iyad Ag Ghali. This movement was, however, short-lived, as a peace agreement was signed in Algeria on 4 July 2006. The so-called Algiers Agreement called for the restoration of peace, security and development in the region of Kidal.

This was, however, not the end of the conflict. The agreement was not implemented properly as the development plan for the Kidal area failed to materialize within the time frame leaders such as Ibrahim Ag Bahanga believed had been agreed to. Tensions also increased within Tuareg society in Kidal. Particularly, the junior commanders who had constituted the rank-and-file vanguard in the struggle became increasingly embittered as the well-established Big Men monopolized the formal as well as the informal economic relationships with the Malian state. Thus, one year later in July 2007, the situation escalated once more. Ibrahim Ag Bahanga and some other former members of the ADC started a new violent insurgency against the Malian state. This rebellion was much smaller in scale than the previous ones; however, this time they were not alone on the battlefield. The al-Qaeda in the Land of Maghreb (AQIM) is trying to establish itself in northern Mali (see also ICG 2004, 2005b), and a new Tuareg rebellion is also taking place in neighbouring Niger under the flag of the Niger Justice Movement (MNJ).[5] These rebellions are taking place in a region of informal trade and smuggling, with little government control over borders and the hinterlands (ICG 2005b; Keenan 2007). The external environment of the latest Tuareg rebellion is therefore not only more violent and dangerous, but also includes the possibility of the forging of new regional networks between aspiring Big Men across the desert. The rebellion is political, but is also fuelled by economic self-interest of current and aspiring Big Men and the desperate social navigation of youth seeking to escape poverty and social death by 'being for somebody' through the use of force (see Bledsoe 1990; Vigh 2006).

The National Pact In reviews of previous Tuareg rebellions (e.g. 1962–63 and 1990–96), as well as the current one, it is striking how they all relate, albeit in different ways, to the issue of control of local administration – should it be under the auspices of the central state or should this control be in accordance with a more decentralized formula?

The National Pact of 1992, signed by the MFUA group and the transitional Malian government of President Touré on 11 April 1992, was an attempt to deal with this issue. The Pact laid out new administrative boundaries and established local assemblies to permit a degree of self-governance of the northern regions (Seely 2001; Ministère de l'Economie de l'Industrie et du Commerce 2008a, 2008b). When President Alpha Oumar Konaré was inaugurated in June 1992, he immediately followed up on the decentralization processes laid out in the National Pact. In fact, Konaré had no other choice but to decentralize. His predecessors, Moussa Traoré and General Touré, had made various concessions to the Tuareg insurgents that were deeply resented in the southern parts of the country. In order to fulfil these concessions – to keep the north within the state of Mali – and to contain the simmering unrest in the south, the only possible policy option was to embark on a process of administrative decentralization in the whole of the country (Seely 2001; Bratton et al. 2002; Hesseling and van Dijk 2005). In order to achieve this, the Decentralization Commission (DC) was established. The DC created new administrative boundaries, not only by renaming existing ones but also by giving villages the opportunity to group themselves into desired communes.[6] This may be read as an attempt to empower local populations, but it also became a tool for local aspiring Big Men to organize their own communes as they saw fit.

Controlling a commune not only gave aspiring Big Men a political constituency, but also represented a possibility for the extraction of resources: spoils from the state and locally generated ones through various designs of patrimonial politics. In short, it constituted the possibility of building political castles – 'castles in the sand'. One example is the aforementioned Ibrahim Ag Bahanga, who after the end of the Second Tuareg Rebellion managed to acquire his own commune, in the border area between Gao and Kidal. This was achieved through a combination of popular support and his ability to use force. Ag Bahanga and some other younger Tuareg commanders were not satisfied with their reintegration package and had therefore kept their guns.

After a month of raiding and creating instability, Ag Bahanga was given his commune.[7]

Apart from Ag Bahanga and a few other younger commanders who used force to fight their way into the decentralization process, what happened in the Tuareg regions (i.e. Gao, Kidal and Timbuktu) was a relatively carefully designed process of co-option. Tuareg senior commanders and other leaders, almost exclusively originating from noble and royal families, were given access to power and economic resources on the local level as well as in the national government and administration. This strategy of co-option worked remarkably well for several years, but as other peace dividends failed to materialize a new undercurrent of discontent started to emerge among those who saw no real improvements in their living conditions. This happened first and foremost in Kidal, the most isolated of the three Tuareg regions. The main reason for this is that control over civil service and local administration has remained unchanged. The quality of administrative supervision is inadequate. Moreover, with few exceptions, those guilty of corruption and abuse of power have been neither punished nor transferred. Rather, rent-seeking and corruption within the civil service and local administration were on the increase, but not everyone was prepared to accept the prevailing social order any more. Emerging leaders from non-ruling lineages wanted access to state power, for the purpose of reform but also in order to take advantage of this for their own personal benefit. The events in Kidal from May 2006 onwards are therefore a combination of increasing local discontent with this development and the emergence of new aspiring Big Men. This is evident in all three Tuareg regions – Timbuktu, Gao and Kidal – but is most explicitly felt in Kidal owing to its isolation. In many ways, it is correct to say that the state of Mali ends where the road stops in Gao. Kidal is somewhere else, not Mali but not another country either; it is something in between, a hinterland lost in limbo between Algeria and Mali (Bøås and Hatløy 2008).

Northern Mali – networks of patronage as elusive front lines in the sand?

The borderlands of the countries in the Sahel region have all come under accusations of harbouring the AQIM or groups allied with this organization. It is therefore clearly a danger that what is essentially a local conflict in Kidal and northern Mali may be locked in a 'war on terror' framework, in which the accusation of al-Qaeda connections becomes a self-fulfilling prophecy as local insurgencies have nowhere else to turn (see also Bøås and Jennings 2005; Bøås 2007a). This is particularly dangerous as connections already exist on a pragmatic, business level, but thus far there is no firm or widespread ideological attachment. The simple point is that these people know each other; they pass each other in the desert and sometimes also trade with each other. However, this does not necessarily suggest that they constitute nodes and hubs in a new emerging illicit regime of terrorism and trafficking based on an ideological framework. Rather, on the contrary, this part of the violent life-world of northern Mali is ad hoc in nature, much more like 'ships that pass in the night' than regularized interactions based on a well-established network of patronage (see also Bøås and Dunn 2007; Bøås 2007a).

Nonetheless, the current Tuareg rebellion is taking place under different external circumstances to those of its predecessors. In addition, the internal environment is also changing. Contemporary Tuareg society is in flux, and the outcome of this process of social transformation cannot be taken for granted. The traditional system of power and property has been breaking down for some time. Nobles from royal families continue to own most of the camels, but the rapid increase in ownership of four-wheel-drive cars makes the camels less important for economic purposes.

Herding is still an economic occupation of high prestige, but has become difficult as a full subsistence-base activity owing to erratic rains and diminishing pastures. The nobles from royal families (particularly those in Kidal) deploy close in-marriage, devotion to Islam and ritual purity to preserve their position, but the youth and others of less prestige, such as clients and people from so-called slave lineages, are less likely to obey them fully. Their traditional subordinates are seeking alternative modes of accumulation and thus, as the traditional rulers' ability to control people decreases, they also possess less 'wealth in people' (see Miers and Kopytoff 1977; Bledsoe 1990), enabling others like Ag Bahanga to become Big Men who those searching for alternatives can 'be for'. This is related to the new economic opportunities of the trans-Saharan trade – opportunities that increase at least the potential for violent upward mobility for those willing and able to use force, and thereby also for changes in the power relations of Tuareg society (see Bøås 2007b; Utas and Jörgel 2008).

The Third Tuareg Rebellion and illicit activities in a borderless region Drugs and the trafficking of people are becoming increasingly important in terms of cross-border smuggling, and offer new economic opportunities as well as the establishment of new networks and nodal points in such networks of governance and control. However, cigarettes are the oldest contraband and also remain the most important one in northern Mali (see also UNODC 2008). The trafficking of drugs and people only became significant at the time that the new rebellion started in 2006. The increasing popularity of these old routes of trade and commerce is also related to recent technological advances that have made desert travel much easier. GPS, satellite phones, cell phones and four-wheel-drive cars are currently the standard equipment of desert travellers. The number of routes and means of communication also means that it is possible to drive from Kidal in northern Mali to Tamanrasset in Algeria in about a day without ever travelling on a marked road. Some of these routes run up and down dry river beds, whereas others are little more than camel paths. In the river beds, good drivers can reach speeds as high as 100 kilometres per hour, while on more difficult camel paths they may have to slow down to about 15 kilometres per hour. However, on average, an experienced driver can drive about forty kilometres per hour in an unmodified diesel four-by-four.

The cigarettes, almost exclusively Marlboro (locals do not talk about cigarettes, only 'Marlboros'), mainly come from Zerouate in Mauritania in big trucks, sometimes in pre-sealed containers, to Kidal. There, the shipment is split into smaller lots and taken across the border to Algeria (mainly Tamanrasset) in Toyota Land Cruiser four-by-four pick-ups. Some of these cigarettes are sold locally in Algeria, whereas others make their way across the Mediterranean to the European market – here, they are still cheaper than those produced locally, even when a considerable number of middlemen have taken their cut since the cigarettes left North Carolina in the United States.[8]

The trafficking of people across the Sahara is also increasing, and Gao is in the process of becoming an important informal hub along this route for Congolese, Cameroonians, Liberians, Nigerians and others who seek to leave the African continent.[9] At Gao they are picked up for a Sahara crossing into Algeria. It has not been possible for the author of this chapter to make any concrete or reliable estimates concerning the number of people trafficked along the Gao-to-Algeria route, but given the demand from desperate migrants it is most likely quite a profitable illicit business.[10]

Drugs, particularly cocaine, are smuggled through northern Mali and Kidal in particular.[11] Successfully making a trip across the border with this kind of drug may earn the driver as much as 3,000 euros. Latin American drug cartels are increasingly using West Africa as an important transit point in their smuggling of cocaine to the European market. Mali is still not a prime target in this business. The three most important transit countries are Senegal, Mauritania and Guinea-Bissau – an estimate published in *Jeune Afrique* in September 2008 shows Mali at the bottom of a list of West African transit countries.[12] However, the cocaine trade is also making its presence felt in Kidal. According to local sources, this started in 2006 – at the same time as the new Tuareg rebellion began. Even if the amount of cocaine and other types of hard drugs smuggled through Mali and Kidal is still quite small compared to the activity along other West African transit routes, there is every reason to be concerned about this development. Mali is still a relatively weak state, and once the forces of international drug cartels embed themselves in such a society it can be immensely difficult to uproot them. The recent history of Guinea-Bissau gives evidence of this, as this country is now infamously known as a *'paradis des narcotrafiquants'* (Diouf with Meunier 2008: 22) or simply a narco-state (Einarsdottir 2007; see also Vigh in this volume). In this regard, Kidal would be the weakest link in a fragile state.

The trans-Saharan smuggling of cigarettes and other contraband, including drugs, people, vehicles and arms, is valuable and for some Tuaregs is an integral part of their livelihood. The majority, however, are not directly involved. According to information obtained from sources in Kidal, the smugglers (i.e. those doing this on a regular basis) are organized in gangs numbering ten to fifteen people, and the total number of people involved is claimed to be less than a hundred. However, even if the majority do not participate, they know about it. They do not necessarily support it, but see it as just another type of the trade that has gone on across the Sahara ever since the first traders crossed this border area and, as such, most are also part of extended networks that benefit economically from eventual profits (see also Keenan 2007).

Kidal – marginal, but still integrated into the illicit global political economy

Kidal is formally a part of Mali, but in reality it is something else. As many Kidal citizens argue, the state of Mali ends where the road stops at Gao. The 350-kilometre track through the sand from Gao therefore cuts across an area caught in a borderless limbo between the Algerian and Malian states. It is a place lost in time and space, where ATT is not an affectionate nickname for the Malian president Amadou Toumani Touré (aka ATT) but rather the local abbreviation for 'arms, Thuraya, Toyota' – the three things a Kidal household cannot do without.[13]

In the context of the Malian state, Kidal is marginal. However, if we consider its place in previous rebellions, it is also a centre – a centre at the very margins of the state. It stood at the forefront of both previous Tuareg rebellions, each led by people either from or close to the royal family of the area. It can still partly be characterized as a traditional society, ruled by the nobles from the royal families. Their position, however, is increasingly questioned – peacefully as well as through the use of force.

The current rebellion is related to the internal policies of Kidal and, as mentioned, started in 2006 when former MPA fighters led by Ibrahim Ag Bahanga, Hassan Ag Fagaga and Iyad Ag Ghali took up arms and established the Democratic Alliance for Change (ADC) on 23 May. Its official aim was to defend the interests of the Tuareg of northern Mali, but it was just as much a reaction to a perception of this group of rebels as being permanently excluded from the spoils of the state, as the previous rebel leadership had come to monopolize key positions locally as well as nationally. Most of the ADC fighters were therefore former MPA combatants who felt marginalized both politically and economically. The original ADC revolt lasted only a couple of months, until a deal was reached in Algiers the same year. This time peace prevailed until May 2007, when Ag Bahanga and some other former ADC members restarted the rebellion from his base around Tinzaoutin, close to the Algerian border.

As mentioned, Ag Bahanga was among the rank and file in the rebellion of the 1990s. He is currently believed to be somewhere in his late forties – thus, too young to have played a decisive role in the 1990s. When that revolt was over, he was offered reintegration into the army at the rank of corporal. He refused this offer and instead, as mentioned, fought his way into local government. Thus, what we need to come to terms with is how his current rebellion is best understood as a combination of political issues and personal ambitions, and how these have been fused into criminal activity as well. Some see Ag Bahanga mainly as a bandit in disguise – someone using the rebellion as a cover to run a profit-making trans-Saharan smuggling racket – but our view is that he is best seen as occupying both roles (see also BBC 2008). He controls part of the smuggling, but also embodies a social and political agenda – thus personifying the Big Man as a social actor, living in a social setting and not only taking but contributing as well. He embodies the authority to command, to instigate action (war), to take, but also to argue a political case and to give (to redistribute).

Ag Bahanga has repeatedly argued for increased equality in Kidal, and his entry by force into the local administration after the end of the previous rebellion was clearly unwanted by the traditional elite in Kidal. He was a young man with no particular background or family, who used force and his ability to attract others to use force for him to upset the natural order of things. Currently, Ag Bahanga is combining various smuggling operations with low-level insurgency, articulating Tuareg demands for autonomy and development.[14] In a recent interview with *El Khabar*, Ag Bahanga argued for the creation of a special status for Kidal that could also be extended to other Tuareg regions in the north and for a reduction in the number of Malian troops in the area. He restated his commitment to finding a peaceful solution to the conflict, and expressed his willingness to release his prisoners as soon as the talks showed progress. In the same interview, Ag Bahanga also denied any links to terrorist organizations and claimed that his men had fought AQIM and chased them out of Kidal towards Timbuktu. It is almost impossible to verify these claims, but it is interesting to note that the release of prisoners did take place on 10 September 2008, when Ag Bahanga set free the forty-four Malian soldiers he had been holding captive. As part of the same deal, the government promised to provide $2 million of development aid to the north.

This may lend some credibility to Ag Bahanga's claim that he is fighting for the development of the north's Tuareg regions. However, it is also clear that Ag Bahanga, if not directly involved in smuggling operations himself, at least provides security for one of the routes from Kidal to Algeria's Tamanrasset. Whereas three of the five main drug routes from Kidal to Tamanrasset are controlled by people belonging to the traditional elite of Kidal, the other two are controlled by people with a similar background to Ag Bahanga's, suggesting that part of what characterizes Kidal is a combination of politics and trafficking. Thus, as in many other places, in this part of the world we cannot draw a firm line between politics and crime. Rather, these activities are integrated in close and complicated ways, and the political struggle involving Big Men and their clients and henchmen is also influencing the battle to control smuggling routes and vice versa. Thus, to a certain degree it is possible that it is the very ability to combine politics and crime, the legal and the illicit and the formal and the informal, which characterizes a successful Big Man in this area. It is the elusiveness of the margin which creates the castles in the sand that promote and maintain the Big Man.

Big Men across borders: the Tamanrasset connection Tamanrasset is a world apart from Algiers and the northern Mediterranean parts of Algeria. It is geared towards the south, and its identity is Saharan and Tuareg. The town of Tamanrasset is situated in the desert, but it is not a historical desert city like Kidal or Timbuktu. Its history is much more closely connected to the birth of the Algerian state than, for instance, its Malian counterpart Kidal.

As a city, it emerged in the nineteenth century as a small but important military garrison in the French attempt to pacify the Algerian desert. It was only after the French managed to establish some sort of nominal control in the 1920s that Tamanrasset became an important transit point for the trans-Saharan trade. Even then, it was more a village than a town of any size – it still had only about four to five thousand inhabitants in the 1960s. Currently, the town is home to more than 100,000 people and has become one of the most important commercial hubs in the Sahara region: an entrepôt for people and goods transiting from sub-Saharan Africa to the Mediterranean and from the coast to south of the Sahara.

For many people from Mali, Niger and even farther south, it has also become a destination in its own right – people come to work and stay for as long as six or seven months before returning home. Both local government representatives and Algerian state security officials are aware of these informal migrants, but they are also greatly valued as Tamanrasset's state-fuelled construction boom far outpaces the availability of local labour (Porter 2008).[15]

Even if the various Islamist insurgency groups have exploited southern Algeria's vast desert to establish bases for the purposes of training and raising money, it has not been a major battle front. This may change, however, with the coming of AQIM's new emir in Algeria's southern provinces. Yahia Djouadi is a former member of the al-Takfir wa'l-Hijra and the Armed Islamic Group (GIA) and clearly a different breed to the previous leader, Mokhtar Belmokthar. Whereas the latter began as a local smuggler and thereafter formed a marriage of convenience with the Salafist Group for Preaching and Combat (GSPC) in southern Algeria, before reportedly redeploying to Mali to take up his former trade as a cross-border trader and smuggler, Djouadi's career path suggests a more ideologically motivated use of force and violence. This change in leadership took place after the GSPC leader, Abdekmalek Droukdel, changed the group's name to AQIM (see ibid. 2008).[16] Exactly how this will be played out on the ground remains to be seen, but the very fact than Djouadi is not from the region may in fact suggest a weakening of AQIM's network and functionality in the Tamanrasset region as well as in northern Mali and Niger.

However, apart from an increase in opportunistic kidnappings as well as profit-related murders, this part of Algeria has seen little of the violent insurgency that continues to create havoc in the north. There is, however, a great deal of illicit activity going on. Some of these activities, such as arms and human trafficking and drug smuggling, circumvent the state because they are illegal, whereas others, such as the contraband trade (e.g. cigarettes, etc.), seek to sidestep the state because taxes, tariffs, bribes and kickbacks erode profit. Ordinary traders are involved in this illicit business, as are rebel groups from Mali (e.g. Ibrahim Ag Bahanga) and Niger (e.g. the Niger Justice Movement, NJM), and the Algerian GSPC and AQIM.

The extent to which the Algerian state and its local representatives actively try to stop these activities, or are involved in them themselves, is difficult to evaluate. Some seasoned observers, such as Keenan (2004), argue that behind the rhetoric of developmental state-building and fighting terrorist activity there is a complex network of family relationships linking senior levels of Tamanrasset's regional administration with smuggling networks in both Mali and Niger. This suggests that the most strategic regional administration in the Sahara-Sahel zone is at the very heart of the illicit trans-border operations and therefore has little if any interest in taking the steps necessary to increase state control of the border and the border areas. Alternatively, Porter (2008) suggests that the inability to effectively police the border and the lack of state presence outside Tamanrasset town are mainly questions of military capacity.

The 6th Algerian Army Division in charge of Tamanrasset province is staffed with only about seven thousand men. Most of the military personnel assigned to the 6th Division are from the north, and are thus unfamiliar with the area. They are generally rotated out of the area after only a short period of service, and do not speak Tamacheq (the local language), suggesting that their knowledge of what is going on is relatively low.

The Algerian state is present in Tamanrasset town and its immediate surroundings, but is absent in the desert. The recently repaved highway connecting Tamanrasset with Mali and Niger is relatively free of military roadblocks, and alternative routes through the desert are numerous. In the hinterland the soil is carved with tracks, some well used and others only barely visible. It is along these latter routes that the Toyotas, well stocked with arms and Thurayas, come and go from the Kidal area.

Some tentative conclusions

As regards the situation in northern Mali and its relationships with both other rebellions and criminal activities, the best approach is to see this particular rebellion as a separate insurgency with quite different, if also somewhat unclear, objectives. The Tuareg rebellion in Mali concerns local grievances over inadequate state response to drought and the loss of pastoral land. They complain of poor representation in their government, and that the national army is dominated by southerners. The linkages that do exist between the conflict in northern Mali and elsewhere in the Sahel region are largely built on cross-border trade, and little else yet (see also ICG 2005b; Keenan 2007). The GSPC and similar groups operating under the banner of 'al-Qaeda in the Land of Maghreb', on the other hand, are groups that, having lost the conflict in Algeria, are attempting to regionalize their struggle. However, there may also be more to this than just international terrorism. The GSPC have undoubtedly pledged their allegiance to al-Qaeda, but some of their activities seem to be more oriented to profit than to the politics of international jihad. They may be committed to a Qutbist form of Salafism that justifies violence, while still influenced by centuries-old Sahelian trade pragmatism (see also ICG 2005b).

There is no doubt that AQIM fighters roam across the border between northern Mali and Algeria, and the local Tuareg population is aware of this. It is also obvious that the coming and going of this group is, if not welcome, at least tolerated. However, this should not lead us to suggest that there are any firm alignments of a political and religious nature between Tuareg rebels and the AQIM. They are known to have fought together as well as against each other in the past, depending on the circumstances.[17] The AQIM units spend money in Kidal and elsewhere in the Tuareg communities in northern Mali, and on the basis of ancient Sahelian trade pragmatism, the local communities trade with whoever passes by. Some sources (see ICG 2005b) have made a huge point of both current and former GSPC leaders marrying Tuareg women. This has indeed taken place; one example is the previous GSPC leader Mokhtar Belmokthar. However, as far as we are aware these marriages have not been with Tuareg women from noble or royal lineages, suggesting that whereas the marriages may serve a practical purpose they do not indicate that GSPC or AQIM leaders have made important strategic alliances through marriage.

The conflict in northern Mali is first and foremost an internal Kidal affair. It is a conflict between old and new powers, between tradition and those who feel that they fought the war in the 1990s but never saw any benefits from their sacrifice. This is further fuelled by the immense isolation of Kidal. It is not Mali, it is an isolated border region left to fend for itself, and as it occupies a strategic position on one of the old trans-Sahara routes, the population have redirected their livelihoods towards the comparative advantage Kidal can offer – a centre of illicit trade in a vast space of little (if any) government control.

This 'ungoverned space' and the new economic opportunities it creates open up new pathways for the illicit and violent manoeuvring of people seeking to escape poverty and marginalization through capturing whatever niche in the global economy is possible. The result is not necessarily a network of patrons as fixed nodal points in alternative systems of governance, but rather ad hoc fluid interactions between a variety of Big Men on the basis of centuries-old Sahelian pragmatism. However, what set current events in the Kidal area of northern Mali in motion was first and foremost the monopolization of position that the National Pact of 1992 constituted and not the illicit trade as such, suggesting that more attention needs to be paid to how processes of decentralization affect local power configurations. If this is not done, current and new generations of aspiring Big Men will see few other options than to continue taking advantage of Kidal's centrality at the very margin of the state, to continue carving out ever-changing castles in the sand.

Notes

1 There are currently about 530,000 Tuaregs living in Mali.

2 See also Vigh in this volume.

3 Azawad, the ancient homeland of the Tuareg, also extends into Algeria and Niger. According to some Tuareg sources, President Charles de Gaulle promised an Azawad homeland in the 1960s. This researcher has not been able to find any credible source that verifies this claim.

4 The FIAA drew its members mainly from north-west Mali's Hassani Arab minority, a group that is closely related by ethnic ties, dialect and culture to the Moorish population of Mauritania and the Sahrawis of Western Sahara, Algeria and Morocco. The Tuareg dominated the other three rebel groups. For example, the MPA was initially formed among Tuareg refugees and exiles in Algeria and Libya. These four militias established the United Movements and Fronts of Azawad (MFUA) in December 1991 and signed the National Pact peace treaty in 1992.

5 On the MNJ, see Guichaoua (2009).

6 The three northern regions – i.e. Gao, Kidal and Timbuktu – are currently made up of thirteen *cercles* (districts), and within these are eighty-seven communes (of which five are urban and eighty-two rural).

7 We will return to Ibrahim Ag Ba-

hanga and his different agendas later in the chapter. Here it should suffice to mention that he was given the opportunity to reintegrate into the army at the rank of corporal. His current rebellion is thus best seen as a combination of political issues and personal ambitions, and how these have been infused into criminal activity.

8 Some of the cigarettes also come from Europe; that is, they are imported tax-free from Europe and smuggled back again.

9 See also *L'Independant*, 14(2034), 2008, p. 1, and Bøås (2009).

10 Other main avenues for human smuggling through the Sahara include a route through Mauritania, Western Sahara and Morocco to Spain, and a route through Tunisia to Italy and Malta. See also ICG (2005b). It is quite remarkable, however, how little is actually known about the number of people using these routes to try to get to Europe. This is particularly the case for the 'Kidal connection'.

11 Cannabis is also smuggled through the Kidal area. In January 2008, Malian law enforcement officers discovered a total of 750 kilograms, the wholesale value of which would have been about US$1.9 million in Egypt. The cannabis trail fol-

lows the Sahel from the west (Morocco) through Mauritania, northern Mali, northern Niger, Chad and Sudan towards Egypt. From there, the drug is trafficked through the Middle East to Europe. This route offers a way of avoiding the increased border control between Morocco and Spain.

12 See Diouf with Meunier (2008).

13 Thuraya is one of the most common brands of satellite phones and, in Mali as in many other places in West Africa, has become the common name for these kinds of phones, with Toyota referring to all four-wheel-drive cars. This should not be read as suggesting that all Kidal households are involved in trafficking – they are not. However, you still need the ATTs to live there.

14 It is difficult to be exact concerning the question of sympathy and support for Ag Bahanga. The views are quite mixed. Some see him as a bandit and opportunist; others believe he also has a political agenda. With regard to the manpower he commands, size estimations differ from a couple of hundred to 3,000. The latter is most likely an inflated figure, but credible sources claim he controls about four hundred cars.

15 With record hard currency reserves – estimated at around US$150 billion, by far the largest in Africa, surpassing those of Egypt and South Africa combined – there is no shortage of money to build new infrastructure and expand public institutions. This has also been confirmed in interviews with Tuareg youth from the Kidal region.

16 Since this change, the AQIM has initiated a new wave of attacks against both the state and foreign interests in Algeria, thus far mainly in the area between Algiers, Boumerdès, Bouira and Tizi Ouzo (see, for example, Erik Selmer in *Dagsavisen*, 25 August 2008), and has also expanded its range of activities in Mauritania. On 15 September 2008, twelve Mauritanian soldiers were ambushed and killed north of the town of Tourine, close to the border with Western Sahara (see BBC 2008). The extent to which the situation in Mauritania after the last coup will affect the rebellion in northern Mali is still unclear, but political instability in yet another neighbouring country may have an impact on trafficking as well as the politics in northern Mali.

17 For example, Tuareg groups and GSPC units have reportedly fought small battles over smuggling routes, whereas at other times they have joined forces against elements of the Malian army that have disrupted their routes. It is difficult to see any fixed pattern in this, most likely because none exists. It is all ad hoc and pragmatic.

References

BBC (2008) 'Troops die in Mauritania ambush', London: BBC.

Berge, G. (2002) *In Defence of Pastoralism: Form and Flux among the Tuaregs in Northern Mali*, PhD thesis, University of Oslo.

Bledsoe, C. (1990) '"No success without struggle": social mobility and hardship for foster children in Sierra Leone', *Man*, 25: 70–88.

Bratton, M., M. Coulibaly and F. Machado (2002) 'Popular views of the legitimacy of the state in Mali', *Canadian Journal of African Studies*, 36(2): 197–238.

Bøås, M. (2007a) 'Vest-Afrika – politisk utstabilitet og ressursrikdom', *Internasjonal Politikk*, 65(3): 107–26.

— (2007b) 'Marginalized youth', in M. Bøås and K. C. Dunn (eds), *African Guerrillas: Raging against the machine*, Boulder, CO: Lynne Rienner, pp. 39–53.

— (2009) 'Leaving West Africa is never easy: the trans-Saharan escape', Paper presented to the 108th Annual Convention of the American Anthropological Association, Philadelphia.

Bøås, M. and K. C. Dunn (2007) 'African guerrilla politics: raging against the machine?', in M. Bøås and K. C. Dunn (eds), *African Guerrillas: Raging against the machine*, Boulder, CO: Lynne Rienner, pp. 9–37.

Bøås, M. and A. Hatløy (2008) *Peace and Security in Northern Mali – Elusive*

Frontlines in the Sand? Report to the Norwegian Ministry of Foreign Affairs, Oslo: Fafo.

Bøås, M. and K. M. Jennings (2005) 'Insecurity and development: the rhetoric of the failed state', *European Journal of Development Research*, 17(3): 385–95.

Diouf, A. with M. Meunier (2008) 'Drogue – le nouveau triangle d'or', *Jeune Afrique*, 2486: 22–7.

Einarsdottir, J. (2007) 'Partnership and post-war Guinea-Bissau', *African Journal of International Affairs*, 10(1/2): 93–112.

Guichaoua, Y. (2009) 'Categories of rebellions in practice: the Mouvement des Nigériens pour la justice in northern Niger'. Paper presented to the Workshop on Understanding Order, Cooperation and Variance among Non-State Armed Groups, Queens University, 4/5 September.

Hesseling, G. and H. van Dijk (2005) 'Administrative decentralisation and political conflict in Mali', in P. Chabal, U. Engel and A.-M. Gentili (eds), *Is Violence Inevitable in Africa? Theories of Conflict and Approaches to Conflict Prevention*, Leiden: Brill, pp. 171–92.

Humphreys, M. and H. Ag Mohamed (2003) *Senegal and Mali*, New Haven, CT: Yale University Press.

ICG (2004) *Islamism, Violence and Reform in Algeria: Turning the Page*, Brussels: International Crisis Group.

— (2005a) *Understanding Islamism*, Brussels: ICG.

— (2005b)) *Islamist Terrorism in the Sahel: Fact or Fiction*, Brussels: ICG.

Keenan, J. (2004) 'Americans and bad people in the Sahara-Sahel', *Review of African Political Economy*, 31(99): 130–39.

— (2007) 'The banana theory of terrorism: alternative truths and the collapse of the second (Saharan) front in the war on terror', *Journal of Contemporary African Studies*, 25(1): 32–58.

Keita, K. (1998) *Conflict and Conflict Resolution in the Sahel: The Tuareg Insurgency in Mali*, Carlisle, PA: US Army War College.

Lode, K. (1997) *Civil Society Takes Responsibility – Popular Involvement in the Peace Process in Mali*, PRIO report 5/97, Oslo: PRIO.

Maïga, M. T.-F. (1997) *Le Mali, de la sécheresse à la rébellion nomade: chronique et analyse d'un phénomène du contre-développement en Afrique Sahélienne*, Paris: Harmattan.

Miers, S. and I. Kopytoff (1977) *Slavery in Africa: Historical and Anthropological Perspectives*, Madison: University of Wisconsin Press.

Ministère de l'Economie de l'Industrie et du Commerce (2008a) *Programme Décennal de Développement des Regions Nord du Mali*, Meguetan Trage: Bamako.

— (2008b) *Conclusions et Recommandations du Forum de Kidal pour le Développment des Regions Nord du Mali*, Meguetan Trage: Bamako.

Porter, G. D. (2008) 'Curtailing illicit and terrorist activity in Algeria's Tamanrasset', *CTC Sentinel*, 1(9): 14–16.

Seely, J. C. (2001) 'A political analysis of decentralisation: co-opting the Tuareg threat in Mali', *Journal of Modern African Studies*, 39(3): 499–524.

Selmer, E. (2008) 'Terror ryster Algerie', *Dagsavisen*, 25 August, p. 14.

UNODC (2008) *Organized Crime and Illicit Trafficking in Mali: Evaluation of Crimes and Priority Problems – Assessment of National Institutions*, Dakar: UNODC.

Vigh, H. E. (2006) 'Social death and violent life chances', in C. Christiansen, M. Utas and H. E. Vigh (eds), *Navigating Youth, Generating Adulthood: Social becoming in an African context*, Uppsala: Nordiska Afrikainstitutet, pp. 31–60.

Utas, M. and M. Jörgel (2008) 'The West Side Boys: military navigation in the Sierra Leone civil war', *Journal of Modern African Studies*, 46: 487–511.

PART TWO

Thematic case studies

6 | Critical states and cocaine connections

Henrik Vigh

'The threat posed by *drug traffickers* is so great that the state is on the verge of collapse ... Guinea-Bissau has lost control of its territory and cannot administer justice,' a UN official said at a meeting of the UN Security Council on 12 December 2007.[1] With a fourth of the cocaine consumed in Europe passing through the region every year,[2] and a large part of the political and military elite being involved in the illegal dealings, it seems understandable that the UN worries about the negative effects the drug cartels have on the already fragile and brittle façade of state in Guinea-Bissau. The statement echoes a general concern with regard to the Upper Guinea coast in general, yet in Bissau the increase has been so dramatic that the UN has designated the small country 'Africa's first narco state'.[3] It is feared that the Guinea-Bissauian state will be corrupted and ruined by the cocaine connection, bringing Bissau closer to an anarchic lack of formal governance. That cocaine connections induce failed states seems, as such, to be the common argument among the international agencies working on the issue. However, if we look at the picture in historical terms, the UN official seems to have misinterpreted the logic of the phenomenon and inversed its causality. The Guinea-Bissauian state is not on the verge of collapse because of the influx of cocaine and the presence of the drug cartels. Rather than inducing a crisis within the state, the cartels have targeted Bissau exactly because of the critical state of affairs. The attractiveness of Bissau as a drug hub is directly related to the consequences and dynamics of factional politics to start with. Instead of destroying the state, the cartels target Bissau precisely because of its merely *nominal* existence (Vigh 2006a [2003]).

Shipwrecked proof

In December 2005 a boat was wrecked near the small city of Ondame on the coast of Guinea-Bissau, West Africa. With one of the world's most drastic tidal extremes, the coastline of the country is no stranger to the occasional vessel running aground on its many underlying reefs and sand dunes. Yet this particular shipwreck was different. As the ship struck the reef, it lost its cargo to the sea and littered the coast with carefully wrapped and sealed packages of cocaine.[4] Being one of the first instances of hard proof of the cocaine connection in Guinea-Bissau, the shipwreck made explicit what had long been the subject of rumours in the country's capital, namely that the country functioned as a transit route for the trafficking of cocaine from Latin America into Europe.

For those with prior knowledge of Bissauian politics the rumours of cocaine trafficking were not new.[5] When I first came to the city, in January 2000, it had been a long-standing undocumented 'truth' that the government of João Bernardo 'Nino' Vieira, the country's former president, had been involved in cocaine trafficking. Cocaine was one of the many points on the list of the illegal ways the *homi garandi*, the Big Man, was said to be making his fortune. In early 2000, just after the ousting of Vieira's regime, during a visit to the Bijagos islands off the coast of Bissau, I was shown where the *branco*, the 'white man', who served as the liaison for the trafficking between the three continents, resided. I was shown where the planes landed and where the drugs were shipped from. 'It would land here,' I was told, 'be brought to that house, repacked and shipped into Europe in goods passing through Bissauian waters.' As President Vieira and his network had just lost the war, it was presumed safe to publicly proclaim what had otherwise been confined to the flow of rumours, meaning that former secrets about his illegal and illicit dealings were openly aired. Long-standing secrets about the former president were, as such, debated loudly, and trading drugs and smuggling weapons were the primary revenues mentioned.

I wrote this in my field notes at the time, but did not pursue the issue further – first of all, because the country's desperate political situation over-shadowed the importance of a cocaine connection. At the time, Bissau was in a state of collapse. The country had just emerged from a period of warfare that had destroyed many areas of the capital, left it in economic and insti-tutional ruin and, not least, left the threat of further war hanging in the air. The constant possibility of conflict, the complete disarray of everything but the military institutions and the large number of militarized youth with no viable livelihoods were such overshadowing problems that the cocaine rumours disappeared into the background. The social and economic crisis was present and tangible, while the accusations of cocaine trafficking were numerous but the proof modest.

New proliferation, old configuration The proof has since become prolific. Within the past five years, Guinea-Bissau has been one of the primary West African transit points for the movement of cocaine from South America into Europe.[6] With many tonnes of cocaine having been impounded in the country since 2005, there is no longer any doubt as to the role it plays in the trafficking of illegal and illicit substances and goods.[7] However, the impounded cocaine has equally clearly demonstrated the level of complicity of the country's leading political networks. Most of the seized drugs have disappeared before being destroyed, and instead of combating the cocaine cartels the police, army, navy and air force seem more intent on assisting them and returning confiscated shipments to their 'rightful owners' (Ellis 2009: 191).

This connection between apparent lawlessness and a booming cocaine trade has moved the otherwise marginal and geopolitically unimportant country into the limelight. Bissau has become interesting news, spurring talk of 'the Cocaine Coast',[8] 'West Africa's Narco State',[9] 'the Afghanistan of Africa' and creative headlines such as 'Out of Africa: the New Cocaine Mules'.[10] Yet though the magnitude of the current cocaine connection may be relatively novel, the political dynamics and networks that support and facilitate it – and directly account for Guinea-Bissau's dominance in this global trade – are not. The cocaine cartels navigate non-state agents of power and politics behind the façade of state, and it would seem that what Bissau has to offer is an enduring state of competing factions, patronized public institutions and negotiable political networks. The country is saturated by political factions and fraction (as cohesive minority and processes of rupture and dissent), creating a scenario that is not only conducive to informal dealings but is actually built on them.

In order to shed light on the cocaine connection in Bissau and its relation to Big Man politics and transnational networks, this chapter moves from the structural to the experiential. It will look at some of the conditions – historical, political, geographical and demographical – that make Guinea-Bissau an ideal location for the cocaine trade before turning to a more experience-led focus, illuminating the cocaine connection and its consequences from the perspective of some of the people caught up in it. The point of departure is, however, historical. The cocaine connection is not just the source of conflict in Bissau, but is built on dynamics and networks that have themselves been created in a context of conflict. As we shall see, the longstanding factional politics, generational dynamics and states of collapse that are central to an understanding of the conflict and crisis in Bissau are equally necessary frames for understanding the booming trade in cocaine. As a historical perspective will show, these dynamics are not new but rather firmly consolidated. The current cocaine trade works through key factions and figures, networks and Big Men that rose to power some forty years ago in the war of liberation.

The historical dimension: faction and fraction

After a long and brutal war of liberation, Guinea-Bissau declared independence in 1973. Through the efforts of the PAIGC,[11] the country became part of the world of free and sovereign states and embarked on a journey to create a country characterized by freedom and equality. The main figure behind the liberation struggle had been Amilcar Cabral, who managed to secure popular support for the PAIGC, initially as a peaceful worker-based independence party that organized unions and civil protest, but after 1961 as an armed revolutionary party.[12] In 1963 the party launched a ten-year armed liberation struggle against the Portuguese army and colonial system as they established themselves in the rural and forest areas of the country. Relying on guerrilla tactics, within half a year the PAIGC were fighting the Portuguese along two fronts, and by 1965 were in control of half the country. They had established their presence on the northern, southern and eastern fronts, creating three relatively independent military formations under the overall command of Cabral, and pushing the Portuguese back to the major cities and the coastal estuaries where they had fortified their interests in the early colonial days. However, though the PAIGC was to gain international acclaim for its innovative and egalitarian political programmes and projects, and its leader and ideologue Cabral was to be iconized as a revolutionary thinker, the PAIGC seems to have been a more divided organization than imagined, and in the final stages of the war the Portuguese succeeded in assassinating Amilcar Cabral. He was shot and killed in Guinea Conakry through the combined efforts of the FLING, the Portuguese secret police (the PIDE)[13] and internal conflicting factions within the PAIGC. It was within this context of conflict and factional strife that Guinea-Bissau declared its independence on 24 September 1973.

Enduring factionalism Looking at the liberation era shows that factionalism was not somehow introduced to the Guinea-Bissauian state but is rather in its very constitution. From the very point of the country's recognition by the international community as an independent, sovereign state, Guinea-Bissau was not 'one-dimensional, formed around a single generic trunk, like a majestic oak tree whose roots are spread deeply into the soil of history', but rather 'a variable multiplicity of networks whose underground branches join together the scattered points of society' (Bayart 1993: 220), with each underground branch – or network – protecting and defining access to resources and authority. This became further noticeable after the war as Bissau turned into a post-colonial nightmare of factional strife and economic decline. The networks and commanders that emerged within these different military formations during the war would show themselves to be enduring. As the war veterans, *antigos combatentes*, demanded recognition for their sacrifices during the years of war – for the well-being they had been deprived of and the youth they had lost on the battlefield – they were given privileges and positions of power within the newly created state, with the most influential of them becoming the Big Men who would define the military and political elite of post-independence Guinea-Bissau.

Though the PAIGC initially seemed intent on rebuilding the country in its ideological image, internal strife quickly rendered the push towards progress impotent and created a state apparatus in which different state institutions, ministries and military positions were handed out as spoils to *antigos combatentes*. Instead of developing towards the envisioned freedom and prosperity, the twenty-five years of official Cabralian Marxism led to growing poverty and a massive gap in wealth between the country's small but divided elite and the general population. This became even more evident as the country moved from a one-party state to a multiparty democracy, and from a planned economy to an economic policy of free market forces. The neoliberal version of capitalist development that took over as Marxist ideology was discredited in the 1990s merely intensified the strife between different political networks. What emerged was not promising futures but rather increasing conflict and turmoil. However, until 1998 the violent potential of these power struggles and socio-political configurations had been relatively restrained, confined to minor outbreaks of fighting and three more serious purges. The war in 1998 highlighted the illegal trade and shadow economies that were feeding the different Big Men and their networks in Bissau, as well as clearly illuminating the regional character of the country's political dynamics, as the onset of war in 1998 was directly related to the trafficking of guns within sub-regional networks.

From conflict to warfare The prolonged period of instability exploded into full-scale warfare on Sunday, 7 June 1998. Having been in power since November 1980, President João Bernardo Vieira, popularly referred to as Nino, was no stranger to coup attempts. In fact, he seemed exceptionally adept at the art of surviving and controlling factional and political conflict. He had himself gained office in 1980 by overthrowing President Luis Cabral,[14] and prior to the coup of 1998 that would be his downfall had survived three alleged coup attempts. In 1983, the current prime minister, Victor Saúde Maria, was dismissed and imprisoned, along with his alleged accomplices, for planning to topple the government; in 1986 Paulo Correia, a hero of the war of independence and the leading figure for a large part of the majority Balanta population, was arrested and executed, together with a handful of other prominent politicians, on charges of plotting to overthrow the government (Forrest 1992: 251);[15] and in 1993 João da Costa, an influential politician, along with the head of the paramilitary Rapid Intervention Force and a dozen soldiers, was arrested on charges of being involved in a military coup.[16] Nino's uncanny ability to manoeuvre through a political terrain as factionally destabilized as that of Guinea-Bissau gave him a reputation of possessing a special ability to see the plotting of coups despite their clandestine and covert character. *I tene odju*, he has eyes, people said of the late president, when referring to his ability to pre-empt political problems.

The coup in 1998 was a consequence of the dismissal of Brigadier Asumané Mané as chief of staff on 5 June. Half a year prior to the start of the war,[17] Mané had been suspended following accusations of arms sales from the Guinea-Bissauian armed forces to the MFDC rebel movement in Casamance, Senegal.[18] During their fight for independence the MFDC have had close connections with Guinea-Bissau, as they have used the northern, Diola/Felupe-dominated areas of the country as a safe haven for tired soldiers recuperating from the war. However, with the Guinea-Bissauian entry into the West African Monetary Union and the gradual alignment of President Vieira's politics with the French field of interest in West Africa, favouring the Senegalese side of the Casamance conflict, there was an increased focus on Guinea-Bissau's role in supporting the MFDC cause through arms smuggling. As a consequence of the pressure from France and Senegal, Brigadier Mané was singled out to bear the blame for the apparent arms sales to the rebels, and a parliamentary investigation was launched on 27 February.[19] Indicative of the regional character of the Guinea-Bissauian conflict, it did not take long before four different military forces were involved in the war. The Guinea-Bissauian army was split in two, with the large majority of the soldiers opting to join Mané's side of the conflict. However, the few hundred men, mostly officers and the presidential guard, who did choose to stay on the presidential side of the conflict got the backing of an artillery battalion from Guinea Conakry consisting of 500 men, as well as 1,300 Senegalese commandos, within less than two days. While avoiding the question of responsibility for the arms sales that initiated the war, it seems necessary to add that during the war, as well as after it, Asumané Mané was able to count on the help of the MFDC guerrillas, indicating that the relationship between the two parties was not a negative one.[20] As it turned out, Nino Vieira's side lost the war as they were overrun by the Junta Militar in the *ultimo assalto,* the last assault.

The war was in many ways a precursor of the past ten years of factional strife and illegal dealings. Rather than looking at a post-war scenario, what we are currently witnessing is more akin to a conflictual plateau, in which the tensions at play have become locked in a stalemate of incessant tension. The war clearly illuminated the instability of the country's political environment, showing the factions at play as well as providing a window on the regional dimensions of their fight for the control of resources and assets. Furthermore, the durability of the regional and local political alliances, which had been shaped during the war of independence with different underlying connectors, such as military camaraderie, ethnicity, lineage, transactions and relations of obligation, came clearly to the fore.

Persistent problems As the civil war 'ended' towards the end of 1999,[21] the economic catastrophe of the two years of fighting became evident. Guinea-Bissau had already seen a rapid decline in development assistance prior to the war, from US$180 million in 1996 to US$124 million in 1997, yet during the war this was reduced to US$96 million in 1998 and was merely US$52 million in 1999 (Einarsdottir 2007: 102). A cut in state budgets by more than two-thirds within three years is drastic in any circumstances. But the terrible effects of the cutback were heightened by the fact that 80 per cent of the state budget stems from development assistance,[22] the economic situation being aggravated by a 50 per cent drop in the international prices of the country's largest export crop, cashew nuts, in 2000. As the flow of resources dried up, the political factions, which had gained control of state institutions as payment for sacrificing their youth on the battlefield, found themselves looking for new resource flows. No longer able to use institutions as points of access to resources in the shape of taxes, bribes and development assistance, they seemingly initiated a general scramble for assets in Bissau.

From the end of the civil war in 1999 up to 2005 the desperate economic situation resulted in a crippling instability and uncertainty fuelled by constant political and factional strife. 'Things are going from bad to worse', *mal a pior*, people said, the statement amplified by a visible decline in living standards and the well-being of Bissau's population at large, resulting in an intense period of societal and political stress and decline, including a coup and an army mutiny as well as a soar in random shootings.

Return of the hyena However, these dismal prospects and the generalized despondency seemed to change as I went back to Bissau during the run-up to the democratic elections in 2005. Before 2005, Bissau had started to suffer from a serious case of election fatigue. *E falla ke es i mocracia, ma i crisi so*, 'they say that this is democracy but it is just crisis', as one of my informants phrased it, as every coup had been followed by yet another election seeking to legitimize a new government's control of state resources.

Yet something changed when ousted ex-president Nino Vieira returned to run for office again in 2005. The fact that Vieira was able to set foot in Guinea-Bissau came as a surprise to many, as his old enemies in the Junta Militar were controlling the country. Rumours were that the ex-president had made a deal with the Junta Militar allowing him to return to power to their mutual benefit. He had promised something in return for amnesty, but people were unsure of what the 'bait' had been. As he was flown into Bissau and landed near the city's stadium, in a helicopter belonging to the Guinea Conakrian air force, I was standing in a crowd of thousands of cheering people welcoming him back. Bissau was alight with tense talk of what would happen next, who would react to his presence, and whether or not he would bring stability and progress. It was an extreme change: from being a hated figure, singled out to bear the brunt of the blame for the civil war just a few years earlier, he returned as a figure encompassing the possibility that the country could return to better times. Even people who had been anti-Vieira were now praising his return, and for the first time in years my interlocutors appeared hopeful. 'Better a hyena that is full than one who is hungry,' people said. The hope was, as it often is in relation to wealthy politicians, that his wealth would prevent him from taking excessive bites out of the meagre state budget.

But Vieira was not full. He had gained his fortune from illicit dealings and illegal trade, and what he had been brought back to milk was his old cocaine connection. The massive boom in cocaine trafficking coincides with his return to Bissau. After Nino Vieira's reinstatement, the number of tonnes confiscated in Bissau started to soar (see Ellis 2009: 192). The cocaine connection moved from minor to massive, a fact which is evidenced by the documentation of the problem: I have not been able to find any written documents mentioning the problem between 2000 and 2004, yet I have located 223 reports, articles and bulletins from between 2005 and 2010 focusing on the issue.

On making his return to power, Nino Vieira promised prosperity and peace. Yet as we shall see, he was able to keep only one part of this promise. Rumour has it that he awoke his slumbering cocaine connections, convinced different key figures and factions to facilitate their exploitation, and subsequently sold the service of the state apparatus and the country's status as a sovereign state to the Colombian cartels, thus ensuring that a steady flow of resources would be directed into the different networks and Big Men controlling military institutions, the police and various parts of the state for the trafficking. In fact, he so successfully kept his promise of prosperity that the profit from the cocaine trade is currently said to dwarf the GNP of the country,[23] testifying both to the poverty of the place as well as the lucrative possibilities of the informal economy. However, Nino Vieira fell short in bringing a minimum of peace and stability to Guinea-Bissau and appeasing the different networks at play. Perhaps owing to the amount of money involved, perhaps to Nino's unwillingness to divide the shares in an acceptable manner, or the greed of the actors involved, the cocaine trafficking did not lessen the level of conflict in Bissau, and rather than being able to control the situation, Nino Vieira was assassinated, mutilated with machetes and shot on 2 March 2009.

Nino was murdered after allegedly having ordered the assassination of army chief of staff Batista Tagme Na Waie the day before. Vieira and Na Waie were both *antigos combatentes* and long-time rivals.[24] They were also the Big Men of two competing political networks within the army and, formerly, within the PAIGC, both of which had formed during the war of liberation, had adapted to the interim period and, not least, to the cocaine trade. Though the killing of the two Big Men decapitated the country's political apparatus it did not diminish the cocaine trade. Indicative of the factional nature of politics in Bissau, what we have seen instead since the twin murders in March 2010 is that Jose Americo Bubo Na Tchuto, former navy chief and, once again, an *antigo combatente*, who was exiled after an attempted coup in 2008, has gained a prominent place in Bissauian 'politics'.[25] So prominent, in fact, that Bubo Na Tchuto and former head of the air force Ibraima Papa Camara, also an *antigo combatente*, have been named 'drug kingpins' under the US Drug Kingpin Act, meaning that US citizens are barred from doing business with them and that attempts have been made to freeze their overseas assets.[26]

Political dynamics and critical states

So what can we learn from this brief foray into Guinea-Bissauian history? First of all, it seems fair to say that the political history of Guinea-Bissau has, since its independence, been characterized by what can be called 'stable instability'; that is, relatively continuous political crisis and conflict. The country falls into the common post-independence scenario of internal conflict becoming visible as soon as the external enemies have been defeated and the image of a radical Other is no longer able to shade fragmented liberation movements (see Chabal 2002). Bissau's inhabitants have, as such, found their lives set in a social environment of flux, greatly influencing their well-being, social possibilities and life chances. Recent change has merely added to the misery and made social life an uncontrollable succession of negative socio-political and economic developments (Vigh 2006b). It is a city characterized by volatile political change, economic hardship, insecurity and uncertainty, making life a constant struggle to deal with 'the actualities of a desperately disturbed everyday life' (Guyer 2007: 410). Yet the instability seems in itself a sign of the political prominence of the network and Big Men politics in question. Contrary to what they seem (Sahlins 1963: 289), Big Men are prime exemplars of the fact that power is never personal. That Big Men constantly have to demonstrate their power through displays of wealth and force is not indicative of their strength but of the very fragility and negotiability of their status. As their worth and authority are socially generated, rather than structurally endowed, they are Big Men only for so long as they are recognized as such. Much like the dynamics of acephalous political systems, where worth must be gained and proved, so the lack of institutionalized authority means that Big Man power is as delicate as it is contested. Though the state apparatus, offices and titles may serve to represent a Big Man's status, they remain secondary to it: in terms of politics Vieira was a Big Man before he was president. He was in the business of winning not votes but clients; not spearheading a party but a political network, meaning that he was locked in constant struggles for resources (symbolic, material or otherwise) to access, distribute and control, and in a constant struggle to maintain his position.

Secondly, Guinea-Bissauian history directs our attention to the constitution and consolidation of factional politics that characterize much of post-colonial African political history. Factions are 'units of conflict activated on specific occasions rather than maintained by formal organization', Mayer states. They are 'loosely ordered' and based more on 'transaction than issues of principle' (1966: 116). Exactly this combination of conflict, flexible organization and transaction can be seen in many parts of West Africa, with political factions within independence movements having become patron–client political networks embedding power in the very grain of society, yet evading the institutionalization of parties and positions. These factions, constituted in the war of independence, have a more enduring character than one would perhaps expect, and they are visible agents not just in the endless series of conflicts that have punctuated Guinea-Bissau's movement through time, but equally in the informal economies and illicit and illegal dealings that have constituted prime local, regional and international transactions through the past half-decade. In Bissau the smuggling of guns, embezzlement of development assistance or trafficking of cocaine show the same factions and figures, networks and Big Men taking centre stage. Their obligations are focused on relations and social ties rather than impersonal orders, and the organization is pliable and plastic rather than institutionalized. Constantly changing yet still relatively enduring, it is exactly the factions' flexibility and ability to adapt to possibility which makes the country an ideal partner for agents within informal, global economies. I have argued elsewhere (Vigh 2006a [2003]) that we need to see the Guinea-Bissauian social environment as wavering and volatile rather than as a consolidated terrain if we wish to make sense of the political dynamics in the country. Yet the larger historical picture equally shows us that it does not make sense to see the cocaine connection as a singular *critical event* but that we rather need to frame it within a historical *critical continuity*.

As should be clear by now, the Big Men networks that developed during the war of independence are the same as those that engaged in war in 1998–2000, as well those that have now directed their interest towards the cocaine connection. Furthermore, the historical insight grants us the possibility of going a bit deeper into the explanations for the cocaine trade and its consequences in Bissau. The very attractiveness of Bissau as a drug hub is directly related to the consequences and dynamics of factional politics.

Like moving into an empty house For the cocaine cartels, moving their business to Bissau was 'like moving into an empty house', another UN official said.[27] Instead of state institutions trying to protect the country from international crime and illegal trade, the cartels encountered a state occupied by competing political factions whose obligations are directed towards personal allegiances and networks rather than institutions, national subjects and sovereign state: not an entity working for the common good of an imagined community, but a fragmented structure, operating beneath its recognition as a sovereign body, yet whose parts are put to work in the interests of specific networks. This fragmentation has been so severe in Bissau that 'the state' seems to be kept in existence only by the life support offered by international relations.

The Guinea-Bissauian state may have pro forma and *de jure* existence as a sovereign body, but in terms of both the Weberian and Hobbesian definitions of the state it is effectively obsolete: there is no monopoly on the legitimate use of force and no state to protect or guarantee the security and well-being of its citizens. It is an environment which counters our 'normal', hierarchical understanding of the state and our normal idea of political structures. In other words, the 'state' as a bureaucratic structure allowing for centralized civic rule and serving to protect its citizens and distribute resources functions as a representation directed towards donors and international organizations, yet its underbelly is cross-cut by and intertwined with patrimonial networks. Much the same scenario has been analysed by William Reno in his work on the 'shadow state', in which rulers rely on global systems and recognition of sovereignty while in fact using state structures and institutions to further their own interests (Reno 2000).

Yet perhaps the concept of the state (shadowed or illuminated) is, in fact, unfavourable as an analytical variable when trying to understand the political dynamics in Guinea-Bissau. The situation, without preconceived ideas of politics proper, is a state of factionalism that is not epiphenomenal to the Guinea-Bissauian state but is rather its mainspring (see Bayart 1993: 233, 240, 268) – not pathology but a historically contingent reality. The state in Guinea-Bissau is 'a plural space of interaction and enunciation [that] does not exist beyond the uses made of it' (ibid.: 252), meaning that we need to see the use it enables and the effects it produces, rather than accept it as an a priori entity, if we wish to understand the proliferation of the cocaine trade and the country's allure for the cocaine cartels. Focusing on the 'state' in a place like Bissau obscures the actual social and political dynamics; it clouds both the local and international dynamics that we really need to get right if we want to change things for the better. The idea of the state presumes the existence of an abstract yet singular political entity; it presumes the existence of a sovereign power and a defined populace. In other words, for my current line of enquiry the statist perspective amounts to looking at political processes through the wrong analytical optic; through the lenses of a superimposed order that does not correspond to the reality of the place we are actually looking at (see Dunn 2000).

However, in his work on shadow states what Reno manages to do is to direct our attention to the fact that the state can serve as an *asset* rather than a hindrance in relation to the informal economy. Offering business opportunities to the different political factions in question, the cocaine cartels have, in Bissau, been able to hide behind the protective walls of a sovereign state recognized and protected by international law.[28] In other words, rather than having to hide from state institutions and authorities, the cartels can hide beneath them. Instead of preventing the Guinea-Bissauian state falling prey to global illegal networks, the Big Men and networks that control the army, security and police forces in Bissau have made them important agents in facilitating the trade. The representation of the state provides the framework – in terms of security, impunity and invisibility – that enables illegal trade and trafficking to continue, uncontrolled by international law.[29] The navy is not actively protecting the territorial waters of the country from the influx of cocaine, but is active in moving traffickers and goods within the coastal waters and island of Guinea-Bissau; the army is busy loading and protecting the illegal cargo in question; the air force provides facilities and possibilities; and the police provide impunity.

Geography and demography

But why, we may ask ourselves, has Bissau been singled out by the cocaine cartels, when the historical and political scenario described, specificities apart, would fit many countries on the Upper Guinea coast? The answer is, of course, that Guinea Conakry and Sierra Leone have also been targeted precisely because they share many of the same dynamics. However, owing to the extreme networked nature of politics in Guinea-Bissau, the country appears currently to be the one offering the least resistance to the cartels in question.

Furthermore, its geography is advantageous for smuggling activity and the trafficking of illegal and illicit goods. In relation to the cocaine connection, Guinea-Bissau is strategically placed along the ninth latitude north, offering the shortest distance to the South American continent. For transport via Brazil or Venezuela, the country is within reach by both boat and plane. It is only a four-hour flight, by light aircraft, to Guinea-Bissau, which furthermore offers approximately four hundred miles of coastline and ninety islands that are unpatrolled by law enforcement agencies, allowing the planes to land and the drugs to be redistributed – once again either by light aircraft or boat.[30] Furthermore, Guinea-Bissau is logistically advantageous once the cocaine is in the country as it offers various routes for redistribution. Though not much is known about the actual process of relocation of the cocaine, part of the reason Bissau is interesting to the drug cartels is related to the multiple possibilities of redistribution the place offers, enabling the cartels to diversify the movement of cocaine and minimize their risks and losses accordingly. First of all, the country is traditionally connected to the Saharan trade route, renowned for its part in smuggling illegal and illicit goods. Secondly, the cocaine is transshipped farther up the coast by boat, including both high-speed motorboats and local fishing vessels. The cocaine trade thus provides an alternative to traditional livelihoods as trafficking the drugs offers a steady income to a population otherwise caught in decline. Fishing provides a case in point: as the fishing rights in Bissauian waters have been sold to Europeans, Russians and the Chinese, the ocean around the country has been emptied, resulting in an abundance of local fishermen who have had their livelihoods taken away (Lucht 2008). 'Fishermen get involved [in drug trafficking] because they can earn more money from illegal activities,' Mody Ndiaye, adviser to UNODC in Bissau, has stated.[31] But fishermen are not the only locals for whom the cocaine trade provides a possible move out of an otherwise trapped situation. Much the same can be said of the *dyulas*, i.e. the traditional Mandingo traders, and, not least, the many smugglers who traffic smaller quantities out of the country. Thirdly, this combination of economic decline, diminishing resources and withering livelihoods is further intensified by the fact that we are not looking just at specific groups of people who see possibilities in trafficking cocaine, but rather a whole population grasping for even the slightest or most risky possibility of gaining a better life.

Generational anomie The specific make-up of Guinea-Bissauian politics offers, as such, the cartels other benefits beyond simply invisibility and protection. Furthermore, the touched-upon economic downturn, which has characterized Guinea-Bissau for the past ten years, coincides with a growing population of young people and a stalled educational apparatus.[32] In Bissau there is an increasing number of young people competing for access to a minimal amount of resources and opportunities, which means that most young people who are coming of age have to struggle to gain an education, job or any other type of access to resources. 'We are seeing an increasingly large generation of young people who find themselves persistently unable to support themselves, look after their families and set up an independent household' (O'Brien 1996: 57, cf. Seekings 1996; Vigh 2006a [2003]). This pairing of crisis and generational inertia in turn makes the country interesting in relation to both the trafficking and the trading of cocaine. Nigerian traffickers are notorious for using youth as mules in their attempts to ship cocaine to, primarily, Europe or North America (Ellis 2009). However, as the drug trafficking has moved farther north, the drug 'industry' is able to offer an enticing way out of the existential impasse that shades the lives of a great many of the area's young people. The inertia of the trans-generational process has had dire effects on the lives of, especially, young men as they find themselves unable to meet social expectations and move from being dependent on others to being independent, or having dependants:

> Young people are tired here. If you don't have work, and your father doesn't, then it's a great tiredness [*kansera*] for you. If you don't work, if you don't have money, you can't get married. My son is there [he points towards Pilun]. I can't take him ... Because I don't have a job, so I have to leave them there. I can't go and look for them ... You know ... women can't suffer like men. They can't sit [for] one day, two days without eating. They can't! So I have to leave them there [with his wife's family].

Buba's statement makes us aware that he, like many other young men in Bissau, is finding it difficult to survive physically: i.e. to find enough to eat. Yet it equally directs our attention to the social tragedy of this lack of resources. As a persistent decline in resources has entailed a retrenchment within family, socio-political networks and state, it has become impossible for Buba and the majority of young men in Bissau to support a family, marry and thereby become a man of respect, an adult. The generational 'misdynamics' are similar to those in many other areas of West Africa. The blocked development and social castration involved in not being able to meet social expectations is caused by the interlocking of poverty and patrimonialism; by Big Man systems in situations of heightened lack of resources. Such systems are not necessarily or straightforwardly exploitative. However, the deeper the crisis or decline, the more the Big Man is able to define the terms of exchange (see Eisenstadt and Roninger 1981). Currently, the cocaine trade and its networks are not just the primary way of gaining access to resources, ranging from a ticket to Europe to a daily meal, but one of the *only* ways. In any case, Big Men provide the social avenues that enable imagined worthy lives. The focus of my informants is, thus, not on charismatic leaders, ideology or religious enlightenment, but on *possibilities* opened in the social terrain by the dynamics of different networks and competing Big Men. The consequence is that Bissau is a city saturated with young men looking for a way to escape their current predicament and move towards a better life of recognition and worth; constantly looking for possibilities and life chances, while all along complaining bitterly about the humiliation of having to act like a boy while in fact seeing oneself as a man. In Seku's words:

> I want to be the man of my [own] head.[33] I want to be a man of respect, a complete man, complete [*completo*]. You understand? I want to have my own house, children, a wife. I want a job. If you've this then no one can tell you you're young. You'll have your own family, your own job. If you're a complete man then you're the [sole] force of your head.[34]

Neither Seku's situation nor his aspirations are unusual. Living one's life at the margins of resource flows, locally or globally, makes one dream of the inclusion that could grant one the possibility of being worthy. 'Being in control of one's head' involves having the freedom to choose, to make up one's own mind and follow one's own desire, all of which is ideally encompassed in the category of adulthood. From a Guinea-Bissauian perspective, neither Buba nor Seku is a proper man as they do not control their own lives, cannot get a wife or support a household, but rather stay dependent on the goodwill of parents and kin. Yet, as mentioned, it is a common complaint, an aggravation felt by all my younger informants, given their remoteness from realizing what they see as their social being and healing their social impairment.

The consequence is a generational anomie in which it is unachievable for youth to attain the role and position[35] that are both culturally prescribed and socially expected of them (see Merton 1968 [1949]),[36] meaning that generations of men are stuck in a position of juvenility. As networks become increasingly difficult to access, youth are willing to do almost anything to gain access to the resources and authority that will allow them to escape this social moratorium. In this situation of having so few options available to them, being exploited by a patron through an unequal exchange of resources, favours and obligations is currently the best they can hope for (see Hinkelammert 1993). Currently, in Bissau, even negative reciprocity induces a social relationship with – at least – the possibility of reciprocation (see Sahlins 1974), granting youth an opportunity to better their lives in the future. Beyond being exploitative, the relationship contains, in other words, a possibility.[37] In Bayart's words, commenting on a similar but not quite so aggravated process of social marginalization in Cameroon: 'Recurrent unemployment prevents those without money from ... being able to choose a spouse – the *sine qua non* of social recognition. The social frustration caused by the economy of survival forces many "little men" to make radical choices' (Bayart 1993: 240).

The situation creates, in other words, a willingness to take substantial risks. Interestingly, the dynamics are exactly the same as those we can see when looking at issues of mobilization and militancy. Young men are in much the same situation during wartime, whereby factions, through the patrimonial workings, offer futures in return for militant manpower (Vigh 2006a [2003]). Furthermore, as we have seen, the same factions that are able to mobilize youth in situations of war are those we are currently seeing take centre stage in relation to the cocaine connection, once again tying together conflict and the informal economy of cocaine.

From cartels to patrimonial networks

This connection between cocaine cartels, factions and patrimonial networks becomes even more evident if we look at the actual movement of cocaine within Bissau – that is, the way drugs move from cartels into factions and filter through patrimonial networks.

It is clear, when in Bissau, that not all the cocaine that enters the country leaves it again, but that the substance has become currency in its own right, feeding into networks as well as individual addictions. The primary capital in the cocaine industry is unsurprisingly cocaine, and although the deals made and prices paid for facilitating the drug flow and enabling the trafficking remain unidentified, it seems clear that services and favours are being paid for in drugs rather than currency and that cocaine moves through networks as payment – a fact which can be seen in the diverse trajectories the traffic takes. The great quantities that have repeatedly been intercepted only to disappear after having been removed or handed over to special police and military forces are most likely not cocaine that is in Guinean hands, but goods en route; seized during what should be uninterrupted movement. Conversely, the many instances of smaller amounts of cocaine being intercepted at airports in Europe are more likely to reflect Guinea-Bissauian networks trying to traffic the rewards gained from protecting the cartels into areas where they can make a proper profit. While the large-scale movement of drugs is an exercise in international shipping and logistics, the smaller-scale drug trafficking works through local networks and global diasporas connecting places through people. It moves illicit and illegal goods through a dispersed and complex web of connection. What we are seeing is thus multiple movements of the same goods connected to the same informal economy, yet working on different levels and scales and through different routes and points of distribution. If we look more specifically at the movement of cocaine through these local networks we see that it trickles through patrimonial networks in much the same way that resources have moved from factional Big Men to the man on the street over the past years. Similarly, the picture of Big Men controlling the present and prospective social conditions of youth has not been disrupted but appears consolidated by the influx of cocaine into the city.

In fact, the cocaine trade seems to strengthen the existing factions in Guinea-Bissau. They may be in a constant state of tension as they struggle for positions of control of remnants of state and resource flows, yet in relation to their control of people, secured through their privileged positions as purveyors of futures, they are as dominant as ever. For the large group of people in the city who are trapped in a situation of abject marginality with barely enough resources to survive the present, let alone create a positive future, the booming cocaine trade provides a possibility of centrality. Just as the situation of warfare entails factions and patrimonial networks opening up for young people as they are mobilized to protect the control and flow of resources, cocaine offers inclusion in terms of distributing, trafficking and pushing drugs. It offers, in this respect, work and livelihoods, and not least a distant possibility of migration. As young men in Bissau are currently willing to do almost anything to survive the present and secure the future, Bissau has become a city of potential 'mules', with a single flight to Amsterdam in December 2006 carrying thirty-two mules.[38] Though the cartels seem to primarily traffic cocaine in larger quantities by plane and boat, there has been an increase in the use of couriers and 'shotgun' trafficking, with groups of mules being dispatched;[39] this practice appears directly related to local networks and their underlying trafficking and distribution of drugs. Nineteen per cent of the traffickers caught in Portugal in 2008 were from Bissau. So, though the amount of cocaine trafficked by mules is in all likelihood far less than what reaches the continent shipped in goods or smuggled by air, it nonetheless means a diversification of the traffic and thereby an increased influx of cocaine into Europe.

For the mules involved, the cocaine trade provides one of their only possibilities of migration. Given both documents and an airfare, becoming a mule provides a possibility that is otherwise out of reach. Yet, as we shall see, it equally provides an opportunity – although with dire consequences – when actually in Europe. Guinea-Bissau not only provides political, geographical and demographical advantages for the cocaine trade, it equally provides a well-consolidated yet flexible and adaptable diaspora for actualizing the last transaction in the commodity chain. This means that Bissau not only breeds a large group of people willing and able to traffic the drugs in question but also offers them the ability to sell them; once in Europe the drugs are distributed and sold via West African networks.[40] In fact, the connection between the cocaine trade and Guinea-Bissau is so consolidated that even prospective migrants take the trafficking and pushing of cocaine into consideration as both stereotype and livelihood. 'If you go to Spain,' Aliu, a hopeful would-be migrant, told me in Bissau, 'you can just as well tell your family you're selling drugs straight away.' The current financial crisis is seen as so severe, in relation to West African migrants in Europe, that selling cocaine is understood as one of the 'jobs' one can actually get as a young Guinea-Bissauian migrant. Cocaine offers an accessible income for those willing to risk selling it. Most of the young men I have followed from Bissau to Lisbon dream of getting good jobs, recognition and the ability to live a worthy life, but within their sphere of possibility the cocaine connection seems to have such a prominent presence that many treat it as a point of departure. 'I don't force anyone to buy it,' Americano told me as we were standing in an alley in Lisbon where he sells cocaine to survive. 'I don't put my hand in your pocket, I don't steal, I don't hurt people. It's just commerce,' he continued, explaining to me that selling cocaine was merely another way of doing business. Similarly, Latino, another Bissauian pusher, said: 'Go over there [points to a bar] and you can buy beer, go over there and you can buy cigarettes; here you can buy cocaine.'

Yet selling cocaine is not business as usual. The pushers I talk to in Lisbon are forced to work nights and long hours for a minimum of payment. They constantly have to deal with the danger posed by other pushers, police and punters, all of which becomes condensed into what they call a *vida di zero*, a life of zero, an empty existence void of worth. What they can attain from the cocaine trade is, in other words, merely a translocation of their hardship: rather than becoming 'a man of one's own head', as Seku said in the quote above, what is gained – when seen from below – is an extended state of social and existential fatigue. So, though they have distanced themselves geographically from the uncertainty and hardship that characterize the critical context of Bissau, the cocaine connection as an informal economy traps people in a situation that is not very different from that which they seek to escape in the first place. The insecurity, suffering and lack of ability to secure for oneself a positive future seem enduring and unavoidable. In Neto's words:

> Look, I stand here all night, but I only make enough to be able to stand here again tomorrow. The Big Men that sell us our drugs [that we sell on]; they sell them to us expensively. Our [own] kin, they sell it so that we can [only make enough] to survive today ... but tomorrow we have to stand here again, only to be able to stand here again the day after that. What a zero-life [*vida di zero*]. Africans here in Lisbon ... I'm telling you, it's a zero-life. There are no possibilities, only a zero-life. Here, if you're black you're nothing [*abo i ka nada*].

Conclusion

This chapter has explored the history of political upheaval, uncertainty and conflict in Bissau and argues that, though we have seen a change in what is being fought over, the political process remains very much the same: the much-commented-on cocaine connection in Bissau represents new political revenue in an old political form. Rather than focusing on the cocaine trade and current calamities as critical events, it has looked at critical continuities. Looking at informal networks and shadow economies, one is generally forced to search the penumbra for information. It is a world of opacity, which reveals itself in glimpses, and which does not lend itself to persistent illumination. What we can see when focusing on the issue in Bissau is a connection between conflict and the informal economy of cocaine that is tied to historical, political formations. Instead of being a novel phenomenon, the cocaine connection has been re-established and strengthened over the past ten years, working through and with political networks that have defined and controlled the flow of resources and power in the country for almost half a century. The increase in cocaine trafficking is related to more constant underlying aspects of the Guinea-Bissauian political environment, namely that it is defined by a Big Man system, rather than to a sudden impact or novel occurrence: that is, to a critical continuity rather than a critical event. The pre-independence struggle was an early warning of the factional strife that has marred Guinea-Bissau since independence, as the commanders and central figures within these different military formations emerged to spearhead the political turbulence we are still witnessing today. What we have yet to see is the effect that the cocaine trafficking will have on Guinea-Bissau in the long run. Some of the consequences are already starting to be felt. As factions and the patrimonial networks they encompass function as the de facto social security system in Bissau, one can hope that the profits of the trafficking will spill over into the pockets of the desperately poor. Yet though the drug trade has increased the wealth of the city's minute elite, it has not brought with it a generalized surge in wealth.

What we are currently witnessing in Bissau is an increased dependency on 'pedra', as crack cocaine is called, among the city's impoverished population, and a surge in drug-related local crime, adding an extra element of uncertainty to even kin relationships and family solidarity. The burden of criminality is as unequally distributed as assets are.

Notes

1 www.unodc.org/unodc/en/frontpage/assisting-guinea-bissau.html. My emphasis.

2 *Observer*, 9 March 2008.

3 www.un.org/ecosocdev/geninfo/afrec/newrels/organized-crime.html.

4 *Sunday Telegraph*, 10 June 2006.

5 This may be true of the whole of West Africa in relation to the trafficking of drugs. According to Stephen Ellis, the sub-region has had a stake in drug trafficking for more than half a century (Ellis 2009).

6 www.unodc.org/documents/data-and-analysis/Studies/West_Africa_Report_2009.pdf.

7 Including arms, counterfeit products, cigarettes and – most recently – heroin (unpan.org/directory/worldNews/include/displayIssueDetail.asp?issueID=32; www.unodc.org/documents/data-and-analysis/Studies/West_Africa_Report_2009.pdf; www.ndu.edu/press/cocaine-instability-africa.html).

8 www.theafricareport.com/archives2/politics/3295045-west-africas-cocaine-coast.html.

9 www.time.com/time/world/article/0,8599,1904997,00.html.

10 www.limerickleader.ie/8272/Out-of-Africa-the-new.3285301.jp.

11 Partido Africano pela Independencia de Guiné e Cabo Verde.

12 Cabral had initially been associated with an independence party, the MING (Movimento para Independência Nacional da Guiné Portuguesa), along with another dominant liberation leader, Henri Labery, in 1954. Yet differences of opinion about the role and intensity of Guinea's union with Cape Verde resulted in the constitution of two new parties, the FLING (Frente de Luta pela Independência Nacional de Guiné) and the PAIGC. The FLING mistrusted the Cape Verdeans (Cabral's ethnic group) for the role they played in the colonial administration and for their past participation in the slave trade along the Guinea-Bissauian coast.

13 Policia International e de Defesa do Estado were the secret police of the fascist Portuguese regime.

14 The half-brother of independence leader Amilcar Cabral.

15 The outrage created by the executions led to the formation, in exile, of the party Resistência da Guiné-Bissau/Movimento Bafata, currently the second-largest party within the political system.

16 Called the Ninjas by the younger section of the population.

17 On 12 January 1998, to be exact.

18 Casamance, the southern part of Senegal bordering Gambia and Guinea-Bissau, has been the scene of a liberation war waged by the predominantly Diola (Felupe)-based MFDC (Mouvement des Forces Democratique de Casamance) since 1982.

19 *Guinea-Bissau: Human Rights in War and Peace*, Amnesty International, 1999, p. 4.

20 The presence of MFDC troops on the Junta Militar side was denied by its leadership; however, I have multiple eyewitness accounts from both sides of the conflict testifying to the opposite, and have also seen video footage from behind the front lines showing irregular, francophone troops pointed out to me as the MFDC.

21 Finality is arguably relative. The past ten years of incessant coups, coup attempts and purges seem, in retrospect, more like a negative plateau – rather than a ceasing – of conflict.

22 daccess-dds-ny.un.org/doc/
UNDOC/GEN/N06/314/74/PDF/N0631474.
pdf?OpenElement.

23 According to UNODC. For an
economy in which 80 per cent of the official revenue comes from development
assistance, however, this probably does
not say much. Yet the point is that the
cocaine business and the subsequent
flow of money it feeds into the country
have become primary sources of income
for groups such as the police, military
and navy, who have otherwise been paid
irregularly, if at all, and feed off the
country's population in order to gain an
income.

24 www.welt.de/english-news/
article3300063/General-Na-Wai-killed-in-
government-building-attack.html.

25 www.bbc.co.uk/news/10412654.

26 news.bbc.co.uk/2/hi/8610924.stm.

27 *Observer*, 9 March 2008.

28 Having only minor geopolitical
significance, the country is without the
protection, or supervision, of a major geopolitical power. In other words, though
the country has a potentially destabilizing
effect on the sub-region, no one's interests are curbed by targeting Bissau as a
primary point of transition.

29 International Crisis Group, *Africa
Reports*, 142, 2007, p. 9.

30 www.talkingdrugs.org/traffickers-
use-western-africa-to-bring-cocaine-to-
europe.

31 www.irinnews.org/Report.
aspx?ReportId=79507.

32 www.un.org/esa/sustdev/publica-
tions/trends_africa2008/demographic.pdf.

33 *Misti sedu homi di nja cabeza.*

34 *Si abo i homi completo abo i poder di
bu cabeza.*

35 See Fortes (1984: 118) and Meillassoux (1981 [1978]), who similarly argue
that young men cannot fulfil themselves
socially until they marry, but locate this
'social shifter' (see Wulff 1995) as a tool in
the hands of powerful elders.

36 The concept of anomie is somewhat
problematic as there will always be a
relative distance between the ideal and

the real, between the *culturally prescribed*
and the *socially possible*. However, there is
a difference between a schism that can be
socially and culturally incorporated and
one that is so significant that it leads to
conflict.

37 Patrimonialism is obviously not
exploitative as a straightforward exchange
of favours and obligation. However, the
interaction on which patron–client relationships are based is between the holder
of capital and positions (symbolic, political or economic) and a person seeking the
particular resource. The deeper the crisis
or decline, the more the holder is able to
define the terms of exchange in relation
to the demand on the resource(s) s/he
controls (see Eisenstadt and Roninger
1981). Currently in Bissau, the terms of
exchange are extremely unfavourable
for those seeking assistance, and we are
thus seeing youth running errands and
showing servility for the mere possibility
of patronage.

38 www.unodc.org/unodc/en/
frontpage/west-africa-under-attack.html;
www.fao.org/sd/erp/documents2007/YEN-
WA%20Newsletter%20No%206%20-%20
September%202007.pdf; *World Politics
Review*, 26 June 2009.

39 www.unodc.org/pdf/research/
wdr07/WDR_2007.pdf; www.cfr.org/
publication/ 13750/in_west_africa_threat_
of_narcostates.html.

40 www.unodc.org/documents/
data-and-analysis/Studies/West_Africa_
Report_2009.pdf.

References

Bayart, J.-F. (1993) *The State in Africa: The
politics of the belly*, London and New
York: Longman.

Chabal, P. (2002) *A History of Postcolonial
Lusophone Africa*, London: Hurst & Co.

Dunn, K. (2000) 'Tales from the dark side:
Africa's challenge to international
relations theory', *Journal of Third World
Studies*, 17(1): 61–90.

Einarsdottir, J. (2007) 'Partnership and
post-war Guinea-Bissau', *African Journal
of International Affairs*, 10(1/2): 93–112.

Eisenstadt, S. N. and L. Roniger (1981) 'The study of patron–client relations and recent development in sociological theory', in S. N. Eisenstadt and R. Lemarchand (eds), *Political Clientelism, Patronage and Development*, London: Sage.

Ellis, S. (2009) 'West Africa's international drugs trade', *African Affairs*, 108(431): 171–96.

Forrest, J. B. (1992) *Guinea-Bissau. Power, Conflict, and Renewal in a West African Nation*, Boulder, CO: Westview Press.

Fortes, M. (1984) 'Age, generation, and social structure', in D. E. Kertzer and J. Keith (eds), *Age and Anthropological Theory*, Ithaca, NY: Cornell University Press.

Guyer, J. I. (2007) 'Prophecy and the near future: thoughts on macroeconomic, evangelical, and punctuated time', *American Ethnologist*, 34(3): 409–21.

Hinkelammert, F. J. (1993) 'The crisis of socialism and the Third World', *Monthly Review: An Independent Socialist Magazine*, 45(3): 105–14.

Lucht, H. (2008) *Darkness before Daybreak: Existential Reciprocity in the Lives and Livelihoods of Migrant West African Fishermen*, PhD thesis, University of Copenhagen.

Mayer, A. (1966) 'The significance of quasi-groups in the study of complex societies', in M. Banton (ed.), *The Social Anthropology of Complex Societies*, London: Tavistock.

Meillassoux, C. (1981 [1978]) *Maidens, Meal and Money: Capitalism and the domestic community*, Cambridge: Cambridge University Press.

Merton, R. K. (1968 [1949]) *Social Theory and Social Structure*, New York: Free Press.

O'Brien, D. B. C. (1996) 'A lost generation? Youth, identity and state decay in West Africa', in R. P. Werbner and T. Ranger (eds), *Postcolonial Identities in Africa*, London: Zed Books.

Reno, W. (2000) 'Shadow states and the political economy of civil wars', in M. Berdal and D. M. Malone (eds), *Greed and Grievance: Economic Agendas and Civil Wars*, Boulder, CO: Lynne Rienner, pp. 43–68.

Sahlins, M. (1963) 'Poor man, rich man, big-man, chief: political types in Melanesia and Polynesia', *Comparative Studies in Society and History*, 5: 285–303.

— (1974) *Stone Age Economics*, London: Tavistock.

Seekings, J. (1996) 'The lost generation: South Africa's youth problem in the early-1990s', *Transformations*, 29: 103–25.

Vigh, H. E. (2006a [2003]) *Navigating Terrains of War: Youth and soldiering in Guinea Bissau*, New York and Oxford: Berghahn Books.

— (2006b) 'The colour of destruction: on racialization, geno-globality and the social imaginary in Bissau', *Anthropological Theory*, 6(4): 481–500.

Wulff, H. (1995) 'Introduction. Introducing youth culture in its own right: the state of the art and new possibilities', in V. Amit-Talai and H. Wulff (eds), *Youth Cultures: A cross-cultural perspective*, London: Routledge.

7 | Bigmanity and international criminal justice in Sierra Leone

Gerhard Anders

Africa has become a veritable laboratory of international criminal justice. The International Criminal Tribunal for Rwanda (ICTR) was established in 1994 to try the perpetrators of the Rwandan genocide and will soon finish its work. The Special Court for Sierra Leone was set up in 2002 as a new 'hybrid' international tribunal, combining national and international elements, to hold those accountable who 'bear greatest responsibility' for war crimes committed during Sierra Leone's civil war. The establishment of the International Criminal Court (ICC) in 2002 as the first permanent international criminal tribunal has further institutionalized the criminalization of specific modes of African politics and warfare. So far the ICC has concentrated on investigations in Africa and has conducted criminal investigations in Uganda, Congo-Kinshasa, the Central African Republic, Sudan and most recently Kenya. As a consequence, international criminal law has become a major influence on current African political debates and many an African politician can fear an indictment by the ICC.[1]

It is as yet unclear how African politicians and warlords will respond to this development, and opinions are divided between those who argue that criminal investigations thwart peace negotiations and those who hold the view that criminal justice will contribute to more sustainable peace and the rule of law in Africa. This case study from Sierra Leone investigates the various attempts of the leaders of the armed factions to convert their military strength into political office and material security after the end of the civil war. The establishment of the Special Court for Sierra Leone in 2002 added a new element to the region's political topography, and the indictments against twelve leaders of the various armed factions and Charles Taylor, the Liberian president at the time, effectively thwarted the attempts of these men to convert their wartime exploits into political or economic capital during the transition from civil war to post-conflict order.

The chapter will first show the relevance of the concept of the Big Man for the analysis of war crimes trials against African warlords and politicians. The second part investigates in detail the attempts of the leaders of the armed factions to find a place in Sierra Leone's social and political order during the aftermath of the civil war. It clearly shows that national political actors continue to pose a most serious threat to former military Big Men's attempts to convert their military strength into political office, social status and material security. The third part of the chapter describes the trials of the two most important accused who stood trial before the Special Court for Sierra Leone: Sam Hinga Norman, former leader of the pro-government militia Civil Defence Forces (CDF) and cabinet minister between 1996 and 2003, and Charles Taylor, former rebel leader and Liberian president between 1997 and 2003.

Big men in Africanist and Melanesian studies

The Big Man, 'one of the figures that Melanesia has given to world ethnography' (Strathern 1991: 1), is often invoked in both popular discourse and academic debates to describe the distinct style of African politics. Like Bayart's 'politics of the belly', the Big Man is not a purely analytical category but also figures in vernacular ideas about politics and social status such as the *borbor bele*, literally the guy with a belly, in Sierra Leone.[2] Médard (1992) draws most explicitly on the Melanesian Big Man model to analyse African politics.[3] He draws mainly on Sahlins (1963), who first coined the term to distinguish Melanesian pre-contact political systems from the more hierarchical and centralized political systems of Polynesia. According to Médard, these African Big Men operate in a similar fashion, converting economic resources into political authority. However, unlike Sahlins' Big Man, who operates in a stateless society, Médard's Big Man uses his access to the state's resources to enrich himself by operating a system of patronage.

This idea of converting capital from one realm into another in the context of personal rule is salient to the present analysis. Of course, first the concept of the Big Man has to be stripped of its evolutionist undertones before it can be invoked to elucidate the downfall of certain types of military and political leaders in Africa owing to the interventions of international criminal tribunals. This analysis, then, does not constitute an attempt to apply a model developed for one geographical area to another or to establish a comparative axis between Africa and Melanesia, a long-running theme of British social anthropology since the 1950s and 1960s (cf. Barnes 1962; Lambek and Strathern 1998; Strathern 1982); nor does it conceptualize the Big Man as a timeless and abstract model. It rather employs the Big Man as a heuristic device to think about the criminalization of certain modes of African rule and warfare due to the expanding scope of international criminal justice.

Like the Melanesian Big Men, the leaders of the armed factions in Africa tend to be self-made men, entrepreneurs who rely solely on their personal skills as military organizers, political leaders and charismatic orators. Both leaders and followers use war as a resource to benefit from personally, to accumulate prestige and wealth. After the cessation of hostilities they try to convert their gains made during war into material security and social status. The leaders of the armed factions tend to seek political office to consolidate their military exploits. The conversion of military strength into political office, however, has been increasingly thwarted by international criminal tribunals that hold them responsible for war crimes and crimes against humanity committed by their armed factions. This is part of a wider movement driven mainly by Western powers to criminalize certain modes of politics and warfare. This development has added a new dimension to African politics, as the interventions of the ICC in political conflict across the continent demonstrate. The idealistic drive to promote the rule of law and global criminal justice has often been at odds with the need to include rebel leaders in peace talks and entice them to form political parties. Hence, the international criminal courts have often been criticized for hindering peace negotiations.

Médard's analysis does not cover Big Man politics during armed conflict. The modern West African civil wars of the 1990s provided African Big Men with the opportunity to accumulate wealth and prestige. The use of war for accumulation and personal enrichment figures prominently in current debates about the economic dimension of African civil wars. Some authors even argue that the main driving force behind the African wars is the exploitation of natural resources and the leaders' desire to enrich themselves (Collier and Hoeffler 2004), while others emphasize the importance of grievances and political demands for participation and distribution (Fanthorpe 2001; Keen 2005; Richards 2005). In any case, the literature on the topic suggests that combatants tended to perceive membership in an armed group as a possible vehicle for social advancement in the highly clientelistic and gerontocratic structure characterizing West African societies (Ellis 2007: 120–32; Ferme 2001: 159–86; Gberie 2005; Peters 2005; Peters and Richards 1998; Richards 2005; Utas and Jörgel 2008; Vigh 2006).

The combatants emulated the behaviour of their commanders – the Big Men – who were role models for the youth,[4] as Ellis (2007: 286) notes, and some even succeeded in becoming Big Men in their own right. But once their leaders had revoked the reciprocal patron–client relationship during the disarmament and demobilization process, the former combatants no longer felt they owed their former commanders loyalty. Quite the contrary: many felt betrayed by their former leaders, who had abandoned them after they had succeeded in converting their military strength into political office and economic advantage. In fact, after the civil war there was widespread resentment among the rank and file against their former leaders because they felt they had been sacrificed and abandoned in the name of peace and reconciliation.

The Big Man's status is unstable since he can rely only on his personal skills in maintaining his position as a patron who redistributes wealth, thus converting economic capital into political authority. This instability is revealed after the successful conversion of his military strength into political office. Having dissolved their armed groups, the former military leaders became vulnerable to the interventions of the international criminal tribunal. They were unable to return to their previous position of strength and their former followers failed to rally to their support. During the election campaign in 2007, several hundred former combatants had succeeded in finding new patrons. Christensen and Utas (2008) describe how they attached themselves to political parties as bodyguards.

Finding a place: the aftermath of the civil war, 1999–2003

The main argument of this chapter is that international criminal justice is a new influence on the transition from civil war to post-conflict order in Africa. Attempts to convert military strength into political authority and social status may fail owing to the intervention of an international criminal tribunal. But international tribunals are of course by no means the only possible threat to the attempts of leaders of armed factions to find a place in post-conflict society, as the history of the Sierra Leonean conflict and its aftermath aptly illustrate.

The time between the signing of the Lomé peace agreement in June 1999 and the end of the civil war officially declared by President Kabbah in January 2002 was a highly volatile and sometimes violent transition period. During this time the leaders of the armed factions and tens of thousands of combatants tried to find a place for themselves in the post-conflict order. Some of the more educated RUF leaders, the 'political wing' (TRC 2004: 335), and the RUF leader Foday Sankoh joined the government headed by President Kabbah to form a government of national unity, one of the central provisions of the Lomé Agreement. By contrast, the RUF field commanders who controlled large swathes of the north and east of the country were reluctant to disarm the force under their command because they feared losing the leverage it afforded them. At this point, their relationship with the political leadership in Freetown was strained and communications were poor. The political leaders around Foday Sankoh, in turn, had an interest in keeping the armed cadres as an alternative option and political leverage.

The reluctance of the RUF leadership to disarm led to several attacks on UN peacekeepers at the beginning of May 2000, and within a week more than five hundred UN peacekeepers had been taken hostage. President Kabbah and Vice-President Berewa considered the attacks on the peacekeepers and a violent incident during a protest march in Freetown on 8 May 2000 as violations of the Lomé peace agreement. As a consequence, they ordered the arrest of 180 suspected members of the RUF. The TRC report criticizes Kabbah's government for using the violent incident as a pretext to end the RUF's participation in the government. The RUF ministers had already been arrested before the demonstration, on 7 May 2000, effectively dissolving the government of national unity even before the shooting on 8 May 2000. Members of the West Side Boys participated in these arrests, which neutralized the RUF leadership (Utas and Jörgel 2008: 502–3). Foday Sankoh was arrested on 17 May 2000 after having been in hiding for nine days. He had escaped during the shoot-out at his residence on 8 May 2000, during which twenty-two demonstrators and fifteen people in Sankoh's residence were killed (TRC 2004: 331–447).

This turn of events effectively thwarted the attempts by some elements of the RUF leadership to convert their wartime exploits into political office. Most of the field commanders under the leadership of Issa Sesay, the RUF's interim leader since May 2000, eventually agreed to resume disarmament after an agreement was signed between the government and the RUF in May 2001 (ibid.: 461). After the disarmament exercise had been completed in early 2002, many former commanders were able to benefit for the moment from the disarmament, demobilization and reintegration (DDR) programme, including the Special Court's indictees Issa Sesay, Morris Kallon and Augustine Gbao. At the time of their arrest in March 2003, Sesay and Kallon were in the process of setting up fishery projects as part of community development initiatives, while Gbao was running an agricultural development project in his home village in Kenema District.[5] Apparently, Sesay was also in negotiations with the Special Representative of the UN secretary-general, Adeniji, for a scholarship abroad before he was arrested at the Special Court's behest.[6] In Sierra Leone, various leaders of armed factions have used this strategy to go abroad. For instance, the leaders of the National Provisional Ruling Council (NPRC) received scholarships to study in Britain and the USA. Valentine Strasser, the former head of state, studied at the University of Warwick and former NPRC strongman S. A. J. Musa received a UN grant to study at Birmingham University. Compared to the more ambitious attempt to convert the RUF's military strength into government positions after the Lomé Agreement, these efforts to carve out a niche for themselves in the post-conflict order are much more modest. Nevertheless, if they had succeeded in setting up their economic enterprises they would have turned from rebel commanders into respected members of the community with a relatively secure livelihood – not a small achievement in a society characterized by abject poverty and few economic opportunities.

The main objective of the renegade soldiers who had toppled the democratically elected government in May 1997 and formed the Armed Forces Revolutionary Council (AFRC) under the leadership of Major Johnny Paul Koroma was to be reinstated into the Sierra Leone Army (SLA). This was the main motive behind their attack on Freetown in January 1999[7] and continued to be their primary objective after the Lomé Agreement (TRC 2004: 387). The AFRC had not been part of the negotiations in Lomé, and the leaders of the AFRC felt left out and marginalized. As a result, neither Johnny Paul Koroma nor any other AFRC commanders (except for Idrissa Hassan Kamara, aka Leatherboot, who had joined the RUF and formed part of the RUF delegation to Lomé) had been rewarded with positions in the government of national unity agreed upon in Lomé (ibid.: 342). Yet at a previous point, President Kabbah had appointed Johnny Paul Koroma chairman of the Commission for the Consolidation of Peace (CCP), the body charged with overseeing the agreement's implementation, in a bid to 'engage Koroma in the peace process in the interests of national reconciliation' (ibid.: 343–4).

Many former AFRC fighters succeeded in filtering back into the SLA, which was being trained by the British, but many others, including former commanders, were less lucky and were still trying to join the army. The largest organized group of former soldiers were the West Side Boys in the Okra Hills east of Freetown. They consisted of former AFRC combatants who had established a base there after their attack on Freetown was repulsed by Nigerian troops in January 1999.[8] The West Side Boys, under the leadership of Special Court indictee Bazzy Kamara and Hassan Bangura, aka Bombblast, professed allegiance to Johnny Paul Koroma, and after Koroma was appointed chairman of the CCP many of them joined him in Freetown, where they acted as his bodyguards. In May 2000, this group acted as an auxiliary force to government troops when the RUF advanced on Freetown after the violent incident at Sankoh's residence (ibid.: 384–9, 428, 459; Utas and Jörgel 2008: 503).

By attaching themselves to their patron Johnny Paul Koroma and assisting the government against the RUF, the West Side Boys wanted to show their loyalty to Kabbah's government. As a reward for their support they hoped to be reintegrated into the SLA (TRC 2004: 330–31). Koroma's and the West Side Boys' realignment in relation to the government paved the way for the leaders of the West Side Boys to rejoin the army or find employment as Koroma's bodyguards, as Utas and Jörgel (2008: 504) point out. A remnant group stayed in the Okra Hills and abducted a group of British soldiers in late August 2000. This group was largely destroyed during a British commando raid to free the hostages. At least twenty-five fighters were killed and eighteen others, including their leader, Foday Kallay, were arrested.[9]

Koroma had been instrumental in neutralizing the RUF as a political force during the events at the beginning of May 2000 and emerged as a key player in the period between 2000 and 2003. In August 2000 he officially disbanded the AFRC and formed a political party, the Peace and Liberation Party (PLP). He was elected as a member of parliament for Wilberforce in Freetown, an area where many soldiers live, in the general elections of May 2002. In January 2003 some of his followers, including Alex Tamba Brima and Santigie Bobor Kanu, who were later indicted by the Special Court for war crimes, were arrested after a failed attack on an armoury in Freetown. Koroma was able to escape. He allegedly fled to Liberia, where he was killed on the orders of Charles Taylor, according to several prosecution witnesses in the trial against Charles Taylor.

Taylor's defence lawyers have challenged this story and presented evidence contradicting the prosecution witnesses.[10]

Koroma's escape came just weeks before his indictment by the Special Court, and in spite of the rumours of his death he is still considered to be at large. There are many rumours about the reasons for the attack on the armoury and Koroma's subsequent escape, but in any case it seems he might have anticipated his indictment by the Special Court. As the leader of the AFRC he was one of the principal suspects and among the first nine persons indicted by the court on 7 March 2003 (the other eight were Foday Sankoh, Charles Taylor, Sam Bockarie, Alex Tamba Brima, Bazzy Kamara, Issa Sesay, Morris Kallon and Sam Hinga Norman).

By contrast, the leader of the Civil Defence Force (CDF), Sam Hinga Norman, then minister of internal affairs, was very surprised when he was arrested on 10 March 2003 as he never expected to be indicted.[11] The CDF was a pro-government militia that had fought against the rebels of the RUF and the renegade soldiers of the AFRC (Hoffman 2007). The militia was committed to re-establishing the democratically elected government of President Kabbah. CDF was actually an umbrella term for several ethnic militias that had emerged during the early and mid 1990s to defend local communities from attacks by the RUF rebels and marauding government soldiers. The CDF leadership was heavily intertwined with the traditional chiefdom political structures, as Hoffman (ibid.) shows. The CDF mainly consisted of the Mende militias known as Kamajors, an anglicized form of the Mende word for traditional hunter (ibid.: 642). After the Mende-dominated Sierra Leone People's Party (SLPP) won the general elections in 1996, Norman emerged as leader of the Kamajors and was appointed deputy minister of defence. In 2002 the SLPP won the general elections by an overwhelming majority of 70 per cent and Norman was appointed minister of internal affairs. According to some observers, Norman claimed a leadership role in the SLPP and was perceived by President Kabbah, a northerner in a party dominated by Mende from the south-east, as a threat to his interests (Abraham 2003). His arrest in March 2003 effectively thwarted Norman's efforts to play a leading role in national politics, as the following section will show in more detail.

Between 1997 and 2000 the CDF had fought against the RUF and the AFRC and sometimes served as an auxiliary force for the West African peacekeeping force ECOMOG (Economic Community of West African States Monitoring Group). After disarmament in 2002, many of its commanders set up development projects and NGOs or joined local politics as SLPP functionaries. Others sought office in the chiefdom administrations with which the Kamajors and the other ethnic militias had been in close contact during the war. Hoffman notes in this respect that 'rural Mende notables with no direct military role or official rank exerted a great deal of influence over the *kamajors* and the

CDF' (2007: 660). Moinina Fofana, former 'Director of War' of the CDF and the second accused in the trial against CDF leaders, for example, was appointed Chiefdom Speaker, i.e. head of the paramount chief's administration, in his native chiefdom. His attempt to convert his high position in the CDF into political office, however, was thwarted by the prosecutors of the Special Court for Sierra Leone, who ordered his arrest in June 2003. Allieu Kondewa, former Kamajor 'High Priest' and third accused in the CDF trial, had returned to his home area, where he operated as a herbalist in his native district before his arrest in June 2003.

Summarizing the experiences of the various armed factions in the civil war in Sierra Leone, it is clear that the majority of their leaders and commanders strove to convert their military strength into political office or social status after disarmament. Some even succeeded, such as the former AFRC commander Idriss Kamara, aka Leatherboot, who had joined the RUF and served as minister in the short-lived government of unity. He was released soon after his arrest and in 2007 joined the leader of the All People Congress (APC), Ernest Bai Koroma, as head of security during the turbulent election campaign. After Koroma won the elections he appointed Kamara head of the presidential guard. Kamara was by no means the only ex-combatant who joined politicians in the run-up to the 2007 elections, as Christensen and Utas show (2008). Hassan Bangura, aka Bombblast, the former commander of the West Side Boys, joined the so-called task force of the SLPP (ibid.: 12).

The attempts by the RUF political wing to convert the military exploits of the RUF in the government of national unity were not stopped by an outside intervention but rather by President Kabbah, Sam Hinga Norman and Johnny Paul Koroma, who used the violent incidents of May 2000 to remove the members of the RUF from the political stage (TRC 2004: 448–53; Utas and Jörgel 2008: 502–5). The Special Court's establishment was a direct consequence of the developments in May 2000. In June 2000, the government of Sierra Leone sent a letter to the UN secretary-general requesting a special tribunal to try Foday Sankoh and other senior members of the RUF 'for crimes against the people of Sierra Leone and for taking of UN peacekeepers as hostages'.[12] In August 2000 the UN Security Council passed Resolution 1315 authorizing the establishment of the Special Court for Sierra Leone.

The events between 1999 and 2003 show that only a few Big Men were blocked from trying to find a place in post-conflict Sierra Leone through indictment by the Special Court for Sierra Leone. The reason for this is the limited mandate of the court, which was set up to hold accountable those 'bearing greatest responsibility' for war crimes and crimes against humanity committed between 30 November 1996 and 2002 in Sierra Leone. As a consequence, only individuals with command authority faced prosecution before the Special Court. From the very beginning the court was designed to try only a relatively small number of individuals. The number of individuals indicted was never intended to exceed twenty, and amid intense speculation David Crane, the court's first chief prosecutor, issued nine indictments in March 2003, about six months after his arrival in Freetown. In the following months only four further indictments followed, bringing the total number of indictments to thirteen. In 2003 two indictments were withdrawn: that against Foday Sankoh after his death in custody on 29 July 2003 and that against Sam Bockarie after his death had been confirmed in May 2003. The trial against Sam Hinga Norman, Fofana and Kondewa, the alleged leaders of the CDF, commenced in June 2004, and the trial against the three RUF leaders, Sesay, Kallon and Gbao, in July 2004. The trial against three leaders of the AFRC commenced a year later owing to financial constraints.

By contrast, the overwhelming majority of combatants benefited from a general amnesty agreed upon in the Lomé Agreement. Article IX of the agreement granted 'absolute and free pardon and reprieve to all combatants and collaborators in respect of anything done by them in pursuit of their objectives', up to the time of the signing of the agreement. This clause had been a key demand by the RUF delegation during the negotiations in Lomé as they feared prosecution for the crimes they had committed. After the violent events in May 2000, however, the SLPP government led by President Kabbah changed its position on the amnesty and sent a letter requesting the UN's support for a special court 'to try and bring to credible justice those members of the Revolutionary United Front (RUF) and their accomplices responsible for committing crimes against the people of Sierra Leone and for the taking of United Nations peacekeepers as hostages' because the RUF had 'since reneged on that Agreement'. The UN Security Council responded with Resolution 1315, instructing the secretary-general to negotiate an agreement with the government of Sierra Leone to set up the Special Court. Resolution 1315 took notice of a disclaimer added by the Special Representative of the secretary-general to his signature on the Lomé Agreement that the amnesty provision would not apply to 'international crimes of genocide, crimes against humanity, war crimes and other serious violations of international humanitarian law'.[13] Subsequently, this provision was included in the Special Court's statute (Article X) and confirmed by the court's appeals chamber in a decision on defence submissions challenging the court's jurisdiction.[14]

The persons indicted by the Special Court for war crimes and crimes against humanity were not the only former combatants who were arrested and prosecuted. In May 2000, the national authorities arrested several hundred members of the RUF under emergency legislation (Amnesty International US 2001). In March 2002, the public prosecutor's office charged Sankoh and sixty RUF members with the murder of the protesters who were killed during the violent incident on 8 May 2000 at Sankoh's compound in Freetown, while the other detainees were released. In September 2000, a group of West Side Boys was arrested in the wake of a British commando raid to free British soldiers who had been taken hostage. Thirty-eight of them were charged with murder, conspiracy to murder and aggravated robbery. Following the attempted attack on an armoury near Freetown in January 2003 about eighty persons, mainly former members of the AFRC and West Side Boys, were arrested. Among them were Alex Tamba Brima, Bazzy Kamara and Santigie Borbor Kanu, former members of the West Side Boys and the AFRC, who were transferred to the Special Court after they had been indicted for war crimes. The public prosecutor charged seventeen of them with treason (Amnesty International US 2004). In December 2004, the High Court found eleven of them guilty, passing ten death sentences and one of ten years' imprisonment. In December 2008 the Court of Appeals overturned the convictions and acquitted the accused who had been found guilty by the High Court because of lack of evidence. In March 2006 the trials against fifty-seven former members of the RUF and thirty-one former members of the West Side Boys were finally concluded. The High Court acquitted forty-two accused and found twenty-six guilty, passing prison sentences of up to ten years. In the trial against the West Side Boys, twenty-five accused were acquitted and six sentenced to life imprisonment (Amnesty International US 2007). The manner in which the government handled the detentions and trials provoked protests from Amnesty International and other human rights groups (Amnesty International US 2003). It also contributed to a widespread sense of being treated unfairly prevalent among the former members of the RUF, the AFRC and the West Side Boys.

The experience of former leaders of armed factions who attempted to find a place in Sierra Leone's post-conflict society between 1999 and 2003 has been mixed. Part of the leadership of the RUF and the AFRC was caught up in the arrests of hundreds of members of the RUF and the AFRC by the national authorities. Many were held for years without being charged and without access to legal representation. The trials against the members of the RUF, the AFRC and the West Side Boys were characterized by massive violations of fair trial rights and dragged on for more than four years. However, the leadership of the RUF and the AFRC was only marginally affected by these arrests, which were carried out in a chaotic and unfocused manner. Most of the people detained were members of the rank and file, with the notable exceptions of Foday Sankoh, former RUF ministers Mike Lamin and Idriss Kamara, aka Leatherboot, former RUF spokesman Gibril Massaquoi and senior RUF commander Isaac Mongor. Unlike the ordinary combatants, Lamin, Kamara and Massaquoi were soon released from prison. Mongor was released in 2004. Massaquoi and Mongor chose a different strategy to use their pasts to their advantage and appeared as witnesses for the prosecution in trials before the Special Court.[15] In 2003, the Special Court indicted a number of persons who had been comparatively successful in converting their military strength into political influence. Sam Hinga Norman was most successful. He had been deputy defence minister between 1996 and 2002 and was appointed minister of the interior in 2002. Johnny Paul Koroma had also been fairly successful. In a surprising move by Kabbah, he had been appointed chairman of the Commission for the Consolidation of Peace and emerged as a key figure in securing Kabbah's success during the violent phase in May 2000. Then he launched a political career, setting up the PLP and winning a seat in parliament in the 2002 elections by drawing on the strong support he enjoyed from the army. In Norman's case the indictment of the Special Court was directly responsible for the end of his political career. Koroma, on the other hand, was wanted by the national authorities in connection with the failed attack on the armoury in Wellington. The indictment by the Special Court only sealed the end of his political ambitions in Sierra Leone.

In contrast, the former leaders of the RUF had already been marginalized following the events in May 2000. Sankoh was already facing trial in the High Court but Sesay, Kallon and Gbao had avoided the wave of arrests by the national authorities in 2000. They had given up on acquiring political authority and had their sights set on a much more realistic and modest objective. Like tens of thousands of former combatants, they participated in the disarmament, demobilization and reintegration process, but it would be wrong to underestimate their achievement. Unlike thousands of their former followers they were in charge of development projects and were important Big Men in the communities where they ran the projects financed by the DDR programme. Becoming a respected community leader with a regular income is not a small achievement in Sierra Leone, where the overwhelming majority of the population lives in abject poverty. Their indictments by the Special Court, however, thwarted their attempts to become Big Men in their communities. The same applies to Fofana, who was appointed chiefdom speaker, and Kondewa, who continued to practise as a healer. With regard to the three former leaders of the AFRC who stood trial before the Special Court, it is more difficult to assess their ambitions, but it seems that they had hoped for the protection of their patron, Johnny Paul Koroma, in their attempts to find a place in the new political order.

Norman and Taylor – African Big Men in the dock

In Freetown the court conducted three trials, all of which are now concluded. Except for Norman, who died in custody, and Taylor, who is still awaiting the verdict of his trial at the time of writing, all accused were found guilty and are serving their prison sentences in Rwanda. The trial against the three remaining leaders of the RUF began in July 2004. The prosecution concluded its case in August 2006 and the defence at the end of June 2008. On 25 February 2009 the trial chamber found Sesay and Kallon guilty on sixteen counts and Gbao on fourteen counts. Sesay was sentenced to fifty-two years, Kallon to forty years and Gbao to twenty-five years. In a decision delivered on 26 October, the appeals chamber upheld these convictions. The trial against three leaders of the AFRC, Alex Tamba Brima (first accused), Brima Bazzy Kamara (second accused) and Santigie Borbor Kanu (third accused), started in March 2005. The prosecution concluded its case in November 2005 after calling fifty-nine witnesses. The defence opened its case in June 2006 and concluded its case at the end of October 2006 after calling eighty-seven witnesses. The trial chamber delivered the judgement on 20 June 2007 and convicted the accused on eleven counts. Brima was sentenced to fifty years, Kamara to forty-five years and Kanu to fifty years. The convictions were upheld by the court's appeals chamber. The trial against three CDF leaders, Sam Hinga Norman (first accused), Moinina Fofana (second accused) and Allieu Kondewa (third accused), began in June 2004. The prosecution concluded its case in July 2005 after calling seventy-five witnesses. The defence called forty-four witnesses and concluded its case in October 2006. The first accused died while undergoing medical treatment in Dakar, Senegal, on 22 February 2007. On 2 August 2007 the trial chamber found the remaining two accused guilty on four counts and sentenced them to six and eight years including time served. The appeals chamber overturned these convictions and sentenced Fofana to fifteen years and Kondewa to twenty years.

This section concentrates on Sam Hinga Norman and Charles Taylor, the two most senior Big Men who stood trial before the Special Court. They were most successful in converting military strength into political influence. Prior to Taylor's arrest, Norman was the most senior Big Man, so to speak, charged with war crimes before the Special Court. He was much older than the other accused and had already achieved a social position commanding considerable respect. Sam Hinga Norman was born in 1940 and belonged to the lower echelons of the Mende political elite in the system of indirect rule established by the British colonial power after declaring south-east Sierra Leone a protectorate in 1896. After independence in 1961 the Mende-speaking areas in south-east Sierra Leone aligned themselves with the SLPP, the ruling party until 1967. Norman joined the army in 1959 and served until 1972, ascending to the rank of captain. In 1966 he obtained a diploma from an officers' school in Britain. In 1967 he held the rank of lieutenant and served as aide-de-camp to the governor general. In this capacity he was involved in a coup led by the force commander, also a Mende. He was arrested after a counter-coup in 1968, tried for treason and imprisoned until 1972. After his release he went to Liberia, where he remained in exile until the political climate changed. In 1989 Norman returned to Sierra Leone and was appointed Chiefdom Speaker of Valunia Chiefdom. In 1994 he became regent chief in Jamaia Bongor chiefdom in eastern Sierra Leone.[16] When the attacks of the RUF intensified during the early 1990s Norman became involved in organizing the Kamajor self-defence groups, soon adopting a leadership role owing to his skills as chiefdom politician and military officer.

The 1996 elections were won by the SLPP and the new president, Kabbah, appointed Norman deputy minister of defence, and in this capacity Norman continued to direct the CDF forces against the RUF and later the AFRC. After the end of the war Kabbah was re-elected president and appointed Norman minister of the interior. At the time Norman was a national icon, considered by many to be a hero who defended the country against the RUF and the AFRC. It was generally believed that Norman, who had a strained relationship with President Kabbah, had set his sights on the presidency, but his political career ended abruptly when the prosecutor of the Special Court ordered his arrest.

Charles Taylor, former warlord and president of Liberia between 1997 and 2003, is the most prominent accused facing trial before the Special Court. He has an elite social background and enjoyed tertiary education in the USA. His family is descended from the Americo-Liberians, freed slaves from the USA who settled on the coast of Liberia in the nineteenth century. At first it appeared that Taylor had successfully converted his military strength into political authority when he was elected president in the 1997 elections, but he soon came under growing international and domestic pressure. International pressure on Taylor had been building up since 1999 (Utas 2003: 251–8). The USA and Britain accused him of supporting the rebels in Sierra Leone, exchanging arms for diamonds (Smillie et al. 2000) and of ties with criminal gangs and terrorist networks. By June 2003 two rebel groups, Liberians United for Reconciliation for Democracy (LURD) and Movement for Democracy in Liberia (MODEL), had pushed back Taylor's forces and laid siege to Monrovia, where Taylor was holed up. When the prosecutor of the Special Court, David Crane, unsealed the indictment against Taylor in June 2003 while Taylor was attending a peace conference in Accra, the pressure on him increased. According to representatives of ECOWAS (Economic Community of West African States), this move derailed the peace process in Liberia and prolonged the fighting and suffering of the civilian population. Taylor finally stepped down in August 2003 and left the country for Nigeria, where he had been offered asylum.

It is important to note that he was not indicted for war crimes committed in Liberia but for war crimes committed in Sierra Leone by the rebels of the RUF and the AFRC, whom he was accused of supporting – especially by the USA and Britain.[17] In March 2006 the pressure on Nigeria's President Obasanjo had become too great and he finally declared that Taylor would be extradited. Taylor tried to leave Nigeria but was arrested on the Nigerian–Cameroonian border.[18] At first he was detained in Freetown, but owing to security concerns was moved to the Netherlands in June 2006, where the trial was to be held. Taylor still commanded considerable respect in Liberia and Sierra Leone, and it was feared that a trial in Freetown could affect the stability of both countries. Like Norman, Taylor is a Big Man who had already successfully converted his military strength into political office, but his violent past became a liability when the prosecutor of the Special Court charged him with war crimes and crimes against humanity.

Taylor's trial commenced in June 2004 in The Hague but was delayed after he dismissed the lawyer representing him because of the inadequate resources made available for his defence. A new defence team with much more substantial financial resources was subsequently appointed by the court's registrar and the trial recommenced in January 2008. The prosecution called ninety-one witnesses, including thirty-one insider witnesses, and concluded its case in February 2009. The defence case started in July 2009 and called Taylor as first witness. Taylor spent more than five months on the witness stand. After he concluded his testimony in February 2010 the defence called twenty witnesses and closed its case in September 2010.

Initially, both Norman and Taylor followed the standard response of all accused in political trials since Charles I: they pleaded not guilty and refused to recognize the court's authority to put them on trial. This is a common strategy of accused persons and was attempted to varying degrees by all accused before the Special Court. However, drawing on their elite background and their skills as senior Big Men, Norman and Taylor mounted the most sustained attacks on the court's legitimacy.

Norman had denied the court's jurisdiction since his arrest in March 2003 and had even briefly undertaken a hunger strike as a publicity stunt in May 2003. At the beginning of the first two trials in 2004, Norman was the most prominent accused in the court's custody. For many Sierra Leoneans he was a national hero rather than a war criminal, and his arrest provoked many critical comments across the country. To general surprise, Norman dismissed his defence team at the opening of the trial on 3 June 2004 and demanded to represent himself. The bench granted Norman the right to self-representation and appointed stand-by counsel to assist him in his defence. But a few weeks into the trial Norman decided to boycott the proceedings because he argued that his fair trial rights were being violated when witnesses were allowed to testify anonymously, shielded from the public. In response, the judges revoked Norman's right to self-representation and appointed a lawyer to represent him.

After the prosecutors had read their opening statement, charging him with eight counts of war crimes and crimes against humanity, Norman decided to make his defence statement. This was highly unusual because the defence would normally make its statement after the end of the prosecution's case and before calling witnesses to testify in defence of the accused. In his brief opening statement on 15 June 2004, which lasted barely ten minutes, he presented himself as an honourable and loyal warrior who spoke the truth and did not need to rely on lawyers' tricks. Norman argued that 'there is or are no charge or charges legally placed before this chamber against me', because according to him the Special Court was unconstitutional and lacked jurisdiction. The public gallery was packed with his supporters, who responded to this statement with cheers. The judges warned them that 'this is not a political forum' and adjourned for thirty minutes. After this interruption the trial resumed. During the first weeks the public gallery was packed with Norman's supporters. Throughout his trial he tried to exercise his influence,[19] but popular support quickly waned after the initial flurry of excitement. The trial was a tedious and protracted affair and had not been concluded when Norman died while undergoing surgery at a military hospital in Senegal in February 2007 (SCSL 2007).

During the first weeks of the trial Norman was defiant. He continued to deny the court's legitimacy but also participated in cross-examining prosecution witnesses. To this end the court provided him with extra resources, including a computer and a printer.[20] During the cross-examination of witnesses he knew personally, he tried to introduce the patron–client relationship that once existed between them into the courtroom. For example, on 15 June 2004 he cross-examined the first prosecution witness who testified under protective measures. Norman addressed the witness by his Mende nickname, which indicated the witness's lower social rank, and reminded him that 'you and I know each other very well'. When asked by Norman whether he was good or bad, the witness conceded that 'when you were chief you didn't do bad'.[21] Norman followed the same tactic during the cross-examination of another witness, whom he addressed as his son. This witness had belonged to a group of children freed from the RUF. Norman had paid his school fees and went to great lengths to try to invoke the personal relationship that existed between them in the courtroom, but the judges soon interrupted him.[22] In this context, it is noteworthy that Norman conducted his defence in English, a clear marker of his high social status as a person who 'knows book', the vernacular for an educated person. These attempts at instantiating his position as Big Man or 'papay' in the courtroom were thwarted by the judges, who repeatedly interrupted him and ordered him to limit himself to questions directly related to the charges in the indictment. By September 2004 Norman was so frustrated that he refused to participate further in courtroom proceedings and left his defence to his lawyers.

In January 2006 Norman returned to the courtroom in a last attempt to get his perspective across. He took the witness stand as first defence witness and testified for several days. In his testimony he presented himself as a loyal soldier who only sought to re-establish the elected government and said he did not have a hidden, criminal agenda. During his testimony, the public gallery was almost filled to capacity for the first time since the beginning of the trial in June 2004. Most of the onlookers were Norman's followers who had come to support their former leader. General interest was much lower than in 2004, however, and most people in Freetown did not seem to take much interest in the trial. It was clear that Norman's appeal to the general public was on the wane owing to his detention and inability to intervene in national politics.

The same can be observed with regard to Charles Taylor, who epitomizes the African Big Man in the dock. Many analysts considered Taylor to be the personification of a new generation of African political entrepreneurs who straddled the spheres of the formal and the informal, the legitimate and the criminal, to create a 'shadow state' (Reno 1998). Taylor's arrest in March 2006 marked his complete removal from Liberia's political landscape. As a consequence, his influence in Liberia has been steadily declining, but he still commands considerable respect, as I learned during fieldwork in 2008 and 2009. Both his advocates and opponents agree that he would be a formidable contender for the presidency if he were to return to Liberia.

Taylor also challenged the Special Court's jurisdiction, arguing that he had enjoyed immunity as head of state when the indictment against him was unsealed in June 2003. His lawyer filed an appeal in September 2003, but on 31 May 2004 the appeals chamber ruled that immunity was not a bar to prosecution when the indictment was unsealed and that he could therefore be tried for war crimes and crimes against humanity. Although the appeals chamber rejected his motion, Taylor has been more successful in dealing with the legal challenge than Norman was. Norman had been out of his depth after his arrest and clearly underestimated the magnitude of the trial against him. He did not anticipate the sheer length of the trial and his defence had run out of steam just three months after it had begun, by the end of September 2004, when he decided to boycott the courtroom proceedings. Norman had been taken by complete surprise as he was arrested on the day his indictment was unsealed and could not plan ahead for his defence before his arrest. By contrast, Taylor had three years to observe proceedings before the Special Court. Consequently, he was in a position to assess the scale of the trials and to be prepared.

Taylor proved much more adept than Norman at achieving his aims. During his initial appearance on 3 April 2006 he was declared indigent, which meant that the court would pay for his defence. Taylor's lawyer at the time, Karim Khan, had complained of insufficient resources for the defence team but his demands were rejected by the court's registrar. After months of haggling that culminated in his boycott of the opening of the trial and the dismissal of Karim Khan at a dramatic hearing on 4 June 2007, the court grudgingly gave in to his demands for more experienced defence counsel and allocated US$100,000 per month to his defence team.[23] The new lawyer, Courtenay Griffiths, was an experienced criminal lawyer and Queen's Counsel from Britain, and was aided by two co-counsels, three assistants and three investigators. The trial chamber granted the new defence team extra time to prepare its case and the trial started in January 2008. Between January 2008 and February 2009 the prosecution called ninety-one witnesses, including about thirty insiders who testified about the alleged links between Taylor and the rebels in Sierra Leone.

The defence case started in July 2009 and Taylor was called as the first defence witness. He testified for twelve weeks and finished his testimony in November 2009. Cross-examination lasted eight weeks and was concluded on 5 February 2010.[24] Then followed a few days of re-examination by Taylor's defence counsel. Including cross-examination and re-examination, Taylor spent a total of more than five months on the witness stand, an unprecedented feat in the history of international criminal justice.

Taylor started his testimony with a flat denial of the charges and accused the prosecution of conducting a campaign of 'disinformation, misinformation, lies, rumours'.[25] With a booming voice, resembling that of a preacher, he denied being a rapist, murderer or terrorist. He visibly enjoyed the opportunity to tell his side of the story after more than three years in detention and having listened to ninety-one prosecution witnesses who spread a 'whole pack of lies', as he charged on 15 July 2009. Even here, in the sterile courtroom on the outskirts of The Hague, it was possible to observe the modus operandi of a charismatic African Big Man. Upon taking the witness stand he immediately set out to forge personal relationships with all participants in a courtroom drama with himself as central character. With a keen eye for hierarchies he addressed the judges by name, adopting a deferential and respectful demeanour towards them, often stating that he merely wanted to 'help' them find the truth. In contrast, towards the prosecutors conducting the cross-examination Taylor adopted an arrogant attitude, accusing them of misleading the judges and refusing to take orders from them. Nothing escaped his attention and he was always abreast of developments in and outside the courtroom. For example, on the day Chief Prosecutor Stephen Rapp was confirmed as the new US Ambassador-at-Large for War Crimes, Taylor congratulated him on his new appointment.

During the twelve weeks of his testimony, Taylor told an alternative story in which he appeared as the victim of an Anglo-American conspiracy. According to Taylor, the Special Court's chief prosecutors, all of whom happen to be American or British nationals,[26] acted as proxies on orders from the US government to permanently remove him from the Liberian political arena and install Ellen Johnson Sirleaf as president in his stead. He presented himself as a trained economist who had only the best intentions for his country. Taylor praised Gaddafi as a fellow pan-Africanist and in his narrative it was only pan-Africanism which had brought him to Libya, where his group had received training.

He dwelt at length on his presidency between 1997 and 2003, presenting himself as a regional peace broker who had nothing to gain by supporting rebels in neighbouring Sierra Leone and who was simply too busy 'running a government'.[27] Courtenay Griffiths quoted extensively from speeches and communiqués to show that Taylor was a legitimate head of state elected in free and fair elections who respected the rule of law. When testifying about the first years of his presidency, Taylor was visibly proud to have rubbed shoulders with world leaders. At times he would create the atmosphere of an intimate gathering where a former head of state granted his listeners a glimpse into the internal workings of international diplomacy usually veiled from the public's gaze.

During his weeks on the witness stand, Taylor dissected the testimony of key witnesses who had testified against him during the previous year. In a highly sophisticated duet with his lawyer he succeeded extremely well in showing inconsistencies and gaps in the testimony of these witnesses, leaving very little of the sweeping indictment intact. In general, he was highly adept at getting and holding the attention of those present in the courtroom – the judges, lawyers and court staff as well as the occasional journalist or observer in the public gallery. Everything in his performance was deployed for maximum effect, including his impeccable double-breasted suits and the flowing traditional African gowns he sported during the last days of his testimony in February 2010.

In painting the image of a statesman, highly educated and striving for the economic development of his country, Taylor tried to show that he was not very different from politicians in the West, even though he operated in a different political and cultural environment in which dependency and the colonial legacy loomed large. He framed Liberia in terms of the patrimonial logic of the post-colonial era when he referred to the country 'as America's little farm, its little brother in Africa', which had been neglected by the USA.[28] He often referred to other African heads of states as 'brothers' and to prosecution witnesses as uneducated 'boys' who were too low in social status to have interacted with him. Acting as a somewhat paternalistic cultural expert, Taylor explained this to the bench in terms of the African custom of referring to each other in terms of fictive kinship. He also invoked this patrimonial logic when explaining the phenomenon of child soldiers. He argued that orphans and displaced children attached themselves to commanders and armed factions, who looked after their well-being but did not use them as soldiers.

According to an often-cited truism, everyone is equal before the law regardless of status or wealth, but it is equally true that social status, education and eloquence make a great difference in courtroom performance. Norman quickly had to admit defeat after he had decided to represent himself. He had simply underestimated the scale of the trial against him and was not able to engage the court with a challenge that matched the prosecution. By contrast,

Taylor used the pressure created by the dismissal of his lawyer to get a new defence team with considerably more resources at its disposal. Norman failed to introduce his status as Big Man into the courtroom and because of his lack of legal expertise the judges took the opportunity to discipline him, asserting their authority instead. His strategy of invoking social hierarchies would have worked in the setting of a Sierra Leonean court but he failed to lift it to the international stage. Taylor, on the other hand, left the defence to his lawyers and opted strategically to testify in his own defence. Drawing on his skills as an orator, he succeeded in telling his side of the story to the judges and audiences in the West and Africa. Whether this will be enough to convince the judges of his innocence, however, is a different issue and remains to be seen. The judgement in the trial against Taylor is expected early in 2012.

Conclusions

Since its advent in the 1990s international criminal justice has become a factor in African politics, but it is important to note that it constitutes merely one in a whole range of influences shaping the political arena during the aftermath of civil war in Africa today, as the experience of former senior members of the various armed factions in Sierra Leone clearly shows. Only a tiny fraction of former commanders and leaders were indicted by the Special Court for Sierra Leone owing to the court's limited mandate to try only those 'bearing greatest responsibility' for war crimes and crimes against humanity. Their attempts to convert their military exploits into political office and material security in the post-conflict political and social order were effectively thwarted by the indictments against them. For most former combatants and commanders, however, the Special Court constituted only a relatively minor aspect of the intense power struggles in the national political arena, where the ability to forge new alliances and draw on existing social networks was more important than the spectacle of global justice in Freetown. During the turbulent reconfiguration of the country's political arena, triggered by the violent incidents in 2000, the former leaders of the RUF and the AFRC were politically marginalized, and several of them were arrested by the national authorities. Hundreds of members of the RUF, the AFRC and the West Side Boys were detained. Some died in custody, while many spent years in prison without being charged. Most prisoners were eventually released without being charged, but more than a hundred faced trial before the national courts, and thirty-two were convicted on charges including murder, conspiracy to murder and treason. Against the backdrop of only thirteen individuals indicted by the Special Court, four of whom were already in the custody of the national authorities before they were transferred to the Special Court, these numbers bear testimony to the importance of national political actors and networks in spite of the establishment of a highly visible international criminal tribunal.

The Special Court's impact was most palpable for the most powerful Big Men, who had succeeded in converting their wartime exploits into high political office and were effectively beyond the reach of their rivals in the national political arena. Norman, then minister of the interior and widely hailed as the defender of the democratically elected government, was utterly surprised when he was arrested at the behest of the Special Court in March 2003. During his trial he tried to defend himself by drawing on the cultural capital of a Sierra Leonean Big Man, but he was not able either to mount a serious defence or to use the stage provided by the trial to his advantage. Taylor fared much better because he was able to transcend the cultural limits of Bigmanity. Of course, it is difficult to assess whether they would have been successful in converting their military exploits into political authority if they had not been indicted by the Special Court's prosecutor. At least with regard to Norman, it seems highly likely that he would have continued to play an important role in the national political arena if he had not been indicted. It is more difficult to assess the influence of the indictment against Charles Taylor. It is hotly debated whether the indictment further isolated Taylor and thus contributed to his departure or actually thwarted the peace negotiations in Accra and thus prolonged the bloody battle for Monrovia. In any case, the indictment and the subsequent diplomatic pressure on the Nigerian government to surrender Taylor prevented him from returning to Liberia as he had promised on the day of his departure, when he announced, 'God willing, I will be back.'[29] African political and military leaders will find it more difficult to keep promises like this in the future, and there are already signs that Big Men across Africa are adapting to the growing influence of the ICC, but the Sierra Leonean case also underlines the continued importance of the national political arena.

Notes

1 On the debate about transitional justice in Uganda, see Allen (2006). On the Special Court for Sierra Leone, see Kelsall (2009). On the ICC, see Clarke (2009). For general studies on the politics of international criminal justice, see Bass (2000), Clark and Kaufman (2009), Chuter (2003), Dembour and Kelly (2007), Peskin (2008) and Simpson (2007).

2 See also Ferme (2001: 159–86) on the concept of big people, *kpako*, among the Mende, the dominant ethnic group in the south-east of Sierra Leone.

3 But see the short piece by Trouwborst (1986).

4 It should be noted that a few women served as senior commanders in the Revolutionary United Front (RUF) in Sierra Leone and the National Patriotic Front of Liberia (NPFL). These women would have adopted the status of 'mammy', the female equivalent of a 'papay' in Krio. Female combatants were used by most of the armed groups, especially the RUF and the NPFL. See, e.g., Gberie (2005) on Sierra Leone and Ellis (2007: 113) and Utas (2005) on Liberia.

5 News reports of 12 March 2003, www.sierra-leone.org/archives/slnews0303.html, accessed on 2 August 2010.

6 Interview with David Crane in Utrecht, 11 June 2008

7 Trial Chamber Judgement, 20 June 2007, *Prosecutor v. Brima, Kamara and Kanu*, SCSL-04-16-T-613: 72.

8 Ibid.: 79.

9 *Daily Telegraph*, 17 September 2000, www.telegraph.co.uk/news/worldnews/europe/1355809/Fire-fight-in-the-Occra-Hills.html.

10 Special Court for Sierra Leone, *Defense Motion for Disclosure of Exculpatory Information relating to DCT-032*, 24 September 2010.

11 Interview with David Crane in Utrecht, 11 June 2008.

12 Letter dated 9 August 2000 from the Permanent Representative of Sierra Leone to the UN, addressed to the president of the Security Council, S/2000/786: Annex.

13 Report of the Secretary-General on the establishment of a Special Court for Sierra Leone, S/2000/915: 5.

14 SCSL Appeals Chamber Decision on Challenge to Jurisdiction: Lomé Accord Amnesty, 13 March 2004.

15 Mongor and Massaquoi benefited from a generous witness protection programme. The court's Witness and Victim Service had spent US$4,800 over the period of a year to support Mongor and his family. The court paid for Mongor's rent, food, medical and childcare expenses, mobile telephones, top-up cards for the mobile phones and travel within Sierra Leone. During cross-examination Mongor claimed that these payments covered only expenses he would have paid out of his own pocket (transcripts, Taylor trial, 7 April 2008). It is unlikely, however, that Mongor would have been in a position to spend US$4,800 a year. For anyone familiar with the situation in Sierra Leone, a total payment of US$4,800 over a year suggests a much more luxurious lifestyle than that enjoyed by the overwhelming majority of the population. The court's support was doubtless a highly attractive offer for Mongor, who had spent four years in Pademba Road Central Prison without being charged.

16 A regent chief acts as paramount chief after the death of a paramount chief until a new paramount chief takes office.

17 The USA and Britain had been promoting sanctions against Liberia since 1999, accusing Taylor of ties to Gaddafi, terrorist networks and criminal gangs. He allegedly supported the RUF and the AFRC in neighbouring Sierra Leone to gain control over the diamond-mining areas in the east. This is also at the heart of the indictment against him.

18 According to the prosecution, Taylor tried to escape when he was arrested at a border post in northern Nigeria. Taylor disputed this in his testimony on 10 November 2009, claiming he had merely wanted to visit his 'friend' Idriss Deby, president of Chad.

19 During his trial Norman made three attempts to intervene directly in national politics. In October 2003 the TRC filed a request with the Special Court to take a public statement from Sam Hinga Norman. As it turned out, Norman had asked the TRC to make a public statement to bring his side of the story to a wider audience. The court's registrar refused, citing concerns that Norman might incriminate himself in a public statement. This led to a heated exchange between the court and the TRC. Eventually the registrar offered to allow the members of the commission to visit Norman at the court's detention centre and take a statement there, but this was found inadequate by the TRC (Nesbitt 2007). In 2005 Norman wanted to participate in elections for the SLPP leadership but again his request was denied, and in 2006 he reportedly left the SLPP and joined another party. But while the first intervention in 2005 stirred the national political landscape the second intervention was barely noticed. By the end of 2006 Norman's trial did not generate much interest in Sierra Leone and even in the south and east of the country he was no longer a force to be reckoned with.

20 Decision on Request by Samuel Hinga Norman for Additional Resources to Prepare his Defence, 23 June 2004.

21 Transcripts, CDF trial, 15 June 2004.

22 Ibid.

23 A considerable increase compared to the US$25,000 per month paid to the other defence teams in Freetown, who all considered this amount to be insufficient (personal communication with members of defence teams).

24 Interrupted by a recess of one month between 11 December 2009 and 10 January 2010.

25 Transcripts, Taylor trial, 14 July 2009.

26 David Crane, a former Pentagon lawyer, served as the court's first chief prosecutor between 2002 and 2005. Sir Desmond de Silva, a British barrister, who had served as the court's deputy prosecutor, succeeded Crane. He was succeeded in December 2006 by Stephen Rapp, an American lawyer and former US attorney in Iowa, who had served as prosecutor at the ICTR. In September 2009 Rapp was appointed US Ambassador-at-Large for War Crimes and was succeeded by Brenda Hollis, a former US Air Force lawyer who had served as trial attorney in the Tadic trial conducted before the International Criminal Tribunal for the Former Yugoslavia and as expert for the Special Court's Office of the Prosecutor.

27 Transcripts, Taylor trial, 27 July 2009.

28 Ibid., 14 July 2009.

29 'Charles Taylor leaves Liberia', *Time*, 11 August 2003, www.time.com/time/world/article/0,8599,474987,00.html, accessed 8 December 2010.

References

Abraham, A. (2003) 'Sierra Leone: post-conflict transition or business as usual?', *News from the Nordic Africa Institute*, 3, October.

Allen, T. (2006) *Trial Justice: The international criminal court and the Lord's Resistance Army*, London: Zed Books.

Amnesty International US (2001) *Annual Report: Sierra Leone*.

— (2003) *Annual Report: Sierra Leone*.

— (2004) *Annual Report: Sierra Leone*.

— (2007) *Annual Report: Sierra Leone*.

Barnes, J. A. (1962) 'African models in the New Guinea highlands', *Man*, 62: 5–9.

Bass, G. (2000) *Stay the Hand of Vengeance: The politics of war crimes tribunals*, Princeton, NJ: Princeton University Press.

Bayart, J.-F. (1993) *The State in Africa: The politics of the belly*, London and New York: Longman.

Christensen, M. and M. Utas (2008) 'Mercenaries of democracy: the "politricks" of remobilized combatants in the 2007 general elections, Sierra Leone', *African Affairs*, 107: 515–39.

Chuter, D. (2003) *War Crimes: Confronting atrocity in the modern world*, Boulder, CO: Lynne Rienner.

Clark, P. and Z. D. Kaufman (eds) (2009) *After Genocide: Transitional justice, post-conflict reconstruction and reconciliation in Rwanda and beyond*, London: Hurst.

Clarke, K. M. (2009) *Fictions of Justice: The International Criminal Court and the challenges of legal pluralism in sub-Sahara Africa*, Cambridge: Cambridge University Press.

Collier, P. and A. Hoeffler (2004) 'Greed and grievance in civil war', *Oxford Economic Papers*, 56(4): 563–95.

Crane, D. (2005) 'Dancing with the devil: prosecuting West Africa's warlords', *Case Western Reserve Journal of International Law*, 37(1).

Dembour, M. B. and T. Kelly (eds) (2007) *Paths to International Justice: Social and legal perspectives*, Cambridge: Cambridge University Press.

Ellis, S. (2007) *The Mask of Anarchy: The destruction of Liberia and the religious dimension of an African civil war*, 2nd edn, London: Hurst.

Ferme, M. (2001) *The Underneath of Things: Violence, history, and the everyday in Sierra Leone*, Berkeley: University of California Press.

Fanthorpe, R. (2001) 'Neither citizen nor subject? "Lumpen" agency and the legacy of native administration in Sierra Leone', *African Affairs*, 100: 363–86.

Gberie, L. (2005) *A Dirty War in West Africa: The RUF and the destruction of Sierra Leone*, Bloomington: Indiana University Press.

Godelier, M. and M. Strathern (eds) (1991)

Big Men and Great Men: Personifications of power in Melanesia, Cambridge: Cambridge University Press.

Hoffman, D. (2007) 'The meaning of a militia: understanding the Civil Defence Forces of Sierra Leone', *African Affairs*, 106(425): 639–62.

Keen, D. (2005) *Conflict and Collusion in Sierra Leone*, New York: Palgrave.

Kelsall, T. (2009) *Culture under Cross-examination: International justice and the Special Court for Sierra Leone*, Cambridge: Cambridge University Press.

Lambek, M. and A. Strathern (eds) (1998) *Bodies and Persons: Comparative perspectives from Africa and Melanesia*, Cambridge: Cambridge University Press.

Médard, J.-F. (1992) 'Le "big man" en Afrique: esquisse d'analyse du politicien entrepreneur', *L'Année Sociologique*, 42: 167–92.

Nesbitt, M. (2007) 'Lessons from the Sam Hinga Norman decision of the Special Court for Sierra Leone: how trials and truth commissions can co-exist', *German Law Journal*, 8(10): 977–1014.

Peskin, V. (2008) *International Justice in Rwanda and the Balkans: Virtual trials and the struggle for state cooperation*, Cambridge: Cambridge University Press.

Peters, K. (2005) 'Reintegrating young combatants in Sierra Leone: accommodating indigenous and wartime value systems', in J. Abbink and I. van Kessel (eds), *Vanguard or Vandals: Youth, politics and conflict*, Leiden: Brill, pp. 267–96.

Peters, K. and P. Richards (1998) ;Why we fight: voices of under-age youth combatants in Sierra Leone', *Africa*, 68(2): 183–210.

Richards, P. (2005) 'Green Book millenarians? The Sierra Leone war within the perspective of an anthropology of religion', in N. Kastfelt (ed.), *Religion and African Civil Wars*, London: Hurst, pp. 119–44.

Reno, W. (1998) *Warlord Politics and African States*, Boulder, CO: Lynne Rienner.

Sahlins, M. (1963) 'Poor man, rich man, big-man, chief: political types in Mela-nesia and Polynesia', *Comparative Studies in Society and History*, 5: 285–303.

Simpson, G. (2007) *Law, War and Crime*, Cambridge: Polity Press.

Smillie, I., L. Gberie and R. Hazleton (2000) *The Heart of the Matter: Sierra Leone, diamonds and human security*, Ottawa: Partnership Africa Canada.

Special Court for Sierra Leone (2007) 'Autopsy shows Sam Hinga Norman died of natural causes', Press release, 28 March.

Strathern, A. (1982) 'Two waves of African models in the New Guinea Highlands', in A. Strathern (ed.), *Inequality in New Guinea Highlands Societies*, Cambridge: Cambridge University Press.

Strathern, M. (1991) 'Introduction', in M. Godelier and M. Strathern (eds), *Big Men and Great Men: Personifications of power in Melanesia*, Cambridge: Cambridge University Press, pp. 1–4.

TRC (Sierra Leone Truth and Reconciliation Commission) (2004) *Witness to Truth: Report of the Sierra Leone Truth and Reconciliation Commission*, vol. 3A, Accra: GPL Press.

Trouwborst, A. (1986) 'The "big man": a Melanesian model in Africa', in M. van Bakel, R. Hagesteijn and P. van de Velde (eds), *Private Politics: A multi-disciplinary approach to 'big-man' systems*, Leiden: Brill, pp. 48–53.

Utas, M. (2003) *Sweet Battlefields: Youth and the Liberian civil war*, Uppsala: Uppsala University Dissertations in Cultural Anthropology.

— (2005) 'Agency of victims: young women in the Liberian civil war', in F. de Boeck and A. Honwana (eds), *Makers and Breakers: Children and youth as emerging categories in postcolonial Africa*, Oxford: James Currey, pp. 53–80.

Utas, M. and M. Jörgel (2008) 'The West Side Boys: military navigation in the Sierra Leone civil war', *Journal of Modern African Studies*, 46: 487–511.

Vigh, H. (2006) *Navigating Terrains of War: Youth and soldiering in Guinea Bissau*, New York and Oxford: Berghahn Books.

8 | Big Man bargaining in African conflicts

Ilmari Käihkö

The Cold War had profound effects on African states. Generous external financial and political backing, chiefly from the two superpowers, enabled African leaders to create and maintain far-ranging patronage networks. However, as the Cold War ended and external patronage resources drastically declined at a time of falling prices for raw materials, on which many African countries were extremely economically dependent, these networks became a source of direct instability. As a consequence, fewer resources were available to maintain patronage networks (Richards 1996). As the formal state was in fact built upon informal flows of resources, such changes involving weakening state capacity following the first post-independence decades, and the post-Cold War liberalization and democratization opened the political space to new actors who challenged incumbent leaders: rival politicians, armed insurgents and a multitude of informal actors rose to challenge regimes in power (Young 2004). Coping with these new challengers was often an impossible task for African leaders. State weakness became obvious as over half of the African states experienced internal conflict or political crises and turbulence during the 1990s (ibid.: 46). New kinds of survival strategies were obviously needed. This became especially clear as the international costs of resorting to coercive measures rose: violence can result in losing foreign aid or in international disapproval. But, perhaps more importantly, forcing rivals into submission was often beyond the capacity of weakened African states. Power-sharing and co-option in the form of integration and appeasement therefore became a more appropriate way of dealing with competition.

Peace-building literature has traditionally investigated power-sharing from another angle. As Hoddie and Hartzell write, '[t]he unambiguous intent behind the creation of power-sharing and power-dividing institutions is to limit the capacity of any one party to the conflict to dominate the postwar state and use its advantaged position to harm the interests or survival of its rivals' (Hoddie and Hartzell 2003: 306). This chapter will show that this intent does not materialize in all such agreements. While many agreements do achieve this goal of limiting the use of power, regimes can also use power-sharing as a tool to do exactly the opposite and in fact strengthen their hold on power. Similarly, power-sharing has been described as levelling 'power relations between contending groups' (Jarstad 2008: 113). While this evening out may in fact occur, power-sharing can also be used to neutralize opponents and to diminish them as challengers. It is especially the kind of power-sharing that materialized as a form of co-option that is investigated in this chapter.

Co-option is often used in situations of political or military deadlock. In practice it has often resulted in elite appeasement, in which challengers are accommodated with access to power. Both insurgents and incumbents can seek negotiations in times of weakness, or in order to buy time to reinforce their position vis-à-vis their enemies. A good example of this is the peace negotiations that involved different Sierra Leonean governments and the Revolutionary United Front (RUF) during the eleven-year insurgency. Both the government and the RUF repeatedly engaged in and disengaged from negotiations before the insurgents finally accepted a power-sharing agreement in Abuja in 2000–01 (Richards and Vincent 2008: 83–7). Power-sharing is never the first choice of participants, who would obviously prefer victory and non-compromise instead of negotiation. Consequently, power-sharing can result in weakened and politically rather fractured governments that have to struggle to survive, let alone govern.

It is not only African leaders who have resorted to power-sharing, as it has also become an increasingly common instrument in internationally mediated peace. It is therefore no wonder that the subject of power-sharing has been the subject of much research, especially from democratization and peace-building perspectives (e.g. Jarstad and Sisk 2008). This chapter seeks first to explore this practice as a strategy for elite survival, and secondly to concentrate on the consequences of power-sharing in the African context. The research for this chapter is thematic in the sense that it contains empirical material for illustrative purposes only. It is also acknowledged that generalization across societies is problematic yet still potentially rewarding.

The structure of this chapter incorporates binary oppositions of formal and informal political realities. The formal part will concentrate on the African state and its institutions. The (in)security of African states is investigated as a result of fragmented society as well as a weakness of formal state institutions. These two are also the main concerns of the formal political context taken up in this chapter. On the other hand, the more informal political context discussed in the chapter includes informalization and personalization in the sense that power concentrates around individuals and their informal networks. Networks, however, are closely connected to formal politics. Personalization and networks set the focus of this chapter on elites and their relations. In a later part of the chapter strategies of co-option are investigated in this wider context, which combines the formal and the informal. Co-option strategies can be both formal and informal, as they build on the informal but can be formalized as power-sharing agreements. Power-sharing often takes the form of public contracts that are the result of international mediation or other international pressure. But power-sharing may also be an internal process and part of informalized politics. In such cases, the informal is equally or more important than the formal.

As will be seen, the binary oppositions of formal and informal are far from watertight. A considerable overlap exists, making it a priority to explore the formal and the informal together in order to gain a more complete picture of the reality. This priority also forms the question this chapter seeks to answer: *What are the results of power-sharing if the reality is informal?* In trying to answer this question this chapter builds on the research of Utas, who has argued that informal networks are the key to explaining contemporary African politics (Jörgel and Utas 2007; and further developed in the introduction to this book).

The structure of this chapter serves as a criticism of the distinct categorization of African political analysis. In fact, the chapter encourages looking beyond state façades and into the more informal venues, where much of the real politics take place. It is argued that this approach is a clear breach with previous research in the power-sharing literature. While the importance of institutions has formerly been investigated and acknowledged, the emphasis has been on *formal* institutions instead of informal ones (see, e.g., Hoddie and Hartzell 2003). Additionally, the focus in this literature has usually been the political party as a more or less unitary actor. The aim of this chapter is to discuss and problematize a number of expectations within previous power-sharing and peace-building literature, which has concentrated on the formal and neglected the more context-specific informal. This chapter argues that it is impossible to fully understand African political realities without considering the role of the informal.

As will be shown, many of the basic concepts and assumptions that are commonly used to describe and interpret African politics can be criticized for not taking into account the less obvious informal. For instance, informal networks penetrate political parties, and can factionalize them. This factionalization explains why members of the ruling government can actually support opposition, even involving the military. It is also possible that while officials change, networks behind them stay the same. This in turn explains why many power-sharing agreements result in little concrete policy change. Power-sharing can also cause a similar situation, whereby the real power is still retained by an all-powerful president and the informal business continues as usual. After presenting the African formal and informal contexts in which power-sharing and co-option are practised, I will discuss a number of different issues that have to do with these practices: the role of the 'opposition', the effects of power-sharing on statehood, the questionable concept of legitimacy, violence as business as usual, and possible problems as well as irrelevance of power-sharing.

The formal reality and the uncertain survival of leaders

The United Nations' stipulated international system has been instrumental in preserving the boundaries and unity of African states since independence. This has partly caused the main contemporary security threats to these states to be of an internal rather than external nature. Reflecting this, most contemporary conflicts in Africa are intra-state instead of interstate. Even so, there are usually strong international aspects present in these conflicts. But the opposite also holds true, as even insurgents that are used as proxies for foreign interests tend to have some underlying local-based reasons for violence. Many African states combine weak formal institutions with socially fragmented societies. This combination makes it difficult to define 'national security', as there are a number of actors and groups seeking security from a plethora of mostly internal threats. As Job argues, it becomes necessary to differentiate the state from the regime, meaning a smaller group of elites that control the state machinery (1992). Similarly, it has been argued that African states can in many cases be identified with their main owners (Clapham 1996); in the highly centralized political systems in many African countries, it is the regime or the head of state that steers the state. It is often (but not always, as exemplified by the situation of Somalia's Transitional Federal Government (TFG)) the regime which has the best means among local actors to provide security, but also income for itself, through its control of the state resources and privileges. Regimes most notably control the security institutions such as the police and military, but also have sovereign rights to natural resources, fishing waters and tariffs.

The Somali example, however, also shows how symmetry is often closer to reality than asymmetry in comparisons of African militaries and insurgents. This is an obvious sign and result of the weakness of formal state institutions, especially the coercive ones. Symmetry often leads to protracted conflict and military stalemates, as neither side is powerful enough to defeat the other through the use of force. Political stalemates after fraudulent elections having resulted in internal violence show not only the weakness of the coercive instruments at hand but also the dependency on foreign political and diplomatic legitimacy. The need to uphold legitimacy in the eyes of foreign countries places more restrictions on the options available to already weak African governments when fighting insurgents. In other words, a purely military solution to political opponents is often thus not plausible.

The most obvious overall result of the weak formal state institutions is the inability of the state to provide services, including security for its citizens. In a society based on access to elite networks the state apparatus controlled by the regime may even become the main threat to its citizens, as regimes themselves feel threatened and constantly at risk owing to lack of popular support (Job 1992). While regimes do usually have a certain number of extremely loyal supporters, attitudes of the majority of the population towards them can range from indifferent to hostile. The relationship between citizenry and regime can thus become one of mutual fear and suspicion, as each constitutes the gravest threat to the other. This in turn leads state and other actors to seek different security arrangements with a variety of actors, including private security, foreign peacekeepers or militaries, militias and rebel groups. Voids of all kinds have a tendency to be filled, which causes a number of new actors to emerge. States naturally have advantages when it comes to gathering resources: they have the legal and sovereign right not only to collect taxes and tariffs but also to enter into agreements with other governments and private entrepreneurs. Income gathered by these various means then enters the state coffers, where its division is ultimately decided by politicians in government positions. As African state budgets are typically quite meagre, the chance to manipulate markets for the benefit of the elite may become an equally important way to raise resources (Reno 2002). While actors during the Cold War were able to exploit rivalries between the United States and the Soviet Union, it is now especially the opposition which has to look for new ways to finance its activities. This has especially led to increased efforts to find domestic resources that can be exploited – often illegally – leading to complex situations in which it becomes difficult to differentiate between political purposes and private gain (Keen 1998).

But even if they control state assets and resources, regimes may reasonably feel threatened: the survival of a regime in a weak state is far from certain, even if it has the state machinery to support itself. The first priority of any regime is to increase its own security and chances of survival, as this is required to initiate other policies. As Job argues (1992), this context makes the use of already scarce resources to buy weapons highly rational, even if these rarely pay for themselves in terms of direct income. The insecurity felt by political elites forces them to be preoccupied with the short term, no doubt at the cost of the long term. Immediate survival does not always go together with continuity. In fact, many of these decisions can return to haunt the elites in the future and worsen already difficult situations. This is a point that is evident in many power-sharing agreements, and to which we will return later.

The need to separate regime from state is the first sign of the necessity to employ a more informal approach to investigating the African state. In fact, it has been suggested that it is often 'the informal that pursues and carries the formal forward' (Jörgel and Utas 2007: 99). While the informal no doubt influences the formal in any other political context as well, this is more pronounced in Africa than anywhere else. Here, formal structures are exploited by the informal to gather resources that are used to secure power over informal networks. This is why we now turn to look at the underlying political context and 'formal informalities'.

The informal reality and the survival of leaders

Much has been written about the political context and culture of post-colonial African states. What follows here will build on concepts of clientelism, informalization and reciprocity, as well as concentrate on personalization and network aspects. Following Utas's introduction in this book, it will be argued that without considering the informal aspects our understanding of the African political reality will remain seriously limited.

Reciprocity and networks Understanding the modern African state requires an understanding of the underlying sociocultural logic driving society. This in turn calls for a historical perspective. Here I refer most to the recent work of Chabal, who argues that before colonialism Africans were not subjects in the same sense as they came to be during colonialism and after. Obligations that had usually been 'fluid and flexible' became concrete as the colonial state 'sought to exercise absolute, unaccountable and largely arbitrary power over virtually every aspect of people's lives' (Chabal 2009: 88). As argued by Mbembe, the post-colony consists of a number of public spaces which the post-colonial subjects can negotiate through the use of several identities, making absolute domination impossible (1992). This was also the case in the colonial state, which was never able to exert absolute control over its subjects; but then again, it did not have to. The main interest of the colonial powers was resource extraction, and the system of governance accordingly had limited interest when it came to accountability (Chabal 2009). Before colonialism, chiefs could be held accountable as they lived among their people and were often selected. In the worst cases, their subjects could remove or even kill them. While the relationship between rulers and clients was based on 'an asymmetrical relation of reciprocity' or 'on a well-understood system of unequal exchange' (ibid.: 93), this relationship was deemed legitimate as long as expectations of reciprocity were met. A major change came with the imposition of the colonial state, which distorted this relationship in order to exploit it for governance. Chiefs became little more than intermediaries and clients of the colonial administrations, most of them being paid by the colonial states. Their authority gone, the chiefs based their rule mainly on clientelism, which in the end became instrumental, losing what little was left of the moral and ethical dimensions it had once possessed (ibid.: 93–5). With the advent of independence, the new national elites found themselves in a situation in which they had little choice but to seek legitimacy through similar means. This effectively reduced incentives to offer public goods instead of private ones. Chabal equates accountability with reciprocity, which makes the way elites had come to power irrelevant (ibid.: 51–2). What truly mattered was how they met this requirement for reciprocity, which became the crucial method of rule (ibid.: 55–6). Facing the uncertainties of the post-colony, 'subjects ... aspired to being clients, since they sought to secure relations of reciprocity with the new political chiefs' (ibid.: 92). These kinds of relationships are important in an informal reality, as independence leaves people without the protection and mediation of Big Men against other people or unexpected misfortune (Bledsoe 1990). But even if these relationships are based on inequality and obviously favour Big Men, they are equally important for both parties and go well beyond economic considerations, as '[t]he social being of an individual is measured by the people with whom one has relations of dependence or for whom one acts as a patron. The capacity to maintain a social network ... is the mark of status' (Hoffman 2007: 651). This reciprocity forms the basis of co-option: rivals are not only bought off, but also become clients in the networks of Big Men. In addition to material obligations, this relationship also carries social and even moral expectations, which have to be considered.

Clientelistic politics Patrimonialism as the underlying logic of governance supposes privatization of public power, making it difficult to distinguish public from private. State affairs became quintessentially personal (Médard 1982). This privatization of the public has several consequences. As political power becomes personified, the state is turned over into private possession. Only those in power have access to state resources. Politics therefore becomes a zero-sum game in which some have and some have not. This often leads to authoritarianism, as those with power seek to protect their power from others. Colonialism makes the state the largest concentration of power and resources available. This makes controlling the state an imperative, as it is the 'chief instrument of patrimonialism' (Chabal and Daloz 1999: 9). Resources in this sense imply not only financial control but also control over military, diplomatic and educational affairs (Bayart 1993). There is also a considerable social element involved, as political posts are allocated to clients. This in effect makes society and state visibly inseparable; the African state is therefore not formally institutionalized, and the state is exploited in order to further private gains. Even if financial considerations are important, political power should not be equated only with them. Political contestation is about not only the distribution of power and wealth but also the representation of identities. What's more, power and wealth also constitute the means and not only the end, as resources are used to generate support and to gain status and respect (Chabal and Daloz 1999). This is also evident in the discussion of networks above. Clientelism also imbues forms of governance: it connects peripheries to a centre, and most importantly, is used to co-opt opponents (Médard 1982), who in turn can continue to have clients of their own. Reciprocity in the form of mutual support thus forms an important function for African politics and has, at least to an extent, been a factor behind the (in)stability of different states.[1] Whether elites have much choice to engage in clientelistic governance or not, clientelism ultimately favours elites and creates a disincentive to change the system (Chabal and Daloz 1999). And as long as the formal institutions of a state cannot provide for its citizens, ordinary people have to rely on alternative solutions, such as clientelism and different kinds of networks, in order to survive. This same dilemma is evident in politics. Formal bureaucratic institutions resemble façades more than Western ideals (ibid.), but these façades are kept from crumbling because they obviously serve the interests of certain people both within and outside these states. As these formal institutions are too weak to exercise efficient governance, it devolves upon the informal institutions, defined by Collins as 'the unwritten rules, norms and social conventions that are rooted in shared expectations and reinforced by social sanctions' (2004: 231), and more specifically the informal networks, where the real political processes take place.

Big Men and networks

Following Utas, the terms *Big Man* and *network* are preferred to patron–client relations or (neo-)patrimonialism, which are concepts often used to describe aspects of the African political culture. One reason for this preference is that these contested concepts have been the objects of criticism. Another is the fact that these networks are qualitatively different from those usually described as (neo-)patrimonial ones. Jörgel and Utas use Big Man and network as 'open relational concepts facilitating fluid descriptions of social settings' (2007: 13). Their networks are both vertical and horizontal, with Big Men constituting nodes in the networks (ibid.). As patron–client networks have commonly been described as hierarchical and vertical,[2] these networks must be understood as constituting a wider concept as they also include the horizontal dimension in the form of peers. Additionally, unlike what is expected in patron–client relationships, clients in these networks belong to different networks and therefore have several Big Men, who in their turn have their own Big Men. Not only can actors therefore be both Big Men and followers in different networks at the same time, these networks can also be very unlike each other. The interlinked nature of economy and politics makes political actors particularly interesting, but it is also state officials who are increasingly able to join and dominate other networks because of their privileged access to resources (Utas, introduction to this volume).

Networks are essentially about personal relations between individuals. This means that resources moved within networks are of an individual rather than a collective nature. Networks are not stable but fluid, in the sense that actors in them can change or be replaced (ibid.). It must equally be stressed that the nodes are individuals and are therefore not fixed in the same way as official positions are, for example. Finally, the reciprocity in these networks is based on the notion of 'being for' someone or having 'wealth in people', respectively, forming a more complicated relationship than that found in Western patron–client categories (Utas 2008: 2–3). Both Big Men and followers thus have reciprocal obligations to each other. In the case of Big Men, they have to continuously channel the resources they extract from their position to their followers (ibid.: 7). In return, followers are expected to be loyal and to perform demanded services for their Big Men (Jörgel and Utas 2007). This culture of Big Men and networks coexists with seemingly bureaucratic states; Big Men hold positions on every level from the presidency to the lowest public servant, using the salaries and benefits they gain to feed their networks, which extend to other parts of society. These networks can also have international dimensions, which become obvious if it is kept in mind that even presidents are not such Big (wo)Men when compared internationally to other statesmen or even heads of multinational corporations. Africa is still at the margin in international relations. While Big (wo)Men may nationally be on top of networks, this might not be the case internationally.

Personified politics

Political culture based on networks has profound effects on politics as praxis. As networks are individual-based, and as Big Men strive to control networks that are as strong as possible, so do politicians compete over followers in a political environment characterized by personification. Personification and the authoritarian tendencies that accompany it often lead to a narrowing of political space. Elites attempt to safeguard the power they have acquired against political opponents; politics is a 'winner takes all' reality. This is precisely why opposition parties often appear to be dormant between elections. There are usually few benefits to be gained from remaining in the opposition. Not being able to access state resources especially affects the opposition's ability to maintain their networks. This also explains why these dormant parties become active again when elections approach: elections offer a way to gain access to the sought-after state power.

As formal social organizations, parties *sans* the networks controlled by their leaders can therefore be argued as being close to irrelevant. They instead constitute vehicles around which these networks can be built. A narrowing of political space has made violent conflict and insurgency not only viable, but sometimes the only realistic way to seek political power. This underlines the famous line by Clausewitz that warfare is merely a continuation of politics. Warlordism thus becomes nothing more than 'a form of person-centered politics' (ibid.: 88). In this sense the differences between political parties and insurgencies can be smaller than could be expected, especially as in many countries insurgencies are led by former incumbents or other elites. Insurgency can thus become the main form of opposition for incumbent leaders, implying that any unarmed alternative lacks the power to challenge the regime. This naturally poses problems for democracy – and is a symptom of problems in a democracy.

Integration into Big Men networks is one way to cope with opposition, whether these challengers come in military, political or economic form. Describing patronage, Reno has argued that it is 'an adequate strategy for pacifying demanding interest groups and co-ordinating diverse and often antagonistic power brokers' (2006: 47). This practice, it is argued, gains a concrete and official form in power-sharing agreements, which constitute a growing trend in African politics. While war constitutes an instrument of conflict resolution (Holsti 1996), power-sharing agreements usually attain only conflict management. Still, they have become the preferred low-cost Western instrument for this purpose since the Cold War.[3] They are also investigated as a survival strategy for African incumbents and therefore from the perspective of the political context described above.

Co-option and the formal and informal strategies of elite survival

Reciprocity of network relations basically means that Big Men can trade resources such as money and goods, but also protection, legal favours and work, for support. Similar arrangements also make it possible for regimes to deal with competitive elements by integrating them into the official state structure. This co-option can be either a straightforward act to neutralize threats to power, or part of a broader strategy of 'divide and conquer'. Co-option can therefore be used to divide challengers and to hinder attempts to join forces. In this case it is enough to buy out certain key figures instead of all of them. Teshome has argued that the fragmentation of opposition is the main reason behind largely unsuccessful attempts by oppositions to gain power through elections in Africa (2009). The same is true for armed opposition as well, as shown clearly in the Battle of N'Djamena in February 2008. After reaching the Chadian capital, the insurgency groups were unable to decide who should replace President Déby, a disagreement that considerably hampered cooperation between the rebel forces and at least contributed to their failure to take power. In other words, agreement between opposition groups may extend to the fact that they want power to change hands, but they have difficulty reaching consensus about the new head of state owing to personalized politics and the privatized nature of power. This makes it a challenge to build coalitions, which according to Teshome are the only realistic way for opposition to challenge incumbents (ibid.). Fragmentation may therefore obviously be beneficial to incumbents, who can employ co-option to further divide challengers. Power-sharing is the most visible top-level way of achieving this goal. Ultimately, the incumbents may also have little choice in the first place, as discussed above. As a consequence of the weak coercive instruments, the co-option may become a strategy of necessity rather than of choice.

Power-sharing is arguably very different when used with non-violent political opponents than with violent opponents in conflict or post-conflict settings.[4] This is no doubt true, as societies and institutions have probably been affected by the conflict in many ways. One of the effects of prolonged violent conflict is mutual distrust between partners, which makes peace negotiations much more difficult (Hartzell and Hoddie 2007). Nevertheless, power-sharing and co-option have been used as strategies in both settings, and the differences between the results of power-sharing in these settings are arguably smaller on the informal than on the formal side. Finally, as has been noted above, even warlordism is about person-centred politics: considering that it is often the same elite who turn from politics to insurgency only to again return to politics, the differences between various kinds of opposition are smaller than can be expected. Perhaps the best example of such a figure is Ellen Johnson Sirleaf, president of Liberia, who returned to the country as a politician in the mid-1980s and supported then-insurgent Charles Taylor in the first Liberian civil war, before finally becoming head of state after the second Liberian civil war. Taylor has a similar background, and therefore also falls into this category.

Dimensions of power-sharing

Power-sharing is usually thought to include four dimensions: politics, economics, security and territory. According to an often-quoted argument of Hartzell and Hoddie, the more dimensions that are included in the power-sharing agreement, the more lasting the peace (ibid.). This thesis is somewhat problematic in the African context, as all dimensions have not been equally relevant in the African power-sharing agreements.

As shown above, the economic and political spheres are difficult to separate in the African context. There has historically been little secession in Africa (Englebert and Hummel 2005), which makes the territorial dimension less important in this context. The security dimension is a more valid concern, considering the fact that many rebel commanders have been content to be integrated into the national armed forces – for instance, in Chad, Mali, Niger and DRC (cf. Böås and De Koning's chapters in this book). Of course, this kind of integration can be very beneficial to the integrated elites, as integration should provide employment possibilities for rank-and-file combatants while at the same time binding these followers to their Big Men, who have given them these employment opportunities in the first place. I propose that power-sharing is first and foremost elite appeasement that usually takes the form of political or security power-sharing. While much of the previous power-sharing literature investigates political parties as actors, the personalization of politics and networks as suggested above arguably makes an elite-oriented perspective necessary for looking at conflicts and conflict resolution in Africa.

With these elites and Big Men come their networks, which are not necessarily limited to party structures.

Power-sharing and 'opposition'

Co-option can be an effective but costly strategy. Power and offices are handed out according to personal criteria instead of professional merits. New office-holders can turn into new Big Men or strengthen their existing status in their networks, drawing resources from their new office and contributing little to increasing the effectiveness of the state institutions. While this is not necessarily anything new, the worst-case scenario entails that the new office-holders continue to support the opposition, effectively employing state resources against the state itself. Menkhaus describes the transitional government in Mogadishu (TNG) in Somalia in 2000–2003, arguing that there were

> many political and business leaders [that] supported the declaration of a transitional government, but not the actual establishment of a functional state. Instead they approached the TNG as an opportunity to create a 'paper state' – one that would attract foreign aid, which they could then divert, but not one that could become powerful enough to enforce laws and regulations that might threaten their economic and political interests. (Menkhaus 2007: 96–7)

Efforts to keep the TNG chronically weak but alive – or these leaders' support of the armed opposition – might explain why the contemporary TFG possibly supplies more arms and ammunition to their opponents than foreign actors do (United Nations Security Council 2010). It is also evident that there was cooperation between military forces of the junta of the National Provisional Ruling Council (NPRC) and the Revolutionary United Front in Sierra Leone in the early and mid 1990s amid an insurgency. At times the military cooperated with the insurgents against civilians, while different groups within the military might even have fought against each other (Keen 2005). From such examples it is clear that there is no unified government side, but rather a number of different and not infrequently conflicting agendas to the extent of an opposition on the inside. The difference with fragmentation is that here the factionalization is internal and does not split the organizations. The case is not necessarily different on the insurgent side either. Hirsch describes the differing agendas within the RUF after the Abidjan peace agreement. The four RUF negotiators supported implementing the agreement while Fodah Sankoh, the leader of the RUF, apparently wanted to use this lull in fighting to rearm before continuing the war. The negotiators were later arrested by the leadership of the RUF after they had declared a coup against Sankoh (Hirsch 2001). One faction within the RUF was also allegedly helping their enemies, the Kamajor militias, because they did not approve of the RUF-induced violence against civilians (Keen 2005).

This makes the concept of opposition problematic if used in the traditional Western sense. As discussed above, opposition mainly exists before and during elections. At other times formal political opposition is usually non-existent. Even further, as political opposition ordinarily refers to groups antagonistic to the government, this concept becomes meaningless if parts of the government effectively oppose it and constitute an opposition on the inside. Instead, I suggest that political parties constitute vehicles for networks built around Big Men and are ultimately little more than the exterior and formal façades of different informal networks competing for political power. These networks can, and in effect do, penetrate governments as well as constitute factions in larger parties because of the existence of different Big Men. It therefore becomes difficult to consider political parties as unitary actors, as is usually done. I agree with Reno when he writes that the wider political context has to be understood before considering the role of political opposition. He suggests that factions 'marked the end of the more centralized patronage network' (1998: 158), which would then make them a consequence of weak networks and actors attempting to become either new Big Men or members of new networks. Political parties are therefore an excellent example of how the informal drives the formal in contemporary African politics.

Results of co-option: changes to statehood

Co-option can be either the result of outside pressure or a more local solution. The cases of Zimbabwe and Kenya in 2008 and 2009, respectively, serve as examples of power-sharing after outside pressure. An example of an internal co-option is the unofficial networks of the military and economic elite that exploited natural resources in the Democratic Republic of the Congo (DRC) after the Ugandan intervention in 1998. These networks did not become a threat to the regime, as they were later assimilated into the Ugandan state machinery (Vlassenroot and Perrot, this volume). The same kind of logic can be found in Sierra Leone, where state officials see the integration of militarized networks into the official structure as a way to increase stability in the country (Christensen, this volume). Co-option is also a common political practice, as it is possible to include parts of the opposition in the government or the ruling party, which then leaves no viable alternative to the regime in the political field and therefore further reduces the available political space. This has happened in Mobutu's Zaire as well as in Zimbabwe. Dorman calls these practices 'inclusionary tactics', which result in 'dominant-party systems … [which] are also notable for increasing centralisation and presidentialism' (Dorman 2006: 1091–2). This practice can also operate the other way around, as incumbents can create 'phony opposition parties' that are then bribed into compliance (Teshome 2009: 3). While posing as an alternative to the regime, these parties are in fact controlled by the incumbents and can be used to strengthen the image of the regime against its political challengers. Co-option is one way to bring these parties under control. A similar phenomenon associated with insurgencies is the division of opposing forces, which as a result become politically and militarily weaker. Both the Chadian and Sudanese governments were involved in an attempt to decrease the influence of the Justice and Equality Movement (JEM) in Darfur by co-opting a group called the National Movement for Reform and Development (NMRD) (Johnston 2007). This kind of co-option that does not lead to political power-sharing is in many ways less problematic, as it does not involve the façades of the state. However fragile these façades may be, most power is still concentrated around them and it is therefore here that the fiercest conflicts are fought.

It may be that the weakness of an already fragmented state requires the incorporation of competitive elements of both formal and informal natures. But at the same time, it may further fragment the state as well as erode its capacities. For instance, the upkeep of networks is based on state resources, the stripping of which has a negative effect on state functions. It is especially under negative economic circumstances that this practice can become more serious. As leaders cling to power they invest more in networks, while at the same time undermining the long-term economic well-being of the state (Reno 1995). According to Reno, this weakening of formal state institutions can be intentional. Rulers opt to use outside actors instead of state bureaucracies in order to deny resources to internal rivals. This is made possible by the network-based governance, as the upkeep of most formal state bureaucracies is unnecessary (Reno 1998). The importance of the informal makes the formal both irrelevant to governance and potentially threatening to rulers. Rival networks may grow stronger as they access state resources, strengthening them to the point where they could challenge rulers. An avoidance of this formal state weakness can be sought as long as sovereignty is upheld, as it makes it possible to maintain legal connections to external actors (ibid.).

At worst, the result of weakened bureaucracies is state failure. Keen observes that this is what happened in Sierra Leone: as the economy of the country was affected by falling commodity prices and increasing donor demands for democratization, the state institutions ceased to function and the government disappeared. Governance failed as state employees and even paramount chiefs were not paid (Keen 2005). From the network perspective, this breakdown of reciprocity was far more important than the dysfunctional formal state institutions. Then again, these negative effects might not materialize. According to Clapham, it would be better to speak of 'degrees of statehood', statehood as a relative concept, instead of absolutes of weak and strong states (1998: 143, 153). The African state has never met the criteria of the Weberian ideal in the first place. On the contrary, the state has remained one actor among others, and the strengthening of other kinds of actors is not necessarily harmful to the state (Tull 2003). From this perspective the formal state is already weak and lacks control over many areas within society, and does not necessarily become weaker by incorporating competing elements but can instead potentially become stronger. Such an expectation seems to exist among some, at any rate, as the power-sharing agreements advocated by international actors arguably constitute a reconstruction effort in which competing elements are integrated into the state, after which elections and financial aid are expected to result in the state being reformed back into a workable one (Englebert and Tull 2008). Of course, the worst-case scenario described above sees this aid going to enemies of the state, which would not be good for future stability.

Co-option can also lead to the rise of new challengers seeking power, which in turn may need to be accommodated. If power-sharing is mainly inter-elite accommodation, it may be expected that the wider underlying causes of conflict have not been solved. This means that opportunities for new challengers remain in place. For instance, combatants may be more than willing to continue armed struggle if mobilized by new elites, bringing new challengers to demand their share. The co-option itself can result in fragmentation, as elements within the opposition are unhappy with arrangements that have failed to benefit them. It is also likely that loosely or poorly organized opposition groups are more vulnerable to fragmentation, creating a potential problem for many power-sharing agreements. Similarly, a fragmented opposition may be more difficult to come to terms with in peace negotiations, as has happened in the case of Darfur, for instance. Finally, some scholars specializing in Africa have been sceptical about power-sharing as an instrument of conflict resolution. For instance, Spears has argued that power-sharing is yet 'relatively unproven as a means of conflict resolution' and that there are 'relatively few examples of successful, formalised power sharing in Africa which warrant its advocacy' (Spears 2000: 106). A more recent critic of this practice is Mehler, who has specifically investigated power-sharing in Africa (2008). Spears blames much of the failure on the lack of genuine desire and commitment to peace, which are both required to achieve successful power-sharing (Spears 2000). Co-option can therefore constitute a vicious circle with long-range consequences, as parties are never fully satisfied with having to share power with others.

A questionable concept of legitimacy

The legitimacy of political actors has often been tied to their accountability before their constituencies. This same reasoning can also be applied to armed opposition. Power-sharing leads to situations in which insurgents are inserted into political posts without any democratic credentials in an attempt to tame challengers with political or military power. This naturally poses problems for accountability, as citizens have little choice in who gains power over them. Power-sharing tends to be the result of inter-elite negotiations whereby constituencies have little say in the matter. While this lack of account-ability definitely poses a valid concern, investigations of this kind of political accountability fail to consider the whole picture: accountability is as much based on informal institutions as it should be on formal ones.

As we have seen, all Big Men get their legitimacy from meeting their ob-ligations of reciprocity to their followers. Reciprocity is especially difficult for opposition groups: Big Men can uphold their networks only as long as they continue to channel resources to their followers. In other words, without networks, opposition would not be able to maintain political power. With-out political power, opposition cannot indefinitely continue to support their networks unless they find other resources, such as foreign backing or raw materials to sell to international partners in their networks. As reciprocity is the main instrument of legitimacy, the traditional notion of regime or state legitimacy often discussed in literature is of questionable value. This seems to be the case in Ghana, where accountability is increasingly regarded as be-ing based on the division of personalized goods by office-holders (Lindberg 2010). Similarly, ethnicity (or rather identity) can have other practical political outcomes than is sometimes expected: for instance, the ministerial position has been considered to serve the interests of co-ethnics and to exploit this position to favour home districts and their residents (Arriola 2009). In real-ity most networks are multiethnic, and other ethnicities can be favoured in order to win their voters, thus reversing the expectation. An example of this is the recent practice in Sierra Leone, where infrastructure was enhanced in the north when a southern-biased government was in power, and vice versa.[5]

Violence as a manoeuvre

If violence is required for a conflict to receive international attention, it is possible that it then becomes a political manoeuvre on its own. Violence has become both a way to ward off electoral defeat by incumbents and for opposi-tion to challenge the result of rigged elections. The use of violence also brings an elevating effect, in the sense that previously insignificant groups come to be recognized as actors. This may unfortunately be an indication that violence will become a more common tool in the future, especially as actors notice that international interest is usually limited until a certain amount of violence occurs. Some armed groups have already made the same observation, which has possibly led to increased violence against civilians in internal conflicts (Hoffman 2004). Similarly, the Darfurian NMRD mentioned above tried to force its way to the negotiating table by violently targeting African Union peacekeep-ers and international organizations (Johnston 2007). Jarstad has also shown that the inclusion of some warring groups may encourage excluded groups to increasingly employ violence (2008). But it might just as well be political parties which resort to militias, vigilantes and other armed groups in order to wreak havoc and internationalize the conflict. For instance, violence has been a political instrument in Kenya since the days of its return to multiparty democracy (Kagwanja 2009). Despite these deep roots, the 2007 presidential and parliamentary elections in the country illustrate another aspect of this practice. As De Smedt describes, the slogan 'No Raila, no peace!' was popular during the violent phase that followed these elections. According to him, 'calm was restored instantly almost everywhere' after the power-sharing agreement was announced (De Smedt 2009: 592–3). The use of violence by political parties in order to reach political goals is in itself a breach of certain definitions of a political party (De Zeeuw 2008). Political parties are supposed to play by peaceful, democratic rules and abandon violence. Through their use of violence, political parties and insurgents are more similar than is usually believed.

Of course, violence may be employed both during and before elections for harassment, terror and intimidation (Höglund 2008, 2009), but the post-election violence perhaps constitutes a more novel instrument. This violence was made possible by democratization movements and power-sharing as a democratic disguise. In some cases violence is used to complement other instruments of governance in peacetime, making it difficult to draw a clear-cut line between when conflict ends and peace begins. For example, in Côte d'Ivoire some militias have been ordered to defend areas from opposition politicians instead of rebels. It was therefore not only territory but additionally the political integrity of territory together with electoral posts which has been protected by force (Banégas and Marshall-Fratani 2007). In the latest elections in 2010 the incumbent President Gbagbo even went so far as to defend his presidency by violently suppressing opposition after electoral loss (cf. Arnaut in this volume). It took four months and an international intervention to unseat him. The remobilization of former combatants during the Sierra Leonean general elections of 2007 offers another insight into the close relationship between violence and politics. Christensen and Utas show how the skills used during war came to be employed as an important part of 'normal' election politics, blurring the line between politics and violence. These electoral 'politricks' also continued into the post-election phase, as those on the winning side were rewarded for their loyalty (2008). Violence has therefore become a common occurrence – in many places simply a continuation of business as usual – in contemporary African politics. The next section will also help explain why some people are ready to die in order to secure an election victory: electoral loss can lead to an almost complete sidelining of political power and therefore to a major loss of resources available to networks.

Irrelevance of co-option

Hartzell and Hoddie have described negotiated settlements in civil wars to imply that no single actor can 'dictate the institutional rules associated with the postwar state' (2007: 12). In the present context this is not automatically – or possibly even usually – so. In many cases power is shared through the handing out of governmental or military positions, whereas the institutional rules remain the same. According to Hartzell and Hoddie, the wider and more encompassing power-sharing agreements are, the likelier it is that they will result in lasting peace (ibid.). This helps explain why many agreements fail to bring peace, not to mention democracy, as they can be extremely narrow. An institutionalist perspective can therefore be less useful, and the actual co-option mostly irrelevant. This is not least the result of the prevailing personi-fication of politics. As discussed above, the society and the state in Africa are inseparable: this state of affairs results in the weak formal institutionalization of the state as well as the heightened importance of informal institutions.

Personified politics and the role of the African states as the main sources of resources make the head of state the Biggest (wo)Man, although it is pos-sible that he or she is only a figurehead for a network. For instance, Utas has argued that when Charles Taylor and Ellen Johnson Sirleaf came to power they returned with their existing Americo-Liberian networks. Johnson Sirleaf's network has succeeded in taking over parts of the network previously owned by Taylor, underlining the fact that her rule is dependent on this support (Utas 2008). Utas has further observed the differences between Johnson Sirleaf and Ahmed Tejan Kabbah, who served as the president of Sierra Leone from 1996 to 1997 and from 1998 to 2007. Both had international careers, but Johnson Sirleaf had much closer political connections in her country as she had first been part of the Tolbert government, then part of the Samuel Doe administration, and later supported the Taylor insurgency. Politically, Kabbah was in the Sierra Leone margins as he lacked these existing networks when he came to power. Neither was he necessarily successful in creating his own networks. This is possibly due to lack of interest or need, as his vice-president, Solomon Berewa, had a more extensive network in Sierra Leone. This would imply that Kabbah became a figurehead for Berewa's network. As with Johnson Sirleaf, Kabbah's advantage was the international legitimacy, which no doubt brought external resources to the government. He never became a very popular president at home, as he was mostly perceived as shying away from public events, did not feed networks sufficiently and subsequently did not act as a Big Man.[6]

Figurehead or not, presidency is still extremely important. Incumbent governments can be willing to share power if they continue to retain the all-powerful presidency post. This way they can continue to control the political agenda, marginalize reformers, veto reform and simply refuse to implement clauses they believe are problematic – not unlike in one-party states. Ad-ditionally, they can maintain political control by retaining the main levers of coercion, such as foreign affairs, home affairs, defence and internal security as well as finance (Cheeseman and Tendi 2010). Even this might be unnecessary, however, as it may be possible to concentrate powers from other ministries in the presidential office. This was allegedly the case in Zimbabwe, where finances were run by the State House instead of the Ministry of Finance (Rotberg 2000). In the Central African Republic President Patassé bypassed opposition ministers by recruiting advisers who formed 'a kind of shadow cabinet where the real decisions were made' (Mehler 2011: 124). According to van de Walle, power in most African states is highly centralized around the president, who therefore controls access to state resources over local governments or executive and legislative branches of the government. As a consequence, formal politics can become symbolic as '[t]he critical drama is taking place off stage' (2003: 310). This goes against the argument put forth by Walter, according to which a would-be dictator would not agree to disaggregate political or military power and influence with enemies (1999). Sharing power might actually have few consequences, as power-sharing and co-option are likely to have little effect on the policies driven by the regime, as long as executive power remains in one group's hands.

As a strategy, the purpose of co-option is to make the regime more secure – not more democratic, legitimate or representative. The personification of politics also affects opposition, which is usually based around a number of single individuals. Joining the ruling coalition in order to gain access to state resources – as well as boycotting elections or resorting to armed struggle if election loss is imminent – thus becomes a rational choice. As argued by Teshome, parties are often little more than a way to receive electoral support that enables a bargaining position with other elites about the distribution of public goods (2009). An independent power base may improve this position, as community votes are useful to the main party (van de Walle 2003). Resorting to arms is just as viable a way to a better bargaining position vis-à-vis the state. This can be done through increased military power or control over territory as well as population, although the control of a country's capital city is still the key to success. Short of victory, deadlock is the second-best option, as it requires negotiations and concessions from incumbent regimes in order to solve the situation. Cooperating before international donors is a better alternative than a deadlock: if the alternatives are that everyone either wins or loses, it is arguably better to win less than to lose everything.

As long as the political agenda is controlled by someone else, however, power-sharing is more akin to an invitation to take a seat at the dining table where the other elites sit than a real chance to change things. This inability to change the political system shows how the informal can restrict the formal. While many agreements do not result in any formal institutional change apart from certain individuals gaining governmental or military posts, it is clear that the *informal* institutions are the ones that affect the behaviour of the participants after these agreements. Therefore, it has to be emphasized that the 'normalcy' after power-sharing means the continuation of *informal* business as usual, only with the inclusion of new actors and resources in the form of post-conflict recovery funds that can be distributed to different networks.

Post-conflict contexts pose additional difficulties, as conflict has worsened official economies, caused suffering and not least affected networks. As shown by Hoffman, it is not only the pre-conflict networks which may become militarized during conflict and continue in the post-conflict phase; conflict also offers new opportunities to become a Big Man with a militarized network (2007). According to Christensen (in this volume), these militarized networks carry on into post-conflict governance in 'domesticated form'. While these networks do not automatically involve violence, they at least have the potential to use it. While successful disarmament at least makes it more difficult for former combatants to reignite armed conflict, the networks still possess violent skills that can be employed even during peacetime; as shown above, in many cases violence constitutes a part of everyday politics. This means that the expected return to 'normalcy' does not mean the end of violence, not to mention legitimate rule or democratic peace. Continuity rather than change is a likelier outcome, which means that it is often the same Big Men who continue exercising power even if they acquire new positions or possibilities. In other words, it is often the pre-conflict conditions that have contributed to the conflict which come to prevail again in the post-conflict period, possibly in a more extreme form than before: for instance, while the private nature of state power makes it ultimately limited in the sense that those who have power do not want to share it with others, even during peacetime, limiting access to power after a hard-fought conflict can take even more extreme forms. The inclusion of other groups in power-sharing deals can therefore become problematic, as seen in the Abuja negotiations between the Sudanese government and three Darfur rebel groups: independents were considered to belong to the enemy camp, and to thus empower the opposing side (De Waal 2006). Polarization is no doubt present in many internal conflicts, but is not least visible during power-sharing negotiations. The optimal power-sharing solution arguably involves the inclusion of 'third forces' that can better represent the interests of the general population (Ohlson and Söderberg 2002: 28). With polarization, however, their inclusion becomes very difficult. Jarstad has further noted that even if political space is later opened, any opposition groups will start far behind the incumbent parties owing to a lack of resources (Jarstad 2008). In the long run power-sharing might change things, but not necessarily significantly, and not always for the better.

Conclusions

In this chapter I have investigated the results of power-sharing in an informal African reality. Power-sharing constitutes a strategy that can be employed by incumbent governments to manage conflicts and threats. This strategy draws from the system of governance based on networks of Big Men, as threats can be integrated into state structures as well as state-structured networks. Big Men expect loyalty in return for resources. This inter-elite appeasement often seems to have worked, at least temporarily. In many cases, power-sharing may also be the only viable alternative for incumbents as formal state institutions may be too weak to render a military solution possible. Power-sharing is today increasingly advocated from the outside, especially from the Western world. This outside pressure can further limit the viable options of weak African regimes. While existing literature has time and time again shown how problematic power-sharing agreements can be, the more context-specific difficulties have not been investigated. In this chapter I have argued that the distinct categorization of African politics should be breached. The African political reality is naturally *both* formal *and* informal, and the two are impossible to separate. This is partly because of the nature of the state, which has advantages when collecting resources, which in turn are needed to maintain networks. But even if it is often the formal which supports the informal, it happens just as often that the informal drives the formal. As a consequence, it is impossible to understand African politics without taking into account the informal. This has rarely been done. Bringing the informal reality into the mainstream as well as problematizing a number of common expectations regarding African politics have therefore been the main aims of this chapter.

Like other aspects of formal politics, power-sharing agreements are not always what they seem in the African political reality. Neither are many concepts that we constantly employ in describing the political sphere of this informal reality. Concepts like legitimacy, political party and opposition do not necessarily have the same content or relevance as they do in other contexts. This also has an effect on expectations of 'normalcy'; continuity after conflict is a far more likely outcome than change. Violence can continue into the post-conflict phase, taking more 'domesticated' forms. It is therefore difficult to draw a clear-cut line between politics and violence, as well as between politics and economy. This difficulty has led some to consider insurgency movements – and to some extent political parties – to be nothing more than organized criminals. This is a far too easy solution to this problem, and is scientifically unsatisfying.

The centralization of power in African politics is also important in power-sharing. This means that the results of power-sharing may be close to irrelevant when it comes to state policies, as these are controlled by the head of state; when politics turn into private matters it becomes difficult to differentiate state from regime. State interest then often equals regime interest – even if the state's interests could be expected to be something entirely different. This centralization can also affect the conflict resolution potential of power-sharing.

If power-sharing is an inter-elite accommodation, it will likely not succeed in solving the underlying reasons for conflict. Some grievances are always left unattended, which leaves the door open to renewed conflict.

The issues brought up in this chapter have both practical and theoretical implications. These implications should not be understood as a reason to be pessimistic about power-sharing, nor should this chapter be regarded as a criticism of this practice itself. As has been shown in other research, power-sharing can lead to peace, and this possibility should not be underestimated. The purpose of this chapter has rather been to illustrate that informal politics have to be taken seriously if we are to understand African politics and political realities. And these realities, as I have illustrated, do affect the results of power-sharing, as well as any other political activity.

Notes

1 For instance, Paul Richards has argued that 'The Sierra Leone war ... is a product of ... [a] protracted post-colonial crisis of patrimonialism' (Richards 1996: xviii).

2 For an example, see Clapham (1982).

3 Tull and Mehler use the term 'conflict resolution', but it is doubtful whether the underlying reasons for conflict are always resolved by power-sharing agreements. Of course, it is just as possible that war can create new reasons for conflict in addition to solving the old ones (Tull and Mehler 2005: 377).

4 The author would like to thank Anders Themnér for making this point.

5 Interview with Mats Utas, 7 May 2010.

6 Interview with Mats Utas, 12 May 2010.

References

Arriola, L. R. (2009) 'Patronage and political stability in Africa', *Comparative Political Studies*, 42(10): 1339–62.

Banégas, R. and R. Marshall-Fratani (2007) 'Côte d'Ivoire: negotiating identity and citizenship', in M. Bøås and K. Dunn (eds), *African Guerrillas – raging against the machine*, Boulder, CO, and London: Lynne Rienner.

Bayart, J.-F. (1993) *The State In Africa: The politics of the belly*, London and New York: Longman.

Bledsoe, C. (1990) '"No success without struggle": social mobility and hardship for foster children in Sierra Leone', *Man*, 25: 70–88.

Chabal, P. (2009) *Africa: The Politics of Suffering and Smiling*, London: Zed Books.

Chabal, P. and J.-P. Daloz (1999) *Africa Works: Disorder as political instrument*, London/Oxford/Bloomington: International African Institute in association with James Currey and Indiana University Press.

Cheeseman, N. and M. Tendi (2010) 'Power sharing in comparative perspective: the origins and consequences of unity government in Africa', *Journal of Modern African Studies*, 48: 203–29.

Christensen, M. M. and M. Utas (2008) 'Mercenaries of democracy: the "politricks" of remobilized combatants in the 2007 general elections, Sierra Leone', *African Affairs*, 107: 515–39.

Clapham, C. (1982) 'Clientelism and the state', in C. Clapham (ed.), *Private Patronage and Public Power*, London: Frances Pinter.

— (1996) *Africa and the International System: The Politics of State Survival*, Cambridge: Cambridge University Press.

— (1998) 'Degrees of statehood', *Review of International Studies*, 24: 143–57.

Collins, K. (2004) 'The logic of clan politics – evidence from the Central Asian trajectories', *World Politics*, 56: 224–61.

De Smedt, J. (2009) '"No Raila, no peace!" Big Man politics and election violence at the Kibera grassroots', *African Affairs*, 108: 581–98.

De Waal, A. (2006) 'I will not sign', *London Review of Books*, 28(23).

De Zeeuw, J. (2008) 'Understanding the political transformation of rebel movements', in J. de Zeeuw (ed.), *From Soldiers to Politicians – Transforming Rebel Movements after Civil War*, Boulder, CO: Lynne Rienner.

Dorman, S. R. (2006) 'Post-liberation politics in Africa: examining the political legacy of struggle', *Third World Quarterly*, 27(6): 1085–1101.

Englebert, P. and R. Hummel (2005) 'Let's stick together: understanding Africa's secessionist deficit', *African Affairs*, 104(416): 399–427.

Englebert, P. and D. M. Tull (2008) 'Postconflict reconstruction in Africa – flawed ideas about failed states', *International Security*, 32(4): 106–39.

Hartzell, C. A. and M. Hoddie (2007) *Crafting Peace – Power-sharing Institutions and the Negotiated Settlement of Civil Wars*, University Park: Pennsylvania State University Press.

Hirsch, J. L. (2001) *Sierra Leone: Diamonds and the Struggle for Democracy*, Boulder, CO: Lynne Rienner.

Hoddie, M. and C. Hartzell (2003) 'Civil war settlements and the implementation of military power-sharing arrangements', *Journal of Peace Research*, 40(3).

Hoffman, D. (2004) 'The civilian target in Sierra Leone and Liberia: political power, military strategy, and humanitarian intervention', *African Affairs*, 103: 211–26.

— (2007) 'The meaning of a militia: understanding the Civil Defence Forces of Sierra Leone', *African Affairs*, 106(425): 639–62.

Holsti, K. J. (1996) *The State, War, and the State of War*, New York: Cambridge University Press.

Höglund, K. (2008) 'Violence in war-to-democracy transitions', in A. K. Jarstad and T. D. Sisk (eds), *From War to Democracy: Dilemmas of peacebuilding*, Cambridge: Cambridge University Press.

— (2009) 'Electoral violence in conflict-ridden societies: concepts, causes, and consequences', *Terrorism and Political Violence*, 21(3): 412–27.

Jarstad, A. K. (2008) 'Power sharing: former enemies in joint government', in A. K. Jarstad and T. D. Sisk (eds), *From War to Democracy – Dilemmas of Peacebuilding*, Cambridge: Cambridge University Press.

Job, B. L. (1992) 'The insecurity dilemma: national, regime, and state securities in the Third World', in B. L. Job (ed.), *The Insecurity Dilemma – National Security of Third World States*, Boulder, CO: Lynne Rienner.

Johnston, P. (2007) 'Negotiated settlements and government strategy in civil war: evidence from Darfur', *Civil Wars*, 9(4): 359–77.

Jörgel, M. and M. Utas (2007) *The Mano River Basin Area: Formal and Informal Security Providers in Liberia, Guinea and Sierra Leone*, FOI, Swedish Defence Research Agency.

Kagwanja, P. (2009) 'Courting genocide: populism, ethno-nationalism and the informalisation of violence in Kenya's 2008 post-election crisis', *Journal of Contemporary African Studies*, 27(3): 365–87.

Keen, D. (1998) *The Economic Functions of Civil Wars*, Adelphi Paper 320, London.

— (2005) *Conflict and Collusion in Sierra Leone*, New York: Palgrave.

Lindberg, S. I. (2010) 'What accountability pressures do MPs in Africa face and how do they respond? Evidence from Ghana', *Journal of Modern African Studies*, 48(1): 117–42.

Mbembe, A. (1992) 'Provisional notes on the postcolony', *Africa*, 62(1): 3–37.

Médard, J.-F. (1982) 'The underdeveloped state in tropical Africa: political clientelism or neo-patrimonialism?', in C. Clapham (ed.), *Private Patronage and Public Power*, London: Frances Pinter.

Mehler, A. (2008) 'Not always in the people's interest: power-sharing arrangements in African peace agreements', *Violence, Power and Security*, 83, Giga Research Programme, July.

— (2011) 'Rebels and parties: the impact of armed insurgency on representation in the Central African Republic', *Journal of Modern African Studies*, 49(1): 115–39.

Menkhaus, K. (2007) 'Governance without government in Somalia', *International Security*, 31(3): 74–106.

Ohlson, T. and M. Söderberg (2002) *From Intra-State War to Democratic Peace in Weak States*, Uppsala Peace Research Papers no. 5.

Reno, W. (1995) 'Reinvention of an African patrimonial state: Charles Taylor's Liberia', *Third World Quarterly*, 16(1).

— (1998) *Warlord Politics and African States*, Boulder, CO: Lynne Rienner.

— (2002) 'The politics of insurgency in collapsing states', *Development and Change*, 33(5): 837–58.

— (2006) 'Congo: from state collapse to "absolutism", to state failure', *Third World Quarterly*, 27(1): 43–56.

Richards, P. (1996) *Fighting for the Rain Forest: War, youth and resources in Sierra Leone*, Oxford: James Currey.

Richards, P. and J. Vincent (2008) 'Sierra Leone: marginalization of the RUF', in J. De Zeeuw (ed.), *From Soldiers to Politicians – Transforming Rebel Movements after Civil War*, Boulder, CO: Lynne Rienner.

Rotberg, R. I. (2000) 'Africa's mess, Mugabe's mayhem', *Foreign Affairs*, 79(5).

Spears, I. S. (2000) 'Understanding inclusive peace agreements in Africa: the problems of sharing power', *Third World Quarterly*, 21(1): 105–18.

Teshome, W. (2009) 'Opposition parties and the politics of opposition in Africa: a critical analysis', *International Journal of Humanities and Social Sciences*, 3(1).

Tull, D. M. (2003) 'A reconfiguration of political order? The state of the state in North Kivu (DR Congo)', *African Affairs*, 102: 429–46.

Tull, D. M. and A. Mehler (2005) 'The hidden costs of power-sharing: reproducing insurgent violence in Africa', *African Affairs*, 104(416): 375–98.

United Nations Security Council (2010) *Report of the Monitoring Group on Somalia Submitted in Accordance with Resolution 1853 S/2010/91*, www.un.org/ga/search/view_doc.asp?symbol=s/2010/91, accessed 5 August 2011.

Utas, M. (2008) 'Liberia beyond the blueprints: poverty reduction strategy papers, Big Men and informal networks', Lecture Series on African Security, 150.227.5.137/upload/projects/Africa/Utas%20Liberia%20Beyond%20the% 20Blueprints.pdf.

van de Walle, N. (2003) 'Presidentialism and clientelism in Africa's emerging party systems', *Journal of Modern African Studies*, 41(2).

Walter, B. F. (1999) 'Designing transitions from civil war', *International Security*, 24(1): 127–55.

Young, C. (2004) 'The end of the postcolonial state in Africa? Reflections on changing African political dynamics', *African Affairs*, 103: 23–49.

9 | Former mid-level commanders in Big Man networks

Anders Themnér

In many contemporary African countries, informal networks play a prominent role in shaping the political, economic and social life of their citizens. In weak or failed states, where state structures have no or limited reach and can, at best, be described as fragile, actors such as paramount chiefs, warlords, politicians and businessmen have much sway over societal affairs. The authority of these elites, or Big Men, stems from their ability to create networks of dependants that can be mobilized to acquire power, resources and concessions. Even if Big Men often seek to gain access to the formal structures of the state, they tend to use these official positions for their own political and economic purposes, rather than to benefit the general public (Utas 2008: 1). The role of informal structures is especially apparent in societies that have suffered from protracted civil strife, such as the Democratic Republic of the Congo (DRC), Liberia, Somalia and Sudan, where state institutions have been undermined and dismantled during the hostilities. In fact, in the aftermath of civil wars the networks controlled by Big Men may be the only source of security and income available to ordinary citizens. With tensions still running high and few economic resources available, social and ethnic groups often prefer to continue to rally behind their old wartime leaders rather than take the risk of awarding loyalty to state institutions that are unable or unwilling to act as neutral arbitrators (Lyons 2005: 43–7). The informal power of such networks – be they socio-economic, political or military – is, however, not confined only to the period immediately following the cessation of hostilities. It is just as often a reality long after the departure of international peacekeepers and observers (Jörgel and Utas 2007). Caught in a Weberian notion of state-building, the international community seldom acknowledges the central role played by informal structures in post-conflict Africa, giving '… external actors faulty maps to navigate from' in their quest for peace (Utas 2008: 1).

The importance of bringing Big Men and their networks into the equation becomes especially obvious when considering the salience of old military structures. Often assumed to disappear once armed groups have been disarmed and demobilized, military bonds generally continue to linger between different wartime actors, ranging from rank-and-file ex-combatants, former commanders and government officials to regional warlords (Themnér 2011). In fact, Big Men often work hard to retain or gain access to such networks, in the hope of using them to further their own political or economic agendas. This is especially true when it comes to engaging rank-and-file ex-combatants.[1] Hardened by their experiences from the previous war, accustomed to working collectively, and used to taking orders, they can be employed by Big Men for a wide variety of purposes: providing personal security, intimidating political rivals, war-making, as well as engaging in economic or criminal ventures. Owing to the flexible nature of such unofficial military structures, it is essential to take them into consideration when conducting peace-building. If they are co-opted they can be used to support peace; if they are estranged they may be used to undermine it.

Within these informal military structures, former mid-level commanders (ex-MiLCs) play a crucial role.[2] Without their services as *intermediaries*, Big Men have few prospects of tapping into the world of ex-combatants. Given that they are situated at radically different levels of the societal hierarchy, the distance between Big Men and former fighters is often too vast. This is mainly due to two factors. First, because of the non-conducive security climate in post-conflict societies, ex-fighters are often inclined to suspicion. This means that they may be reluctant to work for Big Men with whom they have no personal relations. Secondly, after demobilization many ex-MiLCs continue to wield influence over their old subordinates, jealously guarding access to them. For instance, in 2006 – four years after the completion of the Sierra Leonean demobilization process – ex-Revolutionary United Front (RUF) combatants in Makeni did not dare to meet foreigners without receiving consent from their wartime commander.[3] Owing to their role as gatekeepers to ex-combatant communities – in essence making them local Big Men – it is difficult for politicians, businessmen or old warlords to sidestep ex-MiLCs and take direct responsibility for enlisting ex-fighters. The best strategy available for Big Men is therefore often to acknowledge the authority of ex-MiLCs and outsource recruitment to them. This is particularly true since ex-MiLCs can use their influence to ease the misgivings that their former subordinates may have over providing services for different elites. However, in spite of the key role that ex-MiLCs have in countries emerging from civil wars, we still know very little about how they are able to uphold their societal influence and standing as intermediaries. This constitutes a serious lacuna, especially considering their ability to quickly deliver experienced fighters to spoiling elites.

Hence, bearing in mind the influence Big Men's informal military networks have on shaping war-affected societies and our need to better understand the role played by ex-MiLCs in such structures, I aspire to do three things in the present chapter. First, to identify and highlight in more detail how ex-MiLCs – as intermediaries – facilitate the interaction between Big Men and rank-and-file ex-combatants. Secondly, to illustrate the different social settings in which elites seek the services of ex-MiLCs. Thirdly, to assess whether ex-MiLCs, and the Big Men networks that they are part of, not only constitute an obstacle to peace, but can also be utilized to promote peace in contemporary Africa.

Big Men and ex-combatants: the benefits of cooperation

A central theme in many African societies is that power is not necessarily a function of territorial control, but rather a consequence of the number of clients that people possess. This has been described as a 'wealth in people' system, where networks of patronage determine the success not only of Big Men, but also of ordinary citizens (Bledsoe 1990; Jörgel and Utas 2007: 13). In fact, being independent and lacking access to a Big Man can be hazardous, as individuals may thereby curtail their chances of gaining access to different resources (Utas 2008: 2). There are a number of different ways in which Big Men can attract clients. As ethnic or religious figures, they can build relations with their local communities by utilizing these collective identities (Figueiredo and Weingast 1999; Gurr 2000; Horowitz 1985). Networks can, however, just as well be built around the idea that people make themselves subject to a prominent individual (Bledsoe 1990). Jörgel and Utas (2007: 13), for example, hold that elites often seek to '... create networks of dependents that allow the Big Man/politician to manifest his power'. In this context networks can almost be described as what is commonly referred to as patron–client relationships. By working, fighting or voting for a Big Man, clients are rewarded with different benefits such as economic resources or security (see, e.g., Bledsoe 1990). One advantage of controlling such networks is that they can easily be transformed into relationships supporting a wide variety of activities. Depending on the contextual circumstances, Big Men can, for example, use the same networks to engage in politics, economic exploitation or warfare (Jörgel and Utas 2007: 15).

In post-conflict societies, where tensions run high and different actors evaluate the pros and cons of complying with a peace settlement, it can be crucial for Big Men to have access to informal military networks by making ex-combatants their clients. The post-conflict experiences of the Republic of Congo (RoC) constitute a lucid example of this. After the end of the war in 1999, the Ninja warlord Frédéric Bitsangou – more commonly known as Pastor Ntoumi – worked hard to ensure the loyalty of his former fighters. As a self-appointed prophet and spokesperson for the opposition, he was vocal in his criticism of the government's failure to integrate ex-Ninjas into the security forces.[4] This earned him a certain amount of respect as a Big Man from his ex-combatants. When the conflict with the government re-erupted in March 2002, Ntoumi could utilize his good relations with his former subordinates to convince an estimated 1,350 ex-Ninjas to take to arms (Themnér 2011).

It can also be wise for ex-fighters to cultivate close ties to senior commanders and politicians to ensure their own personal security. Without the protection of a Big Man, ex-combatants can run the risk of being harassed by vengeful civilians, former opponents or security forces. This is especially true if there is a resumption of hostilities, as ex-fighters are often among the first to be targeted by different armed actors (ibid.). Another reason for ex-combatants to attach themselves to elites is to increase their chances of finding peacetime employment (Christensen and Utas 2008; Hoffman 2007; Utas 2003: 226). In post-conflict societies, where economic resources are scarce and local economies are in ruins, job opportunities are often restricted to individuals with access to nepotistic channels (see, e.g., Peters 2006).

Former mid-level commanders as intermediaries: recruitment outsourced

It may, however, be difficult for Big Men to penetrate informal networks – irrespective of whether they are military, political or ethnic – all the way down to the grassroots level. Scholars working within the field of military organization theory and business management have, for example, found that elites (such as officers and managers) have few possibilities to personally oversee the daily activities of any larger number of subordinates (Graicunas 1937; Nickols 2003).[5] This is largely a consequence of the human brain's limited span of attention: something which restricts the number of workers or soldiers that a leader can manage. It is, furthermore, not enough for leaders to supervise the bilateral relations between themselves and individual subordinates; they must also oversee the relationships between different employees and also between groups of employees and themselves. It is, subsequently, difficult, if not impossible, for managers or officers to run an organization if there are too many subordinates answering directly to them. The optimal solution to this predicament is to limit the leaders' span of control. This can be done by restricting the number of individuals directly reporting to them and delegating more responsibility to mid-level supervisors, resulting in the formation of a more hierarchical organization (Graicunas 1937; Nickols 2003). The same type of reasoning has been put forth by several other scholars. For example, Deutsch argues that without the active participation of a group of between 50 and 500 individuals, which occupy the mid-level of different organizations (such as governments or armed forces), little can be done (Deutsch 1966: 155). Meanwhile, based on research in Liberia and Sierra Leone, Johnston holds that when armed factions expand territorially, they are often obliged to delegate military authority to sub-commanders (Johnston 2008). This is especially true if there is no acquisition of new technologies.

Just like business managers and army officers, Big Men in post-conflict societies are confronted with problems concerning their span of control when seeking to organize the activities of people at the grass roots. Separated from their potential rank-and-file clients by class and profession, it is seldom possible or efficient for them to personally recruit or manage the work of hundreds or even dozens of individuals. For Big Men it is therefore rational to outsource recruitment to brokers, or *intermediaries*, who can facilitate the interaction between them and the grass roots. This is especially true for Big Men aspiring to become national players; without the assistance of intermediaries it will simply not be possible for them to reach out and mobilize enough followers to compete with other elites. The most efficient intermediaries are those who not only possess a network range that includes Big Men and rank-and-file individuals, but who more or less monopolize contacts between these two actors.[6] The crucial role played by an intermediary hence lies in the fact that without his or her services, contacts between Big Men and the grass roots become 'negligible or non-existent' (Hannerz 1980: 190). In post-conflict societies it is possible to identify a number of such possible mid-level actors – junior army or police officers, local religious leaders, second-tier politicians and ex-MiLCs – who both have access to elites and regularly interact with members of local communities.

For Big Men interested in recruiting former fighters, ex-MiLCs constitute the most efficient intermediaries. Not only do they tend to interact with post-conflict elites, they also function as 'gatekeepers' to ex-combatant communities. In fact, owing to the influence that many ex-MiLCs continue to wield over their former subordinates, it can be difficult for other actors to get in touch with ex-combatants without their assistance. The origins of this influence can often be traced back to the preceding war. When armed conflicts are in progress, politicians and senior commanders frequently lose control over their military units. As previously mentioned, this is particularly true when armed factions expand territorially and when there is a lack of appropriate technology for leaders to control the actions of their subordinates. Under such circumstances combatants generally become more loyal to their closest commanders, rather than the top leadership.[7] This is commonly referred to as a 'stable' mentality, and it appeared among the different armed factions during the war in RoC in 1997–99. After being forced from Brazzaville in October 1997, the Cocoye and Ninja forces were obliged to withdraw to the rural and mostly forested areas in the southern and western parts of the country. Once there, central control diminished as the rebels splintered into dozens of different écuries (stables), each led by a mid-level commander. The size of the stables varied, but they seldom contained more than 200 fighters. Contrary to the orders of their highest superiors, these groups generally refrained from attacking military targets, instead preferring to engage in systematic plundering of the civilian population (Englebert and Ron 2004). Even though most of these units were demobilized between 1999 and 2000, there continued to be a strong sense of loyalty and comradeship between former members of the same stable. In fact, after leaving their forest hideouts many ex-Cocoyes and Ninjas chose to settle down in the same urban areas as their former stable leaders, allowing ex-MiLCs to retain authority over many of their former subordinates (Themnér 2011). This stable mentality is, however, not a phenomenon restricted to post-war RoC. In countries such as Liberia, Namibia, Sierra Leone and Uganda, ex-MiLCs have actively sought and succeeded in retaining influence over their former fighters (Dzinesa 2008: 15; Eichstaedt 2009; Hoffman 2007).

The reason why many ex-MiLCs seek to assert their power over their former subordinates is that it offers one of the few strategies available to prevent peace-time marginalization. During war, MiLCs often attain an important amount of social, economic and political power. By controlling the men and women under their command, they can exploit economic resources and receive social recognition from the local communities (Utas 2003). However, with the arrival of peace and the demobilization of their subordinates, they risk losing their most important asset – their network of dependants. It is therefore rational for ex-MiLCs to counter the threat of marginalization by seeking to ensure the continued loyalty of their ex-fighters. By controlling them, ex-MiLCs can control their labour – a resource that ex-MiLCs can either use to engage in economic activities of their own (such as mining, plantation work or agricultural projects), or resell to different elites (Christensen and Utas 2008; Hoffman 2007; Themnér 2011; Utas 2005). In this sense ex-MiLCs can be seen as Big Men or Women in their own right, with their own clients, who may or may not be part of an even 'Bigger' Man's network.[8] The reason why groups of ex-combatants are so popular as labourers is that – owing to the war – they already have organizational skills and routines in place, making them efficient workers (Utas 2005).

However, even if ex-MiLCs have an interest in maintaining their old networks, they must still convince their former subordinates that it is in their interest to continue loyal to them. One way of doing this is to exploit the feelings of affinity between themselves and their former fighters. As previously mentioned, close ties often appear between combatants and their commanders during war, resulting in the creation of a military comradeship that often survives demobilization. Since many lack other acquaintances, this means that interacting with wartime comrades may be the only social forum where ex-combatants can discuss and address the problems that they face when returning to civilian life. Christensen and Utas describe the living situation for many ex-fighters in Sierra Leone in the following manner: '... former militia networks are still active and many ex-combatants refer to these networks as their only family. Having lost their families in the war or fearing to return to their home communities because of the atrocities they have committed, they live with other ex-combatants who have shared similar experiences' (Christensen and Utas 2008: 525).

In my previous work, I have shown that ex-MiLCs can even use such bonds of affinity to convince their former fighters to resort to organized violence (Themnér 2011). This indicates that ex-fighters will go to great lengths to avoid forfeiting the psycho-social benefits of belonging to an ex-combatant community. Another strategy available to ex-MiLCs is to offer former fighters different material benefits. Hoffman has, for example, vividly described how some ex-Liberians United for Reconciliation and Democracy (LURD) combatants continued to pay homage to their ex-MiLCs in Monrovia, in the hope of getting small sums of money (Hoffman 2007: 418). Hence, owing to ex-MiLCs' influence over their former fighters and their position as gatekeepers to ex-combatant communities, Big Men are more often than not obliged to utilize them in their dealings with ex-fighters.

Another reason why ex-MiLCs are optimal intermediaries is that they are one of the few actors who can overcome the suspicious disposition of ex-combatants. This suspicion is largely a function of the continued sense of insecurity found in many post-conflict societies in general and among ex-combatants in particular. After demobilizing, it is not uncommon for former fighters to be harassed, abused, arrested or even killed owing to their military background. In Uganda, for example, groups of former fighters of the Lord's Resistance Army (LRA) fled into the bush in 2009, owing to harassments inflicted upon them by the authorities (Oketch 2009; see also Lanken 2007). Meanwhile, in 2002 the Congolese government launched a campaign to systematically harass former Ninja rebels living in Brazzaville. The abuses committed by the security forces included raiding the houses of ex-Ninjas, stealing their money, imprisoning them and physically abusing them (Nilsson 2008: 71). One explanation for the behaviour of the Congolese authorities, as well as actions taken by security forces in other post-conflict countries, is the fact that former fighters can be a potential source of insecurity because of their military skills. It can, consequently, be tempting for governments to seek to control or at least keep an eye on ex-combatants (Christensen and Utas 2008: 524–5). Such actions can have repercussions on the attitudes and beliefs of ex-fighters, something which was apparent in Sierra Leone. After demobilizing, many ex-fighters of the armed opposition – RUF and Armed Forces Revolutionary Council (AFRC) – were convinced that they were under surveillance by the secret police, making them suspicious of strangers. Such fears were strengthened by persistent rumours that ex-rebel fighters were secretly being executed by Nigerian peacekeepers and pro-government groups.[9] Hence, aware of the possibility of being tricked, cheated or abused and often expecting the worst, ex-fighters may think twice before agreeing to offers from Big Men to enlist (Themnér 2011). Under such circumstances, one of the only options available for elites is to employ the services of ex-MiLCs. These commanders can use their personal relations with ex-combatants to ease their qualms about working for a Big Man and vouch for their employer's sincerity.

For ex-MiLCs, there are often benefits to be had by becoming an intermediary. By providing elites with the labour of their ex-combatants, former commanders can get access to economic endowments that they would otherwise not have, such as cash payments, employment, valuable goods or free access to loot (Christensen and Utas 2008; Themnér 2011). In fact, my research has shown that economic incentives tend to be the main reason why ex-MiLCs agree to provide fighters for spoiling elites (Themnér 2011). For example, in Sierra Leone ex-MiLCs of the Civil Defence Forces (CDF) were offered cash, and even cars, if they recruited ex-CDF combatants on behalf of LURD. As an extra perk, they were even allowed to engage in pillage once inside Liberia (HRW 2005; Nilsson 2008: 145–6). These findings are consistent with what we know about the preferences of mid-level actors in other social settings. Panebianco has, for example, established that as activists climb the hierarchical system of political parties, they award greater importance to economic incentives (Panebianco 1988: 21–30). However, owing to their military and leadership qualities, former commanders are not always merely seen as an asset. In situations of heightened tensions, they may just as easily be viewed as a threat to the interests and power of certain elites. For example, when the security forces in RoC began targeting ex-Ninjas in 2002 (as mentioned earlier), ex-MiLCs were their prime targets (Nilsson 2008: 79–80). Under such circumstances, an additional advantage of becoming an intermediary is the protection received when working for a Big Man (see, e.g., Christensen and Utas 2008: 524).

Intermediaries for many occasions

Owing to problems concerning span of control, ex-MiLCs' continued influence over their former subordinates, and the suspicious disposition of ex-combatants, Big Men have few possibilities to take personal charge of recruiting former fighters. Post-war elites therefore need to enlist the services of intermediaries, in the form of ex-MiLCs, who can represent them in their dealings with ex-combatants. Having said this, it is still necessary to establish in which social settings ex-MiLCs can exploit their position as gatekeepers to ex-combatant communities and become intermediaries for Big Men. In the following, I argue that Big Men have a particular interest in employing ex-MiLCs when they are engaged in war-making and elections campaigns, as well as legal and illegal economic ventures.

War-making In the aftermath of war, there are often several types of elites contemplating a return to violence. Dissatisfied with the terms of a peace agreement, fearing peacetime prosecution, or unhappy about the loss of incomes generated by illegal economic activities, they may conclude that they have more to gain by returning to conflict than by abiding by an accord. These Big Men are close to what Stedman (1997: 5) refers to as spoilers, or 'leaders and parties who believe that peace emerging from negotiations threatens their power, worldview, and interests, and use violence to undermine attempts to achieve it'. Owing to the military skills that they possess, ex-combatants are usually in high demand by such potential troublemakers. Residing in the same country, demobilized combatants can offer domestic spoilers a ready pool of new recruits (Nilsson 2005: 62–3). It is, however, not only national elites who may take an interest in former fighters. Regional Big Men are often keen to strengthen their military forces with experienced combatants from other countries. For example, former fighters from both sides of the civil war in Namibia fought as mercenaries in neighbouring Angola: both for the Angolan regime and the National Union for the Total Independence of Angola (UNITA) (Preston 1997: 463).

Even if the ability of different elites to personally recruit ex-combatants is always restricted, it is especially so when the ultimate aim is to make war. In fact, the creation of armed groups and recruitment of fighters are punishable offences in most countries. As well-known figures in their communities, it can therefore be both difficult and dangerous for Big Men to try to approach and enlist ex-combatants on their own. This is particularly true when government forces or international peacekeepers have been able to re-establish control over contested territories. In such situations, it can be wise for Big Men to outsource recruitment to ex-MiLCs whose faces are less well known, and who can move more freely and interact with former fighters without causing alarm. Efforts by members of the Liberian regime – headed by former president Charles Taylor – to employ Sierra Leonean ex-combatants in their struggle against LURD (1999–2003) offer an illustrative example of this.[10] At the time, one of the leading Big Men in Taylor's entourage was Sam Bockarie – a former senior commander of RUF.[11] As one of Taylor's most trusted military leaders, Bockarie personally organized the recruitment of suitable fighters. In late 2001 and early 2002 he was able to do this by travelling in eastern Sierra Leone, trying to convince ex-RUF combatants to join him in Liberia. This was possible since the area was still largely controlled by RUF units that had not been completely discharged. However, after the demobilization process came to an end in January 2002, and with the deployment of troops from the United Nations Mission in Sierra Leone (UNAMSIL) and the national army, Bockarie could no longer travel freely in the area. This compelled the Liberian regime to switch strategy, instead hiring former mid-level RUF commanders to enlist ex-rebels inside Sierra Leone. These ex-MiLCs ran less risks of being detected when they approached and interacted with potential recruits. In addition, by specifically targeting their former subordinates, they were able to take advantage of the close ties that existed between them. For their services the ex-MiLCs were given monthly salaries and, at times, valuable goods such as cars. Carrying promises of loot and cash payments, these intermediaries were able to entice as many as 1,200 ex-RUF combatants to Taylor's cause during 2001–03 (Themnér 2011).

It is, however, not only because of aspects of secrecy that Big Men prefer to utilize the services of ex-MiLCs. In many cases, urgency is just as compelling a reason to outsource recruitment. For example, during the 2002/03 fighting in RoC, the Congolese regime – partly composed of former Cobra warlords – initially had no need to remobilize ex-Cobra fighters. In fact, by using the security forces and Angolan government troops stationed in the country, the government was largely successful in its efforts to contain the Ninja rebellion. However, when the Ninjas launched an attack against Brazzaville airport in June 2002, things changed. Caught off guard, the regime soon realized that they needed additional fighters to thwart the Ninja offensive. For them it was natural to turn to former Cobras who had been demobilized a few years earlier. However, since the ministers were not in direct contact with the rank-and-file ex-fighters they had to turn to their former mid-level commanders. As these ex-commanders still had contact with their ex-fighters, they were, in a short period of time, able to rally approximately two thousand former Cobras and get them ready for battle. After a few hours they had successfully repelled the Ninja attack and stabilized the situation. Even though the old Cobra warlords could have personally gone to Talangaï, Ouenzé, Poto-Poto and Moungali – Brazzaville neighbourhoods where most ex-Cobras lived – to assemble their ex-fighters, this would have been not only ineffective but also time-consuming. A more efficient strategy was therefore to delegate recruitment to several former mid-level Cobra commanders who both knew where the ex-Cobras lived and could approach more recruits in a shorter period of time. As compensation for their efforts, both ex-Cobras and their former commanders were given carte blanche to loot opposition strongholds in the capital (Themnér 2011).

Election campaigns Big Men do not seek the services of ex-combatants only when conducting war. Former fighters can also be a valuable asset when running for office. Many post-civil-war countries are emerging, weak democracies. This is either because an opening of the political system is an integral part of the peace accord or because democratic principles and institutions are eroded during the course of a conflict. Holding elections in such societies can be a dangerous process. The competitive nature of elections may exaggerate existing tensions, whereby social groups are mobilized along old conflict lines. This can create a volatile situation, especially if there is no consensus concerning the rules of the game and there are few guarantees as to what will happen to the losing side (Höglund 2009). Under such circumstances, where much is at stake, it can be tempting for the contestants to sponsor different sorts of electoral violence, ranging from attacks and intimidation against voters, election workers and opposing candidates to destroying polling stations (ibid.). For

Big Men planning to enter the political process, it can therefore be appealing to employ ex-combatants. Having much experience in using violence, former fighters can be used either for offensive purposes, such as those mentioned above, or for providing protection for Big Men and their followers against the violent actions taken by other elites.

When seeking the services of former fighters during election campaigns, Big Men often look to ex-MiLCs to find the necessary manpower. By turning to their previous followers, these commanders can hastily deliver 'task forces' that are ready for action (Christensen and Utas 2008). One of the most vivid illustrations of how politicians can utilize ex-MiLCs to create such squads has been given by Christensen and Utas (ibid.) in their article on the 2007 elections in Sierra Leone. During the run-up to these elections the two main presidential candidates – Solomon Berewa of the Sierra Leone People's Party (SLPP) and Ernest Bai Koroma of the All People's Congress (APC) – both contacted ex-MiLCs to provide security for them and their parties. While the former approached ex-commanders of the West Side Boys (WSB), Koroma and APC got in touch with the commanders of the RUF. Owing to Sierra Leone's history of electoral violence and the two leaders' distrust of the police and armed forces, both Berewa and Koroma preferred to mobilize unofficial security guards who would be directly loyal to them. Disillusioned by what they had gained from the peace process, many ex-MiLCs accepted the jobs as intermediaries and security providers. When setting up their task forces, the former commanders could make use of the informal networks that continued to thrive between themselves and their former fighters. By playing on the loyalty of their old subordinates and offering promises of pay, jobs and education, they were refused by only a minority. The task forces were used to protect party offices and high-profile party members, as well as to intimidate voters during the actual elections. On several occasions the ex-combatant squads even clashed with each other, using sticks, knives and cutlasses, creating widespread fears of large-scale violence and derailed elections.

Sierra Leone offers one of the more extreme examples of how Big Men can utilize informal military networks, while officially working within the formal structures of democratic institutions.[12] The political mobilization of ex-combatants does not, however, necessarily have to take violent forms. Old military networks can also be used to quickly gather crowds of people to manifest public support for political candidates. Since the mid-1990s, this has been a common phenomenon in Liberia (Hoffman 2007; Utas 2003: 236). For example, during the 2005 national elections there were reports of political candidates seeking the services of former LURD commanders. For these politicians, ex-MiLCs were indispensable allies, since they could bring together large numbers of ex-combatants to boost political rallies (Hoffman 2007).

Legal and illegal economic ventures Even if ex-MiLCs engage their former fighters in both war-making and election campaigns, the most frequent use of former combatants is in different business ventures. In many cases, these post-conflict enterprises are perfectly legal. For example, while ex-MiLCs in Liberia organized their former subordinates into labour teams for brick-making and plantation work, their Congolese counterparts led ex-fighters in small business ventures in areas such as agriculture, animal husbandry and petty trade (Themnér 2011; Utas 2005). It is, nevertheless, common for ex-commanders to employ their old military units for more malign purposes, such as organized crime (see Vigh in this volume). The informal character of old military structures is well suited to the clandestine purposes of mafia-like organizations. Another advantage of transforming military units into criminal groups is that it allows ex-MiLCs to exploit ex-fighters' experience of using violence. These skills can come into good use when intimidating civilians or during turf wars with competing criminal groups. For instance, evidence suggests that Tuareg ex-MiLCs successfully employed their former subordinates to gain control over parts of the lucrative trans-Saharan smuggling routes in Niger (Guichaoua 2009: 11–15; see also Böås in this volume). However, often ex-MiLCs lead their former subordinates in business ventures operating in the grey zone between what is legal and what is not. This is especially true when it comes to the exploitation of valuable natural resources – such as diamonds, gold, rubber and lumber – which generally requires licences granted by the authorities. In both Liberia and Sierra Leone, ex-MiLCs and their former fighters were heavily involved in the exploitation of such resources (Gberie 2002; Utas 2005; see also Persson's and de Koning's chapters in this volume). For ex-combatants and commanders who have been accustomed to enriching themselves by extracting valuable commodities during the war, continuing to exploit such resources can be an effective strategy to avoid economic marginalization after demobilizing.

When ex-MiLCs mobilize their former subordinates in different business ventures, they often do it on behalf of Big Men or within the confines of a Big Man's network. For elites aspiring to engage in economic activities such as agriculture, it can, for example, be wise to leave the day-to-day management to ex-MiLCs. Thanks to the resilience of old command structures, these commanders are often the perfect foremen. Not only do they know the ex-combatant labourers personally, they can also use their standing as wartime commanders to impose discipline on the group. Uganda constitutes a clear example of this. During 2005/06 the World Bank sponsored a reintegration project called the Labora Farm near the town of Gulu in the northern part of the country. The aim of the project was to help former child soldiers to reintegrate into society via farm work, growing crops such as corn, cassava and beans. The venture was led by Kenneth Banya, the former number-three commander of LRA, who had taken advantage of a government amnesty to

defect from the rebels. To oversee the work of approximately 120 ex-child combatants – who were promised food as compensation for their labour – Banya
hired seven of his former deputies. This allowed him to keep a close eye on
the former child combatants as they worked, supervision that often escalated
into physical abuse. Not only could the ex-MiLCs count on employment from
their wartime patron, they were also able to retain the wives that they had
abducted during the war.[13]

When taking on the role as intermediaries, ex-MiLCs do not always enter
the services of Big Men by working directly under them. In some instances
they engage in economic interactions on a more equal basis. Rather than
providing Big Men with the labour of their ex-fighters, they can use their former
subordinates to supply and sell different goods or resources to elites. This
was evident in Sierra Leone after the cessation of hostilities in 2001. Despite
the completion of the demobilization process, former commanders frequently
employed their ex-fighters in the illicit mining of alluvial diamonds in the
central and eastern parts of the country. In April 2002 it was, for instance,
reported that no fewer than two hundred ex-RUF fighters were collectively
digging for diamonds in the Tongo Fields. Organizing the operation was their
wartime commander, to whom the rank-and-file ex-combatants continued to
show loyalty. However, in order to get the proceeds from the finds, ex-MiLCs
and other diamond prospectors were dependent on wealthy diamond dealers.
These Big Men tended to be Lebanese traders who were based in the country
(Gberie 2002).[14] Similar examples can be found in post-war Mozambique. Not
only were many criminal gangs during the 1990s believed to be run by former
government officers, evidence suggests that these ex-MiLCs often utilized their
previous subordinates to engage in activities such as drug trading. One reason
why such outfits were so prominent was that they tended to be part of larger
national and international networks that enjoyed the support of government
officials and criminal actors in Brazil, the Gulf States, Pakistan, Portugal and
South Africa (Alden 2002; Gastrow and Mosse 2002).

Intermediaries of peace?

Considering their key role as brokers between Big Men and ex-combatants,
there are grounds for suspecting that ex-MiLCs may not only constitute a
source of instability but can, in fact, also be used to promote peace. There
are two reasons for this. First, just as Big Men are constrained by problems of
span of control during elections or war, they have similar problems reaching
out to the grass roots when trying to make peace. This is especially true for
rank-and-file combatants who may have more confidence and faith in their
closest commanders than in politicians or generals with whom they may have
no personal relations. In such instances, elites need to put much emphasis
on convincing commanders at the mid-level that peace is in their, as well

as their subordinates', interests. In fact, as I have argued elsewhere, if such mid-level deputies are brought on board, '... they can play an important role in "selling" peace to their followers' (Nilsson 2005: 79). Utilizing ex-MiLCs as intermediaries of peace can be especially fruitful when trying to convince combatants to disarm. For instance, one of the main reasons why the United Nations Development Programme (UNDP) has been fairly successful in removing weapons from ex-Cobra fighters in RoC is that they have employed former Cobra commanders in their disarmament programmes. These have had a much easier time convincing rank-and-file ex-Cobras that they no longer have any use for their weapons.[15]

Another reason why it is crucial to engage ex-MiLCs is the fact that they can be used to counter the negative influence of spoiling elites. If peacemakers can convince ex-MiLCs to support a peace process, they can sever the link binding war-prone elites to ex-fighters and in essence leave spoilers with no one to do their spoiling for them. Giving more attention to ex-MiLCs therefore constitutes a cost-efficient way to prevent renewed warfare and the emergence of organized crime. This is particularly true when keeping in mind the problems associated with giving universal reintegration assistance to ex-fighters, as well as the possible political repercussions of appeasing warlords (Nilsson 2008: 196). The question, then, is how former commanders can be persuaded to embrace peace. Here it is essential not only to provide ex-MiLCs with reintegration assistance, but also to find ways for ex-commanders to maintain the societal status they obtained during the previous war. In fact, failing to give assistance to ex-MiLCs, or endowing them with inappropriate kinds of help, can have dire consequences. For example, one of the main reasons why former government officers ran many of the criminal groups in Mozambique during the 1990s was because there were no reintegration programmes specifically crafted for them. After demobilizing, they were given start-up kits, hoes, seeds and buckets, and were expected to become small-scale farmers like their former subordinates; something which many resented (Alden 2002: 350). Meanwhile, ex-Ninja commanders in RoC experienced similar problems. After leaving their armed units, many began to question the merits of a peace process that had fulfilled neither their social nor their economic aspirations. Upon joining the Ninjas, they had been given lofty promises of employment in the armed forces or in public administration upon victory. However, owing to the outcome of the war, these pledges had not been fulfilled, and because the UNDP disarmament and reintegration programme lacked sufficient funding, many ex-Ninja commanders were left without reintegration assistance. This is believed to have pushed several ex-Ninja commanders into becoming intermediaries, recruiting ex-fighters on behalf of Ntoumi during the 2002–03 hostilities (Nilsson 2008: 79).

Empirical evidence also suggests that when ex-MiLCs are given proper attention and assistance living up to their 'wartime status' – such as jobs in the armed forces, police or private sector – they can be partners in peace. In RoC, for instance, it appears that those former commanders – both ex-Cobra and Ninja – who had benefited from the reintegration assistance provided by UNDP refrained from remobilizing their ex-fighters during the 2002–03 conflict. The programme was constructed in such a way that ex-combatants of the different factions could pool the money they received, and set up joint micro-projects in areas such as agriculture, animal husbandry and petty trade. In many cases, ex-MiLCs ended up taking charge of these collective business ventures. Hence, by re-engaging in violence, these ex-MiLCs risked forfeiting the social and economic status they had acquired by becoming small-scale business managers. For this reason they not only refused offers to become intermediaries for the Congolese government or Ntoumi, but also hindered their former subordinates from taking up arms (Nilsson 2008). In both RoC and Sierra Leone, another successful strategy was to integrate ex-MiLCs into the armed forces. By giving former commanders employment in the security forces, it was possible to prevent them from recruiting ex-fighters for different national and regional warlords (ibid.: 196).

Not only may business ventures based on informal military networks and headed by ex-MiLCs be used to impede efforts by Big Men to remobilize former fighters, they are also effective when it comes to providing jobs for ex-combatants. In Liberia, those ex-fighters with the greatest success in finding peacetime employment were often those who cooperated economically with their wartime comrades and commanders. By using the organizational skills attained during the previous conflict, they were able to collectively work in areas such as brick-making, gold and diamond mining, plantation work and logging (Utas 2005). Experiences such as these suggest that it could, at times, be fruitful to use armed units as the basis for giving reintegration aid to ex-combatants. This is especially true for the 'hard core' of armed groups, who frequently show greater resilience and loyalty to their commanders. Often members of such units have few acquaintances besides their wartime companions – owing either to the atrocities they may have committed or because they have spent long stretches of time away from their homes – making them more dependent on wartime comradeships. In such situations it may be wiser to find ways to use informal military networks for productive purposes, rather than taking the risk that they are co-opted by Big Men seeking to engage in violence and crime.

It is, however, important to keep in mind that giving special attention to ex-MiLCs may not be completely unproblematic. First, owing to their roles as commanders during the preceding war, ex-MiLCs may very well have been involved in atrocities committed against the civilian population. Providing former commanders with lucrative assistance can thereby endanger efforts at societal reconciliation and judicial reform in some war-affected countries. In such situations, it can therefore be wise to couple reintegration programmes for ex-MiLCs with strategies dealing with transitional justice. This may include anything from war-crime trials for certain ex-MiLCs to vetting procedures seeking to exclude the worst offenders from receiving state employment. It is, however, important to bear in mind that even when seeking post-war justice, ex-MiLCs can also be seen as an asset rather than a liability. By cooperating with, rather than prosecuting, these individuals, it may be easier to bring those who carry the greatest responsibility for war offences – senior commanders, wartime politicians and warlords – to justice. Having taken direct orders from these elites, ex-MiLCs often possess unique and critical information that can bind certain leaders to specific events during which atrocities have been committed. A second problem concerns the integration of ex-MiLCs into the security forces. If former commanders are placed in the same units as their previous subordinates, there is always the risk that wartime norms and behaviours will continue to thrive. This has, for example, been a problem in DRC, where entire militia units, with command structures intact, have been incorporated into the national army (see also de Koning in this volume). During 2009 these units were involved in the raping and killing of many civilians in the eastern parts of the country (HRW 2009).[16] When giving ex-MiLCs employment in the armed forces, it can therefore be wise to separate them from their former fighters and place them in command over new soldiers.

Notes

1 An ex-combatant is deemed to be a person who has taken direct part in hostilities on behalf of an armed group and has either been discharged from or voluntarily left the military faction he or she was serving in.

2 Ex-MiLCs are seen as the category of military personnel that was previously situated between the rank-and-file combatants and the highest military leadership, and who personally led their subordinates in battle.

3 Author's own observation during field research in Sierra Leone during January–March 2006.

4 Before becoming a warlord, Ntoumi was the leader of a peaceful messianic movement, the Ntsiloulous, active near the town of Vinza. The Ntsiloulous, meaning the 'promise', is based on a combination of Christian and local religious beliefs. Claiming to have been sent by

God to be the saviour of the people of the Pool region, he was able to tap into the messianic traditions of the region's different ethnic groups. When hostilities broke out in Pool in August 1998, Ntoumi used his spiritual charisma to attract a substantial number of Ninja fighters to his cause and launched a rebellion against the Congolese government. For a more detailed description of the religious foundation of the Ntsiloulous, see Knight (2007).

5 According to Graicunas (1937), business managers can effectively supervise only a small number of individuals, perhaps as few as four to five subordinates.

6 The definition for intermediary has been derived from the term broker, used by Hannerz (1980: 190).

7 During the first civil war in Liberia (1989–96), it was not uncommon for MiLCs to switch alliances and rally their units to opposing factions. For example,

when MiLCs of the United Liberian Movement for Democracy – Johnson faction (ULIMO-J) defected to the National Patriotic Front of Liberia (NPFL), they were able to convince their subordinates to follow them. This is an indication of how the ties binding rank-and-file combatants to MiLCs are often stronger than those binding fighters to the highest leadership of armed movements.

8 During the Liberian civil war several well-known MiLCs were women, such as Martina Johnson of NPFL (Coulter et al. 2008).

9 Interview with former mid-level AFRC commander, Freetown, 12 February 2006, and Hoffman (2007).

10 By the end of the war a new rebel group appeared in eastern Liberia – the Movement for Democracy in Liberia (MODEL) – after having splintered from LURD. However, since most ex-combatants from Sierra Leone fought in the western parts of the country, they were not affected by the appearance of MODEL.

11 During the late 1990s, Bockarie was one of the RUF's most central figures, second only to Foday Sankoh. However, in 1999 a split appeared between the two, owing to Bockarie's objection to the rebel movement's participation in the Lomé peace process. By the end of the year Bockarie had fled to Liberia, after his fighters had clashed with combatants loyal to Sankoh. Thanks to his good relations with Taylor, Bockarie was incorporated into the country's military establishment and became one of the leading figures in Taylor's Anti-Terrorist Unit (ATU). For more information on Bockarie, see Bøås (2007).

12 This is also a well-known phenomenon in Kenyan politics. See, e.g., Kagwanja (2005).

13 After Uganda's leading newspaper, the *Daily Monitor*, ran a piece on the dire working and living conditions for the children at Labora Farm, Banya and his former deputies were fired from their roles as managers (Eichstaedt 2009: 104–6).

14 For more information on the role

of the Lebanese community in the Sierra Leonean diamond trade, see Fithen (1999).

15 Author's observation during field research in RoC during September–November 2006.

16 See also Eriksson Baaz (2010).

References

Alden, C. (2002) 'Making old soldiers fade away: lessons from the reintegration of demobilized soldiers in Mozambique', *Security Dialogue*, 33(3): 341–56.
Bledsoe, C. (1990) '"No success without struggle": social mobility and hardship for foster children in Sierra Leone', *Man*, 25: 70–88.
Bøås, M. (2007) 'Marginalized youth', in M. Bøås and K. C. Dunn (eds), *African Guerillas: Raging against the Machine*, Boulder, CO: Lynne Rienner, pp. 39–53
Christensen, M. and M. Utas (2008) 'Mercenaries of democracy: the "politricks" of remobilized combatants in the 2007 general elections, Sierra Leone', *African Affairs*, 107: 515–39.
Coulter, C., M. Persson and M. Utas (2008) 'Young female fighters in African wars', *NAI Policy Dialogue*, Uppsala: Nordic Africa Institute.
Deutsch, K. (1966) *The Nerves of Government. Models of Political Communication and Control*, New York and London: Free Press.
Dzinesa, G. (2008) 'The role of ex-combatants and veterans in violence in transitional societies', *Violence and Transition Roundtable*, Johannesburg: Centre for the Study of Violence and Reconciliation, pp. 1–19.
Eichstaedt, P. (2009) *First Kill Your Family. Child Soldiers of Uganda and the Lord's Resistance Army*, Chicago, IL: Lawrence Hill Books.
Englebert, P. and J. Ron (2004) 'Primary commodities and war: Congo-Brazzaville's ambivalent resource curse', *Comparative Politics*, 37(1): 61–81.
Eriksson Baaz, M. (2010) 'The complexity of violence: a critical analysis of sexual violence in the Democratic Republic of Congo (DRC)', SIDA Working Paper on

Gender-based Violence, Stockholm and Uppsala: SIDA.

Figueiredo, R., Jr, and B. Weingast (1999) 'The rationality of fear: political opportunism and ethnic conflict', in B. F. Walter and J. Snyder (eds), *Civil Wars, Insecurity, and Intervention*, New York: Columbia University Press, pp. 261–307.

Fithen, C. (1999) *Diamonds and War in Sierra Leone: Cultural strategies for commercial adaptation to endemic low-intensity conflict*, London: Department of Anthropology, University College London.

Gastrow, P. and M. Mosse (2002) 'Mozambique: threats posed by the penetration of criminal networks', ISS Regional Seminar, Pretoria.

Gberie, L. (2002) *War and Peace in Sierra Leone: Diamonds, corruption and the Lebanese connection*, Partnership Africa Canada, International Peace Information Service and Network Movement for Justice and Development.

Graicunas, V.A. (1937) 'Relationship in organization', in L. Gulick and L. Urwick (eds), *Papers on the Science of Administration*, New York: Columbia University Press, pp. 183–7.

Guichaoua, Y. (2009) *Circumstantial Alliances and Loose Loyalties in Rebellion Making. The Case of Tuareg Insurgency in Northern Niger (2007–2009)*, MICROCON Research Working Paper no. 20, Brighton: Institute of Development Studies at the University of Sussex.

Gurr, T. (2000) *Peoples versus States: Minorities at risk in the new century*, Washington, DC: United States Institute of Peace Press.

Hannerz, U. (1980) *Exploring the City: Inquiries toward an urban anthropology*, New York: Columbia University Press.

Hoffman, D. (2007) 'The city as barracks: Freetown, Monrovia, and the organization of violence in postcolonial African cities', *Cultural Anthropology*, 22(3): 400–28.

Horowitz, D. (1985) *Ethnic Groups in Conflict*, Berkeley and London: University of California Press.

HRW (2005) *Youth, Poverty and Blood: The lethal legacy of West Africa's regional warriors*, Human Rights Watch.

— (2009) *Eastern DR Congo: Surge in army atrocities*, Human Rights Watch.

Höglund, K. (2009) 'Elections and violence in Sri Lanka: understanding variation across three parliamentary elections', in A. Swain, R. Amer and J. Öjendal (eds), *The Democratization Project: Opportunities and challenges*, London, New York and Delhi: Anthem Press.

Johnston, P. (2008) 'The geography of insurgent organization and its consequences for civil wars: evidence from Liberia and Sierra Leone', *Security Studies*, 17: 107–37.

Jörgel, M. and M. Utas (2007) *The Mano River Basin Area: Formal and informal security providers in Liberia, Guinea and Sierra Leone*, FOI, Swedish Defence Research Agency.

Kagwanja, P. (2005) '"Power to Uhuru". Youth identity and generational politics in Kenya's 2002 elections', *African Affairs*, 105(418): 51–75.

Knight, C. (2007) *Brazzaville Charms: Magic and rebellion in the Republic of Congo*, London: Frances Lincoln.

Lanken, C. (2007) *Somebody from the Bush: Rethinking abduction, homecoming and storymaking in war-torn northern Uganda*, Århus: University of Århus.

Lyons, T. (2005) *Demilitarizing Politics: Elections on the uncertain road to peace*, Boulder, CO, and London: Lynne Rienner.

Nickols, F. (2003) *The Span of Control and the Formulas of V. A. Graicunas*, Distance Consulting.

Nilsson, A. (2005) *Reintegrating Ex-Combatants in Post-Conflict Societies*, Stockholm: SIDA.

— (2008) *Dangerous Liaisons. Why Ex-Combatants Return to Violence. Cases from the Republic of Congo and Sierra Leone*, Uppsala: Uppsala University.

Oketch, B. (2009) 'LRA revival fears', *All Africa*, 22 June.

Panebianco, A. (1988) *Political Parties: Organization and power*, Cambridge: Cambridge University Press.

Peters, K. (2006) *Footpaths to Reintegration: Armed conflict, youth and the rural crisis in Sierra Leone*, Wageningen: Wageningen University.

Preston, R. (1997) 'Integrating fighters after war: reflections on the Namibian experience, 1989–1993', *Journal of Southern African Studies*, 23(3): 453–72.

Stedman, S. (1997) 'Spoiler problems in peace processes', *International Security*, 22(2): 5–53.

Themnér, A. (2011) *Violence in Post-Conflict Societies: Remarginalisation, remobilisers and relationships*, New York and London: Routledge.

Utas, M. (2003) *Sweet Battlefields: Youth and the Liberian Civil War*, Uppsala: Uppsala University Dissertations in Cultural Anthropology.

— (2005) 'The Reintegration and remarginalization of youth in Liberia', in P. Richards (ed.), *No Peace, No War: An anthropology of contemporary armed conflicts*, Athens/Oxford: Ohio University Press/James Currey, pp. 137–54.

— (2008) *Informal Realities of Post-War Liberia*, Stockholm/Uppsala: Swedish Defence Research Agency/Nordic Africa Institute.

10 | Big Men commanding conflict resources: the Democratic Republic of the Congo

Ruben de Koning

Since the beginning of the 1990s much attention has been devoted to the negative relationship between natural resources and armed conflicts, particularly on the African continent. The destabilizing effect of unequal distribution of land and the mismanagement of revenues from oil had been known and studied for some time. But the so-called 'new wars' of the time featured something different – that is, warlord/Big Men-style rebel commanders financing their struggle with proceeds from easily marketable and extractable gemstones and precious metals, which have come to be known as 'conflict resources'. Connecting local resources of this kind to transnational trade networks, rebel commanders increasingly brokered commercial interests, in addition to political ones. And making profit out of war, they appeared to have an interest in keeping it going, rather than arriving at a compromise over political issues (Collier 2000). War economies, understood as 'system[s] of producing, mobilizing and allocating resources to sustain the violence' (Le Billon 2005) that thrives on conflict resources, have become a chronic condition of several African countries such as the DRC and Ivory Coast, and risk resurfacing in countries like Sierra Leone, Liberia and Angola.

Mainly through channels of the United Nations (UN), the international community has taken a number of measures to neutralize violent networks of resource control. Special UN representatives have helped negotiate power- and wealth-sharing agreements. The Security Council imposed several commodity boycotts on countries, and numerous travel sanctions and asset freezes on rebel leaders and their business associates, as well as criminal elements within the state army. In addition, UN peacekeepers and other external forces have assisted in intercepting illegally traded goods and in bringing extraction areas back into government hands. Measures that combine rebel accommodation and regulatory and military crackdown on these military and private actors have, however, been criticized for overemphasizing the economic dimensions and for either having a negative impact on local livelihoods or failing to offer 'peace dividends' (Le Billon 2007). Yet there is relatively little analysis of how these actors adapt to or circumvent regulatory and military pressure intended to defuse the war economy.

Like many contemporary wars in Africa, associated war economies have the potential to persist after the signing of a peace agreement. Conflict-based Big Men – that is, military figureheads and their business and political associates, or alter egos – often continue to be plugged into resource sectors after the war, the main difference usually being a strengthened affiliation with the political centre. External interventions such as sanctions and peacekeepers tend to reaffirm the position of regular forces against that of non-state forces, motivating the latter to move farther underground or let themselves be co-opted eventually. It is difficult to see how such a superficial form of state consolidation can lead to a breakdown of the patterns of exploitation that emerged during the war. Furthermore, attempts to break down these patterns are likely to be resisted by non-elite actors, including artisanal producers and shadowy traders, whose livelihoods are connected to those Big Men in either the state or non-state political and military circles that command commercial networks. It is increasingly argued that war economies, rather than simply serving greedy, criminalized rulers, for many people represent spaces of high economic intensity and actual development, in a context of general state failure, deep poverty and chronic instability (Duffield 2002). This means that unless the inner potential and adaptive capacities of African war economies and their key operators are understood and recognized, attempts to defuse them will not succeed in dislodging military players and enhancing post-conflict economic reconstruction.

Conflict resources in Africa: detaching, fracturing and realigning networks of control

The issue of conflict resources in Africa came to the fore during the 1990s, when local high-value natural resources appeared to sustain territorial control by newly emerging non-state armed groups. The loss of territorial control signified an important rupture with post-colonial consolidation of state ownership and control of land and resources in Africa (Alden Wily 2001). Yet the challenges posed by insurgent groups to the territorial integrity of the state are in many ways a consequence of earlier patterns of state resource governance. In the two decades preceding civil wars during the 1990s in countries like Sierra Leone, Liberia, DRC and Ivory Coast, state control over land and resource commodities had become the key element in ensuring political loyalties. Patronage included, for example, the selective attribution of rights, the redistribution of extra budgetary revenue, and the attribution of tax-collecting and law enforcement duties/privileges. As long as resources were sufficiently available to extend patronage networks, these patronage systems did not bring serious challenges to state power, notwithstanding the local power struggles for legitimacy and support from the centre, and the local resentment as a result of state predation on local economies.

Following the drying up of patronage resources and diminishing coercive power of the state – resulting from dropping commodity prices, structural adjustment, and reduction of foreign (military) assistance after the end of the Cold War – elements from within pre-war political networks started to detach themselves in some countries. Commenting on civil war in Liberia and Côte d'Ivoire, Reno notes that 'the leaders of the largest insurgent organizations and their armed rivals previously occupied dual roles as high officials and coordinators of patronage in the pre-war state' (Reno 2009). For instance, Liberia's rebel leader and later president Charles Taylor held a high position in Samuel Doe's government which left him in charge of purchasing for the Liberian government (Huband 1998: 16). The Forces Nouvelles (FN) rebel chief in Ivory Coast, Fofié Kouakou Martin, was an ex-corporal in the regular army before the insurgency, as was Sierra Leone's RUF rebel leader Foday Sankoh. In contrast, DRCs first insurgency, by the Alliance des forces démocratiques pour la libération du Congo (AFDL) in 1996–97, was led by a truly political outsider, Laurent Kabila, who, as an old Lumumba loyalist, had for decades fought a rather unsuccessful guerrilla war against Mobutu. Rebel leaders of the Rassemblement Congolais pour la Democratie (RCD) during the second insurgency of 1998, however, were almost all members of the political establishment under Mobutu, either in Kinshasa or in the eastern provinces (Tull 2007).

Part of pre-war political and military establishments, rebel leaders and other commanding officers either already exercised control over informal commercial activities or could impose themselves on these activities as the new security providers cum administrators. By the time rebel movements emerged in the above countries, trade in diamonds, gold and some other precious resources had been informalized and rerouted to such an extent that insurgents found no need to run trade through state offices and national capitals or uphold any form of officialdom (see, e.g., Reno 1995). Goods from resource-rich areas in border regions were often smuggled across borders and exported through neighbouring countries at lower costs than they could be through capital port cities in the country. Diamonds trade from RUF-controlled areas in the north of Sierra Leone and from Forces Nouvelles areas in western Ivory Coast could be routed through Guinea. Liberian timber during Charles Taylor's insurgency years was exported through ports under his control in the far south-east corner of the country, as well as through Ivory Coast.[1] Presently, precious metals from eastern DRC are exported mainly through the capitals of Rwanda, Burundi and Uganda. In all these cases the control by rebel groups of borderlands and cross-border trade significantly contributed to the build-up of the military strength needed to advance towards the capital.[2]

The availability of easily extractable and tradable resources has greatly contributed to the mobilization and success of rebel movements in the above countries, enabling Big Men rebel commanders to exercise authority by sharing out their wealth (de Smedt 2009). At the same time it has been argued that by using resources to provide material rewards to followers, rebel leaders risk undermining their own political agenda of overthrowing the central government or seceding from it (Weinstein 2003). In contexts where revenues are readily available to mobilize combatants, the movement is likely to be infiltrated by a high number of fighters whose intention it is to pursue immediate gain rather than await distribution of political positions once state power is captured. Their willingness to fight to the end is therefore low. In addition, once individual economic motivations come to override common ideological ones, infighting and fracturing of the rebel movement is increasingly likely, further reducing the chances of successfully overturning the government.

Evidence from the above cases of resource dependence affecting rebel unity is mixed. The RUF in the course of its existence indeed degenerated from an ideologically inspired rebellion into a collection of looting mobs. In order to maintain the insurgent force, which came close to defeat on several occasions, no real attempt was made by the leadership to distinguish between committed fighters and those attracted by short-term economic gain. However, since the movement was dependent on natural resources from the beginning, it is hard to attribute the increasingly chaotic style of warfare entirely to this factor. In Ivory Coast rebel beneficiation from resources did not lead to fracturing. On the contrary, it went hand in hand with coalition-building between two smaller rebel groups in the resource-rich west of the country and the one major rebel party in the north of the country.[3] These parties united under the Forces Nouvelles banner. For the DRC the picture is more complex, as will be shown below. In a nutshell, RCD revenue generation from resources was undermined by the sponsors, Rwanda and Uganda, whose desire to establish exclusive areas of control in eastern DRC led to fracturing. For the other rebel and militia parties there is no evidence that their increasing resource dependency reduced combat effectiveness through fragmenting forces. For example, local defence militia in the eastern DRC increasingly coordinated their operations, in spite of them growing more dependent on mineral resources. So while undisciplined looting is a common feature of resource-fuelled wars in the above countries, the impact on the unity of the insurgent groups is dissimilar.

In the peacemaking process the Big Men networks controlling territory and local resources realign with the central state. But while military and political elites are usually in new administrative and military structures, states that emerge from years of warfare are often not able to accommodate smaller men in the new regime. Limited provisions for reintegration of ex-combatants into society or the army have in many countries led to combatants defecting from the peace process in order to resume their warrior livelihoods, often with the intention of being taken more seriously in the next round of negotiations (Tull and Mehler 2005). This is the pattern many field commanders and their

Box 10.1 Definining conflict resources in Africa

Since 1998 the UN Security Council (UNSC) has sanctioned specific commodity exports from four African countries, but without providing a clear definition. It either banned all trade from the country in question, or, if in place, provided an exemption for diamonds exported under a government certification scheme. In response to the ad hoc basis of commodity sanctions, commentators have repeatedly requested a generalized definition for 'conflict resources' and a permanent body with a standing capacity to investigate and call for sanctions in the context of armed conflict. To date no concrete steps have been taken in this direction.

The closest the UN has come to a definition is a reference in a General Assembly resolution of 2000 that understands conflict diamonds as 'diamonds that originate from areas controlled by forces or factions opposed to legitimate and internationally recognized governments, and are used to fund military action in opposition to those governments' (United Nations General Assembly 2000). Applying this definition to cases other than conflict diamonds in Angola and Sierra Leone would be problematic. In the case of the timber sanctions on Liberia, these were targeted at the incumbent government of Charles Taylor. The definitional issue was avoided by simply banning all exports of round logs and processed timber products from the country.

If one applied the above definition to conflict minerals from the eastern DRC, not all military groups profiting from trade would be targeted. While it would cover Congolese and Rwandan rebels, and foreign forces fighting in the DRC, local defence militia (Mai Mai) would be excluded, since these are not opposed to the government. Another problem would pose itself with regard to the superficial military integration of Congolese rebel forces. These have formally ceased to be opposed to the government, but continue to run parallel administrations and attack or scare off public administrators, thereby undermining the central government.

Although there is no commodity ban in place for DRC, the arms embargo provides scope to freeze assets of 'individuals and entities supporting the illegal armed groups ... through illicit trade of natural resources' (United Nations Security Council 2008). This resolution poses similar definitional problems. Superficially integrated rebel and militia groups would not be considered as 'illegal armed groups'. In addition there is the problematic focus on illicit trade. In DRC as in many other contexts in Africa, legal trade equally risks benefiting armed groups, be they legal or illegal, through military extortion of but also through association with licensed traders.

respective units, dissatisfied with their prospects in the new army in the DRC, have followed in recent years. Often illegal revenues from trade in natural resources are used to sustain independent fighting capacities, thereby postponing rebel demobilization. West Africa has struggled with similar issues. In Liberia, for example, 5,000 fighters of the Movement for Democracy in Liberia (MODEL) pulled back into the Sapo forest for several years after 2003. Fending for themselves by pit sawing, hunting and diamond and gold exploitation, they were able to withstand disarmament (Richards et al. 2005). Still today, the border region between Liberia, Guinea and Ivory Coast attracts many ex-combatants from Liberia and Sierra Leone who operate as borderless mercenaries in search of economic opportunities in cross-border resource trade.

Dealing with the Big Men commanding war economies

Responses to African war economies have expanded since the beginning of the 1990s, combining accommodating and punitive measures to deal with rebel leaderships. Typically, wealth-sharing is part of the political settlement of resource-related conflict. This means that key ministries governing natural resources and resource management agencies are transferred to representatives of opposition parties. Wealth-sharing may also be an implicit consequence of army restructuring when former rebel factions maintain control over resources in the post-conflict army. Punitive measures most importantly involve UN (smart) sanctions – i.e. freezing assets and banning travel – on individuals and entities that trade in embargoed goods or support armed groups through the trade in natural resources. In addition, external military interventions have in several countries been aimed at dismantling rebel control over resources. The above responses have the potential to neutralize the means and motivation to fight, but there are many pitfalls.

Resource wealth-sharing can be a dangerous solution in cases where the political will among the rebel leadership to establish long-term peace is lacking. The Lomé agreement in Sierra Leone – signed a year before the UN export ban on diamonds – allocated important resource management positions to the opposition. Most notably, RUF leader Foday Sankoh received the dual post of vice-president and chairman of the Commission on the Management of Strategic Resources. But rather than dismantling RUF trading activities, Sankoh used his position to commercialize diamonds from RUF areas and channel funds back to the rebels, allowing them to continue to fight.[4] Similarly, in Angola, UNITA came to head the Ministry of Mines, strengthening its control over diamond trading. Off-budget sale of diamonds continued to finance arms purchases after the protocol was signed, owing partly due to its weak enforcement by the UN verification mission.

Sanctions often fail to affect those targeted because of limited control measures leading to continued smuggling through neighbouring countries. Despite sanctions on Angola, illegal exports of diamonds continued mostly through DRC, together comprising half of the countries' output, valued at between $350 million and $450 million.[5] The sanctions on Sierra Leone had limited effect until diamond sanctions were also implemented against Liberia a year later. It must be said, though, that the RUF had already been defeated by this time; that Taylor's regime profited equally from timber; and that smuggling options through Mali, Guinea and Ghana remained.

Besides the problem of enforcement – apparent in all cases – the Liberia timber sanctions also demonstrate a lack of international political will to declare sanctions in the first place. Sanctions were declared only in 2003, several years after the first reports demonstrated the close link between the timber trade and ongoing conflict and human rights violations, and only three months before Taylor went into exile – too little time to have made a significant contribution. In fact, in 2003 timber production was already declining as a result of infrastructure destruction and clear cutting in accessible places in previous years (Hardcastle 2001). France and China, during the Taylor regime the main importers of Liberian timber, were the principal objectors to earlier calls for sanctions in the Security Council in 2001. The absence of sanctions thus allowed the country to legally export hundreds of millions of dollars' worth of timber during Taylor's rule, from which Taylor himself is alleged to have derived about $23 million of extra-budgetary revenues (Coalition for International Justice 2005).

In the DRC, anticipated enforcement difficulties were the main reason for the secretary-general to rebuff full commodity sanctions. Consequently, the UN Group of Experts (GoE) started recommending selective commodity sanctions to stem the flow of resources from certain mines from where militia and rebel parties derive revenues (United Nations 2007: 13; United Nations Security Council 2007). The only regulatory action by the UN has been the freezing of assets imposed on gold traders in 2007 for their alleged support of a non-state armed group, in contravention of the arms embargo. A 2008 UN Resolution explicitly calls for sanctions on individuals or entities supporting illegal armed groups through the trade in natural resources. In addition, GoEs have collected evidence against mineral traders and submitted confidential lists to the UNSC for designation under the sanction regime, featuring at least one renowned niobium trader (Africa Confidential 2010: 4). Nevertheless, no new individuals or entities have been added. The third category of responses to war economies is that of external military interventions, which, *inter alia*, aim to bring resource production areas back under government control. The main pitfall here is that one coercive form of resource control is simply replaced by another. The negative effect of private military companies (PMCs) in the cases of Angola and Sierra Leone on the peace process has been widely reported (see, e.g., Schreier and Caparini 2005). In both cases, the firm

Executive Outcomes (EO) defended the corporate interests of certain extractive companies with which it was linked. In Sierra Leone the granting of mining concessions to these companies even functioned as a partial payment for the services EO provided to the Sierra Leone government (Pech 1999a). The hidden commercial interests and indiscriminate killings involved in EO operations to reclaim strategic resources provoked widespread indignation and sporadic violent reactions, and undermined the role of 'peace-enforcing' which EO was so keen to claim for itself (Pech 1999b).

As with PMCs, neighbouring countries' interventions can also grant foreign forces interests in the resource areas they are supposed to secure. The case where this is most clear is that of the DRC, where intervention by the Zimbabwe Defence Forces (ZDF) was compensated with mineral trading rights and concessions for businesses linked to high military and political officials. ZDF fuelled instability by supporting armed groups opposing Rwanda and Burundi in the areas under control (United Nations 2002).

Multilateral peacekeepers are arguably better positioned to re-establish 'neutral' government control over resource areas. UN interventions in Sierra Leone and Liberia succeeded, although often after an intense struggle, in dislodging insurgents from mines and re-establishing 'civil' forms of governance.[6] However, the DRC case demonstrates what can go wrong. The involvement of Pakistani peacekeepers in the gold trade contributed to negative sentiments against the force. Moreover, MONUC (United Nations Mission in the Democratic Republic of the Congo) has thus far failed to prevent the regular forces it supports establishing extortive and dehumanizing forms of control over mines, adding to civilian populations' growing resentment of MONUC's failure to protect them.

Overall it is hard to estimate the effectiveness of the above responses to war economies. What is clear is that the termination of conflict in Angola, Sierra Leone and Liberia did not benefit from elite accommodation and, owing partly to the limited effect of sanctions, required multilateral and unilateral peacekeeping intervention to end fighting and dislodge insurgents from resource-rich areas. While some commentators continue to regard extractive industries in these countries as a threat to stability, several donors and development NGOs have in recent years engaged in the sector to formalize trade and production, and help producers organize themselves to earn better wages. The approach has moved from regulatory and military crackdown on the sector (to end war financing) to harnessing its contribution to development. Still smaller conflict issues remain, including artisanal miners' and community protests against industrial exploitation, as well as miners' discontent with customary Big Men's and statutory authorities' firm control over allocation of rights, redistribution of revenues, labour and financial transactions. The risk of localized resource-related violence in these countries scaling up to threaten nationwide stability is low. However, it must be realized that informal artisanal sectors have absorbed many ex-combatants and that progressive closure of opportunities here could make a choice to engage in crime, banditry and armed violence more likely.

In contrast with the above three countries, resource-fuelled conflict lingers on in parts of the eastern DRC and in western Ivory Coast. Political accommodation of insurgent parties in neither case included any wealth-sharing formula. Instead de facto territorial control of (national) insurgent groups paid out in the form of integration in the central and provincial government administration and in the national army. In Ivory Coast integration is stalled. Despite a power-sharing agreement that made FN rebel leader Guillaume Soro prime minister, rebels continue to control the legal, police and tax system in the north of the country, in contravention of the agreed process of redeploying public administration.[7] In DRC political and military reintegration has moved ahead but with many difficulties, among them the lack of command and control over underpaid newly integrated brigades and the outright refusal to integrate by some militia that were part of the 2008 Goma peace agreement. Like the FN in Ivory Coast, renegade soldiers and former rebel and militia movements refuse to break up parallel administration and taxation structures. Also, sanctions and military interventions have failed to successfully disband parallel civil administrations by military-led organizations. In DRC real commodity-focused sanctions are absent, while military interventions are primarily targeted at foreign armed groups, since almost all the Congolese ones are 'regularized'. In Ivory Coast sanctions are in place but there is no peacekeeping mission to enforce them and gather information on potential sanctions busters. In effect, no diamond traders have ever been listed by the sanctions committee.

The eastern DRC war economy: between warlordism and network enterprise

The military Big Men of the eastern DRC war economy are more commonly described as modern-day warlords (Reno 1998). The term warlord defines military or political strongmen controlling an area through their ability to wage war, often but not necessarily in opposition to the central government. In contrast to the situation in conflicts over secession or regional autonomy, areas of insurgent control are often 'defined by commercial interests, such as the control of a mine, forest, or drug production valley' (Le Billon 2001: 575). In turn, the warlord's ability to establish de facto sovereignty and keep central authorities and competing groups at bay largely depends on the revenues derived from the local economy. The manner in which beneficiation takes place can involve organized looting, but more stable new forms of governance may emerge, especially where the state has failed to provide security and other collective goods. In the context of the eastern DRC war economy, commentators apply the term 'security governance' to describe the provision of security by an armed actor, or warlord, which is either imposed on or requested by a defined social group, and is compensated in the form of coerced, negotiated or voluntary payments of taxes and other more random fees and contributions (Garret et al. 2009).

The description of the eastern DRC war economy as a warlord system in which military strongmen lucratively control mineral-rich areas through the establishment of the monopoly on violence and the advancement of governance formation goes a long way. However, it presupposes a level of territorial control that is not always needed for armed actors to benefit from resource commodity chains. Alternatively, one can describe the war economy as a non-territorial 'network enterprise', which can generally be understood as the intertwining of economic actors operating at different levels of scale and legitimacy into strategic alliances that cut across international borders to enact business projects (Duffield 2002). Although self-provisioning, the war economy – seen as a network enterprise – has no permanent base and little control over productive assets and markets. Instead the nodal points in the network establish and revitalize long regional chains and circuits through facilitating productive activities and through organizing the downstream movement of these goods towards international markets – for instance, by providing legal documentation, secure passage of goods, transport facilities and links to legitimate enterprises. Such nodal points can include the warlords mentioned above, but may also encompass a wider range of Big Men who engage in interlocking political and economic relationships simply to make economic profit without having a direct interest in or organizing violence. Nevertheless, they are integrated in the same networks, assisting in the provision of the means to those who do organize violence. The key point here is, however, not the ambivalence of the war economy network enterprise – supporting organized violence while providing income to an army of small-scale producers, drivers, guards, (unpaid) officials, etc. – but the non-territoriality of its functioning: working through and around government authorities, and with or without physical control over markets, production areas and traded commodities.

The next sections highlight armed groups' self-provisioning strategies, which include organized looting and parallel illicit taxation, as well as conducting trade, investment and logistics services, which are mostly centred around minerals. These strategies reveal continuities but are also altered by internal and external political and military factors, such as the fragmentation of rebel groups and foreign military interference during the second Congolese war (1998–2002), army integration in the transition phase (2003–06) and more recent military campaigns against illegal, largely foreign armed groups (2009–present). Discussion will first focus on the main Congolese non-state armed groups: the Rassemblement Démocratique du Congo (RCD) and its various offshoots, notably the Congrès National pour la Défense du Peuple (CNDP), as well as the multiple Mai Mai formations. Thereafter focus shifts to the main foreign-armed group, the Forces Démocratique pour la Libération du Rwanda (FDLR).

RCD and Mai Mai insurgencies We pick up the DRC case study in the middle of 1998, when a second rebel movement is mobilized in the east of the country in opposition to the freshly installed government of Laurent Kabila, who had only a year before replaced Mobutu as president. Kabila's former allies, Uganda and Rwanda, with which Kabila had fallen out of favour after ordering all foreign troops to leave the country, supported the RCD insurrection. The movement's advance on Kinshasa was blocked by an Angolan intervention, which led to a revision of the military strategy, which began to focus on seizing control of territory and mineral sites in the east of the country in order to build up a revenue base and gain military strength. By the 1999 Lusaka ceasefire accord Kabila's government acknowledged territorial control by the RCD, but halted its advance towards the diamond areas of the Kasai provinces and the copper belt of south Katanga province.

The Lusaka accord offered the opportunity to build a unified rebel government in the east of the country, which would be economically integrated into the eastern African region. However, composed of an array of political and military figures from different political camps and with different regional power bases, the RCD had already fragmented before the signing of the accord. In the same year as the insurrection, Uganda shifted its support to the Mouvement pour la Libération du Congo (MLC), which came to control much of the north of the country. This shift isolated RCD president Wamba dia Wamba, because Rwanda did not favour the moderate and diplomatic approach he represented. In 1999 the RCD split between (1) a Rwandan-supported faction (RCD-Goma), led by Rwandophone leaders from Kivu trusted by Kigali, and (2) a Ugandan-supported faction (RCD-Kisangani or ML), which could not be held together long under the leadership and soon fragmented again. Uganda furthermore supported the Rassemblement des Congolais Démocrates et Nationalistes (RCD-N), a faction split off from the RCD-Goma, operating in Ituri, the eastern district of Orientale Province neighbouring Uganda.

Of the different factions the RDC-Goma was probably best positioned to exert enduring political and administrative control over the eastern DRC. It left the local administrations intact, but failed to set up a system of official revenues, state budgets and public spending.[8] Meanwhile RCD military units concentrated on consolidating their positions in centres of commerce, rich mineral deposits and crucial transport axes. Illicit tax levying was the main method of revenue collection, meant principally to fund the war effort. Attempts to centralize the revenue stream were undermined by individual commanders (Vlassenroot and Raeymaekers 2008). The multiplication of taxes in many zones lead to exorbitant transaction costs for traders, forcing them out of business or shifting their economic activities to areas controlled and secured by militia opposed to or competing with the RCD-Goma. Traders formerly connected to the Mobutu regime in particular faced high taxes and violence, and were thus forced out of business, to be replaced by other Congolese and increasingly Rwandan entrepreneurs and business entities.

Rwandan interests further damaged RCD tax-levying capacity, whether for private gain or state coffers, demonstrating the subordinate position of Big Men in the RCD against those in the Rwandan Patriotic Army (RPA). In the diamond sector, the Rwandan government's Congo Desk, created by Paul Kagame and headed by senior RPA officials like Major Kazura, allocated monopoly positions to trading companies operating in Kisangani.[9] The RCD-Goma claimed that Rwandese army protection allowed these companies to undervalue diamonds, leading to a reduction in taxes payable to RCD-Goma's public treasury (United Nations 2002: 17). In addition, large quantities of diamonds were allegedly smuggled out by Rwandese army officers and traded in Kigali or even directly sold to the Congo Desk. In the coltan sector the RCD government did at first manage to set up and allocate a trade monopoly to one company, SOMIGL, in return for a monthly tax of US$1 million.[10] A reduction of company exports in 2001 damaged its ability to pay its taxes. Soon after, the arrangement was disbanded and the market 'liberalized'. Yet again the metal-trading houses that colluded with the Congo Desk, such as Grands Lacs Metals and Rwanda Metals, gained the upper hand. UN experts attest that 'the Congo Desk has perennially deprived its junior partner, RCD-Goma, of any significant share in resources and prerogatives' (ibid.: 16).

The main rebel parties' capacity to set up an administration able to capture rents from business operations was also undermined by the various self-protection forces or Mai Mai that proliferated largely in response to heavy foreign influence in the RCD-Goma and the MLC.[11] Although their agendas were principally local – operating on behalf of communities and protecting village and tribal properties and territories – Mai Mai militia started operating in coalition with each other beyond the village territory. A coalition under the leadership of General David Karendo Bulenda, known as General Padiri, extended its reach to Maniema, the northern parts of South Kivu and the southern parts of North Kivu.[12] As the war progressed, local Mai Mai militia grew more powerful as a result of military support from the central government. In many areas they came to play a leading role in local governance by replacing local government agents with their own, affiliating customary elders to their cause, regulating resource access, and taxing lucrative commercial activities in mining – in fact mimicking the conduct of 'alien' forces.

However, the home-grown character of Mai Mai militia made them more likely to serve local security interests, including those of ethnically associated

Box 10.2 Nande traders' self-protection

Incorporating about five hundred entrepreneurs, the Nande business elite of Beni and Butembo had grown rich under the Mobutu regime through the export of gold, the import of manufactured goods, and the takeover of European-owned plantations during the 1970s. In a bid to protect their economic wealth from rebels, the Nande business community, together with the Catholic Church and local civil society, was a driving element in the formation of a local Mai Mai militia. Businessmen arranged, among other things, for the import of weapons to arm the militia (Romkema 2001: 34). In addition the militia protected 'indigenous' land rights against appropriation of land by 'foreign' Tutsi populations (Tull 2005). While operating in the Middle and Far East to sell gold and ship back other goods into DRC, traders maintained a strong sense of belonging and responsibility to their communities. Their investment in healthcare, infrastructure and housing further enhanced support from among ordinary citizens for local militia formation (Kabamba 2007).

The ability of the militia to defend territory, properties and trading routes against the more powerful rebel armies relied not on military force alone, but also on 'diplomatic' efforts. Representatives from the Nande business community travelled to the USA to urge the State Department to put pressure on Rwanda to recall the RCD advance towards the 'Grand Nord'. The local Catholic Church started a publicity campaign against Bemba's MLC, accusing its troops of cannibalism, thereby generating the necessary international outcry that helped to halt the movement's advance towards the area (ibid.).

Another potent military actor in the area, the RCD-ML, could not be kept at bay and was therefore turned into an ally. In 2001, Mbusa Nyamwisi, one of the influential Nande businessmen, ousted Wamba dia Wamba, who had been in charge of the rebel faction. He forged an alliance with the local Mai Mai and harnessed support from the Ugandan army, which had an interest in the gold trade from the area. Through their closeness to local security actors, Nande traders were able to push through a change of the customs regime, replacing tax levying on the basis of value and volumes of traded goods with a system of fee payments, thereby significantly reducing transaction costs.

business operators, rather than prey on economic activities through forced taxation. A good example of this has been documented with regard to the northern part of North Kivu, the so-called 'Grand Nord', where the rich and influential Big Men of the Nande's business community managed to keep the RCD and MLC at bay and avoid expensive taxation by the RDC-ML – in their own interests and that of their community at large. To these ends it developed an ingenious strategy of mobilizing and associating military force, of conducting a public relations campaign and practising unofficial diplomacy, as elaborated in Box 10.2.

In summary, the lack of internal control, foreign military dependence and indigenous opposition reduced the RCD ability to tax mineral traders, particularly those under Rwandan and Ugandan protection. But besides not being able, it can be questioned whether the RCD was even willing to set up a durable administration based on tax collection and public spending. The RCD rebellion was a 'movement for power in Kinshasa', to quote the RCD governor of Orientale province in 2001, rather than an attempt to genuinely create a state within a state (Englebert 2003). This *raison d'être* also explains the fracturing of the movement since its creation in 1998. Rebel leaders would split off to be able to independently negotiate their reinsertion with Kinshasa. The superficial exercise of territorial control only served as a basis for negotiating posts in the transitional government and the new national army (Forces Armées du République Démocratique du Congo: FARDC), according to the all-inclusive agreement that was concluded in December 2002 between the main Congolese rebel parties, the Mai Mai militia and the government.[13]

Settlement, integration and defection The Global and Inclusive Peace Agreement of December 2002 largely accommodated the political and military leadership of the main belligerent groups. As to the future of lower-level commanders and ordinary soldiers, the terms of the agreement stipulated that the armed forces of all signatory parties should automatically become FARDC soldiers, and would be able to choose to enter the voluntary national DDR programme, which would assist them to reintegrate into civilian life, or be integrated into the new army structure. Under the latter option they would undergo a process called *brassage* (intermingling), which is meant to create new retrained, re-equipped 'integrated' regular FARDC units in which government loyalist soldiers and former rebels and militia members serve alongside each other. Importantly, it is also meant to break down the existing command structures of units that enter the process. The integrated units are, in theory, posted away from the locations where their members previously operated.

The army reintegration process has been slow and underfunded, and many units refuse, delay or try to change the conditions under which they reintegrate to continue to pursue particular military-strategic, ethnic and economic objectives. Whatever the combination of reasons, the post-2003 transition period shows several examples of elaborate ongoing and newly established parallel administration and taxation systems conceived by FARDC units, particularly by non- or poorly integrated elements. These cover smaller areas than initial

RCD factors controlled, but can be very successful in generating a continuous stream of revenues, thus providing a further disincentive to fully integrate into new army structures and allow designated authorities to take over control.

Most importantly, the CNDP has for several years governed much of Masisi Territory in North Kivu. The CNDP emerged in 2006 from a breakaway faction of the RCD-Goma that felt that the transitional government and the new FARDC army did not protect Tutsi minorities in the east of the country against the FDLR. General Ntaganda, the de facto leader of the group after former leader Laurent Nkunda was arrested in Rwanda in January 2009, managed to centralize taxation systems established during the previous years to control illegal border posts, charcoal markets and the timber trade. In 2009, UN experts estimated that General Ntaganda's network raises about $250,000 a month from these ground taxes (United Nations 2009b). The political agreement between the government and the CNDP in March 2009, which regulates the integration of the CNDP into the military, police and administration, has not convinced CNDP officials to abandon parallel administration and tax collection posts. It is even reported that new ones have been established since early 2010 (United Nations 2010: para. 12).

Furthermore, the accelerated integration of the CNDP into the FARDC at the beginning of 2009 has opened up new resource taxation opportunities. Given a free hand in the pursuit of the FDLR, FARDC units almost entirely consisting of ex-CNDP combatants quickly established control over the more lucrative cassiterite mining areas in Walikale territory. According to UN experts in November 2009, local officers, under the command of a certain Lieutenant Bin Mashabi, are able to earn up to $60,000 per year from taxes levied on minerals produced in the main mining site of Bisie (United Nations 2009a). Besides random taxation (in cash and in minerals), UN experts allege that local CNDP commanders make additional profits by commercializing cassiterite produced on their own behalf through a relative of the controlling lieutenant, who holds an official licence and is thereby able to sell cassiterite to major Congolese and international trading houses in Goma. Farther down the commodity chain, the FARDC (unit not specified) is also reported to requisition aircraft to fly cassiterite from Bisie from Kilambo airstrip to Goma (ibid.). It has not been ascertained whether these arrangements at production and transport level are in any way coordinated.

The CNDP control system in Bisie replaced and imitated that of another non-integrated FARDC unit, of Mai Mai origin, that had previously controlled the Bisie mine. For several years the unit had not received the order to enrol in the *brassage* process, and could control local resources undisturbed under the command of Colonel Samy Matumo. He effectively lobbied at higher military levels to postpone the call to go to *brassage*, and since early 2009 has been awaiting redeployment in South Kivu, presumably in another cassiterite-rich

238

area around Kasika.[14] Regulating economic operators' access to the mine and extracting taxes from miners, the unit could have generated about US$315,000 per month in cash and in kind during its four-year occupation (Garret 2008). To increase control over commercial transactions at the mine, the ex-Mai Mai unit curiously favoured one trading company, the Groupe Minier Bangandula (GMB), owned by an alleged key financer of the CNDP, to buy from artisanal miners (Spittaels and Hilgert 2008). The territorial administrator approved of the alliance by entering into an agreement with GMB to provide security, presumably through the ex-Mai Mai unit, in return for a share of the company's production and revenues (Garret 2008). This (semi-)formal mandate to provide security in the mine can only have contributed to the unit's capacity to levy taxes and appropriate production.

Another example of a mining area that has in recent years been infiltrated by non-integrated ex-RCD and Mai Mai encompasses the gold and coltan mines of Nyunzu and Kalemie territories in the north of Katanga province. Rather than seeking absolute and permanent control of mines, which has become increasingly difficult because of new deployments of police and integrated FARDC battalions (which likewise prey on the local economy), commanders are developing alternative strategies to profit. On the side of the ex-RCD, non-integrated elements of the 69th FARDC brigade of Kongolo reject calls by military superiors in Lubumbashi to move back to their barracks and frequent mining sites far beyond their bases to shake down miners and traders haphazardly.[15] Alternatively, in the coltan mining areas around the village of Kayebe, one lieutenant by the name of Yanzungu installed a small, unlicensed mining company, SOCOMIN, to organize artisanal mining and transport to Bukavu. This means that the company provides some supplies and tools in return for the lion's share of minerals produced, while the soldiers, who are not permanently present, can be called upon if miners refuse the arrangement (SIPRI 2010). For the Mai Mai, one of the main leaders in the area, Major Tango Fort, used to exercise some degree of control over mines, but now aspires to lead a special Border Guard brigade in order to regain access to illicit revenue opportunities. This brigade was proposed by ex-Mai Mai FARDC general Padiri to help integrate the Mai Mai of north Katanga. Tango Fort, however, refused to move with his followers to the reintegration camp of Kamina, and has assumed authority in Kalemie without proper payment and training.

The above examples demonstrate how the military integration process is both challenged and used by ex-rebel and militia units in order to preserve or strengthen their grip on the local resource-dependent economy. In cases where 'renegade' units are strong enough they tend to continue or establish new parallel administrations, but also seek collaboration with commercial partners to generate revenues. In cases where units are scattered and challenged by other FARDC, they can resort to similar forms of collaboration, as well as organized looting. Neither requires permanent territorial control over extraction areas. In case of (near-)defeat, commanders can try to use the integration process to swap positions that can yield similar illicit revenues, e.g. by being transferred to other mineral-rich areas or along borders. Military commanders can thus manipulate political and military pressure to integrate so that it allows them to continue to profit from minerals even when they lose territorial control.

The FDLR survivalist movement The present FDLR forces operating in eastern DRC are remnants of former Rwanda government forces and Interahamwe militia responsible for the 1994 genocide against Tutsis in Rwanda. The FDLR was formed in 2000 in Lubumbashi in the south of the country and received support from the government of Joseph Kabila to move into Kivu to fight against the Rwandan army and the RCD-Goma. In its surge north it aligned and armed other Hutu militants from among civilian refugees, as well as anti-Rwandan forces of the Armée de Libération du Rwanda (ALIR) already established in the east. Before 2002 neither ALIR nor FDLR was actively involved in the exploitation and taxation of natural resources but largely depended on haphazard looting of villages (Romkema 2007). This changed when the Rwandan army withdrew from Congolese territory in 2003 and support from the Kabila government dried up. Without any serious chance of toppling the Kagame government and reluctant to accept voluntary repatriation, the FDLR had no option but to consolidate its power base in eastern DRC.

For its economic survival the FDLR developed a system of 'non-conventional logistics', which basically left units to fend for themselves through the exploitation and taxation of natural resources, trade in manufactured goods and livestock, and agriculture (ibid.). The system prescribes the share of revenues that should move up the military hierarchy to the 'Etat Major' as a contribution to the overall movement's functioning. In the opposite direction, it allows for the provisions of loans and credit from the central treasury to invest in commercial activities (Action pour la Paix et la Concorde and Life and Peace Institute 2009: 26). The mineral sector, particularly gold, is the most important source of FDLR revenues, yielding the force millions of dollars per year (United Nations 2008: 20).[16] In remote mining regions where capital is scarce the FDLR agents have operated as the most important pre-financers of mining operations. Usually they leave this to private persons, who are taxed. Sometimes combatants even form their own exploitation teams – for example, in sparsely populated areas like Kahuzi-Biega National Park (Action pour la Paix et la Concorde and Life and Peace Institute 2009: 26). Organized looting takes place in mines in hostile environments over which no control is exercised. Where coltan or cassiterite is concerned, local populations have been used as forced labourers to evacuate the material.[17]

There are several options with regard to how minerals produced, looted or taxed by the FDLR are commercialized. Outside traders access FDLR-controlled mines in return for the payment of taxes that serve as protection money. However, the preference is for its own people dedicated to trade to bring goods to markets outside FDLR-controlled areas, connect to licensed buyers in main towns, and even smuggle goods across the border. The ability of FDLR commercial agents to handle minerals, particularly the bulky ones, is restricted, though, because of obvious suspicion of FDLR affiliation on the part of FARDC and state officials, not least because of traders' language differences and lack of identity cards. However, state representatives can be made complicit through bribe payments, or circumvented by deputing Congolese traders to conduct business on behalf of the FDLR agents.[18] For instance, at Lulinga airstrip on the edges of Kahuzi Biega National Park, the FARDC's 18th Integrated Brigade was reported as doing nothing to prevent intermediary traders buying from FDLR agents and associated civilians arriving there with cassiterite and coltan (United Nations 2008: 22). FDLR traders usually part with their goods before arriving in towns or transport hubs by selling them to Congolese unlicensed traders who move the goods farther downstream to legal traders and exporters in Congo and neighbouring countries.

Most of the gold from FDLR territories in South Kivu is smuggled by un- licensed traders to Burundi, where it is sold to a licensed gold exporter by the name of Mutoka Ruganyira, who is responsible for almost all official exports from the country, mostly to the United Arab Emirates (UAE) (912 kilograms, worth about US$30 million, between January and September 2009) (United Nations 2009b). He also receives some gold from a licensed gold trader that officially exports gold from Bukavu, Etablissement Namukaya, which is likewise alleged to source from FDLR areas across the province (ibid.). In North Kivu, a group of traders in Butembo, associated in a trading company called Glory Minerals which recently obtained an export licence, receives most of the gold from joint FDLR–Mai Mai- (of renegade general Lafontaine) controlled areas in Lubero. They smuggle gold across the border to Uganda to sell to two gold exporters who sell in Dubai in the UAE, or they go to Dubai directly. Several other unlicensed traders follow the same route. The trade in cassiterite and coltan is more transparent, as mining authorities register much of it once licensed traders put the material on trucks or planes to transport it to national hubs and across the border. Many export companies operating in eastern DRC are alleged to buy from traders who have purchased from markets such as Lulinga, where goods from FDLR territories arrive.

After many years of cohabitation between FARDC, Mai Mai and FDLR milit- ary elements, the FDLR has since the beginning of 2009 been confronted with three consecutive military surges aimed at their neutralization and/or repatri- ation to Rwanda.[19] Temporal removal of the FDLR from strategic locations has, however, had only a limited effect. In many places forces have been able to regroup and recruit new members to recapture areas lost, bringing populations under control with intensified force, using looting and hostage-taking as a deterrent and a source of revenues. Furthermore, dislocation in some areas only provoked the movement to resurface in other areas, usually deeper into inhospitable forest areas farther away from the Rwandan border, such as in Kahuzi Biega and Maiko National Parks. Representing areas of unexploited resource exploitation opportunities, these moves only complicate military pursuit and make surrender less likely. And even if military pressure could remove the FDLR permanently from mines, this would not severely damage the FDLR's self-provisioning strategy. This strategy is more sophisticated than physical control of deposits and trading routes and subsequent taxation, working through investment in extractive activities and other business operations, often in (forced) collaboration with Congolese labourers and business associates and with the connivance of the state authorities.

Conclusions and recommendations

Of the different post-Cold War conflicts in Africa that were heavily driven by natural resources, that in the eastern DRC is the most persistent. Resource revenues helped to mobilize anti-state insurgence by Congolese rebel commanders and presently complicate the military defeat of Rwandese rebels operating from within the DRC. However, a narrow understanding of 'conflict resources' that focuses on non-state players and illegal activities does not capture the different conflict–resource links that are at play. Besides facing military threats from foreign armed forces operating on its soil, the Congolese state and in particular its people in the east are threatened by modern-day warlords operating within the national army. Their reasons for undermining post-conflict state consolidation and military integration processes may be political and ethnic in nature, but the means and motivation to preserve relative autonomy largely derive from the local resource-based economy.

As indicated, the eastern DRC war economy is far from static but evolves over time. FDLR rebel commanders are increasingly driven into remote forest areas, home to many scattered small resource deposits, as well as into the trade of the least bulky goods, notably gold. Meanwhile former Congolese militia and rebel FARDC officers control main mines and trading hubs. But physical control over deposits, trading hubs and minerals themselves is decreasingly important for military Big Men in terms of benefiting from the resource-dependent local economy. They move beyond the role of local security provider/(tax) administrator, through providing logistics, protecting smuggling ventures, channelling investment, and associating with (semi-)formal business entities – all this in the comfort of official army positions and sitting in urban centres.

Attempts to dismantle military Big Men systems of resource control have to come to terms with both the non-rebel and the non-territorial aspects of the contemporary war economy in the eastern DRC. The conventional commodity-focused responses of wealth-sharing, commodity sanctions and military intervention fail to do so. Wealth-sharing takes the form of allocation of grades on the basis of havoc created during years of opposition. Allocation of high functions in the state army to rebel leadership, particularly that of the CNDP, stimulates and renders more sophisticated rebel leaders' violent strategies of resource appropriation. Meanwhile, smaller warlords, often of Mai Mai background, are likely to obtain only minor functions in the new government or army, increasing the risk of defection and opposition to the new army leadership. Commodity sanctions in DRC are absent and the arms embargo concerns illegal armed groups only. Furthermore, suspect business entities associated with illegal armed groups are hardly ever put on the sanctions list. External military intervention props up regular forces that are no less likely to ingrain themselves in the local economy through taxation or otherwise. UN support to military operations against the FDLR went hand in hand with extended FARDC control over mines. Regulatory action to transform the war economy in the eastern DRC needs to distinguish between two groups. First, punitive action needs to target the military spoilers and economic associates who defy civil authorities and perpetuate war. Secondly, some form of accommodation needs to include those actors who, in order to get by, became involved in the wartime economic activities and who have no interest in war and would probably benefit more from peace (Goodhand 2004).

Punitive action against military spoilers is minimal as there is huge reluctance at superior political and military levels to make arrests in order to avoid a backlash in the peacemaking process. Attempts to arrest are countered with military force, cases are dropped by threatening the use of force, and big fish frequently escape from prison. As a result only petty thieves within the army are brought to trial for economic crimes. Bolstering military, criminal and civil justice systems requires international assistance – for instance, through providing the protection of peacekeepers to military auditors when they are investigating cases and making arrests. But significant restructuring is needed to create transparency in the justice system as well. Because justice procedures are not transparent and give too much power to the magistrates, flagrant cases involving high-level commanders are easily dropped.

Accommodating action needs first of all to include intermediate traders and miners, who are the usual victims of extortion and illicit taxation, although they may enter into a (coerced) relationship with security providers. The formalization of their activities is a first step to enhance their rights – for instance, by establishing legal mining zones and trading centres, secure from the interference of non-authorized military players. But accommodation must also reach out to some controlling military units and their commanders, who have demonstrated willingness to fulfil some governance functions and have a decent track record on human rights – for example, through establishing transparent payment structures to engage them in areas of economic interest strictly for security purposes.

As long as high commanders' violent behaviour in DRC is rewarded with official functions and de facto resources control, and lower cadres are left to their own devices, war economies in the DRC are bound to reproduce themselves. So while the scale of war economies under warlords' command may have diminished in recent years, we can expect ongoing struggles featuring smaller men pulling back into the bush with the intention of rising to Big Man status in order to be co-opted into the realms of power.

Notes

1 These were valued at $53 million per year during the period 1990–94, funding purchase of arms and ammunition from eastern Europe. P. Richards, 'The Mano river conflicts as forest wars', *ETFRN News*, 43/44, 2005.

2 In some cases insurgents captured state power (NFPL in Liberia, ADFL in DRC) and in other cases not (RUF in Sierra Leone, RCD in DRC, UNITA in Angola). In Ivory Coast their success is ambiguous, as the Forces Nouvelles have never been able to make an attempt to take the capital, but were able to establish de facto administrative control over the north of the country that has lasted to date.

3 Namely the Mouvement populaire ivoirien du Grand Ouest (MPIGO), the Mouvement pour la justice et la paix (MJP) and the Mouvement patriotique de Côte d'Ivoire (MPCI).

4 'Sierra Leone one year after the peace accord: the search for peace, justice and sustainable development', Conference report by Partnership Africa–Canada, Ottawa, 21–23 June 2000.

5 www.duke.edu/web/soc142/team7/Social,%20Political,%20and%20Environmental%20Issues.htm.

6 In Sierra Leone UN peacekeepers' attempts to seize mining areas resulted in the RUF taking 500 personnel hostage; they were freed only after the mediation of Charles Taylor.

7 Initially foreseen as taking place by 15 January 2009 (Depagne 2009).

8 In some cases recorded tax revenues during the war were reduced to 10 per cent of pre-war levels (Vlassenroot and Raeymakers 2008).

9 The Congo Desk was an agency within the Department of External Relations of the Rwandan Patriotic Army with a mandate to facilitate business between Congolese, Rwandese and Western trading companies and levy a 10 per cent tax in Kigali on the value of traded volumes.

10 'Le coltan congolais, objet de toutes les convoitises', Afrik.com, www.afrik.com/article2630.html.

11 Although some smaller militia aligned themselves with the RDC-Goma, e.g. Mudundu 40/Front de Résistance et de Défense du Kivu (FRDKI) and the Mouvement de Lutte contre l'Agression au Zaïre/Forces Unies de Résistance Nationale contre l'Agression de la République Démocratique du Congo (MLAZ/FURNAC).

12 The success of Padiri's Mai Mai coalition in establishing territorial control and building a relatively unified armed movement translated in 2003 into its integration into the new military and political structures. Padiri was appointed major general and commander of the ninth military region in Orientale province and later the sixth military region in Katanga.

13 In the transitional government the RCD-Goma and the MLC each took one

of the four vice-presidencies, while ministries and seats in the National Assembly and in the Senate were divided among other rebel factions as well. None of the rebel groups' representatives gained influential positions in the economically important ministries of Mines, Energy, Finances and Industry. Global and Inclusive Agreement on Transition in the Democratic Republic of Congo, signed in Pretoria, 16 December 2002, www.reliefweb.int/rw/RWFiles2004.nsf/FilesByRWDocUNID-FileName/MHII-65G8B8-gov-cod-16dec-02.pdf/$File/gov-cod-16dec-02.pdf.

14 DRC Forces Armées Etat Major General, *Rearticulation et comdt des unités ops Kimia II Sud Kivu*, Bukavu, 12 November 2009.

15 'Axe Kalemie–Nyunzu–Kongolo: la population se plaint des tracasseries des militaires non brasses' [Kalemie–Nyunzu–Kongolo axis: the population complains about harassment by non-integrated militaries], Radio Okapi, 19 May 2008, www.radiookapi.net/index.php?i=53 &a=18685.

16 It should be noted, however, that several of their eleven battalions are in areas without mines, and that the sites they do control are not the most lucrative but rather hold small deposits in remote areas. See, Spittaels and Hilgert (2009).

17 See, for instance, 'Shabunda: libération des 45 otages après de violents affrontements', Radio Okapi, 14 May 2010.

18 It has been reported that those trusted with money and minerals are controlled through the threat of force against family members left behind.

19 Umoja Wetu, by the Rwandan army and the FARDC; followed by the MONUC-supported FARDC operations Kimia II and Amani Leo.

References

Action pour la Paix et la Concorde and Life and Peace Institute (2009) 'Analyse de context du territoire de Kalehe', April.

Africa Confidential (2010) 'The UN looks for the exit', *Africa Confidential*, 51(2).

Alden Wily, L. (2001) 'Reconstructing the African commons', *Africa Today*, 48(1): 76–99.

Coalition for International Justice (2005) 'Following Taylor's money: a path of war and destruction', May.

Collier, P. (2000) 'Doing well out of war', in M. Berdal and D. Malone (eds), *Greed and Grievance: Economic Agendas in Civil Wars*, Boulder, CO: Lynne Rienner, pp. 91–112.

De Smedt, J. (2009) '"No Raila, no peace!" Big Man politics and election violence at the Kibera grassroots', *African Affairs*, 108: 581–98.

Depagne, R. (2009) 'Côte d'Ivoire: peace deal runs into dead end', *allAfrica*, 9 March, www.allafrica.com/stories/200903090003.html.

Duffield, M. (2002) 'War as a network enterprise: the new security terrain and its implications', *Journal for Cultural Research*, 6: 153–65.

Englebert, P. (2003) 'Why Congo persists: sovereignty, globalization and the violent reproduction of a weal state', QEH Working Paper Series no. 95, February.

Garret, N. (2008) 'Walikale: artisanal cassiterite mining and trade in North Kivu', Communities and Small Scale Mining (CASM), June, www.artisanalmining.org/userfiles/.../CASM_WalikaleBooklet. pdf.

Garret, N., S. Sergiou and K. Vlassenroot (2009) 'Negotiated peace for extortion: the case of Walikale in eastern DR Congo', *Journal of Eastern African Studies*, 3(1): 11.

Goodhand, J. (2004) 'From war economy to peace economy? Reconstruction and statebuilding in Afghanistan', *International Affairs*, 58(1): 155–74.

Hardcastle, P. D. (2001) *Proposed Sanctions on Liberian Timber*, Internal brief, UK Department for International Development.

Huband, M. (1998) *The Liberian Civil War*, London and Portland, OR: Frank Cass.

Kabamba, P. (2007) *Capital Accumulation and Emergence of New Power Elite in South Africa and the DRC*, Doctoral research project presentation,

Woodrow Wilson International Center for Scholars, 22 August.

Le Billon, P. (2001) 'The political ecology of war: natural resources and armed conflicts', *Political Geography*, 20: 561–84.

Le Billon, P. (2005) *Geopolitics of Resource Wars: Resource Dependence, Governance and Violence*, London: Frank Cass.

— (2007) 'Geographies of war: perspectives on "resource wars"', *Compass*, 1(1): 1–20.

Pech, K. (1999a) 'Executive Outcomes – a corporate quest', in J. Cilliers and P. Mason (eds), *Peace, Profit or Plunder?: The Privatization of Security in War-torn African Societies*, Pretoria: Institute for Security Studies, pp. 81–110.

— (1999b) 'Executive Outcomes – a corporate conquest', in J. Cilliers and P. Mason (eds), *Peace, Profit or Plunder?: The Privatization of Security in War-torn African Societies*, Pretoria: Institute for Security Studies, ch. 5.

Reno, W. (1995) *Corruption and State Politics in Sierra Leone*, Cambridge: Cambridge University Press.

— (1998) *Warlord Politics and African States*, Boulder, CO: Lynne Rienner.

— (2009) 'Understanding criminality in West African conflicts', *International Peacekeeping*, 16(1): 47–61.

Richards, P., S. Archibald, B. Bruce, W. Modad, E. Mulbah, T. Varpilah and J. Vincent (2005) *Community Cohesion in Liberia: A post-war rapid social assessment*, World Bank Social Development Paper 21.

Romkema, H. (2001) *An Analysis of the Civil Society and Peace Building Prospects in the North and South Kivu Provinces, DRC*, Life & Peace Institute.

— (2007) *Opportunities and Constraints for the Disarmament and Repatriation of Foreign Armed Groups in the Democratic Republic of the Congo: The Cases of the FDLR, FNL, and ADF/NALU*, Washington, DC: Multi-country Demobilization and Reintegration Program.

Schreier, F. and M. Caparini (2005) *Privatising Security: Law, Practice and Governance of Private Military and Security Companies*, DCAF Occasional Paper 6.

SIPRI (2010) *Demilitarizing Mining Areas in the Democratic Republic of the Congo: The Case of Northern Katanga Province*, Stockholm International Peace Research Institute, 15 February.

Spittaels, S. and F. Hilgert (2008) 'Mapping conflict motives in eastern DRC', IPIS, 4 March.

— (2009) 'Are Congo's mines the main target of armed groups on its soil?', *Economics of Peace and Security Journal*, 4(1): 55–61.

Tull, D. (2005) *The Reconfiguration of Political Order in Africa*, Hamburg: Institut für Afrika-Kunde.

— (2007) 'The Democratic Republic of Congo: militarised politics in a failed state', in M. Bøås and K. C. Dunn (eds), *African Guerrillas: Raging against the machine*, Boulder, CO: Lynne Rienner, pp. 113–30.

Tull, D. M. and A. Mehler (2005) 'The hidden costs of power-sharing: reproducing insurgent violence in Africa', *African Affairs*, 104(416): 375–98.

United Nations (2002) *Final Report of the Panel of Experts on the Illegal Exploitation of Natural Resources and Other Forms of Wealth of the Democratic Republic of Congo*, S/2002/1146.

— (2007) *Interim Report of the Group of Experts on the Democratic Republic of Congo, pursuant to Security Council Resolution 1698 (2006)*, S/2007/40, 31 January.

— (2008) *Final Report of the Group of Experts on the Democratic Republic of the Congo, pursuant to Security Council Resolution 1698 (2006)*.

— (2009a) *Letter dated 14 May 2009 from the Chairman of the UN Security Council Committee established pursuant to Resolution 1533 concerning the Democratic Republic of the Congo*, S/2009/253.

— (2009b) *Letter dated 23 November 2009 from the Chairman of the UN Security Council Committee established pursuant to Resolution 1533 concerning*

the Democratic Republic of the Congo,
S/2009/603.

— (2010) *Thirty-first report of the Secretary-General on the United Nations Organization Mission in the Democratic Republic of the Congo*, S/2010/164, 30 March.

United Nations General Assembly (2000) *Role of Diamonds in Fuelling Conflict*, A/RES/55/56.

United Nations Security Council (2007) *Report of the Secretary-General pursuant to paragraph 8 of resolution 1698 (2006)* *concerning the Democratic Republic of the Congo*, S/2007/68, 8 February.

— (2008) Resolution 1857, 22 December, p. 3.

Vlassenroot, K. and T. Raeymaekers (2008) 'New political order in the DR Congo? The transformation of regulation', *Afrika Focus*, 21(2): 39–52.

Weinstein, J. M. (2003) *Resources and the Information Problem in Rebel Recruitment*, Center for Global Development and Stanford University, November.

About the contributors

Gerhard Anders is lecturer in African studies at the University of Edinburgh. His research focuses on the anthropology of emergent regimes of global order in the fields of criminal justice and development, tracking the everyday experiences of civil servants, lawyers and others involved in the production and diffusion of administrative and legal knowledge. He has published on legal anthropology, international criminal justice, good governance and corruption, including the co-edited volume (with M. Nuijten) *Corruption and the Secret of Law* (2007) and the monograph *In the Shadow of Good Governance: An Ethnography of Civil Service Reform in Africa* (2010).

Karel Arnaut is an anthropologist who studied at Ghent, Utrecht and Oxford. After many years at the Department of African Languages and Cultures and the Conflict Research Group (Ghent University, Belgium), Arnaut is now researcher at the Max-Planck-Institut zur Erforschung multireligiöser und multiethnischer Gesellschaften at Göttingen (Germany). The main focus of his work is student and youth movements, political and cultural participation, and the restructuring of public spaces in urban Africa and Europe. Most of his fieldwork took place in Côte d'Ivoire and was published in journals such as *Politique Africaine*, *American Ethnologist*, *Africa and Development*, etc. Arnaut is also interested in post-colonial dynamics in the area of diasporic identity formation, activism and super-diversity in urban contexts in Europe and Africa.

Morten Bøås is Senior Researcher and Head of Research at Fafo's Institute for Applied International Studies. He has published extensively on African politics and conflict. His work has been published in journals such as *Politique Africaine*, the *Journal of Modern African Studies*, *African Spectrum*, *Third World Quarterly* and the *Journal of International Intervention and Statebuilding*. His books include *African Guerrillas – Rage against the Machine* (2007), with Kevin C. Dunn, and *International Development*, vols I–IV (2010), with Benedicte Bull.

Maya Mynster Christensen is a PhD Fellow at the Department of Anthropology, University of Copenhagen. She has conducted long-term fieldwork in Sierra Leone among militias and soldiers, focusing on issues of violence, mobilization and militarization, elections and politics. Her current research deals with the mobilization of Sierra Leonean ex-combatants and ex-soldiers into militarized networks and institutions – both within and outside West Africa.

Investigating the consequences of the privatization of global security politics, her thesis illuminates the dynamics of violent mobilization in a context where the demand for cheap, militant labour is growing.

Ruben de Koning joined the United Nations Group of Experts on the Democratic Republic of the Congo in 2011. From 2009 until 2011 he was a researcher with the Stockholm International Peace Research Institute (SIPRI), working on minerals and armed conflicts in DRC. Prior to this he worked as research associate on land- and forest-related management issues at UNDP and the Centre for International Forestry Research.

Ilmari Käihkö is a PhD candidate at the Department of Peace and Conflict Research, Uppsala University, and a research assistant at the Nordic Africa Institute. He has both civilian and military field experience in Africa, first working on development cooperation in Tanzania and later deploying as a part of the Finnish contingent to the UN MINURCAT peacekeeping force in Chad. His chapter was written while working as a researcher at the Department of Security and Strategy at the Swedish National Defence College. His areas of interest include international relations, expeditionary operations, contemporary warfare, political violence and strategy.

Sandrine Perrot is a senior Research Fellow at the Centre for International Research (CERI) at Sciences-Po (Paris). She joined CERI after a two-year postdoctoral fellowship at CERIUM (Centre for International Studies at the Université de Montréal). Dr Perrot specializes in Uganda and focuses more particularly on armed conflicts, the sociology of armed groups and violent phenomena. She wrote a PhD on *The Reversibility of Chaos: The rebuilding of a political order in Museveni's Uganda* and has worked extensively on the Ugandan military, northern Uganda and the Lord's Resistance Army. Her current research focuses on militia phenomena in sub-Saharan Africa. She is also the co-director of the electronic working paper series *Research Questions*, a member of the editorial board of *Politique Africaine* and *Critique Internationale* and an associate researcher at the Centre d'Etudes des Mondes Africains. She has written numerous peer-reviewed journal articles and contributions to edited volumes.

Mariam Persson is a PhD candidate at the War Studies Department, King's College London, and a research assistant at the Department of Security and Strategic Studies at the Swedish National Defence College. Her current research is focused on ex-combatants in informal security networks and vigilante groups in Liberia. Besides Liberia she has conducted field research in Sierra Leone and the Central African Republic and has published on areas such as informal security provision in relation to security sector reform in Liberia and female combatants in African wars.

Anders Themnér is a researcher at the Nordic Africa Institute (NAI) and an assistant professor at the Department of Peace and Conflict Research at Uppsala University. He has published extensively on issues relating to the disarmament, demobilization and reintegration of ex-combatants and informal military networks in post-conflict societies. His most recent work is *Violence in Post-Conflict Societies: Remarginalization, Remobilizers and Relationships* (2011). Themnér's geographical focus is on sub-Saharan Africa, with special emphasis on Liberia, the Republic of Congo and Sierra Leone – three countries where he has conducted extensive field research. He has previously published under the name Anders Nilsson.

Henrik Vigh is an associate professor in the Department of Anthropology, University of Copenhagen. He is the author of *Navigating Terrains of War* (2006) and has researched issues of youth and conflict in both Europe and West Africa. He is currently studying transnational criminal networks as well as heading a research programme focused on an ethnographic comparison of mobilization processes funded by the Danish Research Council for Culture and Communication (FKK).

Koen Vlassenroot is a professor of political science and director of the Conflict Research Group at the University of Ghent. He specializes in conflict issues in Central Africa and has a particular research focus on militias, land issues, security governance and the management of natural resources in eastern DR Congo. His current research focus is on informal taxation and state-building in the DRC. He has carried out extensive fieldwork in the Great Lakes region and has published numerous peer-reviewed journal articles and book chapters. He is the co-author of *Conflict and Social Transformation in Eastern DR Congo* and co-editor of *The Lord's Resistance Army: Myth or Reality?* (Zed Books 2010).

Index

About Zed Books

Zed Books is a critical and dynamic publisher, committed to increasing awareness of important international issues and to promoting diversity, alternative voices and progressive social change. We publish on politics, development, gender, the environment and economics for a global audience of students, academics, activists and general readers. Run as a co-operative, Zed Books aims to operate in an ethical and environmentally sustainable way.

Find out more at:

www.zedbooks.co.uk

For up-to-date news, articles, reviews and events information visit:

http://zed-books.blogspot.com

To subscribe to the monthly Zed Books e-newsletter, send an email headed 'subscribe' to:

marketing@zedbooks.net

We can also be found on **Facebook**, **ZNet**, **Twitter** and **Library Thing**.